# THE NEW PROTECTORATES

JAMES MAYALL
RICARDO SOARES DE OLIVEIRA
(*Editors*)

# The New Protectorates

*International Tutelage and the*
*Making of Liberal States*

HURST & COMPANY, LONDON

First published in the United Kingdom in 2011 by
C. Hurst & Co. (Publishers) Ltd.,
41 Great Russell Street, London, WC1B 3PL
© James Mayall and Ricardo Soares de Oliveira, 2011
All rights reserved.
Printed in India

The right of James Mayall and Ricardo Soares de Oliveira
to be identified as the editors of this publication is asserted
by them in accordance with the Copyright, Designs and
Patents Act, 1988.

A Cataloguing-in-Publication data record for this book
is available from the British Library.

ISBN 978-1-84904-125-6 *Hardback*
      978-1-84904-126-3 *Paperback*

This book is printed using paper from registered sustainable
and managed sources.

www.hurstpub.co.uk

# CONTENTS

v

# CONTENTS

# ACKNOWLEDGMENTS

The editors wish to thank the Rockefeller Foundation for sponsoring a state-of-the-art workshop held at Bellagio, Italy on 6–10 February 2006. A subsequent event was co-organized with the Global Public Policy Institute (Berlin) and held at the Centre for Research in the Arts, Social Sciences and Humanities (CRASSH), University of Cambridge, on 6–8 June 2007. The Fritz Thyssen Foundation generously co-sponsored this event. We thank Mitja Müller, Philipp Rotmann, Stephan Merganthaler, and James Eley of GPPi for research and logistical assistance.

The editors would also like to thank Gary Bass, Duncan Bell, Thorsten Benner, William Burke-White, Simon Chesterman, Björn Conrad, Devon Curtis, Stephen Ellis, Pierre Englebert, Rosemary Foot, Carlos Gaspar, Antonio Giustozzi, Jeffrey Herbst, Christopher Hill, Ayesha Khan, Daniel Large, Neil MacFarlane, Daniel Pinéu, Amadou Sesay, Brendan Simms, Devika Singh, Krishnan Srinivasan, and Masayuki Tadokoro for participating in the events or otherwise contributing towards this volume.

Ricardo Soares de Oliveira would also like to acknowledge a three-month period as Public Policy Scholar at the Woodrow Wilson International Center for Scholars, Washington, DC, from April to June 2010, which provided the ideal context for working on the book, and thank Robert Litwak and Robert Hathaway in particular for their great hospitality.

# ACRONYMS AND ABBREVIATIONS

| | |
|---|---|
| AACA | Afghanistan Coordination Assistance Authority |
| ACABQ | Advisory Committee on Administrative and Budgetary Questions |
| APRM | African Peer Review Mechanism |
| AQM | Al-Qaeda in Mesopotamia |
| AREU | Afghanistan Research and Evaluation Unit |
| ARTF | Afghanistan Reconstruction Trust Fund |
| ASEAN | Association of Southeast Asian Nations |
| AU | African Union |
| BiH | Bosnia and Herzegovina |
| CARDS | Community Assistance for Reconstruction, Development and Stabilisation |
| CEO | Chief Executive Officer |
| CFSP | Common Foreign and Security Policy |
| CIC | Community Interest Companions |
| CIMIC | Civil-Military Cooperation |
| CIVPOL | Civilian Police |
| CNRT | National Congress for Timorese Reconstruction |
| CPA | Coalition Provisional Authority |
| DDR | Disarmament, Demobilization, and Reintegration |
| DHA | Department of Humanitarian Affairs |
| DPA | Department of Political Affairs |
| DPKO | Department of Peacekeeping Operations |
| DRC | Democratic Republic of Congo |
| ECHO | European Commission Humanitarian Office |
| ECOSOC | Economic and Social Council |
| ECOWAS | Economic Community of West African States |

# ACRONYMS AND ABBREVIATIONS

| | |
|---|---|
| ECHA | Executive Committee on Humanitarian Affairs |
| ECPS | Executive Committee on Peace and Security |
| FDR | Franklin Delano Roosevelt |
| EPC | Existing System of Foreign Policy Co-operation |
| ESDP | European Security and Defense Policy |
| EU | European Union |
| EUFOR | European Military Force |
| EULEX | European Union Rule of Law Mission in Kosovo |
| EUPAT | European Police Academy Team |
| EUPM | European Union Police Mission |
| EUROPOL | European Police Office |
| FATA | Federally Administered Tribal Areas |
| FC | Force Commander |
| FDR | Franklin Delano Roosevelt |
| FRETILIN | Revolutionary Front for an Independent Timor |
| FYROM | Former Yugoslav Republic of Macedonia |
| GEMAP | Governance and Economic Management Assistance Program |
| GOP | Grand Old Party |
| GPPI | Global Public Policy Institute |
| HC | High Commissioner |
| IAEA | International Atomic Energy Agency |
| ICC | International Criminal Court |
| ICG | International Crisis Group |
| ICISS | International Commission on Intervention and State Sovereignty |
| ICITAP | International Criminal Investigative Training Assistance |
| ICJ | International Court of Justice |
| ICO | International Civilian Office |
| ICRC | International Committee of the Red Cross |
| ICTY | International Criminal Tribunal for the Former Yugoslavia |
| IDSA | Institute of Defense Studies and Analyses |
| IFI | International Financial Institutions |
| ILO | International Labor Organization |
| IMF | International Monetary Fund |
| IMTF | Integrated Mission Task Force |
| INGO | International Non-governmental Organizations |
| INTERFET | International Force for East Timor |

# ACRONYMS AND ABBREVIATIONS

| | |
|---|---|
| INTERPOL | International Criminal Police Organization |
| IO | Interventionist Operations |
| IPKF | Indian Peacekeeping Force |
| IPTF | International Police Task Force |
| IRC | International Rescue Committee |
| ISAF | International Security Assistance Force |
| KEK | Kosovo Energy Cooperation |
| KFOR | Kosovo Force |
| KLA | Kosovo Liberation Army |
| KPS | Kosovo Police Service |
| LURD | Liberians United for Reconciliation and Democracy |
| MONUC | United Nations in Mission in the Democratic Republic of Congo |
| MP | Member of Parliament |
| MSF | Médecins Sans Frontières |
| NAM | Non-Aligned Movement |
| NATO | North Atlantic Treaty Organization |
| NEPAD | New Partnership for Africa's Development |
| NGO | Non-governmental organization |
| NPFL | National Patriotic Front of Liberia |
| NTGL | National Transitional Government of Liberia |
| OAU | Organization of African Unity |
| OCHA | Office for Coordination of Humanitarian Affairs |
| OECD | Organization for Economic Cooperation and Development |
| OHR | Office of the High Representative |
| OSCE | Organization for Security and Cooperation in Europe |
| OTI | Office of Transition Initiatives |
| PBC | Peacebuilding Commission |
| PBF | Peacebuilding Fund |
| PBSO | Peacebuilding Support Office |
| PKO/DPKO | Peace Keeping Operation |
| PNTL | National Police of East Timor |
| POLRI | Indonesian National Police |
| PRC | People's Republic of China |
| PRT | Provincial Reconstruction Teams |
| R2P | Responsibility to Protect |
| RAW | Research and Analysis Wing |

# ACRONYMS AND ABBREVIATIONS

| | |
|---|---|
| RC | Resident Coordinator |
| RS | Republika Srpska |
| RUF | Revolutionary United Front |
| SAA | Stabilisation and Association Agreements |
| SAP | Stabilisation and Association Program |
| SCU | Serious Crimes Unit |
| SEATO | Southeast Asia Treaty Organization |
| SEE | South Eastern Europe |
| SFOR | Stabilisation Force |
| SOP | Standard Operating Procedure |
| SRSG | Special Representative of the Secretary-General |
| SSR | Security Sector Reform |
| TNI | Indonesian National Army |
| ULIMO | United Liberation Movement of Liberia for Democracy |
| UN | United Nations |
| UNAMA | United Nations Assistance Mission to Afghanistan |
| UNMIBH | United Nations Mission in Bosnia and Herzegovina |
| UNAMID | United Nations Hybrid Operation in Darfur |
| UNAMIR | United Nations Assistance Mission for Rwanda |
| UNAMSIL | United Nations Mission in Sierra Leone |
| UNDP | United Nations Development Program |
| UNEF | United Nations Emergency Force |
| UNFICYP | United Nations Peacekeeping Force in Cyprus |
| UNHCR | United Nations High Commissioner for Refugees |
| UNICEF | United Nations Children's Fund |
| UNMIK | United Nations Mission in Kosovo |
| UNMIL | United Nations Mission in Liberia |
| UNMISET | United Nations Mission of Support to East Timor |
| UNPOL | United Nations Police |
| UNPROFOR | United Nations Protection Force |
| UNSC | United Nations Security Council |
| UNSMA | United Nations Special Mission to Afghanistan |
| UNTAC | United Nations Transitional Authority in Cambodia |
| UNTAES | United Nations Transitional Administration for Eastern Slavonia |
| UNTAET | United Nations Transitional Administration in East Timor |
| UNTAG | United Nations Transitional Assistance Group |
| US | United States |

## ACRONYMS AND ABBREVIATIONS

| | |
|---|---|
| USAID | United States Agency for International Development |
| WFP | World Food Program |
| WGLL | Working Group Lessons Learned |
| WHO | World Health Organization |
| WMD | Weapons of Mass Destruction |
| WTO | World Trade Organization |

# CONTRIBUTORS

**William Bain** is Senior Lecturer in International Political Theory at Aberystwyth University. He has published widely on the subject of trusteeship and international administration, including *Between Anarchy and Society: Trusteeship and the Obligations of Power* (OUP 2003). He is also editor and contributor to *The Empire of Security and the Safety of the People* (Routledge, 2007). At present he is working on a research monograph entitled *The Political Theory of World Order: God, Man, and the Common Good.*

**Mats Berdal** is Professor of Security and Development in the Department of War Studies, King's College London. He was formerly Director of Studies at the International Institute for Strategic Studies (IISS) in London. He is the author of *Building Peace after War* (Routledge/IISS, 2009) and co-editor with Spyros Economides of *United Nations Interventionism 1991–2004* (Cambridge University Press, 2007).

**Michael Boyle** is Assistant Professor of Political Science at La Salle University, Philadelphia. He was formerly a Lecturer in International Relations at the University of Saint Andrews in Scotland. He holds an MPhil and PhD in International Relations from Cambridge University and an MPP from the Kennedy School of Government at Harvard University. He has previously held fellowships at the Center for International Security and Cooperation (CISAC) at Stanford University and the Belfer Center for Science and International Affairs (BSCIA) at the John F. Kennedy School of Government, Harvard University. Dr Boyle was also a Fulbright fellow at the Department of International Relations at the Australian National University. He is currently working on a book manuscript entitled "The Logic of Violence in Post-Conflict States" funded by a grant from the Airey Neave Trust.

## CONTRIBUTORS

**Richard Caplan** is Professor of International Relations and Director of the Centre for International Studies at the University of Oxford. He is the author of *International Governance of War-Torn Territories: Rule and Reconstruction* (Oxford University Press, 2005) and the editor of *Exit Strategies and State Building* (Oxford University Press, forthcoming).

**Christopher Clapham** is a Fellow of the Africa Studies Centre, University of Cambridge. He has edited the *Journal of Modern African Studies* since 1998. Formerly a Professor of International Relations at the University of Lancaster, he has also taught at the Universities of Addis Ababa, the West Indies and Manchester. He is the author of *Haile-Selassie's Government* (1969), *Liberia and Sierra Leone* (Cambridge University Press, 1976), *Third World Politics* (Routledge, 1985), *Transformation and Continuity in Revolutionary Ethiopia* (Cambridge University Press, 1988), *Africa and the International System* (Cambridge University Press, 1996), and *African Guerrillas* (editor, James Currey, 1998).

**Major General K.J. Drewienkiewicz CB CMG** served in the Balkans, predominantly in BiH and Kosovo, almost continuously from October 1996 to June 1999, first in NATO posts and then in the Office of the Civilian High Representative and the OSCE Kosovo Verification Mission. Since retiring from the British Army he has returned to BiH, in the OSCE throughout 2003 and as Military Adviser to the High Representative and the Vice-Chair of the Defense Reform Commission throughout 2004 and 2005. He lives in Suffolk and is an Honorary Fellow of Sidney Sussex College, Cambridge.

**Spyros Economides** is a Senior Lecturer in International Relations and European Politics at the London School of Economics and Political Science. He specializes in the Balkans, the study of civil wars and European security issues as well as US foreign policy. Economides has published widely in academic journals, most recently in *West European Politics, Journal of Southeast European and Black Sea Studies, Government and Opposition*, and *Survival*. He is the co-editor (with Mats Berdal) of *Strategic Thinking: An Introduction and Farewell. Essays by Philip Windsor* (Lynne Rienner, 2002) and the co-editor (with Mats Berdal) of the *UN Interventionism 1991–2004* (Cambridge University Press, 2007).

**Stefan Halper** is a Senior Fellow at the Centre of International Studies, University of Cambridge, and a Senior Research Fellow at Magdalene College, Cambridge. He directs the Donner Atlantic Studies Program. He is the author of *America Alone: The Neo-conservatives and the Global Order* (Cambridge

# CONTRIBUTORS

University Press, 2004), *The Silence of the Rational Center: Why US Foreign Policy is Failing* (Basic Books, 2007) and *The Beijing Consensus* (Basic Books, 2010). Stefan Halper holds doctorates from both Oxford and Cambridge. He has served four American presidents in the White House and the Department of State and is an expert on US foreign policy, national security policy, China, and Anglo-American relations.

**David Keen** is Professor of Conflict Studies, London School of Economics. He is the author of *The Benefits of Famine: A Political Economy of Famine and Relief in Southwest Sudan, 1983–89* (Princeton University Press, 1994; James Currey, 2008), *The Economic Functions of Violence in Civil Wars* (Oxford University Press/IISS, 1998), *Conflict and Collusion in Sierra Leone* (James Currey, 2005), *Endless War: Hidden Functions of the War on Terror* (Pluto, 2006) and *Complex Emergencies* (Polity, 2008).

**Clare Lockhart** is the co-founder and CEO of the Institute for State Effectiveness, founded in 2005 to find and promote approaches to building good governance. She served in Afghanistan as an advisor to the UN during the Bonn Process and to the Afghan Government from 2001 to 2005, designing a number of national initiatives including a program that provides a block grant to every village in Afghanistan, now present in 23,000 villages. She is co-author with Ashraf Ghani of *Fixing Failed States* (Oxford University Press, 2008) and contributes to the media on issues of peace and statebuilding.

**James Mayall** is Emeritus Professor of International Relations at the University of Cambridge and the London School of Economics and Political Science. He is a Fellow of Sidney Sussex College, Cambridge and the British Academy, and is currently Academic Adviser to the Royal College of Defence Studies in London. He has written widely on international relations and international theory and more specifically on the impact of nationalism on international society and North-South relations.

**Richard Ponzio** is Senior Policy and Strategy Officer in the State Department's Office of the Coordinator for Reconstruction and Stabilization. He has served in UN peacebuilding operations in the Balkans, Africa, Asia, and the South Pacific. He has published in several journals, including *International Peacekeeping, Global Governance*, and *Disarmament Forum*, and his latest book is titled *Democratic Peacebuilding: Aiding Afghanistan and Other Fragile States* (Oxford University Press, 2011).

**Aswini Kanta Ray** is Visiting Professor at Burdwan University, West Bengal. He was Professor of International Relations and Comparative Politics at Jawaharlal Nehru University, New Delhi, until 2003. Previously, he taught at the universities of Calcutta and Delhi. He has also been associated with the universities of Tokyo, Mexico, Colima, Southampton, the LSE and the Sorbonne. His books include *Domestic Compulsions and Foreign Policy* (New Delhi, 1975), *The Global System: A Historical View from the Periphery* (Tokyo, 1996), *Democratic Rights in a Post-Colonial Democracy* (CNRS, Paris, 1997) and *Western Realism and International Relations: A Non Western-View* (New Delhi, 2004).

**Wolfgang Seibel** is a Professor of Politics and Public Administration at Konstanz University and an Adjunct Professor of Public Administration at the Hertie School of Governance, Berlin. His research focuses on the administrative side of politics and the political function of public administration. Recent books include *Networks of Nazi Persecution* (editor, with Gerald D. Feldman, 2005), *Verwaltete Illusionen* (on the governance of large-scale privatization in the post-1990 East-German economy) (2005), and *Macht und Moral. Die "Endlösung der Judenfrage" in Frankreich, 1940–1944* (on occupation administration and the Holocaust in France, 1940–44) (2010).

**Ricardo Soares de Oliveira** is University Lecturer in Comparative Politics at the Department of Politics and International Relations, Oxford University, a Fellow of Saint Peter's College, Oxford, and a Fellow of the Global Public Policy Institute, Berlin. He is the author of *Oil and Politics in the Gulf of Guinea* (C. Hurst & Co. and Columbia University Press, 2007) and co-editor of *China Returns to Africa* (C. Hurst & Co. and Columbia University Press, 2008).

**Shogo Suzuki** is Lecturer at the Department of Politics, School of Social Sciences, University of Manchester. He is the author of *Civilization and Empire: China and Japan's Encounters with European International Society* (Routledge, 2009), as well as articles that have appeared in *European Journal of International Relations*, *The Pacific Review*, and *Third World Quarterly*. He has held appointments at the University of Auckland, New Zealand, and the University of Cambridge.

**Dominik Zaum** is Reader in International Relations at the University of Reading. His recent publications include *The Sovereignty Paradox: The Norms and Politics of International Statebuilding* (2007); *The United Nations Security Council and War: The Evolution of Thought and Practice since 1945* (2008, co-edited with Vaughan Lowe, Adam Roberts, and Jennifer Welsh); and, together with Adam Roberts, *Selective Security: War and the United Nations Security Council since 1945* (Routledge/IISS, 2008).

# INTRODUCTION

## James Mayall and Ricardo Soares de Oliveira

German troops fighting the Taliban in the Hindu Kush; EU judges sitting in courts in the Balkans; UN viceroys governing parts of Oceania; American occupation in the Middle East. In mapping the political landscape of the post-Cold War era, future historians are likely to pay particular attention to attempts by outsiders to administer a host of post-war societies, undertake their physical reconstruction, establish functional institutions and open economies, and ultimately, transform what were deemed to be "maladjusted" political cultures. This is not on account of the long-term impact of these efforts. Although it is too early to pass a final verdict on the effects of international tutelage, one cannot possibly rank it amongst the shaping dynamics of the age such as the rise of the Asian economies, the impact of North-South migration or climate change. Yet few developments in the two decades after 1989 reveal more about the character of the international system, of the gaps between liberal discourse and practice, and the fleeting nature of the Western hegemonic moment. What made this possible? What was it like as an actual political experience? How contradictory was its reception? Why was the process of governing others for their own good so flawed and the outcomes disappointing? These are the questions we address in this book.

We label such instances of direct international tutelage the new protectorates, defined as territories where a medium- to long-term international presence, multilateral yet under de facto Western leadership, was established with transformative goals at their core. The prehistory of the new protectorates can be traced to the Western-led interventionism of the early post-Cold War period that included instances of political and economic conditionality and intrusive peacekeeping. Nonetheless, their establishment was a qualitatively different development, with peacebuilding essentially equated with the construction of a liberal state. The motivation for such ambitious undertakings was a complex mix of ideological commitment to implant and nurture liberal institutions, self-styled altruism and security-inspired concerns, which predated but were catalyzed by the events of 11 September 2001.

Territories that can be deemed new protectorates, under our definition, include those where international trusteeship was declared, as in Kosovo (1999–2008), Eastern Slavonia (1995–98), or East Timor (1999–2002), and some form of explicit executive and/or oversight authority was held by international forces. Beyond such obvious instances, the category also includes states such as Bosnia and Herzegovina (BiH), Afghanistan and Iraq where there was a substantial international military and civilian presence; a foreign proconsul with important (formal or informal) oversight responsibilities for the direction of policy; a number of governance tasks which were performed with significant input by foreigners and often a peripheral role for local officials; and the survival of the state in its current form remained inconceivable without the presence of outsiders.

The new protectorate in our formulation is thus a political, not simply a legal reality. In view of the diversity of contemporary efforts to build states under international tutelage, there is certainly a case for deploying a more precise and differentiated language when discussing the matter: trusteeship, international direct administration, exogenous statebuilding or the somewhat vaguer "peacebuilding" are commonly used denominations, which in the hands of some authors have distinct meanings. The current volume does not seek to challenge these concepts or overstate the coherence of the new protectorates. But we believe that there is equal merit in discussing the several instances of international tutelage, in all their multiplicity, as comparable political experiences occurring at a specific moment in time.

This introduction proceeds as follows. Section one seeks to place the emergence of the new protectorate in the political and discursive context of the early post-Cold War era. A number of themes are underlined as re-enabling the project of directly transforming other societies: a democratic-capitalist dominance matched by the deployment of Western power; the lack of a US or Western grand strategy to make sense of the changed international system, and resulting confusion and ad hoc policy-making; a robust humanitarianism emphasizing intervention and underplaying sovereign statehood; and the fitful Western concern with the threat of "failed states." While the new protectorates have a complex relationship with each of these factors, they are inconceivable without them.

Section two deals with the new protectorates in terms of the reception they garnered from defenders and critics; the historical analogies deployed to make sense of the practices and goals of administering others; and the specifically Western political and economic imaginings of foreign state-builders. The latter, with emphasis on the emergence of a "liberal peace" agenda of post-war reconstruction, is of particular importance because of the "ideational causation"[1] between norms and actions. These norms were inextricably bound with the policies deployed in the new protectorates, as the questions of "how to govern and how to justify it"[2] were inseparable.

The purpose of section three is to look at the new protectorates as a form of governance shaping the lives, at least in the medium term, of those under their aegis. We discuss the institutional apparatus of the new protectorate and attitudes towards state power and the use of state prerogatives; the sociology of the intervening agents and their different goals; the routines of foreign administration and the languages that enveloped them; and relations with the "intervened." We aim to flesh out important recurring traits of the theories of governance of the new protectorates. Far from the implicit consistency of a "liberal agenda" decried by much of the critical literature, we argue that this experience was both conceptually muddled and chaotic in implementation, and failed the first test of strategic planning, that is, reconciling ends and means.

It is important to explain at the outset what the book is not attempting to do. It does not provide a political narrative or exhaustive country case-studies, and neither does it pretend to cover all dimensions of its huge and complex subject. There is already a sizeable literature on the impacts.[3] The book's aim is more modest: to provide readers with a series of authoritative studies on strategic aspects of the enterprise of international governance and liberal statebuilding. In particular, this book is about the motivations of the interveners: the pivotal and thus far under-researched perspective of the "intervened" is dealt with in passing but is not the central concern. Our intentions are also more diagnostic than prescriptive. The book has a further aspiration: to address the peripheral status of the new protectorates in broader discussions about international relations. While the experience of the new protectorates remains largely unassimilated by the generalist literature on contemporary international relations, we argue that they provide an important prism through which to understand crucial dimensions of international life since the end of the Cold

War. Our book, therefore, examines, on the one hand, the domestic life of the new protectorates and the local dynamics of international rule, and, on the other, the broader reception of the new protectorates within contemporary international society.

## The Post-Cold War Moment and its Competing Visions

The end of the Cold War was optimistically welcomed in Western capitals as the onset of what President George Bush famously labeled a "new world order," in which a benign Western modernity would prosper and swell indefinitely. By the early 1990s the expansion of global capitalism, especially towards the former Soviet bloc and much of East and South Asia,[4] was matched by an exponential increase in the number of self-declared democracies as well as the virtual eclipse of the political legitimacy of autocratic regimes. Even the advent of serious conflict resulting from Iraq's 1990 invasion of Kuwait reinforced the view that new US-led and UN-brokered collective security arrangements were available to regulate and eliminate global strife.

This naïve enthusiasm was of course short-lived. The trajectory of OECD economies and those of a growing number of emerging markets remained upbeat throughout the 1990s and the process of increased integration and connectedness referred to as "globalization" was the defining storyline of the age. Simultaneously, it became obvious that other parts of the globe were subjected to a process of violent fragmentation.[5] Throughout much of the post-communist and developing worlds, the end of the East-West rivalry resulted in unforeseen outbreaks of warfare. Almost overnight, high-intensity conflicts in Africa, the Balkans, the Caucasus and Central Asia led to the collapse of state institutions and spawned destabilizing regional developments such as powerful criminal economies, terrorist networks, major refugee flows, and secessionist claims. Analysts were often surprised at the resurgence of nationalist, ethnic and religious identities and the role they played in these bitter disputes. In fact, these particularist attachments always had deep resonance in the affected societies but had remained hidden during the Cold War. The fact that they resurfaced as soon as its constraints were lifted should have surprised no-one. Political entrepreneurs bent on mobilizing dormant agendas for personal gain did the rest. Such dynamics quickly disabused decision-makers in the West of the idea that the end of the Cold War had resolved the problem of international order.[6] In this context, the specter of "failed states" became a key concern in Western geopolitical discussions. Failed states were implausibly defined as both "black holes" escaping virtuous processes happening elsewhere and the source of multiple pathologies that could, if unchecked, engulf the global economy.[7]

## The Role of the US

The growing awareness that international order still needed to be built and maintained[8] did not lead to the emergence of a grand strategy on the part of the leading powers. The 1990s were indeed a decade of American hegemony but the messy geopolitical debates failed to produce a consensus. Early self-congratulatory statements in Fukuyama's "end of history" mode[9] did not provide a roadmap for the troubles ahead. Before long, the upbeat prospects were replaced, in the popular and scholarly arena, with much bleaker assessments.[10] Most influential appraisals shared a sense of tragedy about global politics and a view that certain unpleasant factors about international life were enduring. While disagreeing about where the world was heading, all decried simplistic assumptions about global convergence or the triumph of the West. Such musings were partly attempts at explaining the dynamics of contemporary global politics. More important, they represented a mostly unsuccessful liberal attempt to provide the West, and the US in particular, with a grand strategic vision to make sense of the post-Cold War world. Decision-makers and policy intellectuals yearned for the equivalent of George Kennan's "containment" concept, which had framed Western strategy throughout the Cold War.[11]

Perhaps the reason why a grand strategy did not emerge is that a compelling rationale for it did not exist. Foreign policy experts during the Clinton administration years might have complained that something was amiss in the ad hoc approach to global disorder, but the overarching narrative that defined popular attitudes (as well as those of elected politicians) was that of deepening integration and prosperity in the core states of the global economy. As discussed later in this Introduction, remote tragedies in failed states could elicit a charitable impulse but were not consistently perceived as threatening vital concerns. Even the narrower category of "rogue states" failed to garner the amount of consensus amongst US allies sufficient for concerted action.[12] Some analysts even questioned whether the idea of "dysfunction" was appropriate for understanding the international system in the post-Cold War years. John Ikenberry, for example, saw talk of chaos as misplaced insofar as there was "no systemic failure" and, indeed, the post-1945 liberal global system went on to expand after the Cold War.[13]

US debates on these matters, as discussed in Stefan Halper's chapter, were constitutive of patterns of action and inaction at the global level. Other Western states were unable to project power or waited for US guidance, as Europe's initial passivity on the Balkans showed. One of the earliest attempts at a grand strategic ordering of US policy was put forward by Anthony Lake, President Clinton's first National Security Advisor. Lake sought to replace containment with the concept of "democratic enlargement," by which he meant a world order of open economies and free states.[14] The trouble was that this was not really a strategic vision in the traditional sense but an appeal to peoples, and their governments, assumed to be like-minded.[15] As with many initiatives of the first Clinton administration, "democracy enlargement" went nowhere. The rest of the decade was instead taken up by crippling disagreements as to the nature of the post-Cold War era and the US role in it, ranging from isolationism to liberal interventionism and often cutting across party lines.[16] In retrospect it is tempting to overstate the consistency of a "liberal" US-led agenda, but in reality it never cohered either normatively or from a policy perspective.

## UN Interventionism

These limitations on the part of US leadership and the absence of an overarching strategy did not prevent the exponential increase in UN peacekeeping activity during this period. This is the subject of a vast literature and need not detain us here.[17] Several factors contributed to the unprecedented worldwide blue helmet deployment. These included the unfreezing of the UNSC; the willingness of the former Cold War foes to disengage from now useless client states and multilateralize thorny issues; the increase in civil wars; and the humanitarian impulse among Western concerned publics. These early post-Cold War missions immediately went beyond the limited precepts of UN peacekeeping as developed since the 1950s.[18] Some of the twenty missions between 1988 and 1994 included transitional responsibilities, especially in the case of Namibia and Cambodia. The latter UN mission, which involved extensive governance responsibilities, was the clear precursor to the new protectorates that would materialize later in the decade. The UN was entrusted not only with the usual humanitarian and peacekeeping tasks but also with political authority. In theory, the UN was in control of the foreign affairs, finance, public security and information ministries. In practice, bureaucratic inefficiency (with Prince Sihanouk deeming UNTAC "a terrible cocktail of races"),[19] lack of manpower, a particularly apathetic SRSG, and the pull-out immediately after the elections meant that the mission punched considerably below its weight and allowed the establishment of a barely disguised autocracy.[20]

For despite attempts by then Secretary-General Boutros Boutros-Ghali to enhance the UN's role beyond peacekeeping and into "peacebuilding,"[21] movement in this direction was modest. The other high-profile early attempt at rebuilding order in a failed state, the 1992–94 US and UN missions in Somalia, were nominally intended to rehabilitate the country's "political institutions and economy," in what National Security Advisor Madeleine Albright described as "an unprecedented task aimed at nothing else that the restoration of an entire country."[22] This is the sort of language that would be widespread later in the decade. But the killing of US servicemen by troops loyal to the most powerful Somali warlord, Mohamed Farah Aideed, in October 1993 exposed the thinness of Western moral empathy with victims and its insufficiency for sustaining open-ended, complex commitments to rebuilding the lives of others. The Somalia debacle removed some illusions about the ease with which conflicts could be ended and put a momentary stop to Westerners' willingness to intervene in distant trouble spots. Even conflicts that were neither remote nor unimportant, such as the wars in the former Yugoslavia, were not met with decisive Western action. By 1994, public fatigue with interventionism had already set in. Other disappointments in operations in Angola, BiH and elsewhere resulted in a growing skepticism about the use of peacekeeping (let alone longer-term efforts) to address the problem of failed states and ungoverned territories.[23]

Nor was the urgency of these problems taken for granted. The thesis that failed states were a risk, however prevalent amongst policy intellectuals, had limited traction in the real world of policy-making. Some conflicts were deemed a concern while others (Sierra Leone, Liberia, Afghanistan etc.) were allowed to fester. The first and simplest reason for this was that there were just too many failed states. No sensible commitment could be made to commandeer swathes of the world's land and population and redeem them from poverty and violence. For its supporters, "globalization" was both a process and a desired end-state, but it did not provide a roadmap for creating liberal societies. Secondly, the UN bureaucracy had neither the capacity nor the mandate to engage seriously in addressing the shortcomings of failed states. Thirdly, and more important, it was not immediately obvious to decision-makers that the degradation of states in the developing world was of direct relevance to the lives of Westerners. The urge to bring order to the frontier—a perennial concern of empire builders—was slowed down by the perception that the barbarians were remote. Ultimately the problem of disorder on the frontier was perceived as too marginal to require the transformation of Western foreign policies. As late as 1994, the prospect of an international direct role in the governance of war-torn territories was fanciful.

The New Protectorate

By late 1995, the tables had turned again. The bruised passivity of 1994 became the object of opprobrium on account of the West's unwillingness to halt the Rwanda genocide and the aggressive behavior of the Serbs in the former Yugoslavia that culminated in the July 1995 Srebrenica massacre. The result was a considerable change in attitudes towards peacekeeping, at least in the Balkans, and a much greater readiness to deploy force. Furthermore, *Realpolitik* imperatives (which had earlier pushed for non-intervention)[24] were overtaken by public opinion and media pressure in the industrial states in favor of intervention. In the absence of European leadership, at least until the election of the neo-Gladstonian British Prime Minister Tony Blair in 1997, the Clinton administration underwrote interventionist policies. As a result of the Dayton agreement, the Western states committed themselves to policing the shaky peace in Bosnia. And yet, even at this stage, the idea that they were committing themselves to the long-term running of the new protectorates was not widespread.

Two related normative developments paved the way for the new protectorate. The first enabling factor was the elevation of activist groups with rights-based agendas to the political mainstream. The urge to "do something" had become an integral part of Western audiences' reactions to televised suffering in foreign lands. This humanitarianism was mobilized by key, if disparate, constituencies promoting normative and institutional interests, including the media, the aid industry, NGOs, and Christian activists. Although such coalitions emerged in the heat of particular humanitarian crises throughout the decade, by the end of it there was a distinctive "humanitarian international" that entertained close if ambiguous relations with the foreign policies of home states. In this context, the specter of disorder also presented opportunities for the expansion of mandates and budgets into new operating zones.

A second enabling factor was the growing Western revisionism towards state sovereignty and corresponding permissiveness towards intervention in the 1990s. By the beginning of the following decade, this had resulted in the doctrinal innovation of the "Responsibility to Protect" (R2P) discussed in Wolfgang Seibel's chapter. In short, many influential voices in the West questioned the primacy of sovereignty as the organizing principle of international political life and argued that human rights violators could not hide behind it. This relativism towards sovereignty was, unsurprisingly, anathema to post-colonial states and its deployment remained highly selective and inescapably political. But its rise marked an important shift towards making the new protectorates a political possibility barely a generation after the end of colonialism.

# INTRODUCTION

When did international intervention become something else? It is difficult to pinpoint this accurately. As mentioned before, the very intrusive UNSC resolutions on Somalia, Cambodia and elsewhere had not resulted in the establishment of new protectorates and subsequent peacekeeping operations had seemed to lose momentum and ambition. From the mid-1990s onwards, as Paris and Sisk note, there was certainly an intermittent but growing emphasis on longer timeframes and a focus on statebuilding, partly in response to critiques of the previous, mostly short-term missions.[25] But even if the normative context was appropriate for a qualitative jump in foreign involvement, we should not discount the central role of contingency and improvisation.

The earliest instance of direct UN governance was the mission in Serbian-occupied Eastern Slavonia, which was tasked with the transitional administration of the territory before its return to Croatia. This was an ambitious but relatively straightforward mission, yet the precedent was set. By 1997, the shortcomings of the peace process in BiH had led to the promulgation of the so-called "Bonn powers" which created the role of a High Representative of the international community as the arbiter of Bosnian political life and institutions. And by 1999, the UN had accepted executive authority over two small territories, Kosovo and East Timor, as they wrestled away from occupying forces. The basic precept of the new protectorates—that the internationals' role in peacebuilding did not end with the prevention of a return to war but included the management of reconstruction according to virtuous political and economic lines—was established.

These new commitments were only tenuously connected with peacekeeping. As Richard Caplan wrote, the international administrations that resulted were more akin to military occupations:

Never [before] had peacekeeping operations the authority to make and enforce local laws, exercise total fiscal management of a territory, appoint and remove local officials, create a central bank, establish and maintain customs services, regulate the local media, adjudicate rival property claims, run schools, regulate local businesses, and reconstruct and operate all utilities, amongst numerous other functions.[26]

At this stage, the direct governance of others became a political reality. The new protectorates were, at a superficial level, the *ad hoc* response to the lack of viability of post-war arrangements in the absence of an external coercive role. But they came into existence because they were conceivable in terms of the prevalent norms of powerful international actors and the comparative lack of power of those in disagreement with them.

These prevalent norms also dictated that only a multilateral framework would be deemed legitimate as a basis for interventionist policies, even if the policies themselves were premised on US hegemony and Washington's impatience occasionally led it to disregard the UN altogether.[27] There was a level of expediency in seeking UNSC support insofar as international bodies could be portrayed as serving the "community's interests as opposed to the particularistic interests of self-seeking states."[28] But multilateralizing international action also brings "significant costs," so that efficiency reasons are insufficient to account for this preference.[29] There are several explanations for the multilateral framework, including the existence of the post-1945 international architecture, but the US "legalistic" approach to international relations is paramount here.[30] This has resulted in international agencies playing a central role in humanitarian interventions and/or subsequent international occupations.[31]

No doubt in an attempt to salvage the "good interventionism" from neoconservative distortions, liberal internationalists often presented the wars and occupations that followed the terrorist attacks of 9/11, and especially the 2003 Iraq war, as entirely different from the interventions they had championed in the previous years.[32] The justifications for the Afghanistan and Iraq interventions were certainly premised on security concerns (terrorism; WMDs) that had been secondary or even absent in the 1990s, and the UN's involvement on the ground was far less important in both cases. However, they mirrored "quite closely" their UN-run counterparts in terms of their "moral and practical considerations,"[33] especially once the prospect of short-term solutions withered away and US-led forces in both locations dug in for the long haul.

The Iraq and Afghanistan occupations converted the Bush administration and motley conservative groups, who had decried humanitarianism and nation-building as "social work,"[34] to projects of political and economic transformation suspiciously reminiscent of the sort of emerging Clintonite agenda they had criticized in the previous decade. Thus the hitherto fringe project of international tutelage eventually drew support from diverse ideological corners, even if the justifications offered for exogenous statebuilding were varied to the extent of obscuring their similarity. The commonality was twofold: the origins and objectives of the new protectorates lay in the West; and at least briefly, the only internationally legitimate vision for the transformation of occupied societies entailed a market economy and a democratic political system.

The new protectorates were responses to individual catastrophes and can hardly be interpreted (except for neoconservative imaginings for Iraq as the launch pad for the democratization of the entire Middle East) as the implementation of a broader agenda. As such they were at best unplanned, at worst inchoate ventures. At the same time, it is impossible to see these interventions, and the lengthy international presence that followed them, as merely a functional response to humanitarian catastrophe. The problems that justified the existence of international protectorates—war, refugee flows, havens for transnational banditry—are not new. They have traditionally been addressed by the great powers in a variety of forms, verging from punitive raids and intermittent police action to indirect rule and the establishment of long-term imperial control. In the past such tactical choices would have been subsumed within the grand strategies of competing empires or, after 1945, within the rival ideological camps and spheres of interest of the Cold War. When the Cold War ended, there was no clear grand strategic design that could be discerned, and no single will—or clearly competing wills—to give one shape. None of the traditional responses was available after 1989. The specific manner chosen by leading Western states—expeditionary warfare, postwar occupation and the social and political re-engineering of societies—is consequently best understood as an elective approach that reflects a vaguely defined liberal convergence of views at a certain moment in time.[35]

How then should we understand these largely Western efforts to create an international order in the absence of a grand strategic vision?

## *The Rise of the New Protectorate: Normative Visions and Political Reception*

The motivations for international intervention and direct administration in the post-Cold War era are contested. Because it is difficult to draw any direct links between the normative innovations of the era and the real world of politics, many authors resort to instrumentalist accounts. New norms become "theoretical fillers"[36] used to flesh out policies that make sense from realist or neo-imperial perspectives. The empirical record of the last two decades certainly provides some evidence for this argument. This includes the highly selective character of interventions and callous neglect of some of the worst tragedies of the late twentieth century; the sheltering of notorious offenders from international vilification; and the tendency to "will the ends but not the means" of liberal statebuilding in terms of both long-term political will and needed resources.[37]

Such readings, though good for debunking purely altruistic understandings of intervention, do not take seriously enough the new norms embraced by

Western states in two key arenas: the reasons for and expected results from intervention. Intervention is a permanent feature of international life but its justifications have changed radically over the last two centuries and narrowed down significantly with decolonization.[38] In the early 1990s, a new justification emerged. Western decision-makers came to think, albeit fitfully and inconsistently, of a number of sovereign states which were illiberal, war-ravaged, bellicose and/or internally weak as potential international threats[39] and to contemplate neutralizing them. This turned older notions of realist interest on their head as interventions in what were otherwise viewed as valueless, peripheral spots came to be defined as rational. In the context of this changed notion of interest, poverty was a threat and "the promotion of development [...] synonymous with the pursuit of security."[40]

More important, key Western constituencies also changed their views on what should be achieved by intervening. The point was no longer to get rid of specific troublemakers. The growing Western assumption was that states that are politically free and economically open (that is, like-minded) are the sort that never pose a threat to each other and the international system. The increase in the number of states embracing these arrangements would further expand the global liberal capitalist system. Scholars have referred to this as the "liberal peace" agenda.[41] Many of its defenders viewed the internal organization of the states and societies of concern to them—their social structures, clientelistic political economies, corrupt institutions, factionalism, penchant for violence, patriarchal values, etc.—as the problem that needed addressing. The solution seemed to entail transforming them from their present benighted status into something resembling a Western democracy. This objective was mostly unstated and certainly under-theorized, but nonetheless represented the mainstream tendency in what passed for Western strategic thought.

As mentioned before, the consistency of such an agenda should not be overstated. The support for the takeover of war-torn territories emanated from many different corners, ranging from humanitarians sick of merely bearing witness (the Balkans in particular having turned many a relief worker into an advocate of intervention) to careerist bureaucrats out for turf, without reference to the overarching liberal peace agenda more often articulated in the pages of academic journals. And as we shall see, the realities of life in the new protectorates often bore no resemblance to liberal peace precepts. But at a particular moment, the interests of different Western constituencies were nonetheless broadly aligned in the pursuit of this project.

*Imperial Resonances*

The liberal peace agenda has attracted a fair share of hostility as well as support. Robert Cox bluntly dismissed it as "global poor relief and riot control."[42] Focusing on the outer fringes of the new imperialism, Fred Cooper noted that its goal is "domination, not incorporation, and most fundamentally of all, its political purpose is to mark the excluded."[43] From a liberal perspective, however, these critical readings were unmerited. The self-imagining of the intervener was essentially that of a redemptive presence coming to save people from themselves. Imperial talk was dismissed by US interveners without an imperial memory[44] and denied by Europeans, now working within safely multilateral and unimpeachably modern institutions and keen on sharing the benefits of those arrangements with their Balkan neighbors, as explored in the chapter by Spyros Economides. As Mark Mazower noted, the West's democratic liberalism was "naturalized and presented as the only form of political rationality capable of meeting the challenges of the modern world." It is thus "rendered unviolent and pragmatic—there is nothing very ideological about it at all—and is soothingly detached from its more coercive legacies of empire and domination."[45] One of the ironies of the new protectorates lies in the fact that, while an intensely political project, it is more often phrased by its key implementers as a reasonable, even technical, enterprise with altruistic motivations and little if any connection with the colonial past.

On the contrary, the past experience of Western governance of other societies must be kept at the center of discussions of the new protectorates. This is because that history has a bearing on present-day efforts. Perhaps the most disturbing element of continuity lies in the salience of the language of tutelage—the assumption that some people need to be protected from themselves by a benign civilizing entity,[46] and the return to an implicit "standard of civilization" according to which "barbarian" states do not have the same status as "normal" members of international society.[47] From the perspective of the inhabitants of the new protectorates, historical memories of Western rule (or of any form of foreign occupation) have also played a role in reactions to the international presence. The same applies to intellectual critics of the new protectorates who place contemporary experiences in the broader canvas of Western historical malfeasance in the developing world.

Conversely, advocates of the new protectorates do not engage much with the general record of Western imperialism and, if historically minded, are likely to handpick imperial moments where a progressive agenda of sorts can be discerned. Thus the preferred analogies are some of the League of Nations mandates, a few British and French late colonial efforts whose language of "development" is less jarring than that of high imperialism,[48] and, more than any other, the post-war occupations of Germany and Japan.[49] The embrace of "a didactic history which is pregnant with valuable lessons"[50] has been particularly important in the intellectual reception of the new protectorates, if on occasion to lament the lack of spine of the new "empire-lite."[51] However loosely and equivocally, such analogies have also informed the thinking of some decision-makers even if, at the ground level, most officials are considerably less steeped in the historical background of Western efforts at creating order.

Yet there are at least three reasons why too much should not be made of the theme of historical continuity. The first is that seeing the new protectorates in imperial terms risks giving too much consistency to essentially haphazard and ill-thought out ventures (and coincidentally much more coherence to European imperialism than it ever possessed in practice). Secondly, Western empires were flexible about the sort of governance arrangements that fitted different contexts, verging from the recognition of local potentates and indirect rule to highly coercive direct occupation. Indeed some areas were deemed ungovernable and capable only of being at best contained. The political imagination of the new protectorates is much narrower, assuming instead that familiar Western arrangements are entirely appropriate regardless of context. Finally, if one sees the new protectorates as simply derivative of (or, in some readings, coterminous with) the imperial project, one will fail to understand it as the historically contingent, and highly specific, product of a later age. The moral landscape of the West has irredeemably changed since the end of the colonial era, with Western audiences no longer lusting for empire and indeed revealing a dismally low level of toleration towards medium to long-term nation-building. Nationalism and religious fervor in the developing world are also a major stumbling block for the long-term legitimacy of alien rule.[52] Mayall and Srinivasan underline the limits of the imperial past for an understanding of current predicaments, even if there is something "inherently imperial" to them.[53] In this context, the language and historical experience of empire, while to some extent useful in making sense of the new protectorates, are often deployed in simplistic and inaccurate ways.

### Reactions to the New Protectorate

Stating this is not to underplay the extent to which important strands of opinion, particularly in the formerly colonized parts of the world, have refused to believe the good intentions of today's Western state-builders. For them, the language of empire was entirely apt and professions to the contrary on the part of Western interveners did not amount to much. In view of this, it is a mark of the almost uncontested character of Western hegemony that some of the new protectorates got off the ground with UNSC approval. This happened despite the antagonism that many states of the developing world felt towards the Western agendas of exogenous statebuilding.

The reasons for this opposition have been the subject of ample discussion. Very weak states held on to the fig leaf of juridical sovereignty as the remaining barrier against external impingement. As Christopher Clapham shows in his chapter on the near-absence of the new protectorate in Africa, where the largest cluster of weak and failed states is to be found, they need not have worried: the willingness to take over the worst cases was scant after Somalia.[54] From the League Mandates system onwards, there has been "a historical resonance accompanying the project of trusteeship [...] which goes a long way to explain the peculiar distaste with which it is treated by African ruling elites."[55] Indeed, one has only to consider the lengths to which Commonwealth African governments were prepared to go to avoid censuring Robert Mugabe, let alone approving any effective action against his regime in Zimbabwe, to appreciate the long shadow that Western racism and Western support for minority rule still casts over African politics.[56]

Strong states such as China and Russia[57] opposed the new interventionism and subsequent occupations on account of their own authoritarian domestic practices, secessionist troubles and fundamental antipathy towards liberal expansionism. India was animated by a reflexive anti-imperialism and the fear of creating precedents for external involvement in its own conflict in Kashmir.[58] The examples of such overt opposition to perceived Western agendas are numerous, with the intervention in Kosovo in 1999 and the war in Iraq four years later bringing out vociferous complaints of Western meddling and a concurrent unwillingness to sanction these actions through UNSC approval. In sum, there was a general skepticism amongst non-Western countries about the new protectorates that portrayed them as a Western project and derided their universalist pretensions. Despite all claims to the contrary, the emergence of "a solidarist conception of international society"[59] was still far off, and the new protectorates were more a product of Western supremacy than evidence of an emerging normative consensus.

As the chapters by Shogo Suzuki and Aswini Ray explain, this upfront, principled opposition was complicated by real world developments, the result of which was that, despite a willingness to criticize, non-Western states were mostly permissive of Western actions. The simplest one was the fact of Western power and the momentarily defensive position of critics: as C. Raj Mohan noted, "the [Non-Aligned Movement] and the Third World were no longer the *démandeurs* but the *répondeurs* in the emerging post-cold war debate on managing international security."[60] Secondly, although unsympathetic towards statebuilding by foreigners, many states in the developing world were strong supporters of, and key troop contributors towards, more conventional peacekeeping efforts (for example India, Pakistan, Bangladesh). Regional organizations such as ECOWAS were particularly adept at robust, if seldom wholly effective, peacekeeping. This means that they countenanced some forms of international muscular action even when disapproving of Western transformative agendas. Furthermore, the boundaries between peacekeeping and international statebuilding have on occasion proved elusive, with initially robust mandates lightly pursued in practice (Cambodia) while other operations seamlessly escalated into multinational takeovers.

Thirdly, strategic calculations played a role. In the aftermath of the Kosovo conflict, it was actually Russia that pushed for a UN administration to dilute NATO's clout. In subsequent years, Russia showed no interest in the fulfillment of the UN mandate lest it result in the creation of a new state, a bad precedent for Russia's own restive Caucasian Republics.[61] India and China have found the presence of NATO troops in Afghanistan a boon for their interests. India, now a major donor to Kabul, welcomes an Afghan regime that is not a Pakistani proxy. China is pursuing a $3.4 billion investment in copper mining, the "single largest investment in Afghan history," which necessitates the security umbrella provided by Western troops.[62] Also, while cultivating a ThirdWorldist flavor in some foreign policy areas that entails decrying Western "outof-area" involvements, both India and China have pursued uncomplicated *Realpolitik* in their own vicinities. The result of these calculations is that China as well as Russia, as UNSC permanent members, often preferred to abstain rather than oppose Western sponsored interventions. If a veto was threatened, as in the case of Kosovo and Iraq, the bids to legitimize post-intervention medium-term occupations were successful.[63] India's rapprochement with the US also means that it is rhetorically rather than substantively critical of the new protectorates, although one could be misled by the fierceness of the rhetoric.

Yet, as Simon Chesterman noted, acceptance in practice has emphatically not meant "acceptance in theory,"[64] and this ambivalence is becoming more pronounced as Western preeminence is diluted. Developing states are reaffirming the primacy of state sovereignty in a manner that can only curtail the lee-way of Western states to use IOs, and the UN system in particular, to promote statebuilding policies.[65] This trend can be seen by tracking the fortunes of the Peacebuilding Commission (PBC), which is the subject of the chapter by Richard Caplan and Richard Ponzio. Conceived by the High-Level Panel on Threats, Challenges and Change the PBC's overarching goal was to end the penchant for improvisation of previous peacebuilding efforts, improve analysis and coordination at the mission level, and provide a mechanism for early-warning and monitoring of weak states. Although the PBC came into being in 2005, it was shorn of this preventive role by developing states convinced that industrialized states were trying to "hijack" the UN in order to institutionalize "continuing interventions" in their domestic affairs.[66] This capping of the ambitions of the PBC, together with a more recent record of contrarian UN majority voting on issues as varied as Kosovo, Myanmar and Zimbabwe, was proof that the permissiveness of the immediate post-Cold War period was ebbing.

## *Governing the New Protectorate*

This section deals in turn with the organization and staffing of the new protectorate, some of the major policies they pursue, and relations with the local populations. The avowed purpose of the new protectorates was extremely ambitious in all instances discussed in this book: the transformation of illiberal societies into something akin to what interveners thought of as a Western liberal democracy. In addition to the ambitious core tasks of disarmament, demobilization and reintegration (DDR), repatriation of refugees, physical reconstruction and the running of elections, the internationals sought to write constitutions, reform civil services and courts, restart economic activity through privatization, promote post-war reconciliation and/or war crimes tribunals, fight organized crime, reform police and armed forces, empower women in patriarchal societies, etc. The list goes on. In the Western Balkans, the aspirations were even higher as Kosovo and BiH were meant to become not only passably decent societies but candidates for EU membership.

The UN provided crucial legitimacy for the new protectorates and some operations (such as Kosovo and East Timor) were UN-run. Even in the case of Iraq, the Bush administration saw benefits to the post-invasion drawing in of the UN, with tragic consequences.[67] Yet despite this UN prominence the actual number of intervening actors with traction on the ground was mind-numbingly large. In Kosovo, for instance, NATO, the OSCE and the EU were governing co-principals with the UN. Even while working under a nominal alliance, the armed forces of individual states had their own decision-making frameworks and often acted without coordination and according to very different understandings of the situation.[68] UN-system agencies with their own lines of reporting included UNHCR, WFP, UNICEF, the UN Human Rights Office, UNDP, WHO, DPKO, ILO and OCHA, among others.[69] Other organizations included the IMF, the World Bank, the ICTY, the ICRC, the Council of Europe, the donor offices of individual countries, and a number of NGOs too large to list here.[70] A recent study mentions no less than 24 major peacebuilding organizations involved in an average operation.[71] In addition to this, the new protectorates of course contained the large, inefficient and overstaffed civil services of the pre-intervention state.

## The Structure of the New Protectorate

While foreign intervention and peacebuilding are the subjects of large literatures, the sociology and political culture of the intervening agents are underresearched.[72] The internal functioning of missions is rarely the subject of ethnographic work and, with the exception of the odd uncooperative NGO (such as MSF), policy dissensions and the outright clashing ideologies of the many interveners are ignored or subdued by the assumption that a mainstream, broadly shared peacebuilding culture exists.[73] This assumption is premised on two undeniable facts: the general normative agreement on basic end goals (in themselves commendable and therefore unlikely to draw much principled opposition); and a collective understanding regarding the policies that are conceivable (say, DDR) and those that lie beyond the limits of the politically possible (say, the shooting of unarmed demonstrators). But these perhaps deliberately vague points of agreement do not add up to a shared philosophy for the building of a post-war state. In practice, external interveners have different institutional cultures and political agendas, and often opposing senses of what should be prioritized. More important, they stand in no particular relationship with each other and are under no obligation, except in the broadest of terms, to advance common objectives. "Autonomy, not integration and collaboration," wrote Thomas Weiss, "are the hallmarks of this feudal system."[74]

The governance of the new protectorates was instead ineffectively enacted through a patchwork of loose, decentralized arrangements and ill-defined and sometimes non-existent hierarchical relationships. On paper there were differences in the degree to which authority was concentrated. In Bosnia and Afghanistan, the framework for the occupation was initially unclear and bureaucratic overlap was to be expected, although it complicated civil-military relations and rendered them inefficient, as the chapter by John Drewienkiewicz demonstrates. In Kosovo and East Timor, things seemed simpler as the relevant UN resolutions gave the UN a mandate of "undetermined duration and theoretically almost unlimited powers."[75]

Yet in the field, foreign administration was similarly confusing regardless of mandate, with different actors asserting their independence. This "networked" approach to the running of the protectorate constitutes its most strikingly distinctive factor. It is important to understand this "shift from the vertical world of hierarchies to the horizontal world of networks"[76] as an enthusiastic choice by decision-makers and the organizations that constituted the protectorate's crowd of external actors. The prevalence of the networked approach is aptly described by Mark Duffield: it is very much a choice that fits today's international relations and assumptions about the role of actors and institutions. The present-day system of global governance for poorly governed or ungoverned territories is not "manifest within a single institution" but is embedded in a "number of flows and nodes of authority that bring together different strategic complexes of state, non-state, military-civilian and public-private actors."[77] Their approach is essentially non-territorial and theoretically premised on ever-shifting arrangements with "different organizations, interest groups and forms of authority in relation to specific regulatory tasks." For the actors involved their institutional self-interest (defined as political independence and budgetary autonomy) points to the need for distance from other entities.[78]

The dismal results of "new organizational forms and dynamics outside or at odds with formal legal and political structures"[79] have been recognized since the early 1990s and there have been token efforts at addressing them. These included the establishment of the DHA and later OCHA and the Brahimi report's plea for the creation of "integrated missions."[80] But most intellectual and policy efforts have focused on better "coordination" (which has been a function of punctual convergence of interests and not the product of a common strategic focus), knowing full well that no political will exists for transcending the root problem. The "familiar charade that a pluricentral non-system can be made to function as if it were a centrally-organized system"[81] has been kept, with minor modifications, up to the present day.

The non-hierarchical structure of the new protectorate is strange in view of the constant references to the Western state as the model being emulated. But the new protectorate is not like a modern state.[82] In it, the locus of power is unclear and its wielding is dispersed. The problem transcends the dynamics within the circle of interveners and impacts on dealings with the local state, which is often disempowered and weakened in the process. Despite the familiar language of Western stateness, then, the reality of the new protectorate is characterized not by the mimesis of Western procedures and contemporary modes of life but by the experimentation of new governance methods.[83] Our focus on such organizational deficiencies is not meant to favor a "technocratic" explanation for the disappointing results of the new protectorate. The purpose of underlining such shortcomings is to suggest that the new protectorates saw a fundamental mismatch between nominal goals and the means put at their disposal.

## People

With few exceptions, the hiring practices of the UN system, donor government agencies and NGOs within the new protectorates were remarkably similar. The vast majority of contracts were year-long (in the case of 2003–04 Iraq, three months). The quality of human resources was often at best inadequate, and at worst very poor. Long-term secondment to a mission rarely held career-advancing potential for those with permanent jobs elsewhere. The skills set of the average foreign state-builder often did not include the technical capacities most lacking in the new protectorate, especially at an early stage of the deployment. Many missions had a disproportionate presence of very young people, who are often unattached and therefore more likely to go to dangerous zones. Sometimes they were in unjustifiably senior positions, a problem most often associated with the high-profile Republican loyalists of the CPA in Iraq,[84] but present in an attenuated form in other contexts. Stories of vastly overpaid, transient internationals living a sahib's life in well-guarded, insulated pleasure enclaves became rife (Camp Bondsteel in Kosovo; the Green Zone in Baghdad; the "love boats" Hotel Olympia and Amos W. in East Timor), sometimes undeservedly.

More important, all the missions shared a lack of serious, and sometimes even basic, knowledge about the countries they were trying to redeem. Many commentators bemoan the contrast with professional colonial bureaucracies and their standing competence in the languages and customs of the societies they dominated. Even if one is not misty-eyed about such experiences, it is impossible to avoid the conclusion that, in the words of the Brahimi Report, the "armies of imagined experts" never materialized. A clear urban bias characterized the deployment of the internationals, with overstaffed capital and provincial cities contrasting with a light presence elsewhere. Security concerns in places such as Afghanistan also meant that foreign officials were rarely allowed out of "fortress-like" compounds and therefore spent their tours of duty without acquiring field knowledge of any consequence.[85] The usual obsession of the modern state with the accumulation of knowledge as a means to exercise control is practically not there: to use the language of the anthropologist James Scott, the modern protectorate certainly does not "see like a state."[86]

This is not a problem of individuals, at least some of whom were dedicated and highly competent. Although research on institutional memory and learning in the UN system is limited, it is clear that the systems for organization-wide knowledge, guidance and doctrine development are only in their infancy,[87] and the same applies to most other organizations. There has been no major incentive to create and perpetuate a pool of knowledge about a given country. Individuals have every reason to rotate out of difficult positions and there are no systems for managing and passing on experience. To some extent this has to do with bureaucratic inertia and short planning horizons but there are deeper causes, especially at the level of the UN system and other IOs. As mentioned previously, too many UN member-states are against the creation of anything that can be construed as a colonial service-in-waiting, even at the multilateral level. Wolfgang Seibel is more optimistic about the UN's capacity to learn and emphasizes these political impediments instead.[88] A number of Western states belatedly made arrangements for some permanent expertise,[89] but the extent to which it can be mobilized depends on the vagaries of partisan politics. In the case of Iraq's CPA, for instance, experts on the Arab world were often discriminated against on the assumption that they were unsympathetic to the agenda of the Bush administration.[90]

In the absence of a strong institutional character, it is unsurprising that individual, even charismatic leadership has played a disproportionate role in the new protectorates. Many missions are remembered and assessed by the strong-headed demeanor, and willingness to wield power, of the helmsman. SRSGs such as Bernard Kouchner, Michael Steiner (both in Kosovo), Sérgio Vieira de Mello (East Timor), and Jacques Klein (Eastern Slavonia), and Special Representatives such as Wolfgang Petritsch and Paddy Ashdown[91] (both in BiH) gained a reputation for assertiveness towards the intervened as well as the motley group of statebuilders. This strange emphasis on men (as opposed to rational-legal institutions and statebuilding processes) in the new protectorates led to a backlash and worries about international authoritarianism.[92] This charge certainly sticks in many instances, with Jerry Bremer's 2003–4 running of Iraq the fullest example of a vice-regal style (in this case, with hints of CEO managerialism).

Yet a focus on such occasions does not provide a full portrait of the dynamics of power in the new protectorate. While critics insist on the insensitive and even autocratic behavior of the internationals,[93] in reality they mostly did not indulge in the role of the viceroy or old-style district commissioner. Part of the matter lies in the lack of overall authority over the network of interveners discussed above: in many areas the "man in charge" could deploy his powers of persuasion or even talk tough, but little more. Perhaps as important, however, was the internationals' own ambivalence about the colonial overtones of this role. The memoirs of two British officials in the CPA, for instance, betray serious awareness in this regard, even if their dominant US partner was less prone to this sort of self-reflection.[94] The enterprise itself was pregnant with colonial resonances, as discussed above. When push came to shove, however, the interveners often lacked the self-confidence, ruthlessness or political will to act in an imperial manner. If one accepts the new protectorates in their own terms, the problem was not so much that they were a colonial enterprise, but rather, for all the talk of transformative ambition, that they were not "colonial enough."[95]

## Policies

The governance structure[96] described above and in several of the subsequent chapters was plainly inadequate for implementing economic reconstruction agendas that poorly fitted the new protectorates in the first place. Christopher Cramer dubs this "the great post-conflict makeover fantasy."[97] The two points most frequently raised are, first, that economic policies were ill-thought out for the specific circumstances of each protectorate and, second, that the political objectives of the peace, which in many circumstances dictate economic policies that may be suboptimal, were overridden in favor of "purely economic objectives" with destabilizing consequences.[98] As Mats Berdal and David Keen discuss in their chapter on the dominant economic ideas and actual policies promoted in the new protectorates, it is not clear that outsiders understood their inadequacies, the impact of wartime practices (including their own, for example sanctions regimes) or the effects they would have on the local political economy.[99]

As in other matters, the early US occupation of Iraq provides us with the more extreme examples. The CPA put forward "a supply-side strategy of reducing the role of government industry through privatization, eliminating subsidies for electricity and fuel, cutting tariffs, lowering taxes, promoting foreign investment and enacting pro-business laws," the type of drastic reforms conservatives "long dreamed of implementing in the US."[100] But the Washington Consensus on free markets and lean states informed economic policy in the other protectorates as well. The extensive employment of subcontractors, including the problematic use of private security outfits, far exceeded practice in a "normal" Western context. Premature privatization ended up placing in the hands of elite insiders (sometimes war criminals) vital assets for reconstruction.[101] The plethora of imported statebuilders, for all the talk of local capacity building, ended up working with itself,[102] consuming the bulk of available resources, and even consuming the scarce local human resources that might conceivably staff the state apparatus. As Clare Lockhart shows in her chapter on the relations between the Afghan state and the internationals, far from being complementary, the logic of these organizational solutions is competitive with that of the institutions supposedly being built.[103] They have certainly not resulted in a sustainable recuperation of protectorate economies or sustainable revenue-handling institutions.[104]

The lack of institutionalization of the new protectorates and the vagaries of the networked approach resulted in a foreign effort that was inept and wasteful to a remarkable degree. The period between 1995 and 2010 was replete with appalling, long-term failures in basic areas such as electricity provision and garbage collection.[105] Corruption also acquired a systemic character with operations run on a permanent "state of exception" basis where procedures such as audits do not take place consistently and opportunities for self-enrichment abound. As Philippe Le Billon notes, "nepotism, fraud, over-invoicing, lack of transparency and accountability, and tax avoidance [are] institutionalized within peace-building and reconstruction initiatives."[106] The incidence of criminal behavior by the internationals (as opposed to mere incompetence) is disputed. But the lack of accountability and the opacity of international decision-making invariably resulted is a loss of status vis-à-vis the local population. A prominent example was the 2002 corruption scandal around KEK, the Kosovan electricity utility, one of several high-level scandals rocking the province.[107] The fact that the record of protectorate law enforcement towards the internationals has been episodic at best, even when criminal behavior is uncovered, further contributes to this.

In different ways, the same applies to the intervened. The most conspicuous arena for this legal pusillanimity is the maintenance of public order, as analyzed in Michael Boyle's chapter on policing. In Kosovo and Iraq, the establishment of the foreign presence happened simultaneously with large-scale looting and reprisals against enemies and these continued intermittently in subsequent years. The passivity of the interveners on these occasions created an authority deficit that would haunt the new protectorates. This was also the case with organized crime, the origins of which often harked back to wartime networks, but which was decidedly invigorated by the opportunities brought about by the new protectorate. In some contexts this thriving is linked to flawed or nonexistent law enforcement and the closeness between the mafias and the elites partnering with the internationals (sometimes the organized criminals—for example, the KLA or the Northern Alliance—*are* the elites). More often than not, Berdal and Keen explain in their chapter, the continuing role of "illiberal, violent and exploitative actors" is linked to outsiders not understanding the unintended consequences of their own policies.[108] Confusingly, this ground level legal permissiveness could be matched by a continuing high-mindedness at the macro level of the protectorate. Foreigners thus ended up writing enlightened constitutions with minimal local input in Iraq and East Timor,[109] firing local officials in BiH, and continuing a post-independence oversight role in Kosovo through EULEX.[110] Arguably this pattern results in the new protectorates garnering a despotic reputation without the benefits that a consistently despotic practice might produce.

The shortcomings of the new protectorate in managing the economy and upholding the rule of law bring out a broader issue. Why did interveners shy away from the key arenas where, historically, states have been built? Avoidance of the central task of statebuilding—the creation of a political center of power that is accountable but also powerful—remains the rule. At the root of the serious neglect of statebuilding proper is not only the aforementioned specter of colonialism but, perhaps more important, the antipathy of Western liberals towards state power. This is revealed in the unsatisfactory quality of liberal accounts of statebuilding, especially their preference for engaging with the contemporary state as a final product (with all its normatively appealing traits retrospectively inscribed in its origins) and equivocating about the role of coercion and fiscal extraction.[111] As Samuel Huntington noted, Americans in particular seem more concerned with checking the power of institutions than with building them up in the first place.[112]

Some of this ambivalence is entirely understandable. Historically, the building of states has been a violent, difficult and drawn-out process. In protectorates where the state has traditionally been very weak, it is unlikely that strong state institutions can be built in a way acceptable to Western sensibilities. Conversely, Iraq and the states of former Yugoslavia have had previous experiences of strong statehood but these were authoritarian: not the sort of state legacies that internationals want to cultivate. Perhaps an accurate understanding of the often tragic process of statebuilding would have led to an abandonment of liberal daydreams of "nice statebuilding" to be achieved without organized violence, fiscal extraction and political centralization, the old staples of the historical sociology of the state for which the jargon of peacebuilding lacks synonyms. The optimistic agenda of transformation articulated by Western interveners ignored this, but such fears resurfaced in the Western obsession with exit strategies and with markers, such as the holding of elections, the passing of progressive legislation and tokenistic economic reforms, which in no way provided a closure to the process of constructing a viable liberal state.

## The "Intervened'

This gap between the interveners' professed intentions and the willingness and capacity to carry them out was quickly perceived by empowered locals who did not share the same progressive aspirations.[113] In cases such as BiH the internationals had to cope with particularly uncooperative elites as they tried to preserve a multiethnic state. Even when interventions in Iraq, Afghanistan and Kosovo brought about a turnover in elites, it was not apparent that the new set (which incidentally owed its good fortune to the internationals) was, from a normative perspective, any more liberal than the deposed regimes.

The starting assumption of the interveners was that most of the people subjected to intervention were keen on being remodeled into liberal democrats, and that specific key constituencies ("the Iraqi middle class"; "Kosovan NGOs" etc.) were nearly so. That, plus an acute awareness of the many "legitimacy challenges" confronting the protectorate that are closely examined in Dominik Zaum's chapter, led the internationals to seek a degree of "local ownership" for the project of liberal transformation. There is no doubt that populations wanted stability and security. But it is still unclear whether they have or are likely to internalize liberal values to the extent that one could reasonably claim that, say, the Balkan populations have been "Europeanized" or that their practice of democracy has become self-sustaining. If this outcome is in doubt within Europe where conditions are advantageous, as Economides suggests, the task of transforming the political culture of protectorates in other parts of the world, where there is no equivalent economic pull and both cultural and political traditions have little in common with Western liberalism, will surely be even more formidable.[114]

All occupying powers have to rely to a great extent on pre-existing formal or informal governing structures, even if this limits the downward reach of the occupation. It is unsurprising that local political actors have their own agendas and that, after a period of adaptation, they are capable of thriving in a context of external administration.[115] The awareness that interveners want to leave as soon as possible encourages elites to bide their time. What is noteworthy is the internationals' penchant for cutting corners by reaching an accommodation with these actors, many of whom explicitly stand for political and social projects at odds with the purposes of the new protectorate. In this context, "hard" security concerns provide an alternative rationality and invariably carry the day. A shocking example is the fraudulent Afghan election of 2009, which the internationals ended up swallowing. In particular there is a chasm between the rights agendas used to mobilize Western support and justify the protectorate (saving women in burkas, etc.) and the actual pursuit of social and political reform. This confounds the expectations of genuine local reformists as well as their willingness to risk their necks.[116] In seeking this sort of accommodation with local elites, the internationals are sucked into games they scarcely understand and reconstruction becomes, in the hands of their canny interlocutors, little more than "another external asset to be converted into the political currency of patronage."[117]

It is difficult not to conclude that the new protectorates have been characterized by a "virtual liberalism" with a dangerous disconnect between political rhetoric and progressive aspiration, on the one hand, and the world of action and interest on the other. As one of the editors of this book has written in another context, this goes "beyond the traditional hypocrisy of world politics [...] to threaten the traditional and necessary link between power and responsibility."[118]

## Conclusion

More than a decade after the modern protectorates became reality a measure of stocktaking is possible, as attempted in the following chapters. None of the new protectorates, even those in which the US was not directly involved, could have been established without either the projection of American power or indirect US underwriting. Yet neither the US itself nor other states had a grand strategy for the management of world order, let alone one in which the protectorates feature. Their establishment followed the Western victory in the Cold War. At the time only Western values, suitably disguised in the universalist language of the UN Charter, had worldwide traction. It was hardly surprising that when conflict in fragile states either spilled over international borders, menacing regional or even global security, or threatened to do so, it was to the democratic model that the major powers turned. They were no doubt encouraged to do so by the presence in all these societies of many genuinely patriotic democrats. The trouble is, as the late Ernest Gellner might have put it, that the world is over-endowed with these people in societies that do not meet the criteria for the creation of successful, let alone democratic, nation-states. It is not surprising, therefore, that in the absence of a coherent collective vision, success has remained so elusive.

At the heart of the new protectorates were the Zeitgeist-induced assumptions that a peaceful democracy and functioning state and market would somehow come into existence "naturally" and that all good things go together.[119] Had there been a realistic assessment of the challenges Westerners were getting into, the new protectorates would probably not have come into existence at all. Instead, a naïve, ahistorical optimism carried the day. Some observers were especially critical about the "modular" character of the new protectorates—the way in which the liberal state was thought out as a straightforward finished product that could be delivered wholesale to Dili or Kabul. Yet statebuilding in the post-colonial era has frequently had a modular character, with leaders consciously emulating experiences of development they found useful.[120] The problem in the new protectorates was that the "model" existed only at the level of discourse and never panned out as a credible statebuilding project.[121] The result of an enterprise blithely entered into has been a seemingly endless financial commitment, a substantial international presence that remains when the status of the new protectorate is nominally shifted, and a sense that the foreigners' fragile achievements would collapse overnight in their absence. By the end of the first decade of the twenty-first century, except for the supposedly Europe-bound Western Balkans, where convergence with EU practice was still sought, Western fatigue at these engagements resulted in a marked downplaying of the erstwhile reformist agendas in favor of an exclusive security focus.

Can foreigners build other peoples' states and decent societies, even assuming that their motives are mostly altruistic? This book shows that such an enterprise is both normatively intricate and empirically challenging. In some of the new protectorates, foreigners have ended the fighting, saved many lives, and made a contribution to a sustainable peace, an achievement often overlooked by root-and-branch critics. Indeed, portraits of international peacebuilding as "threatening prospects of economic development"[122] are both unfair and over-optimistic about the character (in normative and developmental terms) of whatever domestic arrangements might have emerged in the absence of the new protectorates.

But in retrospect the internationals' organizational solutions, political commitment, and transformative zeal seem inappropriate for taking purported aspirations any further. Even in the case of the post-9/11 invasions, where the sense of existential threat dictated more than a cursory commitment to change, early setbacks soon led to engagements with fewer ambitions. As already noted, the means put at the service of the new protectorate were painfully inadequate for the ends that were sought. For some experts, this extends considerably beyond practical challenges to include the fundamental contradiction of using autocratic means (a foreign enlightened presence) to deliver freedom and prosperity to the populations of the new protectorates.[123] An analysis, such as the present one, that places some emphasis on the empirical failures of the new protectorates (however egregious) must not underplay the perhaps unsolvable "dilemmas"[124] of exogenous statebuilding and the nagging suspicion that it can't be done.

As an expression of great power clout, the new protectorates are unlikely to perish completely, as shown by the ambivalent Chinese and Indian receptions of its discourse and practice. They may find something like it expedient in the not too distant future. As with the humanitarian discourse more generally, it is malleable enough to be reappropriated: witness Russia's claim that the 2008 Georgia war was an exercise in R2P.[125] But the growing impatience of non-Western states and the increased pluralism of international society mean that the support for more such projects will not be forthcoming. Liberal states will remain involved in intervention and peacebuilding. But they will no longer fall into what have invariably turned out to be costly and long-term commitments which, rhetoric aside, they lack the competence, stomach, and legitimacy to fulfill.

The disappointing results of the new protectorates in apparently manageable statelets such as Kosovo and East Timor mean that they are not seen, even from a "technical" perspective, as a solution to truly complicated large-state conflicts in Sudan, the DRC, etc. Moreover, there are a growing number of often sustainable, domestically-run processes of reconstruction in places such as Angola, Rwanda, Lebanon and Sri Lanka. These are anything but showcases for the liberal peace,[126] with the peace dividend benefiting well-placed actors rather than war victims and the poor. But these illiberal processes of reconstruction provide an alternative model to long-term international involvement. Illiberal peacebuilding can now benefit from international support networks that have no appetite for liberal blueprints and indeed actively contribute towards authoritarian post-war consolidation. Mainstream peacekeeping will remain popular but liberal peacebuilding with vast social engineering ambitions will become difficult to sustain and defend. Sovereignty, it seems, is back.

What will the legacy of the new protectorates be? It is hard to avoid the impression that, despite a number of achievements, these stabs at statebuilding by foreigners will not be foundational or transformative in any intended sense. In fact, they may turn out to be curiously transient moments in the history of the societies subjected to them. This is not to underplay the radical nature of empowering Kosovar Albanians, East Timorese or Iraqi Shiites. But the subsequent political order may not be qualitatively different from the status quo ante. As Toby Dodge dispiritingly notes in his analysis of America's bloody attempts at transforming Iraq's political economy and state-society relations, at the end of the day Iraq retains an oil-based rentier economy and a powerful authoritarian state ruled by an illiberal elite.[127] Afghanistan is no closer to being a modern and cohesive state (never mind liberal or not), Kosovars are no closer to abandoning their clan affinities or respecting their non-Albanian countrymen, and East Timor no closer to viable statehood: so much for the ostensible goal of the new protectorates. This conclusion may seem harsh, but—unless one dismisses the stated intentions of the internationals *a priori* as insincere—it is unavoidable when the realities of 2011 are compared with the original vision.

But perhaps the fundamental legacy of the new protectorates resides elsewhere, in what they tell us about a particular moment of Western hegemony. Surveying the somber ideological landscape of the twentieth century, Jay Winter wrote of "minor utopias"—not the murderous ones that dominated global politics, but the often forgotten, decent and optimistic dreams of human improvement—as "spaces in which the contradictions of a period are embodied and performed, and new possibilities are imagined."[128] They were eventually discarded and are now historical footnotes. It is their heuristic value for an understanding of the age during which they rose to prominence, rather than their meager practical impact, that proved noteworthy in the long run. The time is running out for the new protectorates to escape this outcome.

# 1

# PROTECTORATES NEW AND OLD

## A CONCEPTUAL CRITIQUE

*William Bain*

The resurrection of various forms of international tutelage is significant for what it suggests about a changing world order, and puzzling for what these engagements are said to represent and how they are interpreted. That so-called "failed," "collapsed," and "rogue" states pose an unacceptable threat to world order is commonly accepted as a given in contemporary international relations. The interconnectedness brought about by globalization drains the notion of "local conflict" of much of its meaning. Indeed, "global" and "local" are so deeply intertwined, so the argument goes, that it is no longer possible to remain detached from distant conflicts. An open society, full of innovation and fluid in exchange, is also a society vulnerable to those who do not share in its values. The terrorist attacks on New York and Washington on September 11, 2001 provide the most visible and searing icon of this manner of thinking. Hence the American National Security Strategy of 2002 declares: "America is now threatened less by conquering states than we are by failing ones."[1] Some obvious conclusions follow in train. There is an urgent need to extend political and economic freedom to places where it is absent, and to redeem the inherent and indestructible human dignity that is the birthright of every man and woman, no matter where they might happen to live. International tute-

31

lage manifested concretely as several classes of new protectorate is but one way of advancing this project. In other words, the new protectorates are part and parcel of a political project aimed at fashioning a world order of a particular sort.

Most attempts at interpreting the character of the various forms of international tutelage involve an excursion into the world of history. After all, the problems that the new protectorates are meant to remedy beg no flight of the imagination; they are hardly new, which transforms history from a storehouse of curiosity into a powerful and authoritative language used to articulate many different and often conflicting claims. Two of these claims stand out for want of further attention. The first makes a sharp distinction between past and present; it seeks to separate a disreputable history of domination and exploitation from an enlightened engagement in international governance, the end of which is to redeem the world's oppressed (as opposed to backward) peoples in the truths of human rights, democracy, and free market economy. Indicative of this approach is Robert Cooper's suggestion that "postmodern imperialism," a kind of imperialism divested of the coercive relations that are the hallmark of old-fashioned imperialism and instead, accommodates itself to a world of "human rights and cosmopolitan values" through voluntary arrangements aimed at exporting stability and liberty to the "pre-modern" zone of chaos— the world of failed states.[2] The second also involves a journey through the world of history, albeit one premised on a degree of continuity between past and present. This approach invests the past with an instructive or didactic voice. Here, the concept of novelty, which is often meant to immunize "postmodern imperialism" from the opprobrium that typically attaches to the word "empire," gives way to a rather more utilitarian outlook that transforms past colonial experience into a modern-day classroom for the international bureaucrat. Thus, administering new protectorates is guided by the belief that "much can be learned" from past colonial experience.[3]

It is at this point that a puzzle arises: the tension that obtains between a liberal world order founded on the values of freedom and equality, and what is required to make liberal states. The purpose of this essay is to illuminate this tension by advancing two related arguments. First, I want to argue that the invocation of past historical experience, either to safeguard new protectorates from criticism or to conduct them better than they are conducted at present, ends up concealing as much as it illuminates. In this context, history is mined with a view to providing a justification, rather than to impart understanding, which leaves the "is it empire?" debate blind and deaf to questions presupposed by the idea of international tutelage. Secondly, I want to argue that these questions are intelligible in terms of a discourse of ability that is equally at home in a world of empires, such as those that once defined political geography, and a world of democracies as is the current fashion. The point of interest, then, is located at the intersection of the liberal commitment to freedom and equality and the stark reality that the world is marked by conspicuous inequalities that mock the freedom of some people to pursue self-chosen ends.

Advocates of international tutelage have managed to address only one part of this puzzle. For they are long on what people should be, namely free and equal, but a great deal less adept at explaining the reasons why so many people are neither free nor equal. It is in this sense that the new protectorates struggle for a sound footing. They might be useful and perhaps even effective in expanding the sphere in which liberal values prevail; and yet the condition of inferiority implied by the discourse of ability cultivates a nagging doubt about the legitimacy of these arrangements. Moreover, it is likely that these doubts will persist so long as the discourse of ability is separated from an open and assured account of the reasons why some people are deemed to be incapable of acting according to their rights and for their own purposes. So while it is true that the world has changed, dramatically in some respects, there is reason to believe that it has not changed so much as to render unintelligible the post-colonial objection that inability should not serve as a pretext for withholding independence or, presumably, for extinguishing independence once it has been achieved. In the end, the attempt to build a liberal world order, to vindicate the universal values of human freedom and equality, involves treating some people in some circumstances as if they are less than fully free and less than fully equal. And to that extent the new protectorates are not unlike the "old protectorates": they are the instruments of belligerent civilizations that seek to propagate a superior way of life.

## The Cult of Novelty

The approach that endeavors to distinguish past from present usually proceeds from the (unarticulated) belief that an assessment of motives is necessary to safeguard new protectorates from the ignoble strokes painted by the brush of "empire." The history of empire is then reduced to a sordid account of naked greed, which would suffice for an indictment were it not for the foul stench of racism and religious bigotry that so often went hand-in-hand with imperial mastery. Pithy quotations, such as Bismarck's declaration that European pow-ers "share the wish to bring the natives of Africa within the pale of civiliza-tion,"[4] are held out as ready proofs of deceit. A complete charge sheet might also include any number of shameful acts that are memorialized in the con-science of popular memory. The destruction of the Tasmanians, who were hunted to extinction in a perverse kind of sport, is ripe for inclusion; so too is the massacre of Hindu festival-goers at Jallianwala Bagh in Amritsar, all in the name of maintaining good order throughout the realm; and surely the mil-lions of African slaves transported to work the plantations of the New World merit inclusion. It is against this backdrop that Kwame Nkrumah's denuncia-tion of empire receives a sympathetic hearing: "[b]eneath the 'humanitarian' and 'appeasement' shibboleths of colonial governments, a proper scrutiny leads one to discover nothing but deception, hypocrisy, oppression, and exploitation."[5]

If it were not for acts of sheer brutality we might be impressed by the impe-rial masters' professions of enlightened rule. But with the benefit of hindsight, moved by self-effacing embarrassment or self-righteous indignation, a clear and orderly history reveals the misplaced arrogance that is quick to proclaim a contingent present as the apex of human achievement. Here, T.B. Macaulay's derisive characterization of "Hindoo" and "Mahomedan" learning comes read-ily to mind, the entire worth of which was merely the equal of a "single shelf of a good European library."[6] The same unchecked confidence led Charles Grant to denounce "a crafty and imperious [Hindu] priesthood," which he held responsible for leaving the inhabitants of British India in a sunken state of civilization.[7] And India's teeming but organized masses easily gave way to the depiction of the naked men and women of Africa as the wretched residue of humanity. Their otherworldly condition once drew Henry Morton Stanley into a moment of self-reflection that struggled to escape disbelief:

I saw before me over a hundred beings of the most degraded, unpresentable type it is possible to conceive, and though I knew quite well that some thousands of years ago the beginning of this wretched humanity and myself were one and the same, a sneak-ing disinclination to believe it possessed me strongly, and I would even now willingly subscribe some small amount of silver money for him who could but assist me to con-trovert the discreditable fact.[8]

In this fertile soil grew the image of the noble savage, mysterious and charm-ing, but terribly burdened by an impoverished mind and soul.

The history of empire is rich with such examples, whose harrowing details etch the outlines of a morally bankrupt enterprise that elevated the pursuit of gold and silver, the trade in nutmeg and pepper, and the intrigues of great power rivalry above the needs of the vulnerable. Viewed from this perspective, the word "empire" is reduced to an unalloyed term of abuse. Certainly this narrative is immensely popular, but it is also wrong in so far as it is presented as anything more than one of several cogent narratives of empire. The history of empire is less a line drawing than an intricate tapestry made of many different colored threads, each of which tells a particular story that is inextricably a part of a larger whole. Of course, this tapestry is blemished by many ignominious stains, but it also shows many proofs of genuine care which today would pass for the best kind of humanitarianism. To acknowledge this much does not mean that (self-proclaimed) trustees of civilization were always faithful to their obligations, sincere in their professions, or wise in what they set out to achieve. But then liars, hypocrites, and prophets were no less a part of the project of empire than they are now a part of the fashionable promotion of global citizenship. In other words, the missionaries, traders, soldiers, and administrators that set out for the furthest reaches of the globe sometimes got it wrong just as they sometimes got it right.

More damning, though, is the charge that it was all a charade; that pledges to assist and to care for "backward" peoples were a self-conscious attempt at deception in order to grow rich and powerful on the backs of those who could least afford it. Henry Brailsford conveys this opinion in denouncing the First World War, with no less vigor than did Lenin in his famous tract *Imperialism*, as a struggle for "places in the sun" to service the appetites of wealthy (European) investors and bankers. So too does E.D. Morel, founder of the Congo Reform Association that did so much to bring the horrors of the Congo Free State to light, who openly mocked the humanitarian spirit that Bismarck invoked in convening the Berlin Conference of 1885: "[f]rom the ashes of an international conference, summoned in the name of Almighty God, has sprung a traffic in African misery more devilish than the old, more destructive, more permanently ruinous in its cumulative effect."[9] Like Nkrumah, Brailsford and Morel adopt the doctrine of profit as the organizing principle of an historical narrative that grants no quarter to authentic principle. A.P. Thornton explains the mindset of this narrative as being steeped in base instinct and the ever present danger of abuse: "[b]ehind every profession of a civilizing mission…must lurk in fact only the desire of industrial capitalists, men whose real interest in human welfare must ever be slight, to multiply the number of consumers who are at their disposal within the ring of their system of monopoly."[10]

Confronted with an inglorious history of cunning and duplicity, the champions of the new protectorates are anxious to demonstrate purer motives, lest their project too should fall into disrepute. So it is asserted that the "viceroys" of the present are temporary regents moved, not by a lust for wealth, but by a desire to address genuine humanitarian and security concerns. These newer and purer engagements are then distinguished from "classical imperialism" in much the same way as the biblical shepherd separates the sheep from the goats. They are multilateral and temporary, differences that James Fearon and David Laitin attribute to "changed motivations" arising from the collective action problem posed by failed states. Indeed, a vastly changed security calculus—the "bad externalities" that accompany disorder—and the preferred remedy for disorder—human rights, democracy, and the free market economy—augur very different motives from those which gave birth to the great European empires in an earlier, less salubrious age. Gone too are other grubby motives, such as the search for glory and prestige, the desire to civilize "backward" natives, and the imperatives that go with maintaining the balance of power.[11] Sadly, were it not for an aversion to historically informed inquiry, an affliction that runs deep in international relations scholarship, these merchants of "newness" would know that disorder on the imperial frontier typically went hand-in-hand with projects of expansion and pacification.[12]

The wall between past and present is erected a bit higher by giving civil society pride of place in seeking the salvation of failed and collapsed states. A veritable army of NGOs are lauded for providing (among other things) an informal accountability regime through which the purity of motives is policed, all in apparent ignorance that missionary, scientific, and philanthropic societies enjoyed a similar pride of place in areas like the Congo Free State. Indeed, Oxfam's report of arbitrary violence, forced labor, and gratuitous brutality in eastern Congo calls to mind missionaries' reports on conditions in the Upper Congo a century earlier, which tell stories of a society stricken by unrestrained violence, appalling cruelty, and, as if time has stood still, widespread forced labour.[13] A special place is also given to multilateralism in the belief that obtaining the blessing of the "international community" somehow vacates standard objections to alien rule. That the Security Council made Kosovo a ward is evidently different from Britain's declaration of the Buganda (Uganda) protectorate in 1894, which Joseph Chamberlain—an unapologetic champion of the British Empire—defended on similar grounds of peace and order, and the suppression of barbarous behavior.[14] But if there is merit in this defense, then the privileged status of multilateralism is perhaps less compelling than is often assumed; for protecting people in danger, as Chamberlain described the situation in Uganda, would be no less right if done unilaterally by a single state than multilaterally by a group of states acting as a "coalition of the willing."

The difficulty with the narrative of novelty is that the business of identifying the motives from which human conduct springs is a notoriously unreliable enterprise. Human conduct rarely, if ever, springs from a single motive. To identify any one motive as the primary cause of things promises the simplicity that academics crave and the cover practitioners need, but only at the cost of incurring the same clear-sighted incoherence that left Lewis Carroll's Alice puzzled by the Hatter's remark, which "seemed to have no sort of meaning in it, and yet it was certainly English."[15] Explanations of this sort are useful for little more than rendering the entire history of European empire as a contrived (ideological) story that is worthy of the most adept Whig historian.[16] The events of the past are then transformed into icons of a "pseudo-history" which announce a preferred course of action or a policy that deserves praise or blame. In other words, the approach that makes a sharp distinction between past and present mines (as opposed to interrogating) the past with a view to advancing a moral argument that is dressed in the most fashionable clothes the wardrobe of history can furnish.[17]

## The Seduction of Continuity

The approach that separates past and present makes use of a historical backdrop against which something new is illuminated. In contrast, the approach that joins past and present engages history as a storeroom of wisdom and knowledge that provides guidance for the more effective administration of the new protectorates. This approach assumes a didactic history that is pregnant with valuable lessons and ominous warnings that the international bureaucrat—the contemporary "man on the spot"[18]—ignores at his own peril. So if Lord Lugard's experience with indirect rule can be properly understood and adequately digested it might be possible, for example, to increase "local ownership" in future protectorates.[19] Of course, not all lessons are taken from the "how to" side of the ledger. Some are wheeled out bearing advice on what not to do. Gerald Knaus and Felix Martin shade in this direction, in an article aimed at distilling lessons from the experience of Bosnia and Herzegovina, which complains of a "European Raj" that presides over a system of "indirect rule." The lesson that is of interest warns: "[t]he Bosnian illusion, shared by a large international human rights and democratization community, has been that universal laws of power—including the well-known tendencies of institutions to pursue their self-interest, reject blame for failures, evade hard decisions, and prolong their own tenures—somehow do not apply in the case of well-intentioned international state-building missions."[20]

The appeal of this approach is the endless supply of advice that can be gleaned from the past. As circumstances change so too will our reading of the past change, which is to say that the meaning of history is what we need it to mean. This approach is limited only by variation in contingent circumstances and the wherewithal to make sense of them. Unfortunately, it is no more satisfactory than the first approach, for it also reads the past backwards in order to draw a straight and unbroken line from William Bentinck's scheme of directing the improvement of British India to the modern-day viceroys who have been asked to shepherd so-called "war-torn" territories to a higher state of political, economic, social and moral development. Indeed, the principle that guided Bentinck, turning to "greater [European] intelligence" on occasions when Indian "habits, morals or ways of thinking are inconsistent with their own happiness and improvement," is scarcely different from the principle that guided Paddy Ashdown in Bosnia and Herzegovina: "I have concluded that there are two ways I can make my decisions. One is with a tape measure, measuring the precise equidistant position between three sides. The other is by doing what I think is right for the country as a whole. I prefer the second of these."[21] But this kind of analogy mines the past with no less vigor than the approach seeking to separate past and present. It is an analogy that finds intelligibility and utility in the influence it can exert in the present, which involves repackaging history as a moral argument that exhorts a particular course of action. In other words, context and circumstance are abandoned as the past is made the servant of whatever policy is in fashion.

At this point a highly charged debate about the resurrection of empire takes flight. But there are compelling reasons to doubt that a new age of empire is at hand, unless we are content to have "empire" mean something as loose and imprecise as preponderant power. The character of preponderant power can be teased out in a distinction disclosed in Ancient Greek thought. One notion, *hegemonia*, refers to a kind of legitimate authority; it is authority esteemed by others because it is merited in virtue of particular deeds or in recognition of particular excellence. The other, *arche*, refers to control based on power, manifested in the application of force or incentives backed by threats of coercion.[22] Richard Ned Lebow observes that the predominant status associated with *hegemonia* is that it benefits subordinate parties. In contrast, the characteristic feature of *arche* is power used to compel compliance with the help of rewards and punishments.[23] The motifs of *arche*, force and threats used to exact obedience and control are sure to appeal to enthusiasts of a "new imperial moment." But a narrative that begins and ends with dominant power is still some way off the ideas of jurisdiction and command that are entailed by the Latin root of empire: *imperium*. To have jurisdiction is to have authority (as opposed to power) within a defined sphere of action; and within that sphere of action there exists authority entitled to issue commands. It is in this sense that *imperium* has come to mean what is commonly understood as sovereignty, in terms of a state that is not subordinate to any other authority, or an extended order composed of various sub-orders that is nonetheless capable of acting under the direction of a single authority.[24]

If we look beyond intoxicating or infuriating (whichever the case may be) pronouncements about the dawn of a new age of empire we shall find that our world is far more likely to be caught up in a contest between *hegemonia* and *arche* than in a renaissance of *imperium*. For example, John Ikenberry has expressed worry that "America's nascent neo-imperial grand strategy threatens to rend the fabric of the international community." In contrast, Charles Krauthammer has extolled the virtues of American power, which, he argues, should be used "unashamedly" to maintain American dominance for its own sake and for the sake of the entire world.[25] The character of their disagreement is intelligible not in the question "is it empire?" but in the way in which power is exercised and the ends to which it is directed. It is a disagreement clearly audible in Abdullah Gul's complaint, voiced in the midst of Israel's aerial bombardment of Lebanon in 2006, which raises awkward questions about America's self-defined role in the world. Failure to stop the war, he argued, tarnishes America's credentials as a champion of freedom and justice; and with this failure its image as a "kinder, gentler nation" is blotted by an imposing power which, sadly, has ceded the moral high ground in remaining blind and deaf to human suffering.[26] In other words, the disagreement that distinguishes Ikenberry from Krauthammer is not so much a matter of empire as it is about what can be achieved with raw power, that is, the stuff of *arche*, and the danger it poses to American *hegemonia*.

Making sense of the debate about resurgent empire is made all the more difficult when it is conjoined with an all too pervasive fetish of redefining sovereignty. Indicative of this burgeoning industry is an argument that sees "traditional" or "classical" sovereignty as having been eroded by the rising tide of human rights and ever more intrusive humanitarian engagements, in the form of either voluntary arrangements or armed intervention carried out by an elusive but always righteous "international community." It is no longer possible to act with impunity, so the argument goes, because, today, sovereignty entails responsibility to domestic and international constituencies. Gone is that quaint notion of sovereignty that places the prince above the law, whereby the "power of the sovereign is supposedly not limited by justice or any ideas of good and bad, right or wrong."[27] Indeed, once the deadly reality of failed states had been digested, no doubt with considerable anguish and acute embarrassment, an unequivocal rejection of "unlimited sovereignty" becomes the common currency of yet another new world order. And the speculative carapace of such an order fell to the side once it gained positive recognition in a short but celebrated article penned by Kofi Annan in 1999:

State sovereignty, in its most basic sense, is being redefined—not least by the forces of globalization and international co-operation. States are now widely understood to be instruments at the service of their peoples, and not vice versa. At the same time individual sovereignty—by which I mean the fundamental freedom of each individual, enshrined in the charter of the UN and subsequent international treaties—has been enhanced by a renewed and spreading consciousness of individual rights. When we read the charter today, we are more than ever conscious that its aim is to protect individual human beings, not to protect those who abuse them.[28]

Since then the "sovereignty as responsibility" formula has taken hold, not a moment too soon for advocates of the corollary doctrine of a "responsibility to protect," who are most eager to show the door to an "anachronistic" Westphalian order that equates sovereignty with unfettered power.[29]

As a manifesto for political action this line of argument has obvious appeal, especially for those who are apt to retreat into the present, seduced by the immediacy of this or that problem, only to find themselves groping in the dark for want of perspective.[30] But it makes little sense unless the meaning of sovereignty is equated with the ability to issue and to enforce commands, which reduces the state to nothing more than a coercive order that is intelligible only in the facts of what it does, providing evidence that it really exists.[31] Indeed, the very idea that some person or some assembly has a right to power, the conditions of which are resolved with reference to authority, suggests that the confluence of "sovereignty" and "responsibility" is no achievement of the present. Sovereignty has always entailed responsibility. As far back as the thirteenth century the problem of reconciling legislative sovereignty with constitutional government presented itself to mediaeval jurists, Accursius foremost among them, who confronted many of the same questions that trouble the modern constitutional lawyer.[32] Brian Tierney has explored Accursius' treatment of the Roman legal precept, *Princeps legibus solutus est* (the prince is not bound by the laws), to show how legislative authority can be above the law and still be bound, legally as opposed to morally, by the law. Crucially, then, to say that the prince is not bound by the laws is not to condemn oneself to a kind of absolutism that is indistinguishable from the capricious tyrant. It does mean, however, that the definition of law cannot begin and end with coercive command, in which case there truly is no way of binding the sovereign in respect of rules of law. To suggest otherwise would involve a sovereign binding himself by a command that can abrogated at the sovereign's pleasure, which obviously makes nonsense of the idea of being bound.[33]

The essence of Accursius' argument, as Tierney describes it, follows from the logical precedence that law enjoys as against sovereignty; hence sovereignty is the product of law rather than law being solely the product of sovereign command. In other words, the ultimate basis of law rests on a principle found in extra-legal experience which demands that "law ought to be obeyed"; and from this principle it is possible to determine how the will of the sovereign is to be ascertained. Thus the obligation to obey the law is universal, so that it was possible to say that the sovereign "could change a law by due exercise of his legislative authority but if, in his own person, he broke a law while it actually existed his action was just as illegal as a similar act by a subject."[34] Where sovereign and subject are different is intelligible in the context of punishment. Unlike the subject, who is liable to punishment at the hands of a magistrate, the prince is not so liable although he is legally obliged to obey the law. It is in this context that the question of obedience is for the prince a matter of internal discipline: the prince can trespass against the law as a matter of fact but, as Accursius puts it, he "was 'loosed from the laws' only in the sense that there existed no legal machinery for bringing him to justice if he broke them."[35] Of course, an objection might be lodged on grounds that this example, taken from the thirteenth century, is decidedly remote from our world; but the basic structure of Accursius' argument portrays a fair picture of contemporary international relations: fidelity to international law is expected of states, and yet there is no magistrate with jurisdiction capable of redressing occasions of infidelity.

The point to be made is that the challenges posed by the new protectorates are not resolved by opposing a flabby conception of empire to a mythical conception of sovereignty, which ends up missing the greater part of what exercises at least some people about arrangements of political dependency. This line of argument typically unfolds by postulating a changing conception of sovereignty which, in turn, opens the door to a kind of (external) interference that is said to herald the resurrection of empire, for better or worse. But even if we were to concede that there is genuine continuity between past and present, we are still left to wonder if saying so merits much attention. In an important sense the "is it empire?" debate is something of a sterile distraction. For it may not matter all that much that the United Nations mission which once governed Kosovo can be fitted into an "imperial" frame. The same is true of the various transitional arrangements that have been a part of political life in Cambodia and elsewhere. Saying that these missions look like empire or that these arrangements in some way resemble past practices of colonial administration involves an empirical observation that is denuded of more interesting and far more important claims in respect of how human beings should be treated and what they should become. Indeed, empire is simply one way of addressing these deeper, more fundamental claims as well as redeeming them where they are absent.

## The Discourse of Ability

While reflecting on the problems posed by failed states, specifically terrorism and piracy, Max Boot looks wistfully to a time when European powers imposed the rule of law, at gunpoint if necessary, to pacify territories beset by disorder.[36] The analogy between European imperialism and a new generation of protectorates is certainly not lost on Boot; and to that extent his preferred course of action requires no lattice of linguistic evasion to fasten together the desire for expeditious action and the wish to avoid the embarrassment it might evoke, at least in some quarters of the world. He sees little difference between British rule in Pakistan or Italian rule in Somalia and instances of "imperialism-in-all-but-name" in Kosovo and Bosnia. In fact, he is refreshingly candid in saying that it will be necessary "to place more ungoverned spaces under international administration" if we are to lance the festering boil of failed states. More interesting, however, is his estimate of what is required to get the job done: "[t]he real difficulty with emulating these examples is not a lack of legitimacy. That can always be conferred by the United Nations or some other multilateral organization. Harder to overcome is a lack of will."[37]

That an absence of will rather than legitimacy should be identified as the chief problem is suggestive of an historical amnesia that commonly afflicts those who fancy the trappings of "liberal imperialism"[38] without appreciating, much less answering, awkward questions posed by liberal thought. It is in this context that the distracting referendum on the "new age of empire" ends up obscuring a discourse that is no less common to a world of empires than it is to a world of liberal democracies. For at the heart of classical liberal thought is a commitment to individual freedom and equality, the enjoyment of which necessitates the limitation of executive power. Thus, state coercion is justified in a well-ordered society only so far as it secures compliance with properly enacted and publicly known rules that reflect underlying agreement on this fundamental (as opposed to contingent) condition of freedom and equality. Beyond that individuals are equally free to choose for themselves the ends for which they strive and the goods that are to be accorded value. Furthermore, the pursuit of these ends and goods should be tolerated in so far as it does not infringe the liberty of others to pursue their own self-defined goals. There is, then, no *a priori* reason why different subjective preferences relating to expression, movement, confession, and association cannot coexist with one another, with disagreements being settled voluntarily and according to the principle of consent.[39]

The special emphasis that liberalism places on the free and equal individual, choosing in respect of self-defined subjective preferences, raises especially cogent questions about the individual—natural or legal—who in the course of choosing inflicts harm on others or on himself. It is at this point that the difference between "will" and "ability" comes into focus. The person who willfully harms another is usually branded a criminal and punished accordingly. In contrast, the person who lacks ability is more likely to be seen as either a lunatic or a child, the latter being the category of especial interest in international relations. The liberal answer to the problem posed by children is known well enough: they are to remain under the tutelage and tuition of their parents until such time that they are capable of knowing the law, reasoning for themselves, giving informed consent, and, of course, assuming responsibility for their failures. John Locke gives a classic account of this relation when he says the power parents have over their children arises from the duty "[t]o inform the Mind, and govern the Actions of their yet ignorant Nonage, till Reason shall take its place."[40] This way of thinking is no less intelligible in liberal ruminations about the fit between nations and their political institutions. Best known in this regard is John Stuart Mill's suggestion that representative government will flourish only in the hands of people who are mature in their moral and mental faculties; and they are in the same proportion unfit for representative government when these faculties are undeveloped or deformed by bad government, in which case subjection to the government of a more advanced nation is advantageous until they are "willing and able" to sustain a proper government of their own.[41]

The discourse of ability was part and parcel of liberal justifications of empire in days in an earlier age. That various peoples were differently placed in respect of ability presupposed questions probing the reasons why. Indeed, a world mediated by words like "mature," "develop," "advance," and "progress" also elicited explanations of "backwardness," to use the preferred adjective of the day, without which colonial administrators could not fulfill the duties of their sacred trust. It is against this backdrop that Macaulay's ridicule of "Hindoo" and "Mahomedan" learning comes to life. For his objection was rooted in a world view that is given a reprise in a more recent query posed by Daniel Pipes: "[w]hy is the Middle East so at odds with modern life, laggard in everything from literacy to standard of living, from military prowess to political development?"[42] Macaulay would surely recognize and understand Pipes' answer: "[I] slam's problem is less its being *anti*-modern than that its process of modernization has hardly begun."[43] And so other explanations followed. Despotic government left non-European society languishing in a condition of passive stagnation. Poverty stemmed from ignorance of political economy. False religion cultivated superstition. Irrational systems of law promoted disorder. Inadequate education stifled scientific advancement. And cardinal virtues of civilized life, such as fair play and reciprocity, were largely absent in underdeveloped, child-like non-Europeans. Hence James Mill's description of the typical Indian: "[a]mong children, and among rude people, little accustomed to take their decisions upon full and mature considerations, nothing is more common than to repent of their bargains, and wish to revoke them."[44]

But explanations founded on an estimation of ability were all very suddenly swept away in the rush to decolonization. Armed with the ideas of their colonial masters, people once deemed as the wretched of the earth stood up to claim the rights of men for themselves. They reminded all who would cling to the discourse of ability that "[t]he writings of Rousseau, Jefferson, Marx, Thomas Paine, Machiavelli and other political thinkers have had their influence. Thus, everywhere in Africa, Africans demand freedom, equality, and justice."[45] It was no longer possible to argue that these peoples lacked the attributes of coherent and viable political communities; nor did it matter that they were politically weak, economically impoverished, socially divided, and largely ignorant of the workings of modern government.[46] For the law of decolonization, embodied in General Assembly Resolution 1514 (XV), declared a new order of things in unmistakably plain language: "[i]nadequacy of political, economic, social or educational preparedness should never serve as a pretext for delaying independence."[47] In other words, withholding the speedy granting of independence on grounds of "backwardness" or "underdevelopment" amounted to nothing less than an offence against fundamental human rights and freedoms.

So with alien rule departed the discourse of ability, which together made legal fiction of a little observed part of the United Nations Charter: "[m]embership in the United Nations is open to all other peace-loving states which accept the obligations contained in the present Charter and, in the judgment of the Organization, are able and willing to carry out these obligations."[48]

Of course, the grim reality of failed states has exposed the consequences of adhering too faithfully to this legal fiction, which jettisoned what custodians of empire regarded as the wisdom of experience for the promise of an abstract noun. Thus, a presumption in favor of the widest possible interpretation of equality displaced the wisdom of an older maxim, "[t]o establish by law rights and duties which assume that people are equal when they are not is like trying to make clumsy feet look handsome by the help of tight boots."[49] When we turn to contemporary international relations the problem is clear enough for all to see: the new protectorates cannot be separated from an estimation of ability. They are about helping others found durable courts and parliaments, organize free and fair elections, establish viable arrangements of economic exchange, and develop the habits and virtues required to sustain them over a long period of time. Indeed, notions of trusteeship, international administration, conservatorship, conditional sovereignty, and state de-certification are all directly intelligible in the context of ability—or rather, more to the point, the inability of certain groups of people to do these things by their own rights and by their own effort. Each of these ideas presupposes an engagement that specifies arrangements aimed at transforming these groups of people into what they are not but can in principle become, provided they receive adequate tuition and guidance from those who are further along the road of development.

It is not hard to fathom the fact that the discourse of ability is very much at home in the now vanished European empires of the past as well as in the broad currents of contemporary liberal thought. For there is precious little difference between Lord Hailey's description of the British Empire as a "procession of peoples in which great distances separate the van from the rear guard" and Francis Fukuyama's contention that "rather than a thousand shoots blossoming into as many different flowering plants, mankind will come to seem like a long wagon train strung out along a road."[50] And the end of their respective processions is similarly conceived as an infinitely adaptable flower that will bloom no less vigorously in the rocky soil of the Hindu Kush than it does in the fertile soil of the Germanic plain. The issue, then, is not brought to light by opposing what is widely regarded as a discredited world of empire to a more enlightened world of liberal democracies; it is illuminated in terms of a world marked by conspicuous inequalities that overlay a presumption in favor of abstract moral equality. It is in this respect that Ronald Robinson's view rings especially true: "[t]he problems of trusteeship were the problems of power, of the responsibilities of the strong towards the weak. The unequal distribution of political and economic power in the world, which was the fundamental basis of colonialism, has not been suddenly abolished by the accession of most colonies to political independence."[51] This view, expressed in 1965, is no less true now than it was then. Indeed, proclamations announcing the arrival of an unconditional equality that emancipated colonial peoples from the shackles of alien rule did not at the same time emancipate the world from the very real conditions that called out for arrangements of political inequality.

## For Want of Confidence

It is in respect of this deep and abiding tension between the liberal values of autonomy, understood as the freedom to pursue self-chosen ends, and the duty to assist those who are in need of help that a new generation of protectorates struggle to gain a sound footing. This duty of assistance and the ghastly consequences of failed states have combined to resuscitate the discourse of ability; and with it the idea of alien rule, now dressed in rather more benign clothes, having gained newfound respectability. For example, in an early and influential article entitled "Saving Failed States" Gerald Helman and Steven Ratner put forward the idea of "conservatorship" as a way of assisting modern-day *debellatios*—that is, states that are "utterly incapable" of sustaining themselves as functioning members of the international community. Unsurprisingly, they look to the paternal analogy in order to flesh-out the conceptual basis of this "novel" approach to "nation-saving": "[f]orms of guardianship or trusteeship are a common response to broken families, serious mental or physical illness, or economic destitution. The hapless individual is placed under the responsibility of a trustee or guardian, who is charged to look out for the best interests of that person."[52] This manner of thinking is also evident in the work of Roland Paris, who argues that political liberty presupposes political stability. Government must be reasonably effective or capable before it can be responsible. Thus, the obvious recommendation follows in train: "international peacebuilders have little choice but to act "illiberally" in the earliest phases of a postconflict transition."[53] Of course, his is a study in liberal imperialism cloaked in the jargon of "institutionalization before liberalization," for little separates Paris's gradualist approach, whereby "locals" are drawn into public life as they are progressively capable, and James Fitzjames Stephen's belief, expressed in the nineteenth century: "[i]t is not improbable that in the course of time...native [Indian] habits of life and ways of thought will give way to, and be superseded by, those of Europe."[54]

What does separate their respective positions is discernible not in consideration of motive, approach or aims, but in consideration of intellectual coherence and, crucially, the confidence to pronounce conclusions without falling back on the hand-wringing language of "regrettable but necessary" choices, which are themselves responses to the emotive plea: "something must be done." It is here that the gulf between past and present is relevant. Advocates of the new protectorates have made great strides in working out various strategies of post-conflict reconstruction, but they have not got nearly as far in answering uncomfortable questions presupposed by the discourse of ability. Indeed, it is one thing to observe and to describe state failure; it is something altogether different, not to mention more challenging, to explain the reasons for failure. We may delude ourselves with the "evil man" thesis and the comfort it brings, but too often we exaggerate the influence of evil men, only to look foolish after having done so. In other words, the flower may be robust in being adaptable to many different political climates, but it will not grow without the care and attention of a large number of people because good societies are rather more like well tended gardens than plots overgrown with lush vegetation. And in the current notion of a well tended garden there is an unsightly weed manifested in a tension between the post-colonial idea of equality, which entails the freedom to pursue self-chosen ends, and the idea of freedom entailed by the new protectorates: less freedom now means more freedom later. Advocates of international administration have still to provide a justification of this rationed freedom, a justification that persuasively answers an unnamed African's protest to Margery Perham at the onset of decolonization: "We do not wish for any special treatment. We do not wish to be protected; we want to be allowed to make our own mistakes, and to work out our own salvation, as you did."[55]

More often than not modern-day traders in the discourse of ability lack the confidence to issue a reply denominated in the coin of the trade: "you do not understand the conditions of your salvation" or "you are incapable of achieving salvation on your own." They lack the confidence to say, as Stephens said of the British government in India, that their project represents the aspirations and goals of "a belligerent civilization."[56] That they are unable to say so suggests that the likes of Boot have got hold on the wrong end of the stick when they say that the problem is one of will rather than legitimacy. He may lament America's failure to exercise "effective imperial oversight"[57] in the Middle East, but the post-colonial conception of equality—political, economic, social, and cultural—still exerts a firm grip throughout much of the world. Thus it is a question of legitimacy, not will, when people recoil at descriptions of the Middle East as a "backward" region or of the Islamic world as rife with "wild and unruly passions"; and it is no less a question of legitimacy when it is said that the remedy of this "diseased environment" is a far-reaching transformation induced by the "powerful antibiotic known as democracy."[58] Enthusiasm for the new protectorates is driven by a similar desire to rehabilitate the most "diseased" parts of contemporary international relations, namely failed states. But the paradox of it all is that they indulge a modern-day equivalent of Macaulay's wish to create "a class of persons, Indian in blood and color, but English in taste, in opinions, in morals, and in intellect,"[59] yet in doing so they duck having to give an open and confident account of its superiority, pretending instead to be for ever estranged from his world and from his concerns.

# 2

# THE EUROPEAN EMPIRES
# AND INTERNATIONAL ORDER

## MODEL OR TRAP?

*James Mayall*

The order that was restored after the defeat of the Nazi/Fascist Axis in 1945 was a hybrid. The new plant was a graft of the ideas of Wilsonian liberalism onto the root stock of the traditional international society of states. Surprisingly, Winston Churchill, the old imperialist, understood better than most that the rise of the democratic United States to world power required this change. In a speech delivered at Harvard in 1943 he proposed that "the empires of the future are the empires of the mind."[1] Throughout history the rulers of empires have been obsessed with threats, real or imagined, lurking just across the border, on the frontiers that marked the limits of their power. But if—as Churchill's enigmatic remark seemed to imply—international society was henceforth to be grounded in a system of shared democratic values, how was order to be maintained beyond the frontiers of the democratic world?

At the time, not only was the answer to this question not forthcoming, it was not even asked. This was largely because, weakened as they were by the reverses they had suffered during the Second World War, the French and, more important, the British Empires had survived and their writ still ran along most of the potential fault lines in the non-Western world. At midnight on 15 August

1947 the British quit India, honoring the commitment they had made in order to buy the neutrality of the Indian National Congress in the war. The British government did not accept that this historic event signaled the end of the age of European overseas empire, but with the luxury of hindsight, we can now see that the days of British global authority were numbered.

The frontier question was delayed further by the onset of the Cold War, which for the most part neutralized any strategic threat to the West from decolonization. Indeed, the transfer of power was widely regarded by Asian and African nationalists and their liberal supporters in the West as removing the need for a strategy for the non-Western world. Even after the Chinese invasion of Tibet and the frontier war between India and China in 1962,[2] the Non Aligned Movement did not acknowledge the reality of a general threat arising either from frontier disputes or from what later would come to be seen as failed states. Only after 1989 could the question no longer be avoided—how to prevent anarchy in contested and politically unstable countries threatening the interests of major powers and, more generally, undermining the conventions and institutions of international society?

It is not obvious that in the contemporary world the traditional solutions to this problem are available. Nor is it obvious in what direction new solutions should be sought. Those who look to history to provide them with lessons to guide us through our present predicaments almost invariably learn the wrong lessons. In the first chapter, William Bain has concluded that, within the liberal tradition, this is so both for those who see a radical break between the age of empire and the modern world, and for those who see the present as a continuation of the past. He believes that this is because modern liberals are no longer prepared to follow John Stuart Mill in his robust willingness to confine self-government to those who were equipped by education and enlightened values to exercise it.[3] Instead they shy away from confronting the perennial problem of power, of how those who have it should relate to those who do not, while being unable to establish the legitimacy of their policies in failed states, however well meant they may be.

I have much sympathy with this argument. Yet we are where we are, and it seems inherently unlikely that *a priori* reasoning alone will be a sufficient basis for a new and more appropriate grand strategy. To paraphrase the novelist L.P. Hartley, the past may be a foreign country where they do things differently,[4] but we have no alternative to looking to it, if only to show the reasons why traditional strategies are unlikely to prove effective under current circumstances. This is the purpose of the present chapter. Before doing so it will be helpful to consider, in summary fashion, the political, diplomatic and legal context within which protectorates—or other arrangements that performed the same or analogous functions—were most often established before the twentieth century.

## Context and Concepts

For much of human history, in most parts of the world, empire has been the dominant political form. Until the early twentieth century, most empires were dynastic, the territorial holdings of particular individuals, families or lineages. Most empires were also multi-ethnic and many were multi-religious. Their size was likely to be fixed by the reach of the imperial army and the consequent ability of the ruler to extract tribute. Since those who ruled in his name at the furthest limits of imperial authority were for most of the time out of reach, ideas of suzerainty were more appropriate for describing the political relationship of center and periphery than invoking the concept of sovereignty, with its inference of indivisible power and authority.

Suzerainty is generally regarded as an anachronism in the modern world although two countries—Morocco and China—have tried to exert sovereign control over territories which they had once claimed suzerain rights. Morocco, whose claim to Mauritania on these grounds was turned down by the ICJ, failed and, perhaps for this reason, has since resolutely refused to submit its disputed control over the Western Sahara to international arbitration.[5] China was more successful, forcefully incorporating Tibet in 1951, and subsequently resisting all efforts to internationalize the issue.[6]

When dynastic empires fell, it was generally a consequence of defeat by a usurping dynasty or by a neighboring empire. Without the ruler's theoretical protection, peripheral areas might assert their independence or fall prey to a takeover by a rival and stronger empire, or, if the territory was of little strategic or economic significance, revert to the status of an ungoverned no man's land. The development of long distance trade inevitably influenced—and up to a point stabilized—the way rival empires, and the peoples who occupied borderlands in between, related to one another. So long as caravan routes remained important for the transfer of luxury trade goods, those who controlled the high mountain passes were in a strong position to exert strategic leverage. They could earn revenue by taxing the caravans and convert this into political power by playing off the powers on either side against one another. The mechanization of long distance transport reduced the economic significance of many of these borderlands, but their habitual lawlessness also made them politically more troublesome for their neighbors.[7]

Maritime trade also played a part in the prehistory of protectorates: the great mercantile trading companies often established enclave communities in foreign cities to handle their business. In time this practice led to a mixed legal and cultural regime, whose legacy contributed greatly to contemporary globalization, while along the way enormously complicating attempts to redraw the political map when the multinational empires collapsed at the end of the First World War.[8] The transfer of populations, which in the 1990s was widely identified as the international crime of ethnic cleansing, had previously been regarded by rulers as a legitimate strategic instrument. An example is the granting of land to Christian Serbs in the Krajina as a reward for guarding the frontier between the Hapsburg and Ottoman empires.[9]

In the East the principle of suzerainty survived longer than in the West. Until it was finally absorbed into Japan in 1879 Okinawa, for example, maintained the virtual autonomy of its indigenous monarchy by acknowledging the dual authority of China and Japan.[10] But even in the West, some of these traditional devices by which the great powers arranged international affairs to suit their own interests survived into the twentieth century either unchanged or in modified form. These included the establishment of international cities, whose identity was contested, such as Trieste or Tangier; or the reworking of the idea of suzerainty as a form of indirect empire, as in the British maintenance of effective control over the Gulf sheikhdoms through its system of Resident Advisers.[11]

The essential point to note about frontier policy before the establishment of the League of Nations is that it was an imperial, not an international, issue. There was no unsecured international obligation to deal with the problem of lawlessness and its potential threat to international security. The society of states was a pluralist association in the sense that it included great and small powers, empires, republics, dictatorships of various kinds and even city states; but by the same token it was both an ideologically heterodox and a self-help society. As Mark Mazower has demonstrated in his study of the ideological prehistory of the UN, even the rise of liberal internationalism was grounded on the assumption that the West—and originally the British Empire—would continue to manage the ungovernable spaces and to police the non-Western world for its own good as well as in their interest.[12] The trusteeship principle set out in the League Mandates system and developed further in the UN Trusteeship Council did not threaten this assumption,[13] in the minds of the founding fathers of these institutions. Bizarrely arrogant as it now seems, the assumption of Western superiority at least had the merit of tying the interests of the great powers to their responsibility to underwrite the international order.

## *The Impact of Self Determination on International Society*

Liberal internationalism contained the seeds of its own downfall. The idea that the right of national self-determination could be handed out by the Western great powers as a kind of reward for good behavior came under strain in the aftermath of the Versailles Peace Treaty and had no chance of surviving the post-1945 retreat of European imperial power from Asia and Africa. The near quadrupling of the membership of international society between 1945 and 2009, from 51 original signatories of the San Francisco Charter to the current membership of the UN of 191 states, was primarily a consequence first of the descent from world power of the European imperial powers and then of the collapse of the Soviet Union. But it could not have been achieved without the seductive and near universal appeal of the principle of self-determination, an idea which in 1918 had been endorsed by both Woodrow Wilson and Vladimir Lenin.[14]

The success of the principle of national self-determination in simultaneously de-legitimizing the imperial idea and asserting a new normative standard for international society, nonetheless, had a paradoxical consequence. On the one hand it created a highly conservative association of states, deeply committed to sovereignty, non-interference in internal affairs, and the denial of any right of subsequent self-determination for dissatisfied and therefore potentially secessionist groups.[15] On the other, the proliferation of this egalitarian order of law left the rival principle of hierarchical power essentially undisturbed.

Moreover this paradox concealed another, with fateful consequences for what I have called the frontier problem in international society. The new members were strong supporters of pluralism in international life. What mattered to them was the acquisition of sovereignty—and once acquired, its recognition by other states—not how it was exercised and for whose benefit. The rivalry of the two superpowers was not merely a struggle for power but also a battle between opposing sets of universal and constitutional principles. So long as the Cold War lasted the stalemate forced them into accepting the traditional pluralist conception of the society of states. Where either side was persuaded of the necessity of intervention in areas that did not fall unambiguously into one ideological camp or the other—as the US was in Vietnam after the defeat of the French at Dien Bien Phu, and the Soviet Union in Afghanistan in 1979—the rules of the game were prudential. Only one superpower could be formally engaged at a time, the other confining itself to indirect and covert support to its clients.

All this changed with the end of the Cold War. Not only did the Soviet Union collapse, so did the credibility of a pluralist society of states. One side had won the Cold War, even if by default. In these circumstances it was perhaps inevitable, although unfortunate, that the winner should regard its own world view and vision as a blueprint for what the first President Bush optimistically called the new world order.[16]

Western triumphalism should have surprised no one. Great Powers, regardless of their protestations to the contrary, are never entirely willing to allow international society to take on whatever shape its members choose for themselves. At some level they always want to mould it in their own image. It was so during the heyday of the British and other European empires, and it is so today in an era of at least temporarily unrivalled American hegemony. The problem is that while the dilemmas facing a hegemon are similar to those empires confronted in the past, they are not the same. It is not necessary to enter into the scholarly debates about the definition of empire, the distinctions between formal and informal empires, and the possibilities and dangers of comparative imperial history to establish this point.[17] It is sufficient to note that the functioning of a liberal democracy under universal franchise and within the American four-year electoral cycle imposes much greater constraints on the exercise of American power—above all an unrealizable pressure for a "quick-fix"—than those faced by the British in the nineteenth century. Indeed, it is primarily for this reason, as I shall try to suggest in the remainder of this chapter, that imperial solutions are unlikely to resolve the contemporary problem of lawless frontiers, fractured societies and broken states.

## The Limits of Historical Modeling

Three preliminary points will help to highlight the continuities and contrasts between the dilemmas faced by the British and other European imperial powers in the nineteenth and early twentieth centuries and those faced by the United States and its allies at the beginning of the twenty-first.

The first concerns the place of humanitarianism in world politics. Humanitarian considerations did feature from time to time in British imperial policy, sometimes with relatively benign effect as with the abolition of *sati*, sometimes with much more alarming consequences as when the decision to invest Benin seems to have provoked human sacrifice on an unprecedented scale. Nor, as Gary Bass has recently reminded us, is humanitarian intervention a modern invention.[18] But at no time was humanitarianism allowed to dictate the grand strategy of the British Empire. Nor was it assumed that the provision of democratic or civil rights was necessary for maintaining order, although the establishment of a functioning and respected legal system was certainly a central objective of the colonial state.

By contrast humanitarian concerns have been widely claimed as the justification of most, though not all, post-Cold War interventions. Most recent international protectorates have been established in the wake of humanitarian catastrophes of one sort or another. This was not the case in Afghanistan and Iraq—the two cases where the US and some of its Western allies were most deeply and controversially involved in the first decade of the twenty-first century—but whatever the reasons for these interventions, their continuation has been justified increasingly in terms of helping Iraqi and Afghan citizens build a decent and democratic political order. It is believed by many liberals that democracies do not fight one another.[19] This belief has encouraged the tendency for democracy no longer to be seen as a good in itself, but to be regarded by Western governments—more often than by their military and diplomats, who have more direct experience of the realities—as a strategic goal. Nation-building is no longer viewed as a historical process in which a people engage on their own behalf as an act of self-determination; it has become an instrument of Western foreign policy that will deliver the goal.

Very few students of the subject—and even fewer governments—are prepared to accept that the logic of humanitarian intervention is imperial. Indeed, it is more often presented as a way of securing the fundamental rights of populations that have been brutally attacked, more often than not by their own rulers. And it is certainly true that NATO forces were greeted by the Kosovar Albanians as liberators, when the Alliance, acting without UN authority, ended Milošević's tyrannical rule in 1999.[20] It would not be difficult to find other examples.

Nonetheless the liberal consensus about the anti-imperial credentials of humanitarian intervention is not well grounded. This kind of intervention is inherently imperial in the sense that if the old order really is so degenerate and evil that it can only be removed by intervention, then it seems reasonable to assume that what is required is not a quick surgical operation, accompanied by an exit strategy announced in advance, but a long-term commitment of human and financial resources. The reasons why contemporary governments—including above all the government of the United States—shy away from accepting this logic are not mysterious. Even if there was any confidence in the ability of outside forces to create viable national democracies (which there is not) the task would still be too open ended, too expensive and too politically sensitive in most of the former colonial world to make sense to any government that is genuinely answerable to its own electorate.

The second point is that the two models—post-1945 Germany and Japan—that are often used to illustrate how external intervention can install a new democratic order have very limited applicability to the problems posed by contemporary protectorates. They are unhelpful as analogues for both external and internal reasons. Externally, the victorious powers did accept their imperial responsibilities with regard to Germany and Japan. Their own vital interests were involved and they accepted this liability. They did not stay in direct control for very long but they were prepared in principle to stay as long as it took. Internally, while Germany and Japan were discredited politically, they were not hopelessly divided socially; and they were endowed with substantial resources of human capital even after the war. German and Japanese nationalism was homegrown, not imported. It had proved a threat to the two countries' neighborhoods and ultimately to the Japanese and German people themselves; but no-one could doubt its reality. These conditions are missing in most of the more recent cases.

The final contrast between the imperial era and the twenty-first century lies in the extreme difficulty of forecasting the future shape of the international order. In the mid-nineteenth century De Tocqueville correctly predicted that the twentieth century would be dominated by the rivalry between the United States and Russia,[21] although he could not know that it would be their rival ideological visions of modernity that would provide the toxic new ingredient in the traditional brew of power politics. The most likely challengers to American power in the second half of the twenty-first century—China and India—have not endorsed every aspect of the American vision, but they belong all the same in the capitalist camp.

The new great power politics may be mercifully free from the more corrosive forms of ideological conflict, but it is by no means certain that a consensus will emerge on how to deal with the threats posed by social breakdown and religious and ethnic conflict on the periphery of the international system.[22] The national identities of countries are partly formed by the historical stories about their origins and destiny that are inherited by each generation and disseminated through schools and universities. The political classes in China and India have inherited a narrative that emphasizes their rise from the past humiliation imposed by the West. Although China continues to be governed by a Communist Party, which has deftly shed its ideological commitments while retaining its centralized organization, while India has an entrenched if chaotic democratic system of government, they share a broadly common approach to foreign policy.

China and India have no difficulty in asserting their own hegemony in their immediate neighborhoods, but a profound skepticism about assuming any more far flung role in multilateral policing. This places them amongst the strongest supporters of the traditional pluralist conception of international society. All this may change in the future. Indeed the participation of both Chinese and Indian vessels in the international flotilla that is currently attempting to contain the threat of Somali piracy might suggest that it will. But piracy represents a very direct threat to the trading interests of all countries; it is impossible to say how they are likely to react to more amorphous challenges to interests and values that they may not necessarily share.

## Neo-Imperial Temptations

If these constraints were not enough, even some of those who are broadly in sympathy with the US effort at global management have pointed out that American political culture is peculiarly unsuited to imperial rule. During the heyday of Western imperial expansion, the United States was preoccupied with its own continental consolidation, an imperial project in its own right but one that did not lead to either the development of theories of—or practical experience in—imperial administration. As in so many Western films, trouble on the frontier was dealt with either by organizing a local posse or, in extreme circumstances, by sending in the army. Once the area had been pacified everyone returned to their farms and got on with life the best they could. Arguably this aspect of American political culture has translated into a contemporary preference for the quick-fix, a surgical operation in which American power can be deployed effectively and fast, and the troops brought home at the earliest possible opportunity, and certainly in time to play well in the next presidential election.

The searing experience of the Vietnam war reinforced this attitude to overseas intervention but also revealed its limitations. It is perhaps not surprising, therefore, that once the United States found itself unconstrained by the Cold War standoff, and drawn into a series of intractable civil conflicts, administrations of both major political parties have been tempted by what might be called neo-imperial solutions. The first of these, which arguably underpinned American thinking on its intervention in Somalia in the early 1990s, invoked a political interpretation of the division of labor under which American strike forces would clear the ground for the re-entry of the European imperial powers, with their greater experience in the administration and policing of ethnically and religiously divided societies; or failing that, for the entry of United Nations peacekeepers.[23] After the failure of the US's own Somali operation, and—as Americans saw it—after they had been forced to rescue the UN and the EU from an even more humiliating failure in the former Yugoslavia, they were clearly in need of a strategy which would allow them to underwrite a domestic transition without necessarily having to depend on allies or multilateral institutions.[24] It was in this context that democratization came to be viewed in strategic and instrumental terms rather than merely as a desirable political end state for transitional societies. It was seen, in effect, as a global equivalent to the system of "indirect rule," by which the British had kept order in some parts of their ramshackle empire.

These ideas, particularly the last, are, in my view, anachronistic. Indirect Rule was a system designed to keep the costs of empire down and its illegitimacy hidden. But, even in its time, the idea was deeply controversial. As Lord Hailey's monumental *African Survey* makes clear, the debate was both practical and philosophical. From a practical point of view, Hailey suggested, the question was to find,

the most effective means of inducing native opinion to accept innovations which it does not actively demand. In the solution the emphasis may be laid on the necessity for genuine acceptance or on the importance of rapid development. The former is the end sought in the system of indirect rule, which relies on the appeal to the respect of a people for its own leaders, and its pride in institutions which it can call its own. The latter considers rather how best to make rapidly effective the decisions of superior authority, and sees its most efficient agency either in the council system or in the training of chiefs as subordinate agents of the executive government.[25]

The philosophical divide, which has many echoes in contemporary debates about nation- and statebuilding, was between cultural relativists and those who believed that there was a standard of civilization which needed to be defended against barbarian assaults from any direction. On the latter view the values of civilization are in principle available universally. But this does not mean that they can be enjoyed by all people regardless of the level of their material or moral culture. Those who held this view, let us call them liberal fundamentalists, believed that societies that could not meet the standard should not be granted the right of self-determination.[26] Their modern successors appear to have similar faith in a "one size fits all" solution but, as William Bain has also suggested,[27] they are unwilling to incur either the opprobrium or the expense of assuming long-run imperial control. They are driven by necessity, therefore, towards the relativist option.

The tension between cultural relativists—those who now celebrate multi-cultural diversity—and assimilationist civilizers seems to be a permanent feature of British political culture. In British India, in the first half of the nineteenth century, the civilizers dominated.[28] After the 1857 mutiny the pendulum swung back the other way. Practical, primarily financial considerations no doubt provided the major incentive for the British to pursue policies of indirect rule, whenever it was feasible to do so. But it is also fair to say that as a system of government, indirect rule fitted well with the alternative Burkeian temper of British political culture, with its respect for tradition and ideas of good husbandry, in sharp contrast to the intellectualism of the French Republican tradition. As an imperial grand strategy it worked well enough for a time because, in a largely pre-industrial and pre-nationalist world, there was no shortage of traditional leaders to co-opt. However, it depended on an almost unquestioned belief, on the part of the imperialists, in their own innate moral superiority and historic right to rule. This self-confidence, unattractive as it now seems, conveyed itself to the decolonized peoples, so that until the Second World War, the European imperial powers enjoyed great prestige.

These days there are very few pre-modern leaders to co-opt, and even where they survive they are not insulated from national and populist pressures as they were before the First World War. Moreover, both Western self-confidence and prestige have largely evaporated. To be sure, the United States has a magnetic attraction, but as with some fine wines, its prestige doesn't always travel. The near universal sympathy that the Al-Qaeda attack on the Twin Towers and the Pentagon evoked did not last. Despite the fact that the US government responded with a rare demonstration of international solidarity by paying up its arrears to the UN in full, the sympathy evaporated almost overnight in the wake of the invasion of Iraq and the widely publicized excesses of Abu Ghraib, Guantánamo and illegal rendition flights. The quip attributed to an American-based Indian journalist to describe the attitude of his fellow countrymen—Yankee go home and take me with you!—resonates in public perceptions over much of the rest of the world as well.[29]

It would be unwise to conclude the dangers of neo-imperialism have been removed by the election of President Barack Obama, an avowed internationalist. For the United States, the dilemmas of power are in large part structural, so that neither good will alone nor the rhetoric of burden-sharing and partnership will be sufficient to allow an easy change of direction for a country as dominant and complex as the United States. The fact that it is not obvious how America should engage with the outside world makes it inherently likely that neo-imperial options will be considered from time to time in the future as in the past. It does not mean that they can form a foundation for a coherent US grand strategy for the twenty-first century.

An imperial solution to the problem of world order is fallacious for three main reasons. First, it would require underpinning by a strong nationalism at home and a willingness to discount the interests of conquered peoples and to suppress—ruthlessly if need be—any signs of anti-colonial national consciousness that imperial expansion might provoke. Even China, arguably the last great imperial power to meet these conditions within its historic—although in some cases contested—frontiers would have difficulty in expanding its rule over new territories. It would be impossible for any Western democracy.

The United States certainly projects a powerful national identity, but it is built on the universalist claims of the Declaration of Independence. How would the country that was largely responsible for first popularizing the idea of national self-determination, and then raising it to its current status as an inalienable right under international law, justify a policy of expansion against the wishes of the inhabitants? The tactic of labeling its foreign opponents as extremists and its supporters as moderates is not confined to the United States, but it is certainly widely employed by American commentators. Whoever resorts to it, however, overlooks the romanticism of nationalist psychology. It is for this reason that it is inherently likely to backfire, in southern Afghanistan as elsewhere. Young Pashtoons may or may not be enamored of Taliban philosophy, but are likely to resent foreign occupation, or even an indigenous government that they perceive as a foreign implant.

Secondly, any new imperial or neo-imperial order would have to confront the political power of religion. Traditional empires dealt with this problem by the simple expedient of conversion. As late as 1896 the rebel Afghan province of Kafiristan was converted to Islam by the sword. Liberal empires were more squeamish: they dealt with the problem partly through indirect rule and partly by strictly controlling the activities of their own religious zealots. Any tourist in India can view the contrast between the two approaches for themselves. In Goa, colonized by the Portuguese two hundred years before the British emerged as the dominant power in South Asia, the population was forcefully converted to Catholicism; the small chapels and Baroque churches that still dot the tropical landscape bear witness to an age of faith. By contrast, in the rest of India the legacies of the British Raj are everywhere but largely invisible. They can be traced in the infrastructure of the modern state—its road and rail systems, its civil and armed services.[30] Missionaries were not officially excluded as they were in some Muslim countries the British ruled, but having learned their lesson at the time of the Indian mutiny, by and large the British did not regard the religious beliefs of their subject peoples as being any of their business.

There was another reason why the European imperial powers were wary of involving themselves in religious politics. European states have had first-hand experience of the destructive force of religious warfare. When they finally made peace in the mid-seventeenth century, it was on the condition that religion would be depoliticized as an international issue within the Christian West. The US, many of whose early settlers were religious refugees, inherited the diplomatic and legal tradition forged by the European great powers, but lacked the experience that gave rise to it. Despite a rigorously secular constitution, religion has arguably never been fully de-politicized in the United States.

All the world religions number enthusiasts—or, as they tend to be called these days, fundamentalists—amongst their believers. The only difference between the Judeo-Christian West and other world religions in this respect is that in the West there has always been an unambiguous alternative principle of legitimacy to the mandate of heaven—"render unto Caesar the things that are Caesar's." Other religions, particularly Islam, have no difficulty in recognizing secular power in practice, but do not acknowledge the theoretical distinction between secular and religious authority. A return to the politics of religious confrontation would be dangerous under any circumstances, since, this difference apart, those in possession of revealed truth have always had difficulty in accepting the tolerance on which the politics of co-existence rests; but in the context of the contemporary world of virtual communities and instant information exchange, religious intolerance raises an even more serious threat.

In both Afghanistan and Iraq—less so perhaps in the other recent formal and informal protectorates—we have already witnessed the problem that religion poses for Western views of world order. All heirs to the eighteenth century Enlightenment tend to assume that the distinction between church and state is universally accepted. It is not. The Weberian belief that there is a natural affinity between Protestant Christianity and capitalism feeds all too easily into an assumption that there is no difference between allowing private businesses to compete for market share and religions to compete for souls, within a free market. But there is a difference. It lies primarily in the fact that the church/state distinction is not even accepted by Christian fundamental-ists, many of whom are anxious to seize the moral high ground in domestic politics, let alone by radical Islamists.

Modernist theorists interpret nationalist ideology as the glue which bound society together during the transition from agricultural to industrial society and anchored political identity in the nation state. Following Max Weber, the most distinguished of them, Ernest Gellner, also accepted that while there was no necessary connection, the transition also seemed to be marked by an elec-tive affinity between religious and national identity and the market place.[31] More recently, Manuel Castells has argued that in the information age, this affinity has mutated into an elective repulsion, as the homogenizing social power of the nation-state comes under pressure from sub-state ethnic, religious and regional movements in many parts of the world.[32]

The third reason why an imperial solution is not a basis for the contempo-rary international order is that it cannot be reconciled with democracy. Far from acting as a mechanism of indirect rule, democratic government will inev-itably undermine any attempt to establish a neo-imperial system of govern-ment. Traditional dynastic empires did not require ideological justification: local leaders could be coerced or co-opted into supporting the ruling house by a variety of penalties and inducements, designed to signal the futility of resis-tance and the advantages of loyalty. To use the currently fashionable language of hard versus soft power, indirect rule was able to rely on an effective combi-nation of both. At the local level, provided the rulers understood by what ulti-mate authority they exercised their power, the stories they told themselves and their subjects about why they exercised it (always had and always would) went largely unchallenged. It did not matter that it was not true: everyone under-stood that there was a natural hierarchy and that the rulers sat at its apex.

By contrast, the overseas European empires of the nineteenth and twenti-eth centuries did require ideological support because by then governments were answerable to their national parliaments for colonial policy. The justifi-cations offered, while resting on barely concealed racist foundations, nonethe-less embodied notions of trusteeship. The purpose of empire, it was held, was to prepare subject peoples for eventual self-rule.[33] This justification was not a question of choice: it had to be advanced once it was accepted that democracy itself was an expression of fundamental—and therefore universally available—human rights.

These justifications were required in London or Paris; they did not have to be advanced—or at least not very publicly—in the colonial territories themselves. Nonetheless, the process by which the grand strategy of empire shifted from concern with questions of control and geopolitical competition to political education and development gradually eroded the social foundations of indirect rule.

Elie Kedourie provided an incisive account of the undermining of imperial authority.[34] As he noted, imperial conquest was often accompanied by a far higher level of resistance than was generally acknowledged by contemporary imperial historiography. In most cases resistance was short-lived, however. The children of the conquered elites generally bought into the value system of the conquerors: while traditional rulers continued to exercise authority, albeit under supervision, the next generation were exposed to Western education, first in local schools often but not always run by missions and the Christian churches, and then overseas where they trained as engineers, doctors and above all as lawyers.

In Kedourie's view the roots of Asian and African nationalism are to be found in the discrimination suffered by this assimilated second generation, when they returned home, decked out with professional qualifications, only to find themselves excluded both socially and from all senior positions in the colonial state. The new nationalist parties set themselves against the structures of traditional government, which they regarded as tainted by collaboration with the colonial authorities. Instead they demanded independence and majority rule, even if in many cases they dispensed with regular elections once in power.

The moral of this story seems clear. While there have been democratic empires, they contained within themselves the seeds of their own downfall. This was essentially because democratic accountability was confined to the metropolitan parliaments. British and French citizens could challenge their governments over colonial policy, but their colonial subjects had no such right. Yet colonial elites were provided with a Western education and taught that the values on which this education was based were universal.

How then was empire in a democratic world to be justified? The evidence strongly suggests that only short run justifications were possible. The empires were able to slow down the rate of modernization in colonial societies. For a time some stability could be purchased by co-opting traditional leaders and respecting local customs and religion. Even at the time, this strategy was not invariably successful. Traditional forms of leadership still flourish along the border between Afghanistan and Pakistan, as they did under the Raj, but neither the British nor the Pakistani successor state were ever able to subdue this region on a permanent basis. The best that could be achieved was a kind of stand-off under which the tribes were left to their own devices, providing they did not cross any predetermined "red lines."[35] When, as periodically happened, they got out of line, they were subjected to punitive treatment in response. It was a very rough system of justice but reasonably effective as an ordering mechanism.

Elsewhere, whether in Princely India or over much of colonial Africa, the contradictions between an education policy based on liberal values and a system of colonial government that favored local leaders generally opposed to change were bound to be exposed in the end. There were only two ways in which to postpone the inevitable. The end of empire could be postponed by adopting a theory of trusteeship under which the justification for empire was the preparation of colonial societies for self-rule. It could also be postponed by locking up the educated anti-colonial nationalists that the colonial educational system had helped to create.

The weakness of the first of these strategies was the absence of any set of respectable criteria that would indicate when a particular population was ready for independence. The weakness of the second was that there was an inexhaustible supply of nationalists. Imprisoning their leaders attracted more people, not fewer, to the nationalist cause. Taken together, these weaknesses eventually persuaded the European powers that the empire game was over. It is difficult to see how it can be revived in the twenty-first century. There were indeed major intelligence failures behind the decision to invade Iraq, but better intelligence would have done nothing to overcome the legitimacy deficit that any contemporary imperial project will inevitably encounter. A democratic Iraq and Afghanistan are no doubt highly desirable objectives, just as a democratic Germany and Japan were after 1945. But in these latter cases there were powerful internal incentives to legitimize the new order, most notably the desire of the rehabilitated political class to take their place in the institutions of the Western Alliance.

What are the United States and its Western allies to do if they cannot legitimize their new client regimes from outside? One possible answer might be to use the opportunity created by President Obama's administration in the United States to repair the multilateral institutions of international society. Regardless of who is to be held responsible for the current global economic crisis, the fact that it will undermine the welfare of all countries—and the capacity of the West to engage in expeditionary warfare even where it is so minded—may also induce a new willingness to engage in international and regional co-operation. It must be admitted that while the current emphasis on capacity building for stabilization rather than on democracy is probably an essential first step, the outlook is not particularly encouraging.[36]

# 3

# AFRICA AND TRUSTEESHIP IN THE MODERN GLOBAL ORDER

*Christopher Clapham*

Africa presents a paradox in the context of international trusteeship. On the one hand, the continent includes a disproportionately large number of the states, if states they can be called, in which levels of domestic governance have deteriorated to a point at which some form of external trusteeship might be regarded as appropriate. These extend from the clearest examples of state collapse, in which there has been no effective government at all, through to cases in which the quality of governance has been so low that trusteeship might plausibly be advanced in the interests of the great majority of the indigenous population. As a result of these failures of governance, Africa has likewise figured very prominently, both in the discourse on state failure and in the engagement of the international system in attempts to rectify it. Not only has it hosted an exceptionally high number of United Nations (and other) peacekeeping forces, but it has also come to serve as the major site in the global system for the expression of humanitarian concern and responsibility. It is the principal area of operations for international non-governmental organizations, involved in a wide range of activities from child welfare and famine relief, through explicitly governance-oriented tasks such as human rights monitoring and conflict management, to environmental conservation. Indeed, a "concern" for Africa has become an inescapable element in the expression of humanitarian values within the domestic politics of the more developed liberal democracies, as evidenced for example in the Blair government's Commission for Africa. Extending beyond the purely humanitarian, governance failure in Africa has also triggered external reactions that derive from fears of how this might impact on the dominant states in the international system themselves, through uncontrolled human migration, the spread of disease, transnational crime, and—not least—the danger that zones of weak or non-existent government might harbor global terrorism. On all these grounds, one might plausibly expect the development and implementation of international trusteeships, designed to place problematic parts of Africa under some form of external administration, which would in turn be justified primarily in terms of the welfare of the inhabitants of these areas themselves, and secondarily in terms of the wider interests of the international system.

On the other hand, not one single formal case of trusteeship administration has actually been implemented in Africa, in contrast to the explicit forms of externally-supervised government imposed on parts of the former Yugoslavia, and following external conquest on Afghanistan and Iraq. Throughout the continent, the sovereign independent state has remained the sole model on offer and even in these states themselves—in sharp contrast to parts of central Europe, and of former Soviet western and central Asia—the territorial delimitation of Africa deriving from nineteenth and early twentieth century colonial partition has remained almost entirely unchallenged. The only challenges to be recognized, indeed—formally in the case of Eritrea, informally in that of Somaliland—have involved the restoration of colonial territories that had been merged into neighboring states. An exploration of the reasons for this discrepancy between actuality and reasonable expectation may therefore be helpful in understanding not only the distinctive trajectories of Africa itself, but also some of the wider issues underlying the idea of trusteeship.

This chapter seeks to do this in four ways. First, it examines the peculiar history of the idea of trusteeship in the continent, and the corrosive legacies that this history has left behind it. Second, it looks at the diplomatic assumptions that have guided the African regional system since independence, with regard both to the internal management of the continent by African states themselves and to its treatment by external powers; these differ significantly as between the immediate post-independence period, which coincided at the global level with the Cold War, and the post-Cold War era. Third, it takes two African states, Liberia and Sierra Leone, to which the idea of trusteeship might be regarded as most appropriate, and explores the implications of the de facto mentoring structures that have been introduced, even though these stopped short of formal trusteeship. And finally, it seeks to place the issue of trusteeship within the broader context of the problems of African governance.

## The African Experience of Trusteeship

The African experience has always been, and remains, central to the idea of "trusteeship" in modern global politics. At the heart of that idea lies the belief that states that are more "modern," more "developed," or at the crudest more "civilized," have both the obligation and the capacity to extend the benefits of stable and accountable governance to other parts of the world, in the interests both of the international system as a whole and, most important, of the peoples who are thus for their own good brought within the global project of modernity. Nowhere does that project have deeper roots than in Africa, and nowhere is its conceptual, practical, and (not least) moral ambivalence more evident. The peculiar problems of establishing the legitimacy of some modern form of protectorate in the continent, despite the large number of recent cases to which this might appear to be an appropriate solution, directly derive from the close relationship between trusteeship and empire that Will Bain has explored in his contribution to this volume, and to the carryover of specifically imperial legacies into the project of African governance at the present time. This section explores the origins of the project of global governance in the African context, and the (at best) ambivalent forms that it took, as a backdrop from which to extend the analysis to the problems of trusteeship as a means of managing state failure in Africa in the present era.

As soon as the extension of European power over other parts of the world came to be seen as requiring a moral justification, rather than being regarded merely as reflecting the right of the strong to impose their power on the weak, the idea of trusteeship was articulated as appropriate to this purpose. Amongst its earliest expressions was the motto of the Anti-Slavery Society, "Am I Not a Man and a Brother?," encircling the figure of a kneeling slave, which was reproduced in the seal of the colony of Sierra Leone, founded in 1787 as a refuge for freed former slaves from the New World, and later for those "recaptured" at sea by the British navy. This was the first project of state formation in Africa guided by an explicitly humanitarian agenda, and was joined in 1822 by the foundation of the American colony of Liberia, with its analogous motto, "The Love of Liberty Brought Us Here." It is an irony that these two states became the sites of renewed projects of trusteeship in the early twenty-first century, which are discussed later in this chapter.

Trusteeship in Africa, in short, traces its origins to the era of Atlantic slavery, and to the intensely unequal and racially branded relationships that it implied. Even though the project itself was articulated by the opponents of slavery, and explicitly rejected the discriminatory racial assumptions on which slavery was built, the stench of its origins remained. The trustees were still European or white American; those over whom they exercised power in the name of this trust were still African. It would be virtually impossible to construct any morally acceptable form of governance on such foundations.

When, towards the end of the nineteenth century, the colonial conquest was extended to cover virtually the whole of Africa, the idea of trusteeship was extended with it. Its grossest expression was the establishment under the Berlin treaty of 1885 of the Congo Free State, which in the name of the noblest aspirations of humanity handed control over a vast area of central Africa (now the Democratic Republic of Congo) to the rapacious personal rule of King Leopold of the Belgians.[1] This territory likewise has been the location for later projects of trusteeship, extending to the present time. Other justifications of empire, such as the "white man's burden" of Rudyard Kipling or the "dual mandate" of Frederick Lord Lugard, were less horrifying in their practical implications, but nonetheless carried the message of trusteeship as a deeply unequal relationship between the governors and the governed. The "dual mandate" in particular, which explicitly anchored the moral basis for European colonialism in Africa in the welfare of African people on the one hand and the broader interests of global capitalism on the other, bears an uncanny resemblance to justifications for trusteeship at the present time.

The explicit introduction of the idea of trusteeship into African colonial governance, formally defined and subject at least in principle to a measure of accountability, dates from the disposal of the German colonies in the continent to the victorious powers after the First World War. Since the crude transfer of territory from the losers to the winners was no longer acceptable, especially to President Woodrow Wilson of the United States, it became necessary instead to devise a formula by which, under the purview of the newly established League of Nations, the new rulers (Britain in Tanganyika, South Africa in South-West Africa, Belgium in Burundi and Rwanda, and France and Britain in unequal shares in Togo and Cameroon) were formally entrusted with these territories in the interests of their inhabitants. With no more than slight reservations (France, for example, could not impose conscription in Togo and Cameroon), they actually became colonies like any other. In a continent as extensively colonized as Africa, any project of external governance would inevitably carry with it much of the moral and emotional baggage of colonialism. When the very language in which that project was expressed had already been appropriated by colonialism itself, the connection could only be reinforced.

## The Eclipse of Trusteeship in Post-Colonial Africa

Given these antecedents, it was understandable that the rulers of African states at independence insisted on the principle of unfettered state sovereignty (save only for territories remaining under white minority rule, which were treated as continuing colonies), and rejected entirely any suggestion that these states should be subject to any constraint imposed in the name of higher values, with which the idea of trusteeship is necessarily associated. The Charter of the Organization of African Unity, established in 1963, provided the classic statement of this doctrine. It nonetheless left unresolved the problems of actual African state formation, which were all the more starkly revealed by the total collapse of the government of the former Belgian Congo within days of its independence in 1960, from which it needed to be rescued by large-scale intervention on the part of the United Nations, precursor to the problems of dealing with collapsed states in more recent times.

These problems, certainly, were much more intense in some countries than in others. The trajectory of African states since independence has proved to be extremely varied, a variation revealed as the end of the Cold War left different African states in a very different condition to face the challenges of democratic governance and economic development. This revealed a number of states in which some combination of a favorable political geography, legacies of precolonial statehood and colonial rule, and wise political leadership had established the basis for viable statehood, and overcome the weaknesses to which trusteeship in some form might be posed as a solution. A discussion on this subject necessarily concentrates on the much more difficult cases in which viable statehood was not achieved. In these, behind the rhetorical combination of unfettered state sovereignty combined with pan-African solidarity, a reasonably effective though temporary expedient was found by seeking client status, under the more or less explicit protection of one of the major states in the international system, which then guaranteed not only the continued existence of what in Robert Jackson's term might be regarded as "quasi-states" (which were treated "as if" they were states, despite their inability to match the criteria for effectual statehood that previous conceptions of sovereign statehood has assumed),[2] but also the continuance in office, at whatever human cost, of their current rulers. Client statehood is a device even older than trusteeship in international relations, but with significantly different implications.

Where possible, the rulers of fragile African states sought protection from their own former colonial masters. Even though it laid them open to charges of "neo-colonialism" from more radical African regimes and their allies, this had substantial advantages: the new rulers and the old generally shared solid interests in the maintenance of the former colonial state, in addition to the intangible benefits of common language and often long shared experiences and personal linkages.[3] In other cases, which included a very high proportion of the most problematic ones, it was necessary to have recourse to one or other of the superpowers—whether the United States in the case of Mobutu's Zaire or Doe's Liberia, or the Soviet Union in that of Siyad Barre's Somalia (until the Russians shifted their support to Ethiopia) or Neto's Angola.[4] The differences from a trusteeship regime lay in the terms of the compact between the domestic government and its external guarantor. Whereas in the case of a trusteeship, ultimate power lay in the hands of the external trustee, and had to be exercised—in principle, at least—in accordance with some formula that rested on the welfare of the governed, in that of a client state the key person to be protected was the ruler himself, and the terms of that protection could be (and often were, despite Soviet pressure to establish Leninist party-states, and muted American disapproval of the grosser forms of personal rule) virtually unconditional.

This in turn goes a long way to explain why the African insistence on state sovereignty was shared during the Cold War era, not only by the superpowers but also by the former colonial rulers. African states themselves had in any case formed, around the OAU consensus, a rhetoric of solidarity in dealing with the outside world, which meant that external powers which transgressed African norms in their dealings with the continent (for example, by supporting secessionist movements against existing African states, or publicly promoting the overthrow of African rulers allied with a rival patron) would be weakened in their dealings with the continent as a whole. Clientelism enabled external powers to reap the benefits of controlling a following of obedient governments in the international system—as expressed, for example, in votes in the United Nations General Assembly, where the large number of African states counted as an advantage—while at the same time reinforcing rather than challenging the regional norms of the African state system itself. The doctrine of sovereignty likewise excused the external patrons from direct responsibility for all but the worst abuses in the treatment of African peoples by their own governments.

## Trusteeship and Protection in the Post-Cold War Era

The end of the Cold War removed (or at least greatly reduced) the possibilities for external protection, and led to the imposition of more stringent conditions for its provision, which in turn shifted the terms of the relationship away from simple protection and towards at least an implicit trusteeship: the terms of the deal required African states to adopt multi-party electoral systems, open up their economies, and abide by at least minimal conditions for "good governance." International institutions such as the World Bank and the European Union established "conditionalities" for the provision of badly needed aid, and even states which had previously supported African regimes on a clientelistic basis, such as France and the United States, were in some degree obliged to do likewise. This in turn helped to exacerbate the differences between those states that proved broadly capable of adapting their domestic political arrangements to the new global norms with little threat to their own stability, and which benefited in consequence from greatly increased aid flows, and those that were either unwilling or indeed unable to make these changes without severe challenge to ruling groups at best, or to the very existence of the state at worst. It is these latter cases, presenting the severest challenge to African state-formation, that have then become the targets for a renewed interest in the idea of "trusteeship."

This is not the place to go in any detail into the failures of governance in post-colonial Africa, or the range of cases—including Somalia, which has lacked any plausible central government for some twenty years; the three adjacent West African states of Côte d'Ivoire, Liberia and Sierra Leone; and the perennially problematic territory now euphemistically known as the Democratic Republic of Congo (DRC)—which might make suitable cases for treatment. There is now an ample if uneven literature on state failure, much of it drawing on the African material.[5] The extremely uncertain nature of the external response may then be ascribed in part to the reluctance of external states to become engaged, in part to an equivalent lack of enthusiasm from the African community of states, and in part to the inherent difficulties of the project of external state creation in Africa.

There has certainly been no lack of interest in state failure on the part of the dominant states in the post-Cold War global system. Even before the events of 11 September 2001 drew the attention of the United States to the dangers that zones of statelessness might present to its own security, there had been widespread concern, not least on humanitarian grounds. The US intervention in Somalia from December 1992 onwards, Operation Restore Hope, though initiated on humanitarian grounds by an outgoing President in his final weeks in office, rapidly drew attention to the intractable problems involved, and to the difficulty of assuring human welfare under conditions of anarchy.[6] It also demonstrated that there were winners as well as losers from such anarchy, and that efforts to restore order might well be contested; the costs of such contestation, especially when measured in the lives of its own nationals, were more than the United States in particular was prepared to accept. The US had indeed already refused to become engaged in Liberia when, from late 1989 onwards, the security of that execrably governed state was threatened by an insurgency that was in time to affect the stability of its neighbors. A case can indeed be made that a timely intervention in Liberia, which enjoyed very close historic links to the United States, could have re-established stability at minimal cost, and with a positive impact on the region as a whole. The conclusion here must be that West Africa in particular, and in some degree the continent as a whole, simply did not matter enough to expend the political resources required. There was certainly a dramatic difference in this respect from both central Europe and the Middle East, both of which figured much more prominently in the perspectives of the major global players.

In addition to this, however, external engagement in African projects of state reconstruction, or much more radically any attempt to develop systems of governance that might displace the territorial state, continued to run up against the deep resistance of African elites, intellectual as well as governmental, to any form of external tutelage. From the early 2000s onwards, moreover, engrained African hostility was reinforced by the dramatic increase in Chinese interests in Africa. Though China certainly has a strong commitment to the idea of state sovereignty that is derived from resentment at Western encroachments from the nineteenth century onwards, this doctrine also has a practical utility in enabling the PRC to establish close relationships with mineral-rich African states that notably fail to meet Western standards of "good governance."[7] This has helped to restore the counterweight to Western dominance—and hence to the imposition of an idea of trusteeship necessarily linked to the "good governance" agenda—that was formerly provided by the Soviet Union.

But if a Western-run new protectorate is unacceptable, this still leaves open the question of whether African states might devise some equivalent that they might introduce themselves. There has certainly been some dilution, under the pressure of continental as well as global developments, of the virtually unrestricted insistence on sovereignty of the OAU's Charter. Its successor, the African Union (AU) instituted in 2002, at least in principle significantly modified the sovereign rights of member states, and asserted the right of the organization as a whole to pass judgment on the conduct of their internal affairs, even rescinding the membership of states that refused to comply. Nominally at least, the Charter might be interpreted as extending to the right of the organization to impose its own African form of trusteeship or protectorate over designated states or territories—to a greater extent, indeed, than other regional organizations (apart from the European Union) allow. The creation of an AU African Standby Force and its deployment in Darfur derive from these provisions of the Charter. Almost simultaneously, the promulgation under the aegis especially of South Africa's President Mbeki of the New Partnership for Africa's Development (NEPAD) sought to entrench a continental commitment to "good governance." The most innovative feature of which was the creation of an African Peer Review Mechanism (APRM) under which not only other governments but civil society actors also, would review the governance systems of participating states in order to assess their compliance with NEPAD norms, and make recommendations for their improvement. Several such reviews have now been conducted, though since the states concerned had to invite review, the mechanism has been applied only to those that were successful enough to feel confident in accepting the assessment of their peers.

Despite this change in formal procedures, nonetheless, the cultural commitment to sovereignty remains extremely strong. Indeed, NEPAD has been accused by African commentators from north of the Limpopo of being a means of extending the hegemony of a newly liberated South Africa over the rest of the continent. More plausibly, NEPAD and the AU Charter may be regarded essentially as pre-emptive measures, designed to protect continental regimes against external pressures by assuring the outside world that African states were doing something about the issue themselves. Nowhere was the hollowness of this assertion more embarrassingly revealed than in Zimbabwe, where African governments, including notably that of South Africa, preferred to turn a blind eye to the increasingly evident misgovernment of the Mugabe regime, in the name of the sovereignty of independent states. Despite the deployment of a small and ineffectual African Union force in Darfur, the idea that African governments collectively might act as trustees for the welfare of other Africans remained stillborn. The idea of trusteeship remained obstinately associated with the imposition of external power.

## Two Quasi-Trusteeships: Liberia and Sierra Leone

In order to take a closer look at the possibilities and limitations of trusteeship as a form of emergency governance in Africa, it is instructive to examine the two adjoining states of Liberia and Sierra Leone in West Africa, in which a form of trusteeship has come closest to realization. By enumerating the conditions that made such arrangements at least relatively unproblematic in these two states, it should be possible to assess the potential achievements and limitations of trusteeship under (for Africa) generally favorable circumstances, and indicate problematic features that are likely to be much more marked elsewhere on the continent.

In both countries, a legacy of chronically corrupt and unaccountable government prompted increased resistance from the late 1970s onwards, and eventually resulted in armed challenges to the government—initially at the center, but eventually (and much more dangerously) from insurgent groups in the countryside, which from the early 1990s operated from across international frontiers. This rapidly placed a burden on feeble state institutions that these were quite unable to bear, and led to a generalized breakdown of order over much of the national territory. Both government and opposition forces were in both states very poorly disciplined, and warfare led to appalling levels of human suffering, including mutilation and some of the worst cases anywhere in Africa of abuses both by and of children.[8] First in Liberia, and later in Sierra Leone, regional forces under the authority of the Economic Community of West African States (ECOWAS) intervened to restore order, with partial but only very limited success. In Sierra Leone, the former colonial power (the United Kingdom) intervened militarily to decisive effect in the later 1990s. In both states, UN forces (UNAMSIL in Sierra Leone, UNMIL in Liberia) were deployed under Chapter VII of the United Nations Charter.

In neither case was any formal protectorate instituted, but in each, a basic level of order was restored with the assistance of outside forces, and in each case likewise external actors exercised the power to get rid of domestic regimes of which (for very good reason) they disapproved. Internationally supervised multi-party elections were held, leading to the formal inauguration of democratic domestic governments, which however remained highly dependent on external support, both as the guarantors of security and for the provision of government finance and a wide range of governmental services. Both states could correspondingly be regarded as trusteeships in all but name. The elements that made this outside engagement possible, but also point to the limitations of external rule (in these states and by implication elsewhere), can conveniently be summarized under the three headings of practicability, legitimacy, and sustainability.

## Practicability

The first key question is whether a system of essentially external administration can be imposed, without massively overstretching the resources that potentially interested states and international institutions are likely to be willing to commit to the purpose. In this respect, both Liberia and Sierra Leone are at least relatively manageable. For a start, both of them are very small states, with populations of only a few millions, and have relatively favorable political geographies in the sense defined by Herbst.[9] They differ sharply in this respect from a state such as the DRC, with its vast territory, scattered populations and poor communications, in which on a simple practical basis, external governance is vastly more difficult. Second, the military obstacles to the imposition of external force were likewise well within the capacities of even small numbers of well-trained professional soldiers. Potential "spoilers," such as the RUF in Sierra Leone and the NPFL, ULIMO, LURD and other factions in Liberia, operated at a very low level of military effectiveness. The contrast here is with a region such as the Horn of Africa, where indigenous military forces are vastly more formidable. Third, even though the regional environment is destabilizing to a significant degree, with interlinked conflicts affecting the whole southwest corner of West Africa that comprises Côte d'Ivoire, Guinea, Liberia and Sierra Leone, it is by no means as unmanageable as, for example, the Horn or the Great Lakes.

## Legitimacy

One critical requirement for successful trusteeship is that external supervision will be broadly accepted by local populations, without triggering deep-seated hostility of the kind that has seriously undermined it in, for example, Afghanistan and Iraq. In this respect, both Liberia and Sierra Leone provide a far more conducive environment than would normally be found, not only in Africa but in most of the states where trusteeship is likely to be attempted. First of all, the peoples of both countries had suffered massive levels of violence at the hands of domestic armed factions, of a kind that would be likely to induce them to accept—and even to welcome—any force capable of imposing and maintaining basic levels of human security. Second, the legitimacy of domestic political institutions had been so deeply undermined—both by their failure to protect their people against disorder and, more broadly, by the levels of corruption and incompetence that had led to the breakdown of order in the first place—that these had lost any authority that they might otherwise have been able to mobilize in opposition to external rule. The people of both countries shared a general commitment to multi-party liberal democracy as their preferred form of government, but the actual experience of regimes that—formally at least—embodied this ideal had been disastrous.

Third, and in sharp contrast to many of the states in which serious insurgencies had arisen, none of the armed factions in either case enjoyed enough legitimacy among key sections of the population to be able to present a serious political threat to external peacekeepers. Such support as they possessed, illustrated by Charles Taylor's victory in the 1997 Liberian elections, had been due entirely to their continuing military capacity to create further mayhem if they lost; once this had been removed, political parties that tacitly represented armed factions were able to gain only minimal support, either in the subsequent 2005 Liberian election or in the Sierra Leone elections of 1996 and 2002.[10] Fourth, the indigenous societies themselves were not riven by internal ethnic conflicts of a kind that would ineluctably have led any external administration to be associated with one side or the other. Both countries do indeed have complex patterns of indigenous ethnicity, as is the norm throughout Africa, but these are not beyond management by any reasonably well-run administration. The most obvious contrast here is with states such as Burundi and Rwanda.

Fifth—and very different, for example, from a state such as Somalia—there is in neither case any deep sense of indigenous identity that would lead much of the population to regard any external force with hostility. Both states, as we have seen, owe their own origins to external projects of governance, guided (however inadequately) by humanitarian agendas, and in both (despite the long Liberian record of formal independence) external involvement has been an ongoing element in domestic governance. Finally, particular external forces continued to enjoy a level of legitimacy in domestic society that would to a significant degree lead their intervention to be welcomed, or at least accepted. In Liberia, the United States was looked to by a large part of the population as the country's "natural" protector, and had the US government been prepared to intervene, notably at the crisis of state breakdown in mid-1990, there is every likelihood that a massive amount of suffering could have been averted. The United Kingdom enjoyed a comparable status in Sierra Leone, where the links with the former colonizer went back much further, and were far less resented, than in virtually any other British colony in Africa. There had never been any effective Sierra Leonean independence movement, and the country's independence in 1961 derived more from general trends in the continent than from the strength of internal demand. Given the experience of post-independence governance, it is unsurprising that the British military intervention was widely accepted. There is a marked difference here, for example, from the position of France in neighboring Côte d'Ivoire, where the close and continuing French presence after independence had been devoted in large measure to maintaining a particular domestic power structure closely linked to the former colonizer. In short, one would be hard put to find any two states in Africa, whose people would be more prepared to accept trusteeship.

## Sustainability

Effective trusteeship, however, needs not only to be practicable and acceptable at the moment of initial intervention, but also to be linked to a defined and attainable longer-term political program, which will in turn provide a plausible strategy for resolving the underlying problems that led to the introduction of a trusteeship system in the first place. In contrast to the first two criteria, that of sustainability is much more problematic: there are indeed some elements in the Liberian and Sierra Leonean situations that help to provide the basis for a sustainable mission, but others that significantly undermine it.

First, in each of these cases, the key problem was one of state failure—the mismanagement and consequent breakdown of specific institutions of governance—even though this rapidly led to much broader societal consequences. It could thus plausibly be argued that the key to recovery was the reconstruction of an effective and reasonably well-run state, which would in turn make it possible to rectify other problems, and that this was a task achievable with external assistance. This contrasts with other cases of breakdown in Africa, such as Somalia and the DRC, which had much more fundamental causes, of which state collapse was little more than a symptom, and which did not lend themselves to equivalent projects of externally-supported state reconstruction.

Second, there was in each case a model of what the reconstructed state should look like, which precisely corresponded to the template espoused by the dominant states in the post-Cold War international order. Both Liberia and Sierra Leone have internalized the ideal of liberal multi-party democracy that derived from their own origins, and no serious alternative to this model has ever been advanced. Liberia, indeed, maintained for more than a hundred and thirty years after independence a constitution closely derived from that of its parent, the United States of America, the letter of which was punctiliously observed throughout the long period of effectively single-party government under the True Whig Party, which ended with the coup d'état of 1980. In neither case was there any serious issue of secession or state autonomy.

The problems, however, lie much deeper, and threaten to undermine the project of external state reconstruction, even under the exceptionally favorable conditions of these two states. The first of these is the problem of externality itself. The external takeover of basic state functions, notably those of security and economic management, necessarily undermines the very process of creating viable and accountable state institutions, on which the restoration of effective government depends. It can only foster attitudes of dependence, in states whose exceptionally high level of dependence has been one of their basic weaknesses all along. The high "externality" of the supposedly indigenous government is in any case one of its most visible characteristics: the Johnson-Sirleaf government in Liberia is for example run almost entirely at the ministerial level by Liberians who have returned from often long residence abroad, usually in the United States, and whose linkages with indigenous Liberian society are correspondingly weak. Given the attrition of qualified Liberians within the country, during the long period of misgovernment and civil war, this is entirely understandable, and the dedication and indeed heroism of many of these returnees can scarcely be faulted; but the sense that this is an external government run by Liberians remains. In day-to-day administration, these people must likewise necessarily look to the external sector, rather than to indigenous sources, for the resources—notably in terms of finance, but also in terms of security and expertise—that are needed to run the state. The entire political process is oriented towards the outside.

Still more basically, the reconstruction of viable states on the ruins of failed ones must depend on fundamental changes in governance that address the reasons why these states failed in the first place. In particular, this calls for the creation of public institutions, guided by attitudes and ideologies geared to the provision of public goods, that contrast sharply with the deeply privatized states, essentially concerned with securing the welfare of the very small groups of people who ran them, that existed before (and directly led to) state breakdown. In a December 2004 report,[11] the International Crisis Group recognized this problem, and called for an international engagement lasting for some 15 to 25 years, in order to bring about the necessary structural changes. Such a program however would require a thoroughgoing process of social transformation, deeply inimical to the interests of incumbent elites and ultimately capable of implementation only by force, which would arouse local, continental and global opposition and in the process reinforce the problems of externality already noted. The prospects for creating an effective, democratic and internally accountable structure of governance by such means are minimal.

## Conclusion

The preceding discussion provides no very comforting prescriptions for the role of trusteeship, or of the international community in any guise, in reconstructing failed states. There is, to be sure, a historical resonance accompanying the project of trusteeship in Africa, which goes a long way to explain the peculiar distaste with which it is treated by African ruling elites. Whatever the manifest inadequacies of "sovereignty" as a formula for establishing effective and accountable governance in a continent in which this is desperately needed, there has been an intense reluctance on the part not only of politicians but of African intellectuals to articulate any alternative to it. There has indeed been a slowly increasing inclination on the part of the dominant states of the international system to become involved in attempts to rectify the grossest cases of political failure, signaled initially (however unsuccessfully) by United States intervention in Somalia, and subsequently in Darfur. The Rwandan genocide likewise made a substantial impact in legitimizing what the French activist (later foreign minister) Bernard Kouchner has termed a *droit d'ingérence* or right of intervention in cases of extreme humanitarian need—a claim now backed by the adoption by the United Nations Security Council of a "responsibility to protect" that could be used to justify the imposition of a de facto trusteeship. Despite the proliferation of peacekeeping forces in African conflicts, however, those Western states that have been at the forefront of demands for global governance remain extremely wary of attempting to impose any project of external trusteeship, for eminently understandable reasons. In an era of declining Western hegemony, such a project would both be regarded with extreme suspicion by the majority of African states, backed by rising powers in the global system, and at the same time make greater demands on their own resources than they are willing to commit to a part of the world which remains, in geopolitical terms, of only limited interest.

Still more basic is the question of whether this project would carry any plausible prospect of success. Even in those cases—and in this respect the exceptionality of Liberia and Sierra Leone needs continual emphasis—where objections to trusteeship on grounds of either legitimacy or practicality are muted, it is striking how limited a contribution external engagement can make to the perennially difficult task of state creation in Africa. Whatever the role of European imperialism in spreading a worldwide concept of statehood as the only acceptable model of political organization, and however successfully this model may have been exported to many parts of the world, the project of state formation ultimately depends on indigenous elites who are capable both of selling an idea of the state to their own populations and of behaving themselves in ways that reinforce that idea, not least through their own accountability to it. It must in short be converted from an external to an internal agenda. In some respects, and notably in appropriating and establishing the legitimacy of the territories created by colonialism, African elites have been remarkably successful in this quest. When it comes to the much more difficult task of establishing the internal mechanisms needed to make such states work, often under circumstances that make that task exceptionally difficult, they have been much less successful. It is at this point, where the need for external support may appear to be most urgently required, that its deficiencies are likewise clearest.

## 4

# PATERNAL AUTHORITY, CIVILIZED STATE

## CHINA'S EVOLVING ATTITUDE TOWARDS
## INTERNATIONAL TRUSTEESHIPS*

*Shogo Suzuki*

The post-Cold War era has seen a remarkable comeback of the idea of suspended sovereignty and trusteeship. The increased attention paid to human rights issues resulted in the promotion of humanitarian intervention where a state's sovereign authority is temporarily overruled by the international community to prevent an imminent or ongoing humanitarian catastrophe.[1] The political necessity of eroding sovereignty norms acquired an urgent tone after 9/11. Policy prescriptions emanating from both academic and political circles pushed for liberal democracies to establish new protectorates and reconstruct them in their own image. While the efficacy of these policies has been much

* The research for this chapter was made possible by a generous grant provided by the Universities China Committee, whose support is gratefully acknowledged. I am also indebted to Zhu Tianbiao and the School of Government and Management, Peking University, for hosting me during my research trip to Beijing. Many thanks also to the participants in the writers' conference held in Cambridge in June 2007, especially Ricardo Soares de Oliveira and James Mayall, for their helpful comments and encouragement. Finally, I should like to express my gratitude to the various Chinese analysts who gave their time to answer my questions.

debated, they appealed to both realists and liberals, no doubt spurred on by the threat from terrorism. For the liberals, the global spread of democracy was unquestionably seen as a good which should be encouraged, while for realists, it made sense to promote these policies in order to secure a more stable and peaceful environment for the state.[2] These views have of course been tempered by the perceived failure of the intervention in Iraq and disappointing outcomes in the other new protectorates. However, as we will see below, the idea of transplanting liberal democratic governance across the globe—as embodied in the concept of "Responsibility to Protect" (R2P) which places greater emphasis on preventing civil war and state failure over international military intervention—remains influential.

One state that views these developments with ambivalence is China. On the one hand, the Chinese continue to harbor painful memories of Western invasion and interference by the European-dominated international society, which are kept alive by both the political elite and direct experience among the people. In the nineteenth century, the "legitimate great powers" of European international society often used force to ensure that the non-European polities complied with the standard of civilization, and China's failure to do this resulted in semi-colonization which only ended in the 1940s.[3] Consequently, the People's Republic of China (PRC) has tended to guard its sovereign authority jealously, and any perceived attempt to interfere in Chinese domestic affairs is usually greeted with suspicion and hostility. Indeed, Alastair Iain Johnston has argued that China's view of sovereignty resembles that of the Westphalian ideal-type.[4] It is therefore not particularly surprising that some Chinese commentators, as we will see, have tended to see the re-emergence of international trusteeships as yet another attempt by the Western powers to exercise hegemony over other states. China thus shares a similar outlook and identity with many post-colonial developing states that tend to have misgivings towards international society—which continues to be dominated by the Western powers—and its attempts to impose a particular form of governance and civilized form of life. The sovereignty norm proved to be an essential normative weapon that could be used against the West to bring about the end of colonial rule. It remains of considerable utility to ward off any international criticism and interference in a state's internal governance.[5]

On the other hand, the new international trusteeships provide Beijing with concrete benefits. China shares with many Western states the view that so-called failed states can pose a threat to its own national security, and would like such areas to be stabilized, even if it means the temporary suspension of the sovereignty of the particular state in question. Furthermore, participating in the establishment of the new protectorates provides the Chinese with an excellent chance to establish its long-coveted identity of what I call a legitimate great power of international society. As Gerry Simpson has argued, legitimate great powers are not simply military or economic giants, but are states that have also been given "certain constitutional privileges, rights and duties" owing to their superior power which is "recognized...as a political fact" by other states,[6] and their "relations with each other are defined by adherence to a rough principle of sovereign equality."[7] Simpson's argument rests on two assumptions which are of particular importance for this chapter. First, for a rising candidate great power to be accepted into this club of legitimate great powers, it needs to be accorded the constitutional privileges and rights and fulfill the duties expected of its members. Second, for a state to be accepted it needs to be treated as a social equal with the other legitimate great powers.

As far as acceptance into this exclusive social grouping is concerned, the PRC has arguably been accorded constitutional privileges and rights which its fellow members enjoy. It is given a permanent seat in the UNSC, and enjoys the constitutional privilege of having a say on all important matters pertaining to global governance. Even in less institutionalized settings, China's importance means that most regional issues in the Asia-Pacific cannot be settled without Beijing's consent. China's quandary lies mainly in the duties that come with its privileges, as well as its acute sense of insecurity that it has yet to be accorded the social equality enjoyed between other legitimate great powers. The recent humanitarian turn in international society has not only challenged Beijing's oft-cited belief in the sanctity of the sovereignty norm, but—coupled with China's "othering" by Western powers—also pressured the Chinese to actively participate in efforts to enforce humanitarian norms in order to shore up their identity as a legitimate great power. The post-Cold War protectorates are the embodiment of this dilemma which sets China apart from other developing powers and legitimate great powers, and makes the Chinese case unique. If the PRC wants to secure its identity as a legitimate great power, does it have the duty as a "responsible great power (*fu zeren daguo* 负责任大国)" (as the Chinese are wont to describe their country) to participate? Or should it continue to adhere to its developing state identity and oppose the trusteeships, at the risk of alienating itself from the other members of the legitimate great power club?

This chapter is an attempt to address these questions. As can be inferred from above, Beijing's views of international trusteeships have been very much tied into its ongoing debates about issues of international recognition of its power and dualistic identity as both a member of the developing world and a legitimate great power. The analysis provided here can therefore also be read as yet another episode in the continuing saga of China's quest for an identity in the Western-dominated international society, albeit through the case study of the new protectorates. The chapter is divided into two sections. First, it explores Beijing's views of old international trusteeships, which were established under the auspices of the UN and had an explicit aim of guiding dependent polities to independent statehood. Secondly, it provides a brief sketch of the intellectual backdrop from which the ideas for "new" trusteeships emerged, and examines how the Chinese political elite have viewed this new concept, and how Beijing has participated in the entrenchment of new trusteeships in post-Cold War international society.[8]

Given the inherent difficulty in precisely defining trusteeships, the chapter understands international trusteeships or protectorates broadly in terms of an "intervention by outside powers...to replace malevolent or non-existent governance."[9] The Chinese have tended not to use the term "trusteeship (*tuoguan* 托管)" in their discussions of recent peacebuilding (*weihe xingdong* 维和行动) or statebuilding (*guojia chongjian* 国家重建) undertaken by international society. This could very well be because of the colonial stigma still attached to the term and "a broader uncertainty as to the appropriateness of imposing good governance by force of arms."[10] They do, however, implicitly differentiate traditional, institutionalized trusteeships such as, which explicitly aim for dependent territories to attain independent statehood, from new forms of trusteeship, in which the independent state's sovereignty is temporarily suspended until it is deemed fit for independent statehood once more. I will also broadly follow these distinctions in my own discussions of Beijing's views of trusteeships, although the two do share some common features. The reason for this is twofold. First, both "traditional" and "new" trusteeships share the ultimate goal to lead the host polity/state into a condition of fitness ready for statehood. Second, they are united in their general paternalism. The assumption that undergirds both forms of trusteeship is that the trustees know "what is the best" form of governance for their host states.[11] In this sense, then, they are treating their hosts as children who are unable to make correct decisions on how to live their lives.[12]

## China and "Traditional" Trusteeships

The PRC's views of the system of traditional trusteeships can be found in its actions in the UN, which until 1994 continued to operate the Trusteeship

Council charged with the task of promoting "the political, economic, social, and educational advancement of the inhabitants of the trust territories, and their progressive development towards self-government or independence."[13] At first glance, such a system may appear to be anathema to Beijing. China had regularly denounced the UN as a tool of the imperialist powers in the 1960s and early 1970s. Even after its entry into the organization, the Chinese continued to champion the cause of the Third World, forwarding the "Three Worlds Theory" and calling for the Second and Third Worlds to unite and oppose the imperialist policies of both the US and the Soviet Union.

Despite this ideological commitment, China's entry into the UN had very little impact on the Trusteeship Council. One important reason for this is the fact that the very idea of international trusteeship had been thoroughly discredited in international society by the time China had rejoined it. The 1960 UN Declaration on the Granting Independence to Colonial Countries and Peoples—which the Chinese praise as the "mark that the UN decolonization movement had entered a victorious era"[14]—affirmed "the supreme value of self-determination" and "declared that the denial of independence precluded the full enjoyment of fundamental human rights."[15] Although debates over the Europeans' fitness to rule had existed in various forms,[16] this declaration framed decolonization in terms of human rights. Instead of being seen as a means to help the attainment of human rights, trusteeships were now seen as systems that violated them. Furthermore, the "Europeans found themselves unable to reply in any meaningful way" to these charges "because they could not claim the rights of men for themselves and at the same time withhold them from the men of Africa and Asia."[17] As a result, by the time the PRC joined the UN, most states under UN trusteeship had (with the exception of a small handful of islands in the South Pacific) attained independence, and there was very little room for China to play a role of any substance.

The reports presented by the Trusteeship Council to the UNSC indicate that Beijing generally kept a low profile. In the late 1970s, China was conspicuously absent from meetings. Although it has since attended meetings diligently, China has generally not pressed its ideological agenda of anti-colonialism. China curiously failed, for instance, to support the Soviet Union when the latter charged at a Trusteeship Council meeting on 23 May 1988 that the offers by the US (as the acting trustee in this instance) of Free Associations for the Micronesian Islands were an attempt to convert the trusteeships "into an American neo-colonial possession and military strategic training ground."[18] Furthermore, Beijing appears to have accepted the mandate of the Trusteeship Council fairly uncritically, and has noted that the Council played a positive role in promoting independence and self-determination. In a meeting on 14 May 1993, the Chinese delegate stated that "[o]wing to the protracted and tireless efforts of the international community and the peoples of Trust Territories, a large number had terminated their trusteeship status and had become independent and equal members of the international community."[19]

The reasons for the PRC's relative silence towards traditional forms of trusteeships in contemporary international society are threefold. One simple reason, at least in the 1970s, may be that the Chinese diplomats were aware of their newcomer status in the UN, and chose to stay on the sidelines in order to learn and familiarize themselves with the workings of the organization.[20] Secondly, there was little reason to oppose the Trusteeship Council because the Council's goals did not fundamentally clash with those professed by Beijing. The important point to note here is that the UN Trusteeship system aimed to make dependent territories achieve independence or autonomy, and Chinese scholars also acknowledge this point.[21] As the Chinese delegate noted in a Trusteeship Council meeting, the "Chinese Government had all along supported the demands and aspirations of the peoples of Trust Territories to achieve national self-determination and independence,"[22] and these of course were in full agreement with the ultimate goal of the UN Trusteeship system, which was to "gradually make the territory under trusteeship walk on the path towards autonomy or independence."[23] Finally, and perhaps most important, Beijing saw very little reason to flag its anti-colonial credentials, as it had now attained the international recognition it had sought in the 1960s. During this time, the PRC had attempted to break out of its international isolation by positioning itself as a champion of anti-colonialism and attaining the diplomatic recognition and support of the Third World. While Beijing continued to profess its solidarity and identification with the developing world (insofar as it did not clash with the PRC's own interests), once it was rehabilitated into international society it quickly toned down its radical anti-imperialist rhetoric. All of this pointed to a duality within China's own self-perception. Now that it had joined the UN and been given constitutional privileges (in the form of a permanent seat in the UNSC) to play a key role in the governance of international society, Beijing's long-standing desire for this exalted position meant that it would work towards consolidating political hierarchies among states and go against developing states' egalitarian vision of international politics,[24] despite its insistence on its solidarity with the Third World.[25] This tension within China's identity would again affect China's engagement with the new protectorates after the Cold War; and it is to this point that we now turn.

## *The "New" Trusteeships*

If the more traditional forms of trusteeship do not cause many worries within Beijing, the new forms of trusteeship that have emerged since the end of the Cold War caused greater dilemmas.[26] Trends such as humanitarian catastrophes, terrorism and failed states resulted in new approaches to security.[27] First, traditional security and its policies—with their emphasis on external and internal balancing to ward off threats from other states—were seen as limited in their ability to deal with the new security environment. As the UNSC put it in 1992:

> The absence of war and military conflicts among States does not in itself ensure international peace and security. The non-military sources of instability in the economic, social, humanitarian and ecological fields have become threats to peace and security. The United Nations membership as a whole, working through the appropriate bodies, needs to give the highest priority to the solution of these matters.[28]

Second, this brought about new security policies. The fact that the international community was now expected to deal with humanitarian crises, often emanating from failed states, resulted in the gradual erosion of the need to obtain consent from the host country where the international community was intervening. As the state began to be seen as the source of the threat to (human) security, there were increasing arguments that the sovereignty norm could be overridden in cases of supreme humanitarian emergencies.[29] Furthermore, the need to deal with non-traditional sources of threats emanating from within the state meant that the international community would need to undertake more intrusive policies aimed at social engineering. As UN Secretary-General Boutros Boutros-Ghali stated in his "Agenda for Peace," "[t]here is a new requirement for technical assistance which the UN has an obligation to develop and provide when requested: support for the transformation of deficient national structures and capabilities, and for the strengthening of new democratic institutions."[30]

Following the Iraq invasion, the appetite for this has been tempered. In addition to mounting casualties, the retrospective justification of the invasion on humanitarian grounds was regarded as an abuse of humanitarian norms, and reduced international consensus on the efficacy and legitimacy of intervention and the "credibility of the US and the UK as norm carriers."[31] In its place, we have seen a shift towards the concept of "Responsibility to Protect" (R2P) that emphasizes the early prevention of gross human rights abuses, and ultimately aims to avoid costly and controversial military interventions by the interna-

89

tional community.[32] Nevertheless, it is important to note that the growing currency of R2P does not denote the end of international (non-military) intervention aimed at transforming the host state's domestic governance system. Indeed, Ban Ki-moon's UN Secretary-General 2009 report on R2P states that "when national political leadership is weak, divided or uncertain about how to proceed, lacks the capacity to protect its population effectively, or faces an armed opposition that is threatening or committing crimes and violations relating to the responsibility to protect,"[33] the international community should step in to provide good governance and enhance the state's capacity to protect its populace from harm.

Of course, what constitutes good governance is a highly contentious subject, and this last point brings us to a second post-Cold War development that profoundly influenced the development of the new protectorates. The collapse of the Soviet bloc and the communist experiment, as well as the consequent democratization of Eastern Europe, seemed to suggest the ultimate triumph of liberal democracy and market capitalism. It is in this vein that authors such as Francis Fukuyama declared that international society was likely to become increasingly homogenous as polities across the world discover this single "truth" to attaining the good life.[34] In addition, democratization was seen as the panacea for solving a wide range of global security issues. At the international level, theories of democratic peace served to strengthen the momentum of spreading democracy and market capitalism across the globe. It was argued that democratic systems of governance encouraged non-violent means to resolve inter-state conflicts, as well as keeping warmongering leaders in check. Liberal democratic governance was also seen as an effective way of preventing repressive regimes from abusing their power and harming the people, as well as the emergence of failed states which suffered from weak legitimacy and internal strife. The corollary of this development was an emergent sense of a *noblesse oblige*, or a sense of paternal superiority among the policy-makers and commentators of the world's liberal democratic states.

This has resulted in peacekeeping operations shifting their focus from the traditional one of maintaining ceasefires to peacebuilding, where attempts are made to reconstruct states based on Western models of liberal democracy and market capitalism.[35] In a similar fashion to the paternalism prevalent in the late nineteenth century, Western liberal democracies' command of the "truth" or "knowledge" towards a better (international) life, as well as their superior social standing, was rarely questioned. Post-colonialism had rendered the society "an inclusive arrangement in which there are no barbarians, savages, infidels, or pagans standing outside what is now a universal political order: every one is an insider."[36] The Cold War and the American and Soviet camps' desperation to recruit political allies and clients also meant that the internal governance of a state hardly mattered, and this helped bolster the pluralism prevalent in international society. In the post-Cold War international order, however, international legitimacy became increasingly defined in terms of liberal democratic governance and market capitalism, as well as an increasing belief in "democracy promotion as an international civic duty."[37] Illiberal regimes that were unable to fulfill this new "standard of civilization"[38] were gradually seen as beyond the pale of the rules of international society, in the sense that they could hardly expect their sovereignty to be respected if they chose to abuse their people. Furthermore, such polities had to be remolded into Western-style liberal democracies. As Fukuyama claimed after the 9/11 attacks: "The struggle between Western liberal democracy and Islamo-fascism is not one between two equally viable cultural systems, both of which can master modern science and technology, create wealth and deal with the de facto diversity of the contemporary world. In all these respects, Western institutions hold all the cards."[39]

A similar trait can be observed in Mallaby's argument that an American empire could overcome the inefficient political impasse which has plagued the UNSC and play a crucial role in reconstructing the chaotic world order caused by terrorism and state failure. While noting that international legitimacy is important, Mallaby's argument is characterized by an almost unshakable belief that American-led and designed institutions are inherently legitimate, universal, and would be welcomed by the rest of the world.[40]

Although the more recent attempts to forcefully transplant democratic governance have come under much criticism, the influences of paternalistic non-military intervention continue to linger in the concept of R2P as well. While the 2005 World Summit Resolution on R2P was somewhat vague about how exactly this idea should be operationalized,[41] it is interesting to note that those actors deemed particularly qualified to render "assistance" include various UN "development agencies and the Bretton Woods institutions," which have frequently been associated with the promotion of governance based on free-market capitalism and liberal democratic institutions.[42] Here, we again see the assumption that the host states can potentially lack the capacity to think for themselves, just like children: the international community is the ultimate authority on deciding what constitutes good governance to protect humankind, and the route to a life free from humanitarian threats lies in following the universal developmental path laid down by the civilized West.

## China's Views on New Paternalism and Trusteeships

For a state that has experienced the humiliations of being cast as a semi-civilized state that was ignorant and childlike, it should come as no surprise that these developments are viewed with considerable suspicion in Beijing. The PRC's sensitivity to such issues is especially visible in its defense of the sovereignty norm, which provides states with the freedom to decide their own governance and allows all states to stand as equals. M. Taylor Fravel argued in 1996 that Beijing remained fearful of "any precedent that might erode state sovereignty or increase the likelihood of multilateral interventions in the internal affairs of states."[43] If this argument is to be extended to the new trusteeships, we would similarly expect Beijing to oppose any form of intervention in the domestic governance of other states, especially those which suspend a state's sovereignty over a relatively longer period of time while the social engineering process of turning the host country into a liberal democracy takes place.

A closer look at China's behavior, however, reveals a more complex and confusing picture which is perhaps indicative of the PRC's own indeterminate policies. It is certainly true that Chinese scholars do continue to show considerable suspicion towards new forms of peacekeeping which share similarities with the idea of trusteeship. Lai Zhigang, for instance, voices his concern that the end of the Cold War has resulted in the disappearance of a balancing force to control the West acting willfully in peacekeeping operations.[44] He states somewhat darkly that any "peacekeeping projects which use force and ignore sovereignty, [the respect for independent] domestic politics, and neutrality may win a temporary victory, but it is hard to avoid defeat in the long run."[45]

But at the same time we see China actually agreeing to the very same policies that are, in their eyes, bound for failure. Beijing supported Security Council Resolution 1511 in 2003, which temporarily suspended Iraq's sovereignty and placed it under the CPA until "an internationally recognized, representative government is established by the people of Iraq."[46] This point is particularly worth our attention, as the resolution determined a particular trajectory of development for the Iraqis. The goals of the mission included "the holding of democratic elections" and "establish[ing] national and local institutions for representative government," something which Beijing continues to resist from fully implementing within its own territorial boundaries.[47] Furthermore, despite the fact that the international community—in this case led by the UNSC—was paternalistically deciding on behalf of the Iraqi people how Iraq should develop, the Chinese delegate appeared to be quite oblivious to this normative problem, claiming that "it was necessary for the UNSC to adopt a new resolution so as to help Iraq to achieve peace and stability, restore sovereignty and bring about economic and social development as soon as possible," and expressed his confidence that the "resolution will undoubtedly have a positive impact on the endeavor to promote the political process in Iraq."[48] Interestingly, in recent years we have seen Chinese officials suggesting that PRC personnel could play an active role in these social engineering projects: some have suggested that China's "peacekeeping police" could participate in "rebuilding the judicial system, law enforcement and humanitarian relief efforts."[49]

What causes this seemingly contradictory stance? The clearest illustrations of the ambivalent views held by the Chinese elite towards the emergence of trusteeships can be found in the issue of failed states. The international efforts to reconstruct these states—which are modern forms of protectorate par excellence—are grounded in the belief that they pose security risks to their neighbors and bring about humanitarian catastrophes. For a state like China which shares borders with failed or weak states, an exploration of their views and policies towards failed states will provide interesting insights into how Beijing squares practical security concerns with philosophical commitments towards upholding the norm of sovereign integrity.

## *New Trusteeships and China: The Cases of Dealing with Failed States*

To date, the Chinese political elite has remained reluctant to use the term "failed state" (*shibai guojia* 失败国家),[50] primarily because of the association the term has with Western (particularly US) intervention. An example of highly critical Chinese views towards the concept can be found in a *Renmin Ribao* report in 2002, where the author Huang Qing argues that the idea of failed states serves as a justification for power politics and "openly goes against the spirit of the UN Charter and international law."[51] Drawing an analogy between Nazi policies and state failure, Huang further claims: "When the Nazis came to power their ideology [*jiben guannian*] was based on differentiating between 'superior and inferior' races, and it was on these grounds that they persecuted the Jews. The theory of 'failed states' differentiates between 'superior and inferior' states and gives [the 'superior' states] the right to attack others at will."[52]

Huang's views came under attack from other Chinese scholars, who pointed out that his opinions "ignored the [objective] existence of 'failed states' and went against the 'common sense of contemporary politics.'"[53] This demonstrates that the issue of failed states and statebuilding is still very much a debated issue with no elite consensus.[54] This is of course not to suggest an uncritical acceptance of the concept of state failure or state reconstruction. To date, many analyses still remain critical of unilateral attempts (particularly by the US) at reconstructing states. At the same time, they do acknowledge that there is an "*objective* phenomenon" of state failure,[55] and it is more than a simplistic label to justify ulterior motives. What is more interesting, however, is the fact that while such works remain critical of unilateral undertakings, they are conspicuously silent towards multilateral attempts to reconstruct states through international administration, provided these are sanctioned by the UN. Da Wei and Li Shaoxian argue that "unilateralism has damaged the legitimacy of US state reconstruction efforts in Iraq, as well as influencing other states' enthusiasm for joining them."[56] This of course begs the question of whether the Chinese policy circles are beginning to acquiesce in multilateral forms of international trusteeship and would be enthusiastic about participating in such enterprises, and some evidence suggests that this is indeed the case.[57] For instance, Chen Dongxiao *et al.* argue:

...the responsibility of saving "weak states" or "failed states" ought to be shouldered by the UN. On the one hand, the UN needs to do the overall planning, provide leadership and coordination in the process of state reconstruction. On the other hand, if all processes of state reconstruction want the approval of international society, they must go through the UN to attain legitimacy. In this area, the UN enjoys an indispensable position.[58]

Such acquiescence in international trusteeship is based on pragmatic and limited normative grounds, although it is extremely difficult to ascertain the precise degree to which one factor matters more than the other. First, the Chinese share the concern with many other states that failed states can pose a security threat: if international administration can stabilize their borders they are not likely to oppose such efforts, even though they may be slightly uncomfortable with the dilution of the sovereignty norm this entails.[59] They acknowledge that the PRC shares borders with Afghanistan, which is widely held to be a failed state, and several other "candidate failed states (*shibai guojia houxuanguo* 失败国家候选国)."[60] Men Honghua and Huang Haili for instance, argue that as a result of the increasing interconnectedness of the world, state failure will certainly cause larger spill-over effects such as refugee and economic crises. Failed states could even become havens for terrorists, threatening their neighboring states' "security and stability."[61] From Beijing's point of view, instability and state failure in Afghanistan can have some security implications if

Islamic groups there infiltrate or link up with secessionist movements in Xinjiang, which has a large Muslim population.[62]

Secondly, China's increasing integration into international society has brought about a more subtle understanding of sovereignty. As noted above, historical memories and fears of foreign intervention certainly do color Beijing's interpretations of sovereignty. Chinese scholars at times paint a rather dark picture of international politics, stating that "[m]any powers continue to engage in fierce competitions and struggles in the area of economics and politics…[and] hegemonism and power politics continue to exist."[63] Beijing's continuing territorial issues concerning Taiwan or the South China Sea also motivate many Chinese analysts or politicians to advocate a highly restrictive understanding of the sovereignty norm.[64] In spite of these concerns, an increasing number of Chinese scholars have noted that "the boundaries of sovereignty are not timeless or static. It must develop alongside the development of history, and will evolve in accordance to the objective needs of society."[65] The implications here are that the PRC would have to reach a more flexible understanding of sovereignty, and surrender part of its sovereign authority to meet the demands of increasing interdependence, and in practice Beijing has already consented to this by joining a plethora of multilateral institutions.[66] This has undoubtedly taken place because of China's desire to integrate itself into international society and the international economy to attain economic growth.

Thirdly, the PRC's increasing interactions with the global human rights regime have meant that the Chinese elites are gradually—and at times reluctantly—accepting the view that sovereignty may have to be suspended in the face of a humanitarian catastrophe. This process of accepting international intervention has been accelerated by Beijing's growing awareness of the norms that govern legitimate membership in this community, as well as an increasing desire to conform to these norms because they are seen as rightful and legitimate. As legitimate membership in post-Cold War international society has become increasingly defined in terms of a willingness to uphold human rights norms, China has found it increasingly difficult to adhere to a rigid, absolute conceptualization of sovereign authority without risking international criticism, particularly from the Western powers. In practice, this often means a grudging acceptance that a state's sovereignty may have to be suspended and placed under international tutelage if it continues to inflict grievous harm on its own citizens.[67] Indeed, a position paper issued by the Chinese Ministry of Foreign Affairs states that "[w]hen a massive humanitarian crisis occurs, It [sic] is the legitimate concern of the international community to ease and defuse the crisis."[68] The Chinese government also supported the 2005 World Summit resolution on R2P, and played an instrumental role in the UNSC's endorsement of this resolution.[69]

At times, the PRC has even tacitly acknowledged the need for military intervention. The most unambiguous example of this can be found in Beijing's reactions to the 1999 Kosovo crisis. Some scholars forwarded highly polemical accusations that the West's privileging of human rights over sovereign integrity was a "fallacy" (*miulun* 谬论) and used to mask "hegemonism, invasion and war."[70] The Chinese government, however, while highly critical of NATO military action (partly fuelled by a sense of moral outrage at the bombing of the PRC embassy in Belgrade),[71] adopted a more subtle view. It argued that NATO failed to obtain authorization from the UNSC, and that this violated the UN Charter and international law.[72] The thrust of China's criticism was based on procedural grounds, and reflected its deep-seated suspicions towards military intervention not authorized by the UN. However, it is important to note that China's protests were not directed against intervention *per se*, and this indicates that it "felt unable to veto two chapter VII resolutions that demanded Yugoslavia respect its international humanitarian obligation."[73]

Consequently, Beijing has become increasingly flexible towards intervention, and this is reflected in its stance towards state failure and international administration. Like many post-colonial states, China remains uneasy about some aspects of these new protectorates. As noted above, unilateral intervention lacking UNSC authorization—known as *ganshe* (干涉) in Chinese—"has a very pejorative connotation and implies that an operation is...coercive,"[74] and is more likely to be viewed as a form of neo-imperialism. However, China has tended to be silent and unobtrusive on the particular form the reconstructed state is going to take.[75] While there is some skepticism towards reconstructing the failed state along the Western liberal democratic model,[76] one analyst stated with reference to the attempts to reconstruct Cambodia: "As far as changing the domestic structure of governance was concerned, I don't think China really cared, as long as Cambodia was stable."[77] Humanitarian and international image concerns serve as an additional catalyst for China to accept the necessity of international trusteeships in certain cases. Chinese scholars acknowledge that one characteristic of a failed state is that it is "unable to promote the public interest and protect people's lives."[78] In the context of Beijing's growing sensitivity to international human rights norms, it becomes difficult for the Chinese policy elite to advocate the protection of sovereignty while ignoring blatant human rights abuses.

## Putting Paternalism Into Practice: China's Participation in International Administration

While it may not be particularly surprising that the PRC may free-ride on international trusteeships if they provide greater security by stabilizing failed states (particularly those close to its own borders), a more interesting development is Beijing's increasing role in such activities in recent years. In a surprisingly candid statement, Zhuang Liwei argues:

In spite of the fact that American governance over failed states has been the product of selfish desires—which stems from its fear that these states harbor or give rise to anti-American terrorists—objectively speaking, these measures have actually helped these states. On the whole, this is much better than sitting on the sidelines and doing nothing except accusing others motivations [for intervening in failed states] as being corrupt.[79]

Zhuang's study has some interesting implications for China's policy towards new trusteeships in international society. It is possible to see in this statement an acknowledgement that refusal to participate in these undertakings may lead to a somewhat negative image, as active participation is regarded as something that ought to be done, especially if it is for humanitarian reasons.

Naturally, Beijing's ambivalence towards new trusteeships means that Chinese contributions have been selective. To date, most of China's participation has been in UN peacekeeping, which is consistent with its emphasis on multilateral forms of intervention. Chinese analysts also tend to point out that obtaining the host state's consent is very important for Beijing,[80] and this reflects the discomfort the political elite may feel when suspending another state's sovereign authority even if it is perceived to be for the "international good." As one Chinese analyst put it:

The PRC has participated primarily in traditional PKO (East Timor, Lebanon, or Haiti), which has three principles: consent, no use of force, and neutrality. As for non-traditional PKO, China is very sensitive about this. In non-traditional PKO, there is no consent, and neither is there an international agreement to carry it out. Furthermore, it is not carried out by the UN, and is undertaken by some great powers or superpowers...[81]

Despite this typical official line, the PRC has not found it easy to maintain its principled differentiation between traditional and non-traditional peacekeeping. As noted previously, in the cases of state failure it is hard to determine who can legitimately give their consent to international administration, and in many cases consent is not always given under perfect conditions of freedom from power or coercion. In many cases this means that Beijing has (inadvertently or not) ended up participating in the new international trusteeships. It sent a military unit to the state-reconstruction efforts at Cambodia, a police unit to Kosovo, and has more recently "financially and politically supported peacekeeping and peacebuilding efforts in post-Taliban Afghanistan,"[82] even though it has not sent any personnel there. Beijing's principled stance towards suspending other states' sovereign authority is therefore not as strictly adhered to as it may seem.

The primary cause for this disjuncture between rhetoric and practice appears to be linked with China's own unique institutional position as a legitimate great power of international society, as well as its self-perceptions as a great power.[83] In the post-Cold War international society where legitimacy was being increasingly defined in terms of democratic governance, respect for human rights and market capitalism, the PRC was increasingly being seen as an Other.[84] This resulted in a contradictory situation for the Chinese. On the one hand, there was little question that most states—including the Western legitimate great powers—continued to accept China as a legitimate great power with managerial responsibilities in the society. The PRC retained its institutional privileges as a legitimate great power in the UNSC and has increasingly become a key player in a plethora of global and regional institutions. On the other hand, it found itself seen as alien to the Western legitimate great powers. China's poor human rights record resulted in Western states and legitimate great powers viewing it with suspicion, and at times almost as a semi-civilized entity. The underlying unease towards the rise of China was to find its ultimate expression in the "China Threat" thesis, where the PRC was painted as a revisionist power similar to Hitlerite Germany which other powers should fear.[85] The result was an increasing sense among the Chinese political elite that the Western legitimate great powers had not accepted China as an equal.

Setting aside the issue of whether both Western or Chinese perceptions of each other are accurate or not, this labeling comes as a significant psychological blow to the Chinese political elites, who have traditionally assumed that China's growing economic and political profile should and would result in it occupying a position of equality with the Western legitimate great powers. Beijing's need to counter this negative image resulted in the forwarding of the concepts of responsible great power and later "China's peaceful rise" (*heping jueqi* 和平崛起), which was "[d]esigned to provide a credible vision of a cooperative future in China's foreign relations."[86] In practice, the cultivation of a responsible great power image has meant that Beijing has had to avoid behaving in a belligerent manner in the international community and become a status quo state abiding by the core norms of international society and accepts the given distribution of power,[87] even though it has not abandoned the policy options of using force and is sometimes selective in the international norms it chooses to adhere most closely to.[88] More important, Beijing's self-appointed status as a responsible great power has also entailed a growing awareness that the PRC needs to participate in certain activities intended to prevent conflict and humanitarian catastrophes. Such actions, it is argued, will improve China's and its military's image and enhance the PRC's soft power.[89]

This goal poses a fundamental dilemma for Beijing, however. As Wu Xinbo has argued, China has had a dual identity in which it sees itself as a great power and simultaneously a poor country of the developing world because "its levels of economic development and technological prowess lag far behind those of Western countries and some of its Asian neighbors."[90] As noted above, this identity has sometimes been invoked to advance Beijing's pragmatic interests,[91] but—as noted above—nevertheless finds its origins in China's traumatic encounter with and entry into European international society, and should not be trivialized either. As their state was labeled semi-civilized and subjected to unequal treaties and semi-colonization, it is hardly surprising that the Chinese are ill at ease with participating in new trusteeships and go to great lengths to state that they do not agree with unilateral suspension of other states' sovereignty. Furthermore, they are selective in their participation, and attempt to demarcate themselves from Western powers (such as the US) by refusing to join coalitions of the willing in undertaking military activities. China also shuns participating in long-term international administrations which suspend a polity's sovereign authority indefinitely. Rather, the Chinese political elite express a preference for short-term international administration operations with clear exit strategies and goals of independent statehood.[92] This is consistent with Beijing's attitude towards old trusteeships which explicitly aimed to assist dependent territories attain independence as soon as it was feasible to do so.

It is because of these contradictory goals that Beijing finds UN peacekeeping operations a highly useful way to let it "have its cake and eat it." In the minds of the Chinese political elite, playing an active part in international trusteeships helps demonstrate that China is doing its duty as a legitimate great power (or responsible great power as the Chinese like to put it) willing to uphold the humanitarian norms of the post-Cold War international society, thus refuting the "China Threat" theses put forward by Western critics.[93] This distinguishes the PRC's motives for participation from other states like Fiji or Bangladesh, which take part in these operations to subsidize their military budgets.[94] Many Chinese analysts are aware that China's participation in international administration (and UN peacekeeping operations that accompany them) is closely linked with identity politics, and this is visible in their scholarly writings. Men Honghua and Huang Haili argue that "great powers have special responsibilities to actively provide international public goods." Crucially, they then go on to state that these responsibilities "have already been given expression in the area of state failure."[95] China, it is argued, has demonstrated its "outward looking, enterprising foreign policy in state reconstruction" by "training civil servants, reducing [the host nation's] debt and providing economic aid"[96]—all of which is "the usual way in which great powers usually express their spirit of responsibility and create an image for themselves."[97] Tang Yongsheng comes to a similar view when he states that "further participation in PKO is a responsibility that China *ought to shoulder as a great power*,"[98] which effectively calls for China to demonstrate "the *noblesse oblige* that is part and parcel of the identity of a 'legitimate great power' today."[99]

Naturally it is important to note that this recognition game plays to the rules of the legitimate great power club and is inevitably aimed primarily at a Western audience and ends up reproducing social hierarchies within international society. Here, we can again see the tension within China's identity as a legitimate great power and a member of the developing world, which was already visible in China's engagement with more traditional forms of trusteeships administered by the UN during the Cold War. The PRC's participation in new trusteeships has the potential to harm China's identity as a developing power, as well as its relations with the Third World. This danger appears to be felt by the political elite as well, although this is certainly not acknowledged. However, Chinese works are often at pains to square the PRC's competing identities and demonstrate that it is "different from other Western 'legitimate great powers,' creating terms such as 'developing great power' (*fazhan zhong daguo* [ 发展中大国])," although what exactly this means and how it differentiates China from the other great powers is never really specified."[100] Most importantly, the multilateral nature of the UN and its operations means that Beijing escapes accusations of engaging in hegemonic or neo-imperial acts when partaking in the suspension of other states' sovereign authority, despite complaints by the host countries of authoritarian behavior by the UN. As one Chinese analyst noted in an interview, UN-led "international protectorates are much fairer today than in the past, because they are multilateral and regional organizations often play a role. Even within the UNSC, the P5 play many different roles, and this helps overcome the problem of unilateralism too."[101]

It is also important to note, however, that these views conveniently skirt over the philosophical problem of paternalism and treating the host state and its peoples like children who are incapable of determining the direction of their own development, despite Chinese assertions that multilateral UN-led international administrations are "fairer."[102] The political elite of China has yet to confront this issue. In similar fashion to many Western political elites who reject criticisms of neo-imperialism in their attempts to reconstruct failed states, Chinese analysts similarly argue that UN-led international administrations are not paternalistic. It is also worth mentioning that Beijing has a track record of paternalistic behavior, evident in the sense of superiority it adopted towards many developing states, even at the height of the PRC's anti-imperialist campaign.[103] When questioned on this point, one Chinese analyst simply stated that "when China participates in PKO it participates in PKO, and it has no other intentions, and it has no intentions of partaking in paternalism."[104] But at the same time, the same analyst noted that at times when the "host state" may not be aware of what is good for it, the international community and China needed to ignore/suspend its sovereign authority. Even if China did not intend to treat the host state like a child, he stated, "...if China agrees to send PKO, it means that it thinks that PKO would help them. It is not interference (*ganshe* 干涉) if the outcome (*xiaoguo* 效果) is good for the Chinese military, the UN PKO force, and the host country, even if the host state doesn't agree."[105]

This is of course a classic expression of paternalism, as the host state's wishes are seen as having inferior judgment. What matters is that the Chinese and the UN agree that international administration is going to do the host state good. Furthermore, it seems that the cultivation of an image of a responsible great power also entails projecting a paternalistic image of an ability to guide weaker others out of their misery and show them the path to happiness. As one analyst put it:

A "good great power" (*lianghao daguo* 良好大国) is a powerful country which helps its poorer brothers. Just imagine if you were the richest in your neighborhood and the rest were poor; if you didn't help them out at all, they might be forced to steal and harm the safety of the neighborhood. It'll actually benefit everyone if you helped everyone become rich, as it would make the neighborhood a much safer place. A "good great power" does something similar at the international level.[106]

Although paternal relations are not mentioned *per se*, paternalism is again evident in this statement. This is no brotherhood amongst equals: it is perhaps more accurate to say that an unequal, almost big brother relationship is being invoked here.

## Conclusion

Beijing's evolving views on the new protectorates in many ways mirrors its tortuous process of socialization into international society. China's first full encounter with international society was with a Janus-faced European international society. The Chinese elite's relations with this society was a schizophrenic one,[107] where the European states were admired for their advanced scientific knowledge, industrial strength, and system of governance, yet simultaneously hated for their encroachment on China's territory and patronizing attitudes towards the Chinese, all in the name of civilization. Unfortunately, China was in no position to challenge the military power of the European powers, and was grudgingly forced to conform to the standard of civilization and become a Western-style state.

Arguably, China now faces another "Janus-faced" post-Cold War international society, where the civilized are increasingly taking on the role of teaching or telling the weak and failed how they should run their states along civilized lines. The context, however, is very different from the late nineteenth century. Today China is not a semi-civilized entity whose membership is in doubt. Furthermore, it now knocks on the door of the legitimate great power club which plays a privileged role in determining the governance of international society. Nevertheless, the two sides of the society continue to pull the Chinese in opposite directions: on the one hand, there continues to be considerable ambivalence towards the intrusive face which demands homogeneity among its members; on the other hand, China seems to have a curious infatuation and desperate desire to belong to the very exclusive grouping of states which stand at the forefront of the society's demands for conformity.

In order to belong to this group, the PRC has been increasingly compelled to follow the membership rules to become a legitimate great power which will help it to be treated as a social equal with the other Western legitimate great powers. The irony here is of course that by doing so the Chinese end up reproducing and strengthening those very norms that they profess and appear to dislike: and here we are again reminded of the continuing Western dominance of international society which has continued for more than a hundred years.

On balance, it is likely that the desire to become an equal to the Western states will continue to play a dominant role in China's foreign policy, and to this extent its (ambivalent) support for and participation in international trusteeships looks set to continue. Beijing's desire for economic growth means that it continues to integrate itself with the international community and avoid confrontations with the Western powers, particularly the US. But perhaps more significantly, China's own desire for legitimate great power identity and social equality with the West means it will continue to play some sort of role in upholding and protecting the core norms—at times superficially—of the Western-dominated international society.

Of course, we should also keep in mind that the target of membership of the legitimate great power club is a moving one, and whether or not the new member feels socially accepted and equal to other members depends very much on the murky, subjective realm of perceptions. It is certainly possible that continuing frustration with its perceived inability to attain social equality with other legitimate great powers would result in Beijing refusing to play by the Western-created rules of international society. This, however, will probably not spell the end of China's image of itself as a great power, and we can expect its paternalism to continue. The "true path to happiness" it preaches, however, may be one quite different from the West.[108] As Gill and Huang have recently noted, China's economic success "presents the developing world a recipe for success" which is "the antithesis of the Washington Consensus,"[109] and there are already some concerns that Beijing's paternalism may be more accepted in some areas.[110] Whether two fathers will emerge in post-Cold War international society will depend very much on the outcome of China's longstanding, difficult process of integration into a community that has often treated it as an outsider.

# 5

# INDIA AND THE CHALLENGE OF
# THE NEW PROTECTORATES

*Aswini K. Ray*

International protectorates, as a concept, whether new or old, hardly ever figure in India's diplomatic or domestic political discourse. This is unlikely to be a case of normative insensitivity of Indian diplomacy or scholarship, both of which are otherwise responsive to most normative global concerns. More likely, it is another instance of the asymmetrical salience of diverse concerns within the global hierarchy of sovereign states, all increasingly affected by the process of globalization, but in different ways. Understandably, the historically advantaged sections of the new globalization process within the Western nation-states are more concerned with global order within the macro-level than the less advantaged sections still primarily preoccupied with order and governance at home rather than the relatively remote global problems, however pressing otherwise.

Though India admittedly is not among the best examples of the least advantaged, it shares with many of the less advantaged states of the postcolonial world a paranoid infatuation with the principle of national sovereignty, and a love-hate relationship with the Western states inherited from the colonial era. This was reinforced in the Cold War era through a deep distrust of the global role of the US-led military alliances, particularly their policies on India's dispute with Pakistan over Kashmir. In the perceptions of large sections of Indian public opinion until 9/11, the US and many of its Western allies even winked at the cross-border Islamic terrorism unleashed in Kashmir and various other parts of India from Pakistan, its regional military ally. There was also a belief that the emergence of "Islamic Fundamentalism" as a global threat resulted from the US policy of using Pakistan as a conduit-pipe for arms aid to the Mujahedeen guerrillas against the Soviet occupation in Afghanistan.[1]

In fact, against the global military alliances of the Cold War era, India innovated its foreign policy of nonalignment which, in the course of its evolution, developed a pronounced pro-Soviet bias.[2] The collapse of the Soviet Union in 1991 eliminated this global crutch to the Indian economy and diplomacy, leading to its economic liberalization the same year. But the skepticism vis-à-vis US global policies, as I will substantiate in due course, continues within the political culture and throughout civil society.

In a democracy like India this necessarily influences official policies. Although, like China, India has aspirations to great power status within international society, as we shall see, until recently there has been no comparable policy tension between maintaining the rhetoric of anti-imperialism and that of global responsibility, of the kind discussed by Shogo Suzuki in Chapter 4 of this volume. In the Indian case, the relative paucity of reference to the new protectorates in its diplomatic discourse suggests that deep down they are still viewed as yet another version of "Western Imperialism," replacing the Western military alliances and activities in the so-called Third World during the Cold War.[3] The widely-shared Indian perception of the post-Cold War international system remains that of Western domination under US hegemony.

Even in the Western discourse, the ideas and practices informing the new protectorates still remain contested, as Stefan Halper makes clear in Chapter 7. The new protectorates are different from their earlier comparable counterparts such as the Mandates of the League of Nations era or the Trust and Non-Self Governing Territories of the UN-system; both were administered with global accountability guiding them towards self-government. They are also different from the weak and unstable states of the Third World of the Cold War global system, which abhorred any real or potential vacuum in its rigid bipolarity, and hence inducted them within either of the two power blocs, leaving out only the group of the nonaligned states pioneered by India.

The new protectorates are only understandable in the context of the post-Cold War global system, and its spawning of so-called failed states. Despite their acknowledged aberration from the normal pattern of sovereign states, in the absence of any global consensus on the criteria defining "failure,"[4] or in some cases their failure to be constituted as international protectorates, there is rarely any agreement on which states qualify, with the partial exception of UN-authorized transitional administrations in Bosnia, Kosovo and East Timor. It seems likely that originally the criteria of failure and the identification and labeling of failed states emanated from discussions within the Western donor agencies, the World Bank, IMF, the WTO or the IAEA, with all of which Indian diplomacy has had a long history of equivocal relationships for their alleged Western bias, control and domination. This history in turn influences India's abiding skepticism around the concept of failed states and attempts to save them, and ambivalence towards the experience of international protectorates.

Whatever the reasons, in the relative absence of empirical data on India's official response to the challenges posed by the new protectorates, for the purpose of this analysis we are left with few other options than deducing it from the general thrust of India's foreign policy to comparable questions in a historical perspective. We would also use another aperture to deduce India's response to these challenges: India's policy in its South Asian neighborhood, in which, according to the *Foreign Affairs* classification based on twelve criteria, all of them, except India and Maldives, are at different levels "failed states"[5] and consequently "basket cases" for the funding agencies, though not yet strictly termed as protectorates, possibly out of politeness. Even within India, 172 out of the country's 600 administrative districts that are under insurrection by radical Maoist groups are only nominally under government control, as are parts of Kashmir and some parts of India's North-East and central belt inhabited by its large tribal population; there are also other signs of "failure" in India's governance and in the social sectors of literacy, healthcare, AIDS control, corruption, crime, disaster management, water supply etc. Yet unlike China, India manages to survive as a democracy with regular elections under universal adult suffrage, and civil and political rights for its citizens; and despite its large Muslim population, it endures as a secular state. In spite of all its acknowledged deficits in the sphere of governance and democracy, India's struggle for survival as a secular democracy, now with sustained economic growth, and in an adversarial neighborhood of failed or failing states regardless of their comparable inheritance, may be of considerable interest for the global community faced with the challenges of the new protectorates.

## India and International Intervention

The axiomatic corollary of India's historically inherited political culture of postcolonial nationalism was inspired by the Gandhian edict "good governance is no substitute for self-government"; and not just for India, but for all the colonial peoples involved in their liberation struggle. This is in sharp contrast with the egregious historically inherited Chinese nationalism rooted in its "Middle Kingdom" worldview. Even before India's emergence as a sovereign state in 1947, the Congress Party leading the liberation struggle helped in many ways in the liberation struggles in Asia and later Africa, including sending a medical team to China during its mass struggle against Japanese colonial rule. India's first Prime Minister, Jawaharlal Nehru, the architect of the foreign policy of nonalignment, attended the Brussels Congress of Oppressed Nationalities (1927) as the official delegate of the Indian National Congress; later he organized two Asian Relations Conferences (1947, 1949) in New Delhi, later still the Afro-Asian Conference (Bandung, 1955)[6] and the summit meeting of the Non Aligned Movement (Belgrade, 1961).[7] All these conferences were aimed at helping in the dismantling of the colonial system to ensure sovereign statehood for the former colonies, the creation of a more equitable global economic order for the disadvantaged newly emergent states, and "widening the area of peace" within the erstwhile rigid bipolar global divide. India played a proactive global role in all these conclaves of the newly emerging states, as in the various UN fora, and often acted as an "honest broker" between the two superpowers with locked horns or as a troubleshooter in their many global disputes such as those in Korea, Indochina and the Suez crisis, resulting in its emergence as a global soft power.

It was in this phase of India's proactive global diplomacy that India was included in most of the UN peacekeeping operations in the global proxy wars of the superpowers through the Cold War, as in Korea, Suez, Gaza, Congo etc., thus enabling the Indian armed forces to develop considerable professional experience in such operations, which has been used to advantage in more recent times in civil war ravaged countries such as Sudan, Sierra Leone, Liberia, Somalia and Kosovo. Such operations have enabled Indian diplomacy to remain high profile, while the armed forces also find it rewarding to enjoy better service conditions under UN assignments. The Indian armed forces have therefore emerged as a potential pressure group within India's domestic politics on the question of global peacekeeping assignments. A UN peacekeeping force drawn from a nonaligned Asian country has been politically less unacceptable in the new troubled regions, largely located within the non-Western world. The highly professional, multicultural and multi-religious contingent of Indian armed forces from one of the few functioning secular democracies outside the Western world has emerged as an asset for peacekeeping. There is also considerable approval for these classic peacekeeping assignments from within civil society in India, but only when they are under UN aegis.

For, as already mentioned, within large sections of the media and civil society, considerable skepticism still persists toward US foreign policy, despite India's economic globalization and the substantial development of strategic relations between the two countries, including periodic joint military exercises, which would have been unthinkable in the Cold War era. Even now, the entrenched love-hate relationship with the US enables India's Left parties to whip up considerable populist passions against any official attempts by the government to forge closer relations with the US, which, by implication, would apply to political tolerance of (let alone support for) the new protectorates. And, by coincidence, the new protectorates of the global system emerged simultaneously with weak coalition regimes in India's domestic politics dependent on the support of the Left parties for survival. In fact, during the 2004–08 coalition government, the Indo-US Civilian Nuclear Agreement was held to ransom by the Left parties with the threat of withdrawal of political support. Their argument, shared by some other coalition partners, was that any such agreement with an "unequal" partner such as the US would mean "dependence" and surrender of "state sovereignty."

In this regard aspects of the Indian policy on post-2001 Afghanistan could be a pointer to its broader attitude on the issue of protectorates. Departing from its tradition, India supported the UN war against the Taliban, even though it was US-led and unpopular with the Left. India's even more unusual offer of military support was turned down in favor of the geopolitically more critical Pakistani help—which, in the long run, turned out to be a blessing in disguise for India. This was borne out by its impact on the Pakistani Armed Forces under General Musharraf, which were accused of being "un-Islamic" for siding with the US. With its large Muslim population and secularist credentials, India's military involvement could have become a serious political liability. But although not involved militarily and despite suffering periodic collateral casualties, India is active in many Afghan reconstruction projects either by the private sector or through the government with its aid program. India is particularly concentrating its reconstruction efforts in the sphere of infrastructure like roads, railways, power-grids, and educational institutions, including personnel training in public administration both within Afghanistan and in Indian institutions.[8] In the seven years that followed the US-led invitation, India poured more than a billion dollars in aid into Afghanistan, making it Kabul's fifth largest donor, and its footprint in the country was a high-profile one, with no less than four consulates in addition to its embassy.[9] The change of regime in Afghanistan is clearly seen by New Delhi as adding to India's interests.

Since India remains committed against military involvement for the reasons given above, the extent of its involvement makes it by default an accomplice of the Western-led semi-protectorate in Afghanistan. Indeed, if the US and UN forces withdraw before the country has been stabilized—and it remains a distinct possibility that they will—India will confront a difficult dilemma about what to do to protect its diplomatic and economic investment.

For the time being, however, despite India's involvement on the ground, the benefits of US intervention for India's rivalry with Pakistan, and the targeting of international terrorism as a high level bilateral priority, India has rejected the US offer to be associated with its broader war on global terrorism. This is because of "bitter memories of the past," "divergent priorities" on the nature of threats posed by global and regional terrorists, and the "fear of US counter-intelligence" that forces India to prevent sustained contacts between officials. "It is no use saying friends don't spy on friends, because they do everywhere. India does it itself."[10] Furthermore, a section of the mainstream Indian media has been critical of the Western donor countries' policies with regard to the reconstruction of Afghanistan. For example, on the eve of the Paris conference on Afghanistan Development Strategy in June 2008, India's largest circulating English language daily published a center page article headlined: "Donor Politics Undermining the Welfare of Afghans."[11] It welcomed the quantitative increase in Western donor countries' commitments, but was highly critical of its "delivery and effectiveness." This was because such aid "is inevitably tied to the interests of the donor nations, and does not reflect the priorities of the recipient country. In Afghanistan, donor politics has come at the cost of the welfare of the Afghan citizens." The article also referred to the Western countries' "cut-price reconstruction" in Afghanistan compared with the European protectorate of Kosovo, policies with an eye on the taxpayers back home. The focus is on short-term projects which are implemented shoddily to ensure quick delivery to provide "photo-ops," despite their economic unsustainability. For example, despite 70 per cent of its population depending on agriculture, only $400-$500 million has been invested in it. Consequently, people have switched back to traditional cultivation of poppy, whose production has increased along with the percentage of people in Afghanistan below the poverty line from 30 to 35 per cent of the population since the beginning of reconstruction.

The report goes on to offer a positive take on the Indian commitment. The Indian government, though not a traditional donor, is currently administering $850 million in its aid program; its record of local disbursement at 54 per cent is higher than most other donors; its long-term development planning is largely in the infrastructure sector such as roads, dams, electric grids and technical training. At the Paris meeting India's deputy foreign minister promised more aid for Afghan reconstruction.[12]

On the same day as India's largest circulating daily was expressing its criticism of Western aid policies with regard to Afghanistan's reconstruction, India's principal security concern in the region was reflected in the lead editorial column of the same paper, with its headline: "To Stabilize Afghanistan, Shift Focus to Pakistan."[13] Expressing concern at Pakistani covert support for the Taliban and its role in the "maintenance of a balance against India," it argued that "unless the Taliban bases in Pakistan can be eliminated, the international efforts to stabilize Afghanistan cannot succeed." In fact, soon thereafter, the NATO forces under US command bombarded the Taliban and Al-Qaeda militants within Pakistani territory along the Afghan border. Predictably there was an uproar within the newly-elected Pakistani parliament with Prime Minister Jilani expressing outrage at the violation of its "state sovereignty." The Pakistani Army, for long virtually spoon-fed by the US, reacted sharply, terming the incursion as "outrageous," "unprovoked" and "unacceptable," as reported in a BBC World News program on 12 June 2008.

Pakistan is a Western ally, yet the strains that the Afghan conflict have imposed on Pakistani society have brought the state to the brink of failure, while the immunity that American forces enjoy (from sanction if not from criticism) when operating within Pakistani borders might suggest that the country is already a de facto American protectorate. At the same time the strength of popular anti-Americanism on this as on other similar occasions provides dramatic evidence of the lasting appeal of the notion of state sovereignty, which still persists within the political culture of the non-Western world. Since, apart from the Balkans, this constitutes the major catchment area of the new protectorates, any form of governance by the international community requires considerable sensitivity to this concern. Both from introspection as well as from experience of involvement in its own neighborhood, India has learned to be hypersensitive on this issue.

Although India was predictably critical of Saddam Hussein's occupation of Kuwait, it also criticized the US-led second Iraq war, fought ostensibly against the non-existent WMD but actually—or so it was perceived within wide sections of Indian public opinion—to ensure regime change in the oil-rich country. However, India has been involved in many of the reconstruction projects in Iraq, both officially and in the private sector, as in Afghanistan. Indian assistance has concentrated on infrastructural projects in which it has considerable technical expertise. At least one Indian company, associated with the then foreign minister Natwar Singh, was involved in the scandal around the UN-sanctioned "oil for food" program, leading eventually to his resignation. Officially the Government of India has remained pragmatically ambivalent or silent on the US role in post-war Iraq, but many civil society organizations and the media are critical of it. For example, one of the country's most prestigious newspapers[14] recently railed against the Iraqi government's willingness to countenance, and indeed to actively secure, the continued "neo-colonial" presence of US troops in the country.

## India's South Asia Policies

It is an ironic feature of contemporary Indian foreign policy that, despite its continuing suspicion of any revival of the concept of international protection—in part a legacy of its strong Cold-War anti-Americanism, in part due to the vibrancy of domestic public opinion—the Government of India's approach to what it perceives as disorder within its own region has a striking resemblance to US policy on the global level. A brief examination of India's South Asian policies will reveal parallels to the American policies towards contemporary protectorates and the dilemmas associated with them that are discussed by Stefan Halper.

If, at first sight, this seems strange, in part the explanation is that within India's domestic political discourse, the post-war reconstruction of Iraq does not figure as prominently as previous Western induced crises in the earlier period of the high-profile and pro-active phase of Indian diplomacy. During the 1970s, though it was only fitfully visible before the collapse of the Soviet Union and India's economic globalization in 1991, a diplomatic shift had occurred, away from the country's global involvement around the normative concerns that had characterized the Nehru era and towards a more pragmatic focus under Prime Minister Indira Gandhi on India's regional neighborhood, based on *Realpolitik*.

Historically, the shift began with India's disastrous Border War with China (1962) and the 1965 war against Pakistan, followed by the more decisive war against Pakistan over Bangladesh (1971). This series of events influenced Non-aligned India's Treaty of Peace and Friendship with the Soviet Union (1970) as a prelude to the Bangladesh war, and the innovative military planning and execution of the war that led to the decisive defeat of the US military ally, Pakistan. Discounting Indian criticism of the US foreign policy, these achievements fuelled the demand within the country's domestic discourse for the transformation of India's role from a global soft power to a regional military power, in the same mould.

It is within this context that India, like China but without the advantage of P5 status, has sought recognition by the international community with a seat at the UN high table as a permanent member of the UNSC. In pursuit of this goal, the Government of India considerably mellowed its erstwhile high-profile rhetoric against US global diplomacy, which in its official policy (in contrast with Indian public opinion) had almost disappeared after the collapse of the Soviet Union. In 1974 India exploded its first nuclear bomb, ten years after the first Chinese explosion. At the time, India described it as a Peaceful Nuclear Explosion, a one-off event. Much later, in 1998, after further tests India transformed itself into a full-fledged nuclear power with missile technology delivery capacity, vastly increased military strength and corresponding modern fire-power, an Air Force equipped with the latest supersonic aircraft, and a miniature "Blue Water Navy." The semi-official American-style think-tank the Institute of Defense Studies and Analysis (IDSA), along with Research and Analysis Wing (RAW) for CIA-like external intelligence, emerged in the early 1970s, and were later followed by a National Security Council.

As its military power developed from the 1970s onwards, Indian diplomacy shifted gear to play a more focused role as a regional power. Since then, the experience of Indian diplomacy, intelligence agencies and armed forces has emerged as an asset that the international community can draw on in overseeing the governance of what could be regarded as a number of new quasi-protectorates in the region.

This is not how the matter would be presented in Delhi. India has no difficulty in asserting its "natural" regional hegemony, but remains publicly reluctant to share responsibility for the security of its "near-abroad." In 1978, India annexed the Himalayan Kingdom of Sikkim and incorporated it as a constituent state of the Indian federation; and Sikkim remains among the better administered and less violent states of the Indian federation. This was India's response to a potential failed state. With Bhutan, India has consolidated its close friendly relations with economic aid in pursuit of the King's innovative indigenous model of development based on maximizing the people's "Gross National Happiness." In more recent times, a new constitution and the kingdom's first general elections have been helped by some technical expertise from India. Bhutan and India closely coordinate their foreign policies, and Indian economic and technical assistance helps this sovereign Himalayan state with a traditional monarchy to emerge slowly towards democracy and remain stable in the process, unlike its neighborhood. This has been another version of a pre-emptive Indian response against a potential South Asian failed state.

In the neighboring kingdom of Nepal, India has had to face more complex and prolonged problems. In the early 1950s, it intervened politically by providing asylum to the King against the autocratic feudal clique of the *Ranas*, and with its military and economic aid helped to establish a constitutional monarchy and a friendly regime. However, this was accompanied by a highly unequal Treaty of Peace and Friendship in 1951 which has been increasingly resented by large sections of Nepalese civil society, particularly since the democratic movement that developed during the 1990s and more recently during the Maoist-led coalition politics against the monarchy.

In all this turmoil, Indian official policy has remained low-key. The government has deliberately sought to avoid controversy, only periodically expressing its desire in support of the unexceptionable goal of democratic governance. On the other hand, India's civil society groups have been officially nudged to help the democratic movement, and in the actual conduct of the elections. But India's discomfiture with the Maoist domination within the present ruling coalition, which engineered the ouster of the monarchy, has been muted. It has only been partly compensated by the strength of the pro-India lobby within the Nepali Congress Party with its close links with India's scattered social democratic political groups, which themselves have varied levels of presence in contemporary India's coalition politics. Within India's civil society groups there is considerable sympathy with Nepalese sensitivities around the unequal Treaty of 1951, and the government does not seem to be averse to the idea of suitably revising it to accommodate the economic compulsions of this poor, landlocked, and potentially failed state.

In the only recently ended ethnic turmoil and civil war in Sri Lanka, Indian experience has been less successful. Sri Lanka was never a suitable candidate for protectorate status, but India certainly entertained hopes that it would be able to influence the course of the country's political development. These hopes were dashed after India's failure to contain the civil war unleashed by militant Trotskyite groups in Tamil-inhabited Northern Sri Lanka close to its maritime border with India, through a series of diplomatic agreements with the government and military aid through air strikes against the insurrection in the early 1980s. By the end of the decade India had switched gear, goaded by the pressures of Tamil politics within India. In 1980, Indian troops trained the rebel Tamil Tigers in Sri Lanka against the regime. But when the rebel Tigers went out of hand, India pressurized the Sri Lankan government to invite an Indian Peacekeeping Force (IPKF) to fight the Tigers within the country. This disastrous decision, in one fell swoop, alienated both the secessionist Tamils in the North and large sections of Sinhalese people, who resented India's transgression of state sovereignty, although it had been requested by the Sri Lankan regime. It was an Indian version of the US Vietnam experience, and much worse; for while the IPKF had to beat a hasty retreat, the intervention led directly to the assassination of the Indian Prime Minister Rajiv Gandhi by a Tamil terrorist suicide bomber in India.

Since its withdrawal from Sri Lanka, Indian influence over the country has declined. It was never, in any case, a failed state of the kind that has led to the creation of protectorates elsewhere. The Sri Lankan Government's final defeat of the Tigers in 2009—and its dismissive attitude towards the international community's concern about the post-war human rights situation—provided ample evidence of its effective sovereignty, although it was in fact facilitated to a considerable extent by Chinese support.

Despite their setback in Sri Lanka, in the neighboring Indian Ocean island state of Maldives, with its large Muslim population, the Indian armed forces helped to quell an armed rebellion in 1988, capture the coup leaders and restore the friendly Gayoom regime. The Maldives has remained among the few sovereign states in the Indian neighborhood that is not problematic, partly as the result of India's considerable economic and technical aid, particularly to its offshore service industries in the financial sector.

The conclusion seems inescapable: the role that India has played within the region is not so different from the role that a prominent section of the Indian public accuses the US of playing globally. India's decision to become a military nuclear power in 1998, followed by Pakistan, has not helped change India's image in this regard. But the difference in India's present attitude, compared with the earlier Indian sensitivity with normative concerns as a soft power, is that Indian diplomacy now seems perfectly willing to live up to this image in pursuit of its goal of being formally acknowledged as a great power. It follows logically from an assessment of recent Indian diplomacy in the region that India is now willing to take the lead, within its neighborhood, in overseeing the security and governance of potential new protectorates on behalf of the international community.

According to a former Indian Foreign Secretary, "as global power struggle shifts to Asia [there is] a new role for India as a major regional military and economic power is to provide a new Asian equilibrium," along with the USA, Russia, China and Japan. While "foreign policy", he argues, "begins with neighbors ... unfortunately (for India) the neighborhood is on the boil."[15] According to a former Indian Defense Secretary,[16] "South Asia is one of the most violent regions of the world...next only to Iraq, South Asia has seen the largest number of deaths caused by terrorism over the past several years."[17] He continues: "the binding force linking the security perceptions of India's smaller neighbors is their abiding angst regarding its perceived hegemonic ambitions which guide and underpin their foreign and security policy." Moreover, according to him, "in the region, states, acting in concert with armed groups, promote dissidence and insurrection in neighbors with broad spans of territory having no government control." This includes the Afghan-Pak border, Baluchistan, Waziristan, Pakistan's Federally Administered Tribal Areas (FATA) and its North West Frontier Province along with Kashmir, the Northeast and central India's tribal region, now under Maoist insurrection. The former Indian Defense Secretary sees "distinct signs of state failure" in these regions and comments:

The coexistence of functioning national or provincial authority, alongside virtual lack of control on broad expanses of its territory has become a distinguishing feature of violence in South Asia... [which] along with Sub-Saharan Africa and Middle-East, is among the most conflict-prone regions of the world [...] states [from this region] are likely to pass on "weapons of mass destruction" to non-state actors and religious groups.[18]

Within this grim scenario of failed states in the neighborhood, India's increasing willingness, and ability, to play the role of a regional troubleshooter for the international community have been manifested most visibly in the case of its historical adversary, Pakistan, and its one-time client, now not-so-friendly Bangladesh. For a start, India has learnt to live with military regimes in the region in preference to chaos and instability, rather than insist upon the fine print of the criteria of "good governance" in the form of democracy and civil and political rights of the citizens in these states. But when movements for democracy have emerged in any of the neighboring countries, India has been the preferred sanctuary for its votaries threatened with persecution at home. Officially correct—often cordial—relations with non-democratic regimes in the region, along with measured periodic utterances in favor of democratic options and sanctuary for those options' activists, have been fine-tuned as an instrument of Indian diplomacy.

This new Indian policy suits the other major powers, which trust India as they did not during the Nehru era. Arguably, the experience of the Border war with China (1962) after the prolonged bonhomie of the *Panchsheel* era seems to have been the first eye-opener for Indian diplomacy in the direction of such *Realpolitik*. Thereafter the Bangladesh war against Pakistan (1971), followed by the military coup in 1975 and the subsequent coldness in Bangladesh's relations with India, led that country, along with Pakistan, to become another conduit-pipe of "Islamic terrorism" against India. It also became a sanctuary for terrorists from India's North-East, possibly reinforcing the realist underpinnings of India's South Asian diplomacy. Now that this region has also emerged as a major concentration of failed or failing states, India seems well equipped to play a diplomatic role in these potential protectorates on behalf of the international community.

India's official response to the military-backed "interim regime" which ruled in Bangladesh between 2007 and December 2008 was measured, in contrast to its proactive role after the 1975 assassination of Mujibur Rahaman that was also followed by a period of military rule. Pressed by the media to respond to the new regime's arrest of the leaders of the two main parties, both former Prime Ministers, a spokesperson of India's Ministry of External Affairs commented: "the early and full restoration of democracy, due process of law, and respect for individual rights will contribute to the evolution of a stable, democratic, and prosperous Bangladesh."[19] This unexceptionable emphasis on the importance of democracy has been accompanied by measures to improve relations with the regime and foster broad-basing bilateral contacts among the civil society in both countries, including cultural and business groups. While the rebel Bangladeshi author Taslima Nasreen was given asylum in India, she was restrained from airing her high-profile secularist and feminist views; similar restrictions were imposed on the numerous Tibetan exiles in India.

This restraint has surely had the desired effects in the neighborhood. India has also always rushed massive aid, at times of the periodic natural calamities that so often visit disaster-prone Bangladesh. Most important, officially the Indian government has not given in to the demand of a section of Indian public opinion to take any drastic measure against the large-scale infiltration of illegal immigrants from Bangladesh, except the fencing of the borders, which still leaves them porous enough for contraband in human and goods trafficking.

India's recent diplomatic relations with its historical adversary, Pakistan's military regime, more strikingly underscore its potential role as a regional troubleshooter for the international community. An important role in this "critical" case of a potentially failed state as a major breeding ground of "Islamic Fundamentalism," nuclear proliferation (as committed by the nuclear scientist A.Q. Khan) and "global terrorism." So long as he remained in power the Pakistani military leader General Musharraf's relations with the leaders of most of India's mainstream political parties—including the Hindu nationalist BJP— were impeccable; while at home, all his adversaries fighting for civilian rule in Pakistan accused Musharraf of being India's "closest friend." At the same time, India provided sanctuary to most dissidents escaping his regime's incarceration. And throughout the period of military rule, the democratic movement against the military regime in Pakistan relied on the Indian electronic media, in preference to their own gagged press, as the major communication channel for all Pakistani political and civil society leaders. Along with the proliferating "Track-2" diplomacy between the two countries, civil society groups have helped to widen the social base receptive to democratic governance in Pakistan, so long under military rule. This has now become an asset for Indian diplomacy in its adversary's new civil society.

Even more striking evidence of the new pragmatism in Indian diplomacy in the neighborhood is provided by its relations with Myanmar's military regime and the house arrest (now ended) of the Nobel Peace Laureate Aung San Su Kyi. While there were widespread protests against her arrest by many admirers within Indian civil society and the media, and numerous exiles have been welcomed in India, the government maintains close friendly relations with the junta leaders. It has resisted pressures from within and outside the country to snap relations with the junta. For example, shortly before the meeting of the ASEAN Foreign Ministers on 19 May 2008, an Indian think-tank exhorted the Indian government to "act in concert" with China and Japan so as to "intervene on behalf of the people of Myanmar,"[20] but the government was unmoved. Soon afterwards, when Cyclone Nargis devastated Myanmar and the junta refused to allow foreign aid in, many Western leaders were baying for the blood of the military leaders; when US ships with aid materials were refused entry, President Bush demanded extending sanctions against the country, and European countries were equally vehement; but while other foreign aid ships were refused permission to anchor, India's "quiet diplomacy" enabled Indian medical and food aid to enter.[21] In the face of international pressure on India to use its goodwill with the military junta in a pro-democracy direction, foreign minister Pranab Mukherjee explained Indian policy: "It is not our job to determine what kind of government is there," but "economic development and peace should go side by side. We want to have good relations with China, Bangladesh, and Myanmar so that trade between (India's) North-East and ASEAN countries is promoted."[22] Since the foreign minister specifically mentioned the three countries—each of them under different versions of non-democratic regimes—these remarks can reasonably be interpreted as an indication of Indian policy towards any such regime. At a time when the Western policy of democratization is in such obvious disarray, this makes the present Indian diplomacy better equipped to play the role of a regional trouble-shooter for the international community.

## Conclusion

In this context, it may be useful to summarize the Indian experience of dealing with some of the problems in the region, which are comparable to those that have arisen elsewhere in the new protectorates. The former Indian Defense Secretary drew the implicit comparison succinctly in May 2008[23] by stating that a) "Peace processes in South Asia are easier to initiate than to sustain"; this has happened in Kashmir, Afghanistan, Sri Lanka and India's North-East; b) "agreements are observed if their benefits are demonstrable," as in the case of the Indo-Pakistan agreement on Indus Waters (1960) aided by the World Bank, which has survived four rounds of war between the two countries, and the "composite dialogue" on Kashmir, Hot-Line, missile flights, nuclear accidents and cross-border transport, all between India and Pakistan; c) Nurturing extremist groups to counter moderates in opposition is counterproductive; they go out of control to become the problem rather than the solution, at the cost of the "the hearts and minds of the citizens," as happened in the countries of the region—two most glaring instances being India's Operation Bluestar in Amritsar's Golden Temple in 1984 and Pakistan's Lal Masjid siege in 2007.

In conclusion, we should note that, possibly even more than China, India remains committed to the original pluralist conception of international society as set out in the UN Charter. As power gradually but inexorably shifts eastwards, Indian attitudes toward the problems posed by the new protectorates—that is, those unstable areas on the periphery of the international system where intervention and some kind of international oversight seem unavoidable—are likely to command both more attention and respect than in the past. A summary of the guidelines relating to governance of the new protectorates that would be likely to find favor in India might include the following:

1. In the absence of any robust institutional mechanism of accountability, or clearly defined schedule of sovereign statehood, the legal and moral legitimacy of the new protectorates remains somewhat suspect within the "hearts and minds" of the citizens of these regions as also within some sections of the liberal intelligentsia, particularly in the non-Western world.

2. To win credible respect for their legitimacy through demonstrable measures of welfare and public service is the first task of governance of these protectorates. In this context, the actual composition of the interim regimes is crucial for their credibility. To the extent possible, the visible public face of such interim regimes ought to be inclusive of the least controversial representatives of the diverse local identities.

3. External advisers, kept at the unavoidable minimum, should ideally be from nationalities in conformity with the local sensitivities of the protectorates.

4. The goal of such interim regimes ought to be the shortest route to sovereign self-governance, cutting corners if necessary in regard to the ideal criteria of "good governance," in the spirit of the Gandhian ideal. More than that, the interim regimes must be popularly perceived to be interim, and also representing the international community in the sense of being accountable to it, ideally through the United Nations as the "harmonizer of the actions of humanity," as envisaged in the Preamble of the Charter.

# 6

# THE EUROPEAN "PULL" IN THE BALKANS

*Spyros Economides*

The general perception of the Balkan region which developed over the last two decades was primarily shaped by Yugoslavia's wars of disintegration. They molded the views and beliefs among policy-makers, analysts and general publics alike of what the Balkans supposedly were and are: a geographical prosthesis to Europe consisting of "fringe Europeans," captives of long-held ethnic and nationalist animosities, hell-bent on achieving anachronistic political and territorial goals through the indiscriminate use of force. In short they cemented and perpetuated the idea of an "imagined Balkans."[1]

The influence of the European Union (EU) in the Balkans cannot be overstated. Perhaps the greatest success of the EU in this region is effectively to redefine the region geographically and through the use of what are considered to be less pejorative terms. While immediately following the collapse of communism the region was almost always referred to as "the Balkans," very quickly the use of the term "Southeastern Europe" became readily accepted as standard. Following Slovenia's accession to the EU, and as Romania and Bulgaria, "the Eastern Balkans," moved steadily towards EU membership, what remained as the region quickly became widely and officially known as the Western Balkans.

While the EU's influence in the Balkans cannot be overstated, the coherence and consistency of its policies should not be overemphasized. Yugoslavia's wars of disintegration and the EU's inability to cope with them, highlighting both diverging interests among member-states and lack of institutional capacity, provide the context for all subsequent EU foreign policy towards the region. Different member-state interests, whether those with regional concerns such as Greece, Italy or Austria, or those more broadly defined such as Germany, France or Great Britain, have provided a constant obstacle to consensus building. Similarly, the lack of appropriate instruments or application of policy such as conditionality—which was seen to succeed in the neighboring countries— has posed consistent problems for the EU in its Western Balkans policies. If there has been an overarching "EU approach" to the region it has been based on securing and stabilizing. But, as we shall see, there are different interpretations for the EU's motivations (or those of its member-states, as they are not always one and the same thing); there is uncertainty over what constitutes the Western Balkans's "European perspective," and to what extent the EU can shape rather than merely react to events in the region.

The success of the EU in these terms has been to address, and partially redress, the common perception of the Balkans as Western Europe's nasty "other." The effects of the EU's long-term engagement in Southeastern Europe, since the early 1990s, have been real and not confined to the altering of perceptions through presentational sleight of hand. They might not have been as successful as many would have liked, or what success has been achieved might not have come as rapidly as many would have wanted. Many would argue that successful international policy towards the region, especially in terms of security, has come about through the influence of the US, and its ability and willingness to act militarily. But there can be no doubt that the European impact on the development of the Balkan region since the collapse of communism has been immense.

What this chapter seeks to address is the type of impact the EU has had in the Balkans as well as the nature of the policies it has employed in achieving this impact. What is it that the EU and Europeans have attempted to create in relation to Southeastern Europe? Has it been a "European civilizing process," where the establishment of peace and the transcendence of national identities are the intended norms?[2] Can it be characterized in terms of continuation of the argument of EU enlargement as "empire building," where EU enlargement into the Balkans is a further manifestation of the assertion of "political and economic control over the unstable and impoverished eastern part of the continent"?[3] Or is it best to categorize the EU's influence in the Balkans in terms of its "transformative power," its aspiration and capacity to "Europeanize" other states through the use of selective policies and instruments?[4] Would it be safer to argue that indeed Europe's greatest success in the Balkans has been not to establish peace or transform states, but rather to secure against the recurrence of violence?

Whichever version one prefers, what is sure is that the Balkans, in whatever of the regional forms mentioned at the outset, have played a significant role in the evolution of a variety of EU policies and instruments of external action. In return, the impact of the EU on the region has been second to none. The key activity of the EU in the region has been that of statebuilding. This may be a controversial statement in that many would argue that statebuilding has not taken place in the region. But this chapter argues that in practice, the EU has engaged in statebuilding in the Balkans inasmuch as the term is a flexible one which allows us to take into account the variety of different types of states and state-like entities with which the EU interacts and has played a fundamental role in sustaining and developing. In this case a major differentiation ought to be made between the types of EU policies that have resuscitated ailing states, suffering from the rough transition process in tandem with the shock of the Yugoslav wars, and those that have propelled states into further level of democratization and economic development. In other words, the process of EU statebuilding in the region can be divided into those policies which have provided the wherewithal for reconstruction, those which have furthered the processes of transition and democratization, and those which have promoted or resulted in Europeanization. In effect we could argue that a key element of EU action in the Balkans which needs to be addressed is whether the EU efforts to provide security and prosperity amount to statebuilding in the more traditional sense or whether they amount to member-state building (which is a rather different process, and may not be possible in other regions in which the EU is active).

Therefore this chapter will assess what it is that the EU has attempted to accomplish in the Balkans, the types of policies it has used to achieve these goals, and the impact of these policies. Europe's goals have been mixed and hinge on a combination of security related issues and those of transformation of states and societies. The instruments used and policies pursued have been varied, and range from conditionality to coercion. After a brief outline of the history of EU involvement in the Balkans, the chapter examines the premise that EU policy in the region has been mainly pursued through containment and conditionality (and more latterly coercion). States and state-like entities have been shaped and sustained in a variety of different ways to meet goals and according to what instruments are at play. The chapter then examines the extent to which the EU has wanted either to create states in its own image through the transformation process, or to promote democratization in the broader sense of the term, or simply to contain existing and potential security threats through a pragmatic rather than idealistic approach. The chapter concludes, that while security provision and the promotion of prosperity are laudable—and achievable—goals, and while the EU can impose its views through various types of statebuilding, it still remains unclear whether the EU provides a civilizational pole of attraction beyond "Europeanization" and in line with the image of "normative power Europe."

## A Quick Look at Contemporary History

The recent history of the Balkans is deeply intertwined with the evolution of the EU as an international actor. In the context of the wars of Yugoslavia's disintegration, the EU was thrown in at the "deep end" of the foreign policy pool and found itself floundering. Through a combination of institutional inadequacies, diverging member-state interests, and the physical inability to act, the Yugoslav drama quickly became a painful formative experience for the EU. The EU was confronted with an extensive range of hard security issues and growing humanitarian concerns which initially it could do little about. Self-praise aside, the EU was ill-equipped to offer serious mediation which could bring about a meaningful cease-fire in the short-term and prepare the ground for a long-term peace. Nor was the EU able to back up its diplomatic efforts with a convincing show of strength in its effort to bargain a cessation to the hostilities. The reliance on the provision of good offices backed up by civilian instruments of deprivation or punishment—the suspension of aid and the imposition of sanctions—did not carry the needed clout to bring the warring parties closer to a negotiated settlement.

The EU was also hampered by a procedural problem of a different sort. The existing system of foreign policy cooperation (EPC), which was replaced by the Common Foreign and Security Policy (CFSP) during the Yugoslav wars through the Maastricht Treaty, proved an inadequate mechanism to resolve diverging Member-State interests. It also showed that the EU lacked an "early-warning" institutional capacity to be able to foresee crises and plan accordingly. As a result the EU was shocked to be faced by real security threats on its borders, with different states wishing different outcomes, and without much understanding and appreciation of the complexity of the causes of the violent breakdown of federal Yugoslavia.

The humanitarian dimension of war in the Balkans also became an equally serious concern. As war spread from Croatia to Bosnia, the outside world, and especially the EU which was charged with dealing with the Yugoslav wars on behalf of the international community, became increasingly aware of the large-scale humanitarian crisis which was looming. Of course, atrocities such as those committed in Srebrenica, along with the general policy of ethnic cleansing, dominated the concerns. Large-scale deaths were accompanied by large-scale displacement of people. These refugees, many of whom sought refuge within the confines of former Yugoslavia, also sought safe haven across international borders: at least the threat of this was enough to command the attention of the EU.

Consequently, much of the EU's policy towards collapsing Yugoslavia, and subsequently what became known as the Western Balkans, was driven by the need to contain real and perceived threats emanating from the region's wars. What became imperative was the need to ensure that Yugoslavia's wars would not spread further into the Balkans and especially not into the territory of the EU and potential EU members.[5]

Kosovo proved no different a threat during the intervention in 1999. Unlike in Croatia and Bosnia, the EU was not the lead intervening organization; nonetheless it faced the same dilemmas of defending "hard security" interest in the region and meeting the demands of humanitarianism. As a result, EU member states were at the forefront both of the NATO intervention and, more important, of the post-war efforts at peacebuilding in Kosovo.

Ultimately, the experiences in the Balkan context in the 1990s were enormously significant in shaping the subsequent policies of the EU towards Yugoslavia's successor states and the region as a whole. As we shall see, stability has been the predominant initial goal of all EU initiatives towards the Western Balkans. What is less clear is what the EU wished to achieve following the stabilization of the region: to rest on the success of relative peace and stability or to push on in a transformative mode not only to achieve real regional peace but also to draw the states of the Western Balkans into the EU's embrace. In effect what persists throughout the EU's post-conflict policies in the Western Balkans is an uneasy coexistence between the needs for security—both hard and soft—and demands for the creation of the basis for "the good life" based on the values and norms embedded in the EU and its foreign policy.

## Containment and Conditionality

The EU's ability to influence the states of the Western Balkans has, as we shall see, been conducted through a variety of different instruments and agencies. Nevertheless, two core features underpin all EU policies towards the Balkans since the early 1990s, containment and conditionality. Arguably, since the deployment of ESDP military and policing missions in the region, coercion has also become a key feature of EU policy. It could be said that containment and conditionality (and perhaps even coercion) are features each of which define specific periods in Europe's Balkan adventures, and as a result they are chronologically sequential and offer no real analytical framework.[6] I argue here that containment and conditionality have been individually prevalent at particular times throughout the EU's engagement in the Balkans, but they are not mutually exclusive, nor do they feature as discrete policies operating in isolation from each other. They are parallel strands of policy which—whether the product of conscious decision-making or of spontaneous evolution—have coexisted in EU strategy towards the region throughout the 1990s and beyond (with the prevalence of one or the other at specific times). The relevance of these features is that they reflect the concerns of the EU in terms of securing against instability and potentially even conflict, while also setting guidelines and conditions for acceptable practice and behavior of the states in the Western Balkans within the framework of Europeanness. The outstanding question is whether the EU has reached a clear consensus and opinion on whether the phases of containment—and, more important, conditionality—have been achieved satisfactorily to enable a progression to transformative policy towards the region: is the EU confident enough in its ability to influence thus allowing it to move beyond creating a "stable and violence-free" region and into building states able and willing to accede to the EU? Hence the "European pull" in the Western Balkans has been a mixture of incentives and punishments, carrots and sticks. But is there something more overarching than this traditional policy mix which allows the EU to bear influence of the states of the region? In attempting to answer that question it would be useful to delve into the features of containment and conditionality which underlie all of the EU's Balkan policies to show the very essence of the EU's concerns and its ability to influence.

## Containment

What does containment mean in the context of the EU's Balkan policies? A quick assessment suggests four different understandings of this feature.

Firstly, containment for the EU—as for the rest of the international community—had a clearly pragmatic dimension. Throughout the 1990s and beyond, the EU was primarily concerned with the physical containment of existing and potential Balkan wars. Whether one looks at EU (the EU and the EC are used interchangeably) policy towards war in Slovenia, the Serbia-Croatia conflict, war in Bosnia and unrest in Albania, or conflict in Kosovo and the FYROM, the foremost EU concern has been to prevent the spread of conflict to other areas in Southeast Europe (SEE) and beyond.[7] This most fundamental form of containment, stopping the physical spread of war, can be illustrated in a variety of different ways and at different stages of Yugoslavia's disintegration and beyond. From the initial determined effort made to maintain Yugoslavia as a single state—and subsequent policies of stopping the further disintegration of rump Yugoslavia[8]—through to the wars in Bosnia, conflict in Kosovo and ethnic violence in the FYROM, the EU's major goal was to ensure that fighting did not spill into neighboring territory. And this goal was not always well received.[9]

In the context of the Bosnian War, as suggested by Gow, "[C]ontainment was seen as an alternative to direct intervention."[10] He goes on to suggest that "it was containment of both the conflict and the diplomatic damage caused by it, and about simply, bringing the war to an end."[11] In the case of Kosovo, while NATO, and subsequently the UN, were the organizations tasked with making and enforcing peace in 1999 and after, the EU was party to the decision to keep Kosovo as part of what remained of Yugoslavia (and subsequently Serbia) through UNSCR 1244, while pursuing avenues of discussion, reconstruction and institution-building which could lead to an end state satisfying the demands of the Albanian population.[12]

The EU's reaction to the situation in the FYROM in 2001 could also be characterized as one of containment. Inter-ethnic fighting gave rise to the possibility of a partitioning of the FYROM, with the ethnic Albanian community demanding a separate state or union with their neighbors in Kosovo. Needing to ensure that fighting in the FYROM did not spill over into neighboring Kosovo, Albania or even southern Serbia (let alone Greece, an EU and NATO member), the EU emphasized that the FYROM's "European perspective" would be dramatically set back if fighting did not cease immediately. The Ohrid Framework Agreement which was negotiated under heavy pressure from the EU, and Javier Solana more specifically, did bring stability but at a cost. The main aim was to keep the country together, hence the decentralization and other measures of relative autonomy.[13]

Secondly, an equally pragmatic reason for the evolution of the EU's policy of containment with respect to SEE was to forestall the spread of the effects of war in the Balkans. Wars in SEE—in conjunction with the traumas of post-communism—provided the EU with a formidable problem: war refugees, displaced peoples and economic migrants fleeing under the cover of war sought safe haven and a future outside the Balkan region. The vast majority were displaced by war or were the product of what quickly became known as "ethnic cleansing."[14] Nevertheless, not all flows comprised those displaced by war, nor were they confined to the war years of 1991–95 (and the war in Kosovo in 1999). Many refugees fled the Balkans for political reasons, or more importantly as the result of structural economic deficiencies which obliged them to seek economic succor beyond the confines of the Balkans. Other trans-border flows were the product of less well intentioned, criminal activities centering on the illicit trafficking of goods and people.

Hence a crucial aspect of the EU policy towards the region has been one of refugee returns, a form of containment. Policy in Croatia, BiH and more recently Kosovo has always had as a central plank the idea that those displaced by war should be returned to their towns, villages and land. This was supposed to safeguard their right of abode and the return of their property, but it also was an effort to forestall the possibility of these people seeking permanent settlement elsewhere beyond their states, and especially to stop them seeking it beyond SEE. In many respects, EU aid to these states became conditional on population returns and often the reconstruction of their homes if destroyed. In conjunction with this form of containment, very specific to those Balkan states visited by war, a different form of this same policy was adopted and applied to all SEE states: a very strict visa regime restricting travel to the EU. This measure was highly unpopular with the people of the Balkans who rightly saw it as exclusionary. And while the policy has become less restrictive as countries such as Romania and Bulgaria join the Union and others enter into contractual arrangements with the EU in the form of Stabilization and Association Agreements (SAA), controls still remain tight and are a way of containing socio-economic issues within the region.

One could even make the argument that many of the broader EU policies towards the region, short of accession of course, are shot through with this idea of containment. One of these most often referred to by locals is the insistence of the EU on regional cooperation. The EU had set out a road map for reform in the region—and individual states—laying down guidelines for eligibility to receive EU aid and to open up the region's "European perspective."[15] A key element of this road map and a form of conditionality imposed on the recipient states was the idea of regional cooperation. In economic terms this made perfect sense; the reconstruction of local trading patterns along regional lines or the rebuilding of infrastructure such as roads and electricity grids regionally would create important economies of scale.[16] But this was also seen locally as a way of constructing regional activities which would not be the precursor to the "European perspective" but the logical conclusion of a policy limiting this perspective. In other words, Balkan states would be shunted into a regional arrangement outside the EU (perhaps with a special relationship with the EU), in which there would be no prospect of EU membership. The idea was that this policy would alleviate certain economic problems but would also contain others within the region, rather than build the strong politico-economic foundations which would allow for EU accession. Europe's backwater would remain just that, and all its problems would be contained within the region rather than being ingested into the EU.[17]

Thirdly, there is an "ideas" or "ideology" component to containment. While the containment of violence and human flows always topped the EU agenda, equally important was the containment of what were viewed as pernicious and anachronistic ideas stemming from the perceived causes of conflict in SEE (and the use of violence in the pursuit of goals). Nationalism, ethnic animosities and conflict seated in distant historical differences, resolved through the use of force, ethnic cleansing and rape were all deemed features of societies and states that not only did not meet the criteria of the modern European mainstream (and certainly not the ideals and practices of a European project which had long since eradicated violence as a method of state interaction), but had to be kept out of the life of the EU. Thus, for example, the emphasis on the illegality of the changing of frontiers through the use of force, which has led the EU (and the international community in general) into a series of problems with respect to permanent and acceptable resolutions to conflict in Bosnia and Kosovo respectively. This practice was not only contrary to the spirit and ethos of the EU but also went against international practice and understanding established in Europe since the mid-1970s; it also became a threat to a vulnerable post-Cold War international system which was in a formative stage of a "new World Order" (based on respect for law and principles of good behavior and not the selfish pursuit of national interests likely to bleed tension into the system). If war were to produce territorial and frontier change in the Balkans, and remained unchallenged by the EU, then a dangerous precedent would be set for similar action elsewhere in Europe. Therefore containment of ideas took its place alongside the more pragmatic dimension of containment outlined above.[18] A more popular manifestation of these concerns was aired by Huntington, who drew his civilizational fault line through the heart of the Balkans.[19]

Lastly, there is of course the persuasive argument that containment came about by default: the EU could do little or nothing else and hence tried to contain conflicts and crisis. The lack of continuity and coherence between the interests of member states of the EU, and that of the EU as an organization, meant deadlock and inertia. The fact that the Common Foreign and Security Policy (CFSP) was still being negotiated when war broke out in Yugoslavia, and in its infancy subsequently, meant that the EU had no tried and tested foreign policy-making mechanism to meet the crises.[20] The means of enforcing peace were unavailable and so containment became the only feasible option. That there was a minimal understanding of the root causes of strife in the Balkans did not aid the situation. In short, Yugoslavia's demise was "too much, too soon" for the EU's foreign policy-making system.

## Conditionality

The EU's own vision of its international role as a civilian actor, that it would pursue its goals and spread its values through non-coercive means, and its reliance on economic instruments of foreign policy led the EU to develop extensive aid policies. It also resulted in conditionality becoming a central feature of the EU's external relations, particularly with respect to aspiring members, and in the context of the end of the Cold War.[21]

However one defines EU conditionality, it became a key instrument of EU foreign policy, a means to an end. It has now become more than a means to an end: a "norm, or standard, for Community/Union foreign policymaking."[22] But why is conditionality central to the EU's relationship with SEE?

Firstly, "the hour of Europe" necessitated a clear definition of what the EU should/would do. What Europe should and would do was predicated, in turn, upon what Europe could do. Yugoslavia's wars caught the EU institutionally unprepared and instrumentally inadequate. Faced with violent conflict and a series of humanitarian crises, the EU had to rely on its economic might in conducting its foreign relations. This was not conditionality as a "guiding norm of the Community/Union's policy,"[23] but conditionality as policy resulting from the reality that the EU had little else by way of leverage. For example, the EU's attempts to achieve a cease-fire and subsequently end hostilities in the wars in Slovenia, Croatia and subsequently Bosnia centered on "negative conditionality" in that it both swiftly imposed economic sanctions and supported the International Financial Institutions (IFIs) in suspending all aid and financing packages.

Secondly, conditionality has also been a mainstay of EU policy in the Balkans owing to circumstance. While punitive measures, such as economic sanctions, provided a key element in the EU's Balkan policies from the beginning of Yugoslavia's disintegration, "positive conditionality," offering inducements, has played the key role in long-term policy. The EU's economic clout allows it to attach strict conditions to economic assistance and grants offered to any state in SEE. The rise of economic interdependence in the post-Cold War world has also put extra emphasis on the use of economic tools of foreign policy. As it is an "economically based" institution deriving its international role from the strength of the outcomes of economic integration and common commercial policy, the new vision of international relations based on interdependence and the rise of the economic factor suited the EU very well. Throughout the range of the political conditionality extended by the EU towards individual countries in SEE since 1991, or towards the region as a whole through the EU's Regional Approach initiated in 1997, the primary rewards have always been economic in nature. The ultimate reward, that of accession to the EU, is more than economic, but the road to candidacy for accession is one littered with conditionalities which, if met, are rewarded with economic benefits.

"Micro-conditionality" with respect to the conditions attached to reconstruction, infrastructural programs and economic development is supplementary to the more important form of "macro-conditionality" or political conditionality. Conditions range from politico-economic reform, judicial transparency and general institution and capacity building to refugee returns and the arrest of individuals indicted as war criminals by the International Criminal Tribunal for former Yugoslavia (ICTY).[24] This kind of headline political conditionality has been and is employed in all bilateral relations with SEE states. Bosnia provides a most valuable example, where reform and restructuring of the police forces, as stipulated by the EU, proved extremely problematic and became a highly controversial issue in relations between the EU and Bosnia. The EU conditioned the signing of the bilateral SAA with Bosnia on, amongst other things, a police reform package. In mid-April 2008, these reforms were finally enacted and adopted, after much delay; this paved the way, according to the EU's Commissioner for Enlargement Ollie Rehn, for "practical benefits in trade and thus for the economy of Bosnia and Herzegovina, but it is also the gateway towards candidate country status for EU accession."[25]

Thirdly, conditionality is also the product of the foundational principles and rationale of the EU, particularly in its international relations, and as epitomized by its ultimate and most potent foreign policy instrument—enlargement. Here what matters is not what the EU could/can do—and what powers it has at its disposal to attain goals—but what it should do. The assumption is that the EU should represent certain values and norms in its international behavior, reflecting those very norms and values for which the European project was initially pursued. Peaceful interaction, democratization, the protection of human rights, and economic prosperity were formative goals of the EU, and were pursued within the boundaries of the Union, and as such they should be pursued outside of the EU's boundaries as well. And, in pursuit of these goals, the EU should use instruments appropriate with the principles governing the attainment of those goals. Force and the threat of the use of force were not deemed to be appropriate instruments outside the remit of territorial defense: the means had to be in accordance with the ends. Hence the emergence of civilian power Europe. In addition, its most powerful foreign policy tool was to offer membership. If the idea was that "to join us you must behave like us," this was readily extended to "to engage with us you must behave like us."

Perhaps the starkest and most problematic use of political conditionality employed by the EU towards SEE, arising from the basic principles espoused by the EU in its founding treaties and framework governing its external relations, has been that of full cooperation with the ICTY. The basic principle of the protection of human rights is one that has become vital in the EU's external affairs and especially in its relations with states aspiring to contractual agreements with and/or membership of the EU. This is clearly laid out in all EU agreements and accession negotiations as initially laid out in the Copenhagen criteria. As a result, the EU's relations with Balkan states have included clauses in all agreements and prospective agreements (since the mid-1990s) stipulating strict compliance and full cooperation with the decisions of the Tribunal.

Created by a UN Security Council Resolution in May 1993, the ICTY has jurisdiction over those crimes committed on the territories of former Yugoslavia since 1991. Its main objective is to provide justice to the victims of genocide, war crimes and crimes against humanity, as well as to punish the perpetrators of those crimes and deter future crimes of this kind. The ICTY indicts, prosecutes and reaches judgments on those who have been accused of committing the stated crimes. It has pursued indictments against individuals in Croatia, Bosnia, Serbia and Kosovo. The ICTY's weakness is that it is reliant on others to enforce its decisions, mainly on two sources being: the international actors on the ground in the Balkans such as the NATO contingent in Bosnia, and the Balkan states themselves. The most memorable indictment was that of Slobodan Milosević, whom the Serbian authorities arrested and handed over to the Tribunal in The Hague, after much pressure, in June 2001. More recently, Radovan Karadzić was arrested in Belgrade, handed over to the ICTY and is currently being tried on eleven counts of genocide, crimes against humanity and war crimes for his part in the Bosnian war.

The EU has used conditionality in its relations with all SEE states partly as a result of circumstance and necessity. But there is EU conditionality based on virtue rather than circumstance or necessity: to engage with Europe means accepting European standards through conditionality. As one commentator notes with respect to accession negotiations, these "are not about future relations between 'us' and 'them' but rather about relations between the 'future us.'"[26]

## Coercion?

As an addendum to the dualism of containment and conditionality as underlying features of the EU's actions in SEE, we must also consider the role of coercion or the use (or threat of use) of force. A common starting point for examining the EU's Balkan involvement was its inability or unwillingness to use force in the early to mid-1990s. Whether because of lack of common interest among its members, institutional weakness or sheer inability to project force, the EU stood aside—militarily—while Yugoslavia crumbled violently. Some EU members, France and Britain for example, played a major role in the UN peacekeeping mission, UNPROFOR, during the Bosnian conflict. Subsequently, they among others also played key roles in assisting the US-led NATO intervention against the Bosnian Serbs. Other states, such as Germany, were bound by historical and constitutional constraints: the image of German forces operating in SEE was not one that would be welcomed by many in the region, and was anyway impossible owing to the constitutional constraints placed on German forces, limiting them to operations within Germany's borders. This was not helped by Germany's provocative stance in the early recognition of Slovenia and Croatia, which best illustrated the problems of consensus building in European foreign policy formulation and rekindled the debate on Germany's interests and the motivation behind its "Eastern" foreign policy.

Therefore the EU's record as an enforcer of the "international will" was—in the context of Bosnia—virtually non-existent.[27] Its record on achieving agreement of the merits of coercion was equally weak. Nevertheless, many EU members, through the NATO alliance, were willing to consider the use of force against the Bosnian Serbs—and also Milosević's Serbia—to bring them to the negotiating table.[28] Throughout the 1990s, coercion figured in debates only inasmuch as it was launched as a criticism—if not an indictment—of the EU and its inability/unwillingness to actively pursue military intervention; or else it figured through the use of force by individual EU member-states through units operating in UN/NATO operations in the region.

In the longer term, we can arguably trace the emergence of ESDP to this critical assessment of the EU record in the field of coercion in the Balkans during the 1990s. While taking into account the internal dynamic of EU integration pushing forward the idea of a common defense policy, the EU's dismal Yugoslav experience must not be discounted as a key driver in the establishment of the ESDP. It is no coincidence that the deployment of the early ESDP missions has been heavily skewed towards the Balkans. A combination of proximity and geopolitical interest, as well as complementing other civilian EU actions in the region—and no little sense of guilt over the inadequacies of EU policy in the 1990s—meant that Bosnia and the FYROM were the early hosts of ESDP missions. In Bosnia, EUPM was deployed in 2003 and ALTHEA followed in 2004, while in the FYROM, CONCORDIA (2003) was followed by PROXIMA (2004–5) and subsequently EUPAT. Since 2008, the EU has also deployed its biggest mission to date since ALTHEA, through EULEX in Kosovo. In EU parlance these are a mixture of civilian and military ESDP missions, combining policing, training as well as more traditional military enforcement missions. Of the latter, the more "coercive" mission EUFOR ALTHEA is the most significant, which was initially a deployment of some 7,000 troops, replacing SFOR which had guaranteed stability and security in Bosnia since 1996. This has now been scaled back to about 2,000 personnel, nevertheless still playing a key role internally.

Despite the distinction between civilian and military missions in the context of ESDP, they form part of the coercion argument inasmuch as they promote stability and security through means other than the politico-economic methods promoted through the EU's contractual agreements with states in the region. This is especially true in Bosnia and Kosovo, where the EU presence is readily identified as having a "heavy," coercive presence that is not strictly speaking playing the role of a transformative catalyst, and highlights the criticism that what the EU attempts to achieve in the region is often imposed rather than agreed. In some respects, therefore, the "European pull" in the region is colored by these missions and the role they play in the broader EU policy in the Western Balkans. Of course, more is examined in this vein in the context of Bosnia and Kosovo than in that of Montenegro, Croatia or Albania, where there is no such presence and the pressures and influences are different. Nonetheless, it is indicative that military and policing missions not only form a key part of EU policy in the potentially more unstable parts of the Western Balkans, but they are key in that they place a premium on security (absence of violence) and order (as stability), rather than any other capacity.

Indeed, an interesting point for consideration is whether conditionality has been more onerous in these areas of quasi-direct rule, which to some extent form the protectorates at the center of this volume, than in other parts of the Western Balkans. This may be so, but it may well be because the starting point for "transformation" is so much lower or is characterized by a deep-seated instability which many in the EU member-states do not want to see go unchecked. The "political and economic" conditionality of the SAP, for example, may be equally felt across the Western Balkans, but the day-to-day presence of military police units and civilians who "direct" conditionality may make the process seem—and be—qualitatively different. Even in terms of perception, and in the ubiquitous jargon of the internationals, local ownership in the presence of ESDP missions makes conditionality in these cases a radically different process than elsewhere in the region.

### What Is at Stake for Europe? What Do the Balkan States Expect?

Containment and conditionality, it has been argued, are two sides of the same coin in terms of the EU's policies towards the Western Balkans. On the one hand, the continuing policy of containment is part of a process of conflict suppression and management which provides a degree of stability enabling the regulation of a variety of potential spill-overs (as discussed above). Containment is an ongoing process of order maintenance which is self-serving, meets the national interest of a range of EU member-states, promotes the idea of the EU as a powerful actor in the international arena in the terms of security, and arguably provides the basis for further EU policy in the region.

Conditionality, on the other hand, is ostensibly a more forward looking, "creative" policy which strays beyond order maintenance. It is concerned just as much with issues of statebuilding as it is with peacebuilding: it promotes norms, values and codes of behavior as well as building institutions and structures of liberal democracy. It is not only concerned with the security of the existing EU by containment of "external sources of threat," but with the creation of a zone of peace for the well-being of the states and peoples of that region as well as that of the EU.

Consequently, there are two parallel processes that the countries of the Western Balkans have to consider in their relationship with the EU. The states of the Western Balkans are simultaneously the objects of a pragmatic policy aimed at security and stabilization and the subjects of an idealized policy of transformation and statebuilding. The two are not mutually exclusive. The long-term transformation of the region will build on the short-termism of stabilization with the added intended outcome of a just peace and prosperous societies.

But the central question of relevance to this particular volume is to discern what exactly these processes are achieving in terms of how they are perceived by the targets of this policy and not only by the instigators. That is, what is the real influence of the EU in the region and what is it really achieving? In short, what is the European "pull" for the region?

The starting point is that the EU is concerned with security; as said at the outset the goal has been to secure against the recurrence of violence. This is a goal shared by many in the region. The memory of the 1990s is a collective burden on the people of the Western Balkans and the remote possibility of another outbreak of mass violence acts as a strong enough incentive to seek outside intervention to forestall such a possibility. The problem which arises here is that even though this pragmatic version of peace is welcomed it is also, according to some, imposed rather than interactive. It seeks to deal primarily with the concerns of the interveners and only as a consequence with the needs of the recipients. It is an imposition of will rather than agreement on objectives. The EU—which has emerged as the dominant security provider in the Western Balkans even though in military security terms it is a latecomer to the scene—is portrayed as an actor determined to gain control of the region. The EU's policies are an indication of "imperial tendencies" rather than expressions of an idealized future for the region. This is felt most acutely in Bosnia.[29]

Therefore, the "pull" or influence of the EU in this particular interpretation is not "progressive." It is an interpretation which emphasizes the imposition of the EU—as an external actor—on the region through a variety of different policies and instruments. As a starting point one only need examine the titles and labels of official policies and organizations established by the EU (or with the EU as a prime driver of the initiative) to get a sense of this specific view. For example, the word "stability" crops up as a headline delineator in the very first EU initiative towards the post-Yugoslav conflict Balkans, through the creation of the Stability Pact for South Eastern Europe in 1999. Though it was created to deal with a series of issues including human rights and economic development, the main focus of the Stability Pact was on security and reconstruction.

The same language—and to some extent logic—is at the core of the latest predominant EU policy towards the Western Balkans, the Stabilization and Association Program (SAP). Though this is a far more reformist process, making strong use of the principle and policy of conditionality, the language indicates a dedication to the idea of stability and security. It is no coincidence that the initial package of financial support of this program was called Community Assistance for Reconstruction, Development and Stabilization (CARDS).

Some see the SAP as the natural precursor to EU enlargement into the Western Balkans; states sign and meet the conditions of the Stabilization and Association Program, and subsequently enter into the process of acquiring candidate status for EU accession and finally enter into negotiations for full membership of the EU. That is the aspiration of all Western Balkan states, whether realistically achievable in the short term or not. Croatia is the most often cited example of this process. Nonetheless, many in the Western Balkans and beyond argue that the SAA may be a meritorious process but it is an added obstacle along the road to EU accession. Why is it, they ask, that the states of the Western Balkans were not nudged towards the type of Europe Agreements agreed with countries which entered the EU in the last round of enlargement? Instead, the EU has added an extra layer of contractual obligation to precede the process of candidacy for membership and accession negotiations, which is unique to the EU's relationship with the Western Balkans. The EU, it follows in this logic, is not primarily concerned with creating the conditions through which Western Balkans states will be ready to accede, but would rather ensure that the EU's control is established over the region through the SAA's. The promise of future membership usually referred to as the Balkans' "European perspective," which many see located in the "Thessaloniki Agenda," is an unsure prospect. And if it does come to fruition it will be only so as to allow the enlargement of the Union in its "imperial mode."[30]

Therefore the discussion moves from one of containment to meet basic security needs through processes of stabilization to one of control (perhaps leading to enlargement) in the mode suggested by Zielonka. Is there any evidence of this? Some would argue that there is, especially in the role that Europe—and the EU specifically—have played in two specific cases, Bosnia and Herzegovina and Kosovo. In both cases, what was called the international administration of war-torn territories were clearly modern manifestations of protectorates. In Bosnia, the High Representative reigned supreme according to the power ceded to him by the Bonn agreements and the Peace Implementation Council. In Kosovo, UNMIK ran the province in all its aspects by the powers granted it under UNSCR 1244. In both cases, and for some length of time, the civilian aspect of international administration was secured by a substantial, Western-led military presence. And in both cases the EU played a significant role in terms of funding but also in personnel and organizationally.

In the case of Bosnia, and especially during Paddy Ashdown's tenure as High Representative, the international administration of Bosnia was compared not only to a protectorate of the Western world from a bygone era, but more strikingly to an outpost of the Raj.[31] This is striking exactly because this colonial/ imperial analogy as applied to Bosnia is logically not too far a distant from the argument that indeed the EU's eastern enlargement is almost a form of "empire building." Of course, when this comparison was made the prospect of Bosnia's accession to the EU was faint. But even now that Bosnia has signed its SAA, and is firmly on track in this specific process of European integration—and perhaps even enlargement—the controlling powers of an external actor are immense. And they will not recede as Bosnia has to fulfill conditions imposed through its contractual obligations embedded in the SAA, which will be closely monitored and assessed by the European Commission.

Therefore, as argued above, one understanding of the European influence on the countries of the Western Balkans is that of containing existing and perceived threats and problems. The security and stabilizing dimensions of the EU's policies are not only discernible from the content of the policies, and the instruments employed, they are also clearly communicated from the very titles of the policies themselves.

An alternative understanding is that the European influence on the Western Balkans, mainly through the EU's policies in the region, have amounted— and will continue to amount even if enlargement does take place—to a pervasive dominance akin to Europe's imperial past. No matter how well intentioned and benign the EU's presence in the region, the relationship between the EU and the Western Balkans remains unequal. Consequently, not only is the EU's influence dominant, it also leaves no room for any meaningful notion of local ownership of processes of stabilization and change.

The second main type of European influence in the Western Balkans can be categorized as transformational. The EU, through the use of a selection of policies and instruments, is attempting to "Europeanize" the states of the region, especially in the context of pulling them into the orbit of the European project. In one sense this is a highly functional project involving the creation of viable and sustainable democratic systems and institutions of governance, as well as viable and sustainable systems of economic development. Through its role as a civilian power and its substantial economic and institutional capacity, the EU has embarked on a long-term commitment to move beyond stability and construct a regional state system which is truly peaceful and prosperous in the mould of the EU itself.

In this instance the full array of EU instruments have been deployed in the Western Balkans centering on a policy of conditionality. Through this policy, the EU is aiding the Western Balkans states in financial, economic, technical and human terms on the condition that the recipients carry out extensive reforms in an extensive array of policy areas. This systematic attempt at transformation could be defined as democratization in the broadest sense of the term. It aims to institute constitutional democracies with transparent judicial systems protecting basic rights and liberties and affording the possibility of welfare creation and maintenance. This basic provision necessitates reforms throughout the existing system of governance: from fundamental guarantees of human rights, through to free and fair elections, "clean" government, judicial reform, fiscal and monetary responsibility and much more. It is not merely about eradicating crime and corruption, training police forces, reshaping government structures and toying with interest rates or tax brackets. It is about instilling a sense of duty in constitutions and institutions which serve the interests of the people through fairness and transparency, through processes that are inclusive, and about training people not only to carry out their jobs more effectively and efficiently, but to do so in the name of the whole and not certain (limited) parts of society. It is one thing, for example, to set up an independent judicial system, and quite another to create belief in the fairness of the system and the honesty of those working within it. It is taking time but it is in the interests of the EU to create a zone of peace in the Western Balkans, and it can do so by cementing democracy as the uncontested form of political and social organization in the region. But in tandem with this it must also cement belief in democracy as the uncontested form of political and social organization and not as a scheme imported from abroad and of no intrinsic domestic value. This, in a limited sense, is linked to the idea of a European "civilizing mission" as described below, through a combined effort at statebuilding and democratization without which the EU will neither continue to sponsor the transformation nor feel easy about the regional situation.

But there is a deeper connotation to the EU's efforts at democratization; not only is it endeavoring to build democratic states, but it is engaged in preparing the states of Western Balkans for EU accession. There is here a qualitative difference between statebuilding and member-state building. This is where the concept of Europeanization also becomes relevant. If the process is one of member-state building then what is happening is the transformation of values and norms of behavior as well as institutional capacity and politico-economic systems. In this case, the influence of the EU is that it is changing the behavior of states and the values that underpin that behavior. The strict conditionality relating to the arrest of alleged war criminals indicted by the ICTY has many effects and clearly illustrates this point. When indictees are put on trial, justice is served and perhaps truth and reconciliation promoted. But it is primarily indicative of what is morally acceptable in the European sphere and what isn't. So whereas a narrow interpretation of Europeanization may refer to adaptation and convergence to EU standards and policies, by states upon which contractual relations with the EU have had a deep impact, a broader one is centered on behavior arising from ethical norms and moral values that underpin European behavior. The EU, in this understanding, is not only a civilian power but a normative power as well. Arguably this is the most potent transformative impact of the EU, but it is also that which is most difficult to measure. The influence of the EU, in this case, is not always readily accepted and can give rise to antagonisms towards all EU efforts.

## Conclusion

There is a deeper question about the type of influence being exerted by the EU which has been termed "civilizational." Conditionality imposed by the EU or even the promise of eventual accession to the EU, can only go so far in its transformative capacity. Civilian and normative power Europe had a tremendous impact on the development of post-communist states and societies in South Eastern Europe. But a question still remains. Countries and people of the region aspire to the stability afforded by EU involvement and ultimately the material gains to be had from interaction with and potentially membership of the EU. They may even accept certain principles and institutions of governance and economic management. But has the European influence in the Balkans been strong enough in "civilizational" terms to push the agenda beyond one of security and prosperity in general terms, to one of values and beliefs in specific terms? Can the peoples of the Western Balkans be conditioned by a civilian, normative power Europe into being Europeanized? Or is that a process that cannot be achieved through a narrowly defined policy mechanism but needs a longer time frame, and a trust and acceptance that cannot be instilled institutionally? In essence, are European values something more than the transformative capacity of the EU can provide or the recipients are willing to accept?

One may ask why it is that Europe may have a "civilizing mission" towards the Balkans, and whether this is an explicit or implicit part of its policies towards the region. In the first instance we should concentrate solely on EU relations with the Western Balkans. When discussing the nature of the EU's containment policies in the Balkans, one of the points highlighted was that containment was also intended to affect ideas as well as actions: in the context of the Yugoslav wars, extreme nationalism linked to violence was seen (within EU member-states) as inimical to political life in late twentieth century Europe. As a logical consequence, part of Western Europe's attitude towards Southeastern Europe has been civilizational to the extent that it has wished to share its values and beliefs in peaceful reconciliation of differences through cooperation and integration, and the refutation of extreme nationalism as a valid source of political conduct. This context cannot be underestimated. The imprint that the wars of Yugoslavia's disintegration left on the EU's idea of what constitutes the Balkans cannot be overemphasized, and that imprint was a highly negative one which to a great extent has triggered this civilizing mission towards this European sub-region. As a result this civilizing element, specific to the Balkans, is explicit in the EU's policies.

In the second instance, a more implicit set of civilizing principles arises out of the EU's general normative and ethical concerns, with respect not only to institutions and organizations of political and economic life, but also to behavior. Arising out of Europe's turbulent recent past, and not from some external—exogenous—provocation such as war in the Balkans, these concerns had come to dominate the EU's foreign policy agenda. Implicit in all its external relations was the idea that the EU had evolved from a specific set of historical events, and that its establishment was meant to ensure that these events could never be repeated; the EU was not simply an international institution intended to carry out practical tasks, it had a moral and ethical ideal to fulfill. This ideal, in the case of its external relations generally and the Balkans specifically, can be subsumed within this idea of a civilizational pull: "we can assist you to overcome your problems but you will do it in a manner concomitant with our principles and values which have evolved from out own historical experiences." The civilian power Europe of the 1970s has transformed into the normative, moral power of the late twentieth and the early twenty-first century.

In conclusion, this does not always sit easily with a European Union which is a "power" and needs to react as well as to shape events in its own interests. Thus, to recast the Balkans in the EU's own image fits neatly and laudably with the aspirations of the fathers of European integration. But Europe's short-term interests need to placate the demands of order as well as justice. And, in addition, it is not always clear whether the EU's Balkan partners are willing to accept the principled side of the EU's policies or aspire only to the material benefits that EU membership may bring.

# 7

# US FOREIGN POLICY AND THE NEW PROTECTORATES IN HISTORICAL PERSPECTIVE

*Stefan Halper*

Over the course of the twentieth century, the United States inherited a world leadership role of unprecedented proportions. Its dominance grew so great that by the 1990s, Les Gelb observed that the US "loomed as the sole superpower and probably the strongest power in history, both absolutely and relatively."[1] Unlike previous world powers the US had no serious rivals as France and Britain had formerly had, nor was its reach limited by distance and logistics as with Rome and China. Yet strong forces constrain American power. Limitations of will and circumstance have shaped how America conceived of and administered overseas protectorates at the turn of the twentieth century and more recently in the context of stabilization and nation-building measures. These included a quixotic public whose opinion of these engagements shifts rapidly, ever changing assessments of national security and geopolitical priorities, and, indeed, contradictions inherent in the nation's self-conception as a benign yet evangelizing force.

This chapter argues that America's approach to old and new protectorates reflects the paradox characterizing its roles as both the most powerful nation on earth and yet an enduring anti-imperial voice. As the sole superpower, America's approach to such troubled areas as Iraq, Afghanistan and Kosovo remains riddled with aspiration and contradiction. The evidence of successive administrations suggests that "American Exceptionalist" spasms have too often captured policy, trumping the distilled, pragmatic policy required for stabilizing regions convulsed by ideology and ethnic differences, so that in the end neither political ideals nor geopolitical objectives are satisfied.

Since its inception, America has projected its values and "mission," together with its economic, cultural, and political influence, across the North American continent, reaching continuously westward to the Pacific. With each step, territories were mapped, populated and absorbed, becoming a part of the greater American story. Federal law was extended and sovereignty was claimed. With the twentieth century, this process changed dramatically when the US acquired territories through conquest and purchase that it would not absorb as integral and complete parts of the nation. Geographically isolated and culturally distinct from the American continental homeland, these possessions posed difficult policy questions: how does a nation forged in the furnace of revolution, an exponent of Enlightenment freedoms, rule over far-flung peoples and places without becoming itself infected by the imperial assumption of superiority—if only to provide "good government"—and accepting the fruits of exploitation? The answer, from the Spanish-American war to the second Gulf War, has been varied and inconsistent as leaders and their publics vacillated between shifting world views: sometimes isolationist, sometimes internationalist, sometimes unilateral—dare we say "neoconservative"—and at others more communal.

A telling expression of this ambivalence is the failure to establish either the administrative means, of the kind provided by the UK's Colonial Office, or a consistent unifying purpose such as France's *mission civilisatrice*. America's global posture reflects this inconsistency and yields a peculiar track record: successes have been few, with little agreement on the lessons taken from failure, leaving only modest guidance for today's policymakers. With the advent of America's post-Cold War hegemony, the need for an effective model of administration in post-conflict zones has grown. Administering these spaces as autonomous territories and affording them diplomatic and military protection from the currents of irredentism, ethnic claims and communal animosities, not to mention claims by neighboring states, is a daunting challenge in its own right for which the US is not equipped.

## Administering an Accidental Empire

America's post-Cold War interventions have an antecedent in the Spanish-American war.[2] The victory over the Spanish empire yielded possessions in

Cuba and the Philippines. Post-war planners at the time faced a dilemma: what rights and responsibilities arrived with victory? Inconsistent responses continue to plague the administration of American foreign policy today. Unsurprisingly, leaders failed to reconcile American values with empire, discovering what Les Gelb made explicit a century later, that "like any great power, America has worldwide responsibilities that conflict with its ideals."[3]

The Filipino nationalist leader Emilio Aguinaldo claimed that Dewey had assured American support for independence, a claim Dewey denied, but the confusion over the Philippines' status soon embroiled American policymakers. The scope and length of America's occupation remained in doubt. McKinley "agonized and prayed" over the issue before acceding to the demands of his more jingoistic deputies—a group with plans not unlike today's neoconservatives. Early policy towards the archipelago, guided by Teddy Roosevelt and his pro-annexation allies, would be called "benevolent assimilation."[4] Filipino and American domestic resistance quickly combined to scuttle these idealistic hopes to Americanize the Philippines, as if it were the old continental frontier. Isolationist sentiment under the banner of the Anti-Imperial League resisted the acquisition of empire as un-American, preferring to advance American interests abroad through example ("a shining city upon a hill").[5] The steel magnate Andrew Carnegie offered $20 million, the American price paid to Spain, to set the islands free. Though some figures like Grover Cleveland and Mark Twain viewed empire as incompatible with America's self-conception, other opponents reduced the matter to the cultural and racial incompatibility of "Asiatic hybrids" with America's "English-speaking and Teutonic peoples." Aguinaldo, who agreed with the anti-imperialists that both would be better served apart, took up arms when political entreaties failed. The US occupation fulfilled Kipling's prophesy about engendering "the hate of those ye guard."[6]

A blend of pragmatism and benevolence came to characterize the American occupation. The US was resolved to possess the islands but unsure of the meaning and the nature of its new-found ownership. In a pattern that would be repeated for more than a century—and in Afghanistan today—the army had neither the manpower to patrol 7,000 islands nor a coherent strategy to combat the *insurrectos'* hit-and-run tactics. Moreover, there was no apparent way to apply democratic governance in the new dependency over time while mounting a counterinsurgency.

## With No Established Precedent

Legal debates in the major law journals over the status of the new possessions echoed the public debate between the likes of Roosevelt and Carnegie. The American government had three available courses of action: to establish self-government and renounce claims, to prepare the possessions for eventual absorption into the corporal United States through assimilation or settlement, or retain indefinitely, as separate and distinct, territories as "possessions" or "dependencies" that had neither a path to statehood nor a path to independence.[7] The answer, in keeping with American ambivalence toward empire, was all three—the particular course chosen as much by circumstance, domestic politics, and international necessity as design. Hawaii would achieve statehood, Cuba independence, while Puerto Rico, Guam, and the Philippines fell into a nebulous category: of but not in the United States.

Congress considered various options modeled on its own administration of lands on the North American continent—Alaska, Oklahoma Indian Territory, organized and incorporated territories—and foreign governance types like those of Britain: crown colonies, colonies with representative but not responsible government, and self-governing colonies. Congress found all these models lacking, from a deep aversion to expressly imperial models. Puerto Rico's military governor George Davis, charged with producing a model for governance, conceded the obvious, "We have no American precedent to which we can refer as an aid to decide the form of civil government that should be set up."[8] This lack of acceptable precedent continues to vex contemporary planners more than a century later, since the US is still bereft of coherent purpose and means to administer protectorates in the Balkans and Middle East.

Cuba garnered the most benevolent attention from its American occupiers, who left after only three years. Assured that the occupation was temporary, the US military disbanded the Cuban rebel armies with a one-time payment of $75 and then initiated a nation-building campaign "distributing food to a hungry populace, staging a sanitary campaign, erecting thousands of public schools (modeled on those of Ohio), rooting out corrupt officials, building roads and bridges, dredging Havana harbor, to 'recast Cuban society.'"[9] Though the US allowed self-government from 1902, it exacted heavy concessions from the "independent" Cuban regime: reserving the right to intervene at will, veto any foreign treaty, and regulate its debt level. The 1901 Platt Amendment, which also provided for US naval bases on the island (Guantánamo Bay), constituted "a considerable abridgment of Cuban sovereignty," rendering the island "in effect an American protectorate."[10]

In a singular historical moment, the varied currents of American domestic politics and its foreign needs produced a multi-layered approach to protectorates and nation-building. Unreconciled to formal empire but compelled by circumstance and desire to attain world power status, the United States established an uneven regime of suzerainty over foreign possessions. These conflicted obligations and ideals vexed the administration of American protectorates in the decades to come.

## Protectorates and the Consent of the Governed

Theodore Roosevelt's ascent to the presidency entrenched what historian Samuel Bemis considered the "great aberration"—foreign interventionism at odds with American tradition.[11] Roosevelt declared that "chronic wrongdoing, or an impotence that results in the general loosening of the ties of civilized society" in the American sphere of influence required the US "to exercise an international police power."[12] For the next thirty years, the United States declared its right to bring transgressor states to heel.

Roosevelt's policy, pursued by both Taft and Wilson, recast the Caribbean as "an American Lake"—an arrangement similar to the Platt Amendment for Cuba, making the region subject to intervention at the pleasure of the US to secure US or foreign interests with little intent to shape the countries beyond the bare necessities of stability and solvency. That second component motivated many interventions in the first three decades of the twentieth century. "Dollar Diplomacy," backed by an itinerant Marine Corps, sought to stabilize the region through increased US investment and loan guarantees to improve the prosperity and benevolence of the subject regimes.[13]

The American commitment, though earnest, was short-term, pragmatic and of limited effect. Almost as soon as Americans relinquished direct control of their protectorates, the states slipped back into the abyss that drew Marines there initially. Observers might note the ephemeral impact US occupations have had on indigenous political cultures when contemplating the efficacy of Western-style institutions in Iraq and Afghanistan.

These short-term efforts to police and control but avoid outright annexation rooted themselves in a greater American tradition—an empathy for the weak and a call to righteousness. Was it not better to realize strategic political and economic aims alongside a greater moral purpose? In this context, Roosevelt's quiet encouragement of Panama's independence in 1903 served both functions. Colombia's government in Bogotá disfavored its isthmusian compatriots, and rejected renewed entreaties for an American canal, which would enrich the isthmus.[14] When a Panamanian revolt erupted, the US gladly accorded the new state recognition. As in Cuba, America helped to secure Panama's independence but expected favorable terms. Panama granted the US exclusive rights to build a canal, at a steep discount, and ceded full sovereignty over 550 square miles that stretched the length of the Canal.[15] The American control continued, with minor concessions under the 1955 Treaty and 1979 restoration acts; American sovereignty remained absolute in the Zone until the 1999 handover to Panama.[16]

## Mr Wilson's Conception

As President, Woodrow Wilson sought to fulfill America's promise to the world even at the apparent expense of competing American interests. This "Wilsonian Conception" represented a break with his predecessors but proved no more effective at exporting American governance. America's southern neighbor Mexico tested Wilson's resolve. Embroiled by strife after the Mexican despot Porfirio Díaz was ousted in a coup, Wilson pushed for a different paradigm for intervention: justice. Mexico's revolving door of despots threatened American interests. Though Wilson disavowed "material interests" as a debased motivation for intervention, he sent the Marines to seize Veracruz, a hub for American oil interests.[17] Of greater importance in the public presentation was the suspicion that the port was a point of entry for German arms for the Huerta regime.[18] The short occupation of the port proved ineffective, as the arms arrived nonetheless, but the Marines again dispatched their administrative mission, improving sanitation, roads and schools. Max Boot contends, "it was probably the best administration the city ever had."[19] Wilson's effort brought "regime change," delivering power to Venustiano Carranza, and the Marines left. Then Veracruz, like so many other former occupied sites, reverted to its corrupt and insanitary ways. Wilson's efforts to foster democratic institutions in the Americas succeeded only as long as American troops were on the ground.

## Isolationism, New Imperialism and Good Neighbors

During the inter-war years America's new overseas obligations required a new bureaucracy. The US Marines could "fix" problems in the short term but were not an effective substitute for a professional foreign service. The US lacked a model for administration; as the turn-of-the-century historian Robert Wiebe noted, "the paraphernalia for action simply did not exist.[20]

Roosevelt's adventurism and the Great War doubled the size of the military, and a civil service grew to exert softer power in the wake of its conquests. The State Department had increased by five times and universities established programs to prepare the new foreign service for its expanded task. The economic dominance and political capital that had accumulated after the war allowed the United States a unique position in world affairs—involved but apart. The Senate's refusal to join the League of Nations did not stop American diplomats from coordinating some of the most significant diplomatic pacts of the 1920s—to reduce armaments and renounce war. Domestic opposition and diplomatic objections kept the US out of the World Court as well. America could lead the world but would not be bound to it.[21] This isolationism, born of disgust with the utter waste and devastation of the European conflict, did not deter American forays into its Latin American sphere of influence. Harding and Coolidge continued the Roosevelt-Taft-Wilson policy of limited engagements to "re-order" unstable and dangerous regimes—to little effect. As Niall Ferguson observes, by 1939, the "only one true democracy in the entire region...was Costa Rica, where the United States had never intervened."[22]

## Interwar Imperial Hiatus: The League

Reluctant to assume a world leadership role and the messy responsibilities it entailed, the United States left administration of the dismantled German and Ottoman empires to its imperial allies. Wilson called for a system benign in purpose and international in administration, to spread "civilization" more widely. Isolationist sentiment in the US and Wilsonian internationalism found rare agreement that, despite America's new-found preeminence, direct US political control over new territories was unwelcome. Since America's withdrawal from the world stage and unrest within the defeated empires (Germany, Ottoman Turkey and Russia) precluded a truly collective contribution to administration, Wilsonian internationalists sought out other means to administer former colonies.[23] An imperfect resolution was found in the League of Nations mandate.

The Great Depression compounded America's lack of will to act internationally. Franklin Roosevelt further promulgated a policy of isolation and non-interference, declaiming the League of Nations as contrary to "fundamental American ideals." Roosevelt even withdrew America's informal protectorate over much of Latin America with the "Good Neighbor" policy that pledged non-interference and quick recognition of regimes Wilson would have deemed "illegitimate."[24] In so doing Roosevelt foreshadowed the American Cold War strategy of working with in-place regimes to affect US objectives. On withdrawing troops from Nicaragua, Roosevelt remarked that the newest despot Somoza was a "son-of-a-bitch—but he's our son-of-a-bitch."[25] America's protectorates would be administered indirectly, through a policy of tolerance and material support. Elsewhere, with both left- and right-wing opinion allayed against intervention abroad, the US chose to ignore malfeasance and unrest entirely. Far ahead of American opinion, Roosevelt perceived the Axis threat and embargoed oil exports to Japan after the Japanese expansion into French Indochina in 1941, and later sent arms to the Allies without Congressional authority.[26] Aggression and expansion soon overtook the US's own protectorates—the Philippines and Guam—which fell in quick succession to imperial Japan after the attack on Pearl Harbor.

## *The War's Inheritance: New Strategies and Responsibilities*

In the immediate aftermath of the Second World War, the United States faced two large tasks, one practical—to administer the defeated powers and their possessions—and one strategic, to foster a world system conducive to peace and prosperity. Since the elite and later popular consensus held that America's isolationism, the state system, and unresolved grievances contributed to the war's outbreak and scale, the post-war order required American leadership to guide the world toward a cooperative and collective framework.[27] Roosevelt had hoped to render the defeated Axis empires full-fledged members of this new framework. Roosevelt and Truman's "paraphernalia for action"—the World Bank, the IMF, the United Nations and later the Marshall Plan and NATO—suggested an inspired intent, collective, interventionist, constructive. Although the institutional mechanics assured American dominance, the decision to create and participate in these institutions both expanded and constrained the expression of American power. While the scope of these institutions expanded America's global influence, the mechanics of participation and the responsibilities of leadership imposed limits on American initiatives.

As a practical matter, the US island-hopping war strategy produced a slew of dependencies on the Pacific Rim including Japan, half of Korea, and island chains between Alaska and New Guinea. In Europe, Germany and Italy required large occupation forces to rebuild their shattered economies and infrastructure. These new possessions, like the Philippines before, posed the same problem—how to defend and administer distant and "foreign" places.[28] As after the Spanish-American war, post-1945 planners chose the "all of the above" option in devising the terms of administration.

In occupied Japan and Germany, military officials harnessed indigenous institutions (in Japan, the Emperor and the *Zaibatzu;* in Germany, the corporate leaders) to restore normality, leading to disengagement. In about five years, US officials had almost no role in the public life of the defeated powers. That both had possessed democratic institutions in living memory was a benefit. In less developed but geographically large possessions, the US avoided direct occupation and instead relied on antebellum or wartime institutions to assure stability. In established areas of American influence, the Pacific and Latin America, planners preferred a more direct role. Senator Vandenberg, a Republican ex-isolationist and Senate shepherd of the UN Charter, won assurances that the Monroe Doctrine and "full control of most of the Pacific bases taken from the Japs" would be respected.[29]

Influenced by George F. Kennan to accept that "a defeat for democracy anywhere is not a defeat for democracy everywhere," Truman committed the nation to the defense of free peoples everywhere, in theory, but engaged communist initiatives in practice where he could be successful—and was in Greece, Italy and France among others. The pragmatic quality of the Truman-Acheson policy is seen in the Administration's willingness to "do business" with illiberal but non-communist regimes to blunt the spread of communism. These regimes ringed the Soviet sphere and, aided by American military, clandestine and civilian support, acted as a barrier to further expansion.[30] Where national liberation movements were advanced, Washington propped up the remains of European colonialism. Initial Cold War policy would make use of whatever institutions or means were available as long as the US involvement remained indirect and limited and kept the Soviets at bay.[31]

Just as American strategic needs dictated US policy in Guam, Oceania and the Pacific also fell under American administration. Officially the islands, administered by the US as a United Nations trusteeship, but classed as a "strategic trust," fell under the purview of the Security Council. US veto power there ensured that US "control of the islands was, for all practical purposes, absolute."[32] In the Pacific, at least, the guise of internationalism offered America a preferred format for administration. Although the US Navy lobby failed to deliver direct military control through Congress, military considerations remained paramount. Islanders were evacuated and resettled to make way for atomic testing or to enable the US's self-defined mission to "promote the development of the inhabitants of the trust territory toward self-government or independence ... [in accord with] the freely expressed wishes of the peoples concerned."[33]

In East Asia, American policy accepted illiberal governance in South Korea under Syngman Rhee and in Taiwan under Chiang Kai-shek. Chiang's government made little effort to reflect liberal democratic traditions but provided a vital platform for US operations in Korea and, at various times, against the Mainland. On the international stage, Truman and his successors through Nixon refused to recognize Red China, taking care to veto its UN membership whenever the matter arose.[34] Nations within the United States' orbit acquired the economic, military, and diplomatic benefits of the American relationship without having to uphold its political ideals. This broad arrangement seen in Indonesia, South Korea, the Philippines, Thailand, and elsewhere in Asia created wards more than allies, since the United States provided diplomatic cover and assurances associated with SEATO which carried the promise of assistance in event of war, without exacting a political price from the ruling classes. These wards, or "protectorates" in the broadest sense, reflecting market-authoritarian systems of government, often proved capable of suppressing communist sentiment within their borders.

The growing American security guarantee to "bulwark" states and use of international institutions under US influence increased the range of states that could be seen as protectorates but limited the duties of the American minders. The competing strains of American overseas commitments proceeded in an uneasy ad-hockery, one alongside the next—fashioned both by public will and geopolitical circumstance.

## From Expediency to Transformation

In the decolonizing world, pressed to offer an alternative to communism, Washington experimented with several templates—theories of modernization—designed to preserve US pre-eminence while guiding non-communist nationalist leaders from their colonial relationships to independence. Harvard Professor Walt Rostow, an adviser to Eisenhower, Kennedy and Johnson, advanced perhaps the most prominent theory called the "Stages of Growth: A Non-Communist Manifesto." Proceeding from the notion that poverty and deprivation fuelled radicalization, he provided a guide to economic development identifying five stages of growth ranging from primitive society to modern metropolitan economy. One flawed assumption was key to its acceptance at the time, and later its dysfunction; Rostow's America-centrism assumed that all societies sought to become, and could be, like modern day America. He assumed the universal applicability of American values and priorities—and further assumed that with growth and material prosperity, communism would be kept in check. Rostow's theory provided a framework for US economic and political development efforts in Southeast Asia in which efforts were made to impose, from the top, a transformation that in Vietnam's case sought fundamental changes in the nation's political and economic culture. Its universalism, benevolence, and strategic promise made developmentalism, or modernization, palatable to both planners and the US public. Importantly, it linked American idealism with strategic interest in a way that seemed to justify American involvement and protection in transitioning environments.

## Back to the Future: Containment, Cooperation, Wilsonianism

After Vietnam, the United States again approached the matter of protectorates indirectly, albeit in quite different ways at different times. The Nixon Doctrine in 1969 proclaimed, "America should fight only when its national interests were at stake; imperiled regimes looking for US sponsorship would henceforth have to do the dirty work themselves."[35] Nixon defined national interest narrowly, and shunned intervention, inverting Kennedy's "bear any burden" paradigm. America might pay the bills, but it would not clean up the mess. Augusto Pinochet's 1973 coup d'état in Chile and continued US backing for Israel and South Africa illustrated a renewed commitment to proxies.

Carter's declaration that "an inordinate fear of communism" no longer dictated US policy, in a certain sense, expanded on Nixon's policy. But the new caveat threatened to cut off US support for its allies unless they restructured in accord with a model reflecting American values. Carter narrowed America's protective sphere to those who observe "internationally recognized human rights."[36] Nascent liberal regimes fell to communist expansionism as Carter played by the very rules—non-interventionism and non-interference—that his Soviet rivals discarded under the Brezhnev doctrine. His late conversion to anti-communism after Afghanistan fell under Soviet influence came too late to prevent his defeat. American will, expressed at the ballot box, agreed with Carter's sentiments but rejected his methods.

## Reagan

Following a consistent pattern, Ronald Reagan's approach to foreign policy borrowed some elements from previous administrations but overturned others to carve out a new doctrine. The Reagan Doctrine adopted Carter's emphasis on human rights and freedom as paramount objectives but rejected his suggestion that illiberal anti-communist regimes were the moral equivalent of their communist counterparts. Utilizing the American story with its themes of opportunity and equality as a strategic instrument, Reagan gave rhetorical support in his first term to John Foster Dulles' "rollback" policy.[37] Unlike Nixon whose China and detente policies signaled his acceptance of communist spheres of influence, Reagan discarded the preservationist model in favor of an expanded Western sphere. Both the United States and its allies underwrote this anti-communist push in rhetoric and dollars. The Contras in Nicaragua and the Mujahedeen in Afghanistan stood in for American Marines and Radio Free Europe exerted pressure on Eastern Bloc regimes, where Carter had used the UN.[38] Reagan's few direct interventions—Libya, Beirut, Grenada—were extremely limited by either design or disaster. He preferred indirect and ad hoc, events-driven opportunities to realize his goals. Bound to the conflicted American tradition, Reagan offered no particular innovation on "protectorates." Within the described framework, policy remained pragmatic and event-driven; he pushed for freedom but tolerated repression, fought limited engagements without clear resolution, and used institutions to exert indirect control over the American sphere.

## The Post-Cold War Era

As political and economic turmoil diminished the Soviet Union, observers advanced two scenarios for a post-Cold War world; one group anticipated a multilateral world, and another believed that power would be concentrated in the hands of one superpower, the United States. The division reflected the views of analysts about the nature of American power and liberal internationalism and their hopes for the future as much as it reflected any deeper understanding of global evolution circa 1989. Paul Kennedy's *The Rise and Fall of Great Powers* boldly predicted that in defeating its communist adversary, the United States had weakened its own international position through economic profligacy and would experience "relative decline" as its former allies rose to challenge its predominance.[39] Kennedy's counterintuitive assertion that America's success marked its apogee prompted a flurry of responses from a more optimistic cohort. Francis Fukuyama suggested that America's victory was much larger than just a strategic and political victory for the anti-communist bloc, it was an affirmation of the idea of the West—and therefore much more powerful than economic or military power.[40] These two theses carried divergent implications as the emerging world order was either predisposed to American power (Fukuyama) or a direct challenge to its continuance (Kennedy).

Policymakers sympathetic to Fukuyama's view embraced the traditional doctrine of American Exceptionalism—that the US experience was incomparable with and implicitly superior to that of previous great powers—to discount Kennedy's prophesy of impending decline. This took two forms, one derived from the Wilsonian Conception of obligation to better the world (neoliberalism) and another (neoconservatism) that contended that maintenance of American power required intervention to defend American values and interests.

The neoliberal Joseph Nye propagated his own notion of soft power—that American might was found not in missiles but in cultural power and prestige accumulated through the wealth and moral standing that enabled the defeat of the Soviet Union. American interests, in Nye's conception, could be furthered through flexing this muscle subtly against allies and enemies alike. The American way of life had universal appeal that could be translated into diplomatic pressure and guide other nations by example and through multilateral institutions. Brute force was largely unnecessary and often counterproductive since the Cold War result had imbued the American brand with political capital that could be spent liberally without alienating other states.[41] In contrast, neoconservatives assumed a realist framework that American hard power should be used to affect American interests when possible but, like their neoliberal counterparts, broadened the definition of American interests to include the propagation of American values. Charles Krauthammer, the neoconservative who coined the term "unipolar world," rejected Nye's approach as passive and ineffective. Krauthammer argued that by negotiating as equals with lesser powers, America's power was reduced to "moral suasion, and farce. Why then this obsession with conventions, protocols, legalisms? Their obvious net effect is to temper American power."[42] The divide between neoliberal and neoconservative elements was not over whether American power should be used to affect American values but over how to do so.

The first occupant of the White House in this unipolar world, George H.W. Bush, had little sympathy for either the neoliberal or neoconservative factions, and little belief in the counter-intuitive thesis of Paul Kennedy and the declinists. Instead Bush perceived himself as the manager of what he viewed to be a "New World Order." As George H.W. Bush guided communism through a carefully engineered demise, America's network of alliances and protectorates lost its purpose and, despite Mr Bush's contention, was replaced by drift.

American foreign policy without a clear adversary seemed uninspired and unfocused and, most important, failed to analyze and grasp the rise of China which would fundamentally alter the global commons within the decade.[43] As Cold War antagonism subsided states left the US and Soviet spheres—a tumultuous process planners were unprepared institutionally or strategically to address. Illiberal US allies grew into vibrant democracies (for example Taiwan, Korea, the Philippines and Chile) that had less need for American protection—a point dramatically underscored by the US withdrawal from Subic Bay in 1991.

In Panama, Bush faced his first test amidst the post-Cold War chaos. Not unlike his Republican forebear Teddy Roosevelt, Bush defined US objectives in terms of damage control and spheres of influence. Bush sent 26,000 American troops to oust the Panamanian dictator Manuel Noriega, "to safeguard the lives of Americans, to defend democracy in Panama, to combat drug trafficking, and to protect the integrity of the Panama Canal treaty."[44] Operation Just Cause owed more to the Roosevelt Corollary than to the Wilsonian Conception that divided neoliberals and neoconservatives. Yet Bush's intervention did not follow the pattern of Roosevelt or Wilson in one key respect: the situation reverted to the ante bellum status quo once Noriega was displaced and US interests in the Canal Zone were again secure. There was little effort to remake Panama into a "little America" once the Bush administration was satisfied that Panama no longer posed a threat to US interests and Hemispheric order.

Outside of the Western Hemisphere, however, Bush pursued a different strategy in critical situations, namely US-led multilateralism. Saddam Hussein directed a regime that violated international conventions and threatened critical US economic interests—a secure oil supply in the Middle East. Unlike tiny Panama, Iraq possessed the much-touted "fourth largest army in the world" and an arsenal of Cold War weapons. Moreover, Saddam Hussein aroused concern across the region and the globe that the world's economic lifeblood might be constricted and the sovereignty of nations might be imperiled by the precedent of the occupation of Kuwait. When threats and diplomatic overtures failed to move Saddam, Bush assembled a forty-member "Coalition of the Willing." The coalition of autocracies and democracies had a single purpose, to restore the Emir of Kuwait and "contain" Hussein's military adventurism. Kuwait, Saudi Arabia and the Gulf States that supplied the West's oil fell under US protection by default. After the 1991 war, the strategically important Gulf States hosted US bases to prevent aggression in the region and their illiberal regimes were tolerated as points of stability.

Bush's New World Order transformed the United States, momentarily, into a global policeman tasked with preventing lawbreaking and punishing the transgressors of international norms, particularly those norms that affected US security or economic power. In the early 1990s, the Bush Administration practiced a kind of high-level "damage control"; Washington saw off America's Cold War adversaries without much fanfare and checked the rise of rogue states. As Les Gelb noted, "Bush's team performed better in putting the old world's problems to bed than in getting ahead of the new ones."[45] Those new ones were every bit as much a legacy of the Cold War as the nuclear stockpiles in Eastern Europe. Failed states, as they came to be called, were humanitarian disasters and too often propagators of regional wars containing few economic or strategic assets of interest to the US or its allies. But that did not mean they couldn't impose real costs on Washington.

In Somalia, Bush dithered as the African nation starved to death under the thumb of criminal gangs. Public pressure came to bear on Bush who, in 1992, faced an election wrapped in a recession. After the United Nations agreed to support a Somali relief mission, Bush (by then defeated by Clinton) ordered a contingent of US troops to the Horn of Africa. Bush framed the mission in terms of restoring order—only. "The outlaw elements in Somalia must understand this is serious business," the US would commit a limited commitment of US forces who "will not stay one day longer than is absolutely necessary."[46] Bush said the troops would be removed before his successor took office six weeks later. Of interest to us is that Bush's reluctance to accept yet another category of protectorate proved prescient.

Bill Clinton's approach to failed states as new protectorates was more aggressive; he expanded the scope of US efforts in Somalia despite the UN's failure to assume American responsibilities there. Clinton, largely freed from the responsibilities of managing the Cold War's twilight, embraced a cooperative approach to protectorates, apparently willing to extend their duration and scope at least in Somalia. His Secretary of State Madeleine Albright declared the new US mission "an unprecedented enterprise aimed at nothing less than the restoration of an entire country as a proud, functioning and viable member of the community of nations."[47] Rostow's ghost hovered unhappily over the doomed US effort in one of the world's most backward countries.

Amitai Etzioni entitled his 2008 book *Security First* to describe the nation-building process the US had come to embrace. After months of negotiations and small firefights with Somali warlords, security remained elusive and the US goal to feed and stabilize Somalia beyond reach. Envisioned as a law and order operation, the disastrous "Black Hawk Down" incident precipitated a US withdrawal cutting short what would have been an extended effort to pacify and rebuild the country. Two years later turmoil in an even smaller and more obscure African country, Rwanda, demonstrated how deeply the imagery of the stranded and eventually mutilated troops in the Mogadishu incident had cut the American public. Fear of additional casualties in an attempt to stop war in the center of Africa, when added to the absence of an exit strategy, made intervention politically impossible. Even as Clinton received reports that the fighting had devolved to a "genocide," neither he nor his European counterparts chose to act.

Subsequently he sought to accelerate Bush's "New World Order" of peaceful, democratic, and prosperous states through action. In support of this, he sent Marines to Haiti in 1994 in "Operation Uphold Democracy." In Haiti, US planners thought they could establish a lasting "good," and expanded the scope of the intervention and length of the operation. Under international auspices, "the intervention included organizing a force of 1,200 people from 20 countries to monitor Haiti's police and oversee the transition of a professional law enforcement organization. The effort saved lives, calmed would be rioters, helped to clean prisons, painted police stations, and provided relief for storm victims."[48] After the US forces pulled out and were replaced by UN peacekeepers, Haiti, in little time, reverted to its familiar chaotic, impoverished condition. Ten years later it was classified by Freedom House as "unfree" and by Transparency International as the third most corrupt country in the world ahead of two other American protectorates, Somalia and Iraq.[49]

Following Somalia and Haiti, the Clinton administration faced a dilemma—it could not act with the expectation of decisive results, nor could it remain a bystander without the opprobrium of history. A potential way forward from this conundrum seemed to emerge as the Bosnian war deepened. Instead of American soldiers risking their lives for ill-defined objectives, technology and regional allies could stand in with limited consequences for American power and prestige. Scholar Andrew Bacevich argues that through "gunboats and gurkhas" American policymakers remained at the helm but distant from the outcomes on the ground.[50] Instead of using indigenous troops armed with US weapons to ensure communism's defeat, foreign non-American troops backed with American firepower (missiles and aircraft) could police humanitarian crisis zones at the behest of American planners. Clinton funneled $95 million to the European Rapid Reaction force in June 1995 to circumvent the GOP controlled Congress which refused to back American military aid to end the war in Bosnia.[51] After Bosnian Serb atrocities gave Clinton more public backing for intervention, US-backed Croat "gurkhas" turned the tide on the Serb offensive and "gunboats" in the form of NATO-led airstrikes forced the combatants to the negotiating table.[52] The Dayton Accords were drafted in the vortex of this new US strategy which combined limited culpability but near omnipotence in war. Thus the US ended the war, but could it keep the peace?

To enforce the Dayton Accords 20,000 Americans (of a total of 60,000 multinational troops) occupied Bosnia.[53] These peacekeepers fell under a complicated command structure. Their mission was sanctioned by the UN but they operated under NATO commanders. They were slowly drawn down but never withdrawn. As of 2011, a few thousand multinational troops remain in Bosnia, 200 of whom are American.[54] Nearly a decade and a half later, US and international troops patrol Bosnia as a heavily armed and mechanized police force akin to the long-term US Marine contingents across the Caribbean eighty years earlier, whose exit eventually brought the return to antebellum politics and instability.

To avert this outcome in the Balkans, Clinton chose another path—indefinite occupation. American troops in cooperation with international forces established a paradigm that limits US protectorate burdens. US military intervention halted the Bosnian war but the US/international force mechanism remains sixteen years later in a state that relies heavily on foreign aid and security guarantees. America subsequently accepted another Balkan state as a protectorate, Kosovo, in 1999. The air war against Serbia spared America the burden of "boots on the ground" during the conflict while ensuring an indefinite commitment of "boots" to the region. In 2006, the Brookings Institution scholar Michael O'Hanlon suggested the US copy this approach of "controlled realignment of population groups in order to minimize communal violence and set the stage for a stable political settlement."[55] O'Hanlon's assumption is twofold: either a political settlement is possible, something the Yugoslav dictator Tito failed to achieve, or the US presence is sustainable or desirable. Thus the great unanswered question of American protectorates in the Balkans, Iraq, and Afghanistan is under what conditions, if any, can the US leave?

Critics of Clinton's Balkan policy concurred with Buchanan's assessment of the post-Gulf War arrangement, namely that open-ended commitments were unsustainable and undesirable. After the failures in Somalia and Haiti, prominent critics in the Republican Party, then in control of both houses of Congress, rejected Clinton's ameliorist approach. Appropriately Clinton likened his detractors to Republican isolationists after the First World War, casting himself in the role of Wilson:

As the Cold War gives way to the global village, our leadership is needed more than ever because problems that start beyond our borders can quickly become problems within them. We're all vulnerable to the organized forces of intolerance and destruction, terrorism, ethnic, religious and regional rivalries, the spread of organized crime and weapons of mass destruction and drug trafficking. Just as surely as fascism and communism, these forces also threaten freedom and democracy, peace and prosperity. And they too demand American leadership.[56]

To this a GOP critic, Tom Delay, replied that Clinton's "feel-good" foreign policy had no direction and, most important, no exit strategy.[57] Without these requisite conditions, GOP leaders balked at taking on new commitments and roundly condemned the Kosovo war as needless, further underscoring the absence of agreement on what America's role, if any, should be in such situations.

Clinton's liberal internationalism, cooperative and neoliberal in tone, faced fierce criticism on the right. In addition to the isolationist sentiments of Buchanan and Delay, the neoconservatives, dormant throughout much of the early Clinton years, re-emerged to assert that Clinton's limited approach did not go far enough. In his essay "Kosovo and the Republican Future" Robert Kagan also scolded Republicans for offering few alternatives and an "abdication of leadership."[58] In the end, with the help of other neoconservatives like Senator John McCain, Clinton was able to defeat efforts in Congress to scuttle his interventions in the Balkans. In a deep irony, one of the most prominent critics of "nation-building" in the Clinton years was Governor George W. Bush, who said in one of the 2000 Presidential debates, "I think what we need to do is convince people who live in the lands they live in to build the nations. Maybe I'm missing something here. I mean, we're going to have kind of a nation-building core from America? Absolutely not. Our military is meant to fight and win wars. That's what it's meant to do. And when it gets overextended, morale drops" (Bush, 2000 Presidential Debate Transcript). After 9/11, the most prominent nation-builders and advocates of transformation had President Bush's ear in policy towards Iraq and Afghanistan, and now occupied top spots in the Departments of State and Defense.

## Delegating Administration by Degrees: Afghanistan and Iraq

Over the past century, US planners have offered competing visions of American protectorates but have yet to offer a single coherent means to administer these possessions. Most recently, planners have opted for a novel but unproven approach: delegation. Not unlike the indirect influence exerted through indigenous, but allied, leaders like Rhee or Pinochet, delegation relies on allied leaders, American or international institutions to directly administer protectorates whose security is guaranteed by the US. At the strategic level, the US has entered into a series of agreements with international actors as junior partners subject to a collective will. US troops may be under American command in the Balkans but the larger administrative objectives are set by KFOR and the UN.

Both Afghanistan and Iraq can be seen, in broad terms, as contemporary protectorates. Both are being administered by governments supported by Washington and both owe their current status to US arms and financial support. Of course they are quite different in practical terms, but US policy towards these two nations offers particular insight into Washington's view of protectorates. Though the wars in both Afghanistan and Iraq are wars of choice, the reason for US involvement is found in fear rather than advantage. America was attacked on September 11th and resolved to eliminate the base from which the attack was launched. Now, eight years later, the war grinds on, slowly transforming to a nation-building effort with no end in sight. In this sense Afghanistan is an accidental protectorate which offers no commercial, geopolitical or strategic advantage.

Is Iraq a protectorate? After it invaded in 2003, administered the country directly for over a year, and then installed the present regime, the role of the US remains pivotal. Iraq is indeed a protectorate and will remain so until the US military departs in 2011 or later. From that point on, neither the Iraqis nor Washington is likely to seek a close continuing relationship. The same holds true for Afghanistan. When US troops have withdrawn, follow-on relations will depend on circumstances. But a "protectorate," in the sense we use the word, is unlikely. Both Iraq and Afghanistan, for different reasons, are misbegotten efforts. In neither case will the US depart leaving behind a legacy of democratic pluralism. In neither case will the American people be able to embrace the values and principles informing these governments. Both are costly examples of ill-conceived policy in which objectives are unclear, resources are inadequate and the technology of nation-building—which became the objective in both places—is not understood.

More broadly, American protectorates were initially administered by the "blunt instrument" of the US Marine Corps with apparent success in improving sanitation, education, and governance in some states. This proved illusory as by 1939, none of these states resembled a progressive democracy along US lines. Rostow's "take-off" theory met even less success in Vietnam as instability and war erased any gains his development agenda had made. Latterly, Haiti and Somalia are generally agreed to be failed states whose situation in the case of Somalia threatens US national security now more than before. In the Balkans, the US commitment has no apparent end-date, with only wishful thinking supporting the notion that Western institutions and imposed stability will survive the withdrawal of international forces.

Proponents of nation-building point to three general success stories in post-War Japan and Germany and the Philippines.[59] As discussed earlier, Japan's and Germany's indigenous institutions were harnessed in a highly-charged Cold War environment to quickly place economically and politically mature nations back on a steady footing.[60] For the Philippines, granted independence in 1946, its subsequent history represents neither a vindication for the half-century US occupation nor a failure—as the new state has vacillated between benign despotism and imperfect democracy. These three examples suggest that long-term and deeper commitments in resources and manpower yield more productive results. As an anti-imperial global force, the US has proved unwilling to support indefinite operations once circumstances sour. Public will, when met by difficult circumstances, wilts especially when the purpose and means of administering a US protectorate are confused, as they so often are.

The United States continues to seek a workable equilibrium in its global role. The pursuit of an elusive balance has produced a variety of interrelated and competing strains of American foreign policy and overseas administration, from Teddy Roosevelt's robust benevolent imperialism to the Wilsonian Conception, to Rostow's "stages of growth," to illiberal proxy rule. Circumstances and the public have dictated that these concepts live side-by-side. This fundamental incoherence, reflecting a reluctance to accept the position of empire and lack of successful models, has led American planners to reinvent foreign protectorate administration at each new interval, without success.

# 8

# PEACE OPERATIONS
# AND MODERN PROTECTORATES

## THE LOGIC OF SUCCESSFUL FAILURE

*Wolfgang Seibel* [1]

"We have these conflicts where no one really wants to get involved, powerful countries with means will not touch it with a barge pole, they will support weak, ineffectual initiatives by others, sometimes by a sub-regional or regional organization, to create the impression of action."

Kofi Annan, UN Secretary-General 1995–2007, quoted in the *New York Times*, 21 March 2008.

This chapter addresses the political coping patterns that result from unresolvable dilemmas at the heart of the United Nations' peacebuilding efforts. These dilemmas are the product of the UN's double character as a multilateral institution and an international bureaucracy. While much of the UN's deficiencies—not exclusively but particularly in the field of peacebuilding—have been connected to the organization's bureaucratic character, neither the interplay of multilateralism and the UN core organization nor the secretariat's performance in terms of learning and adaptation since the mid-1990s has attracted much scholarly attention.[2] The failure of the United Nations in Rwanda (1994) and Srebrenica (1995), where genocide and mass murder were committed under the very eyes of UN troops, triggered a learning cycle within the secretariat resulting in intensified doctrine building and improved governance of peacebuilding missions. The adoption of the R2P principle by the General Assembly in 2005 and the Integrated Mission Task Force scheme developed by the UN Department of Peacekeeping Operations were key elements of conceptual improvements during the first decade of the new millennium.

The progress was, however, crippled by a changing geopolitical environment. The notion of the UN as proactively identifying risks of massive human rights violations and mobilizing the international community for the protection of people whose governments are unable or unwilling to protect their own citizens became elusive when, after the turn of the millennium, Russia and China, two non-democratic powers among the five veto-carrying members of the UN Security Council (re-)emerged as determined international actors. While the UN as an international bureaucracy turned out to be adaptive and prone to learn, pivotal stakeholders in the UNSC became unwilling to implement the consequences.

This poses an unresolvable problem, especially for democratic UN member states that endorse the humanitarian values on which principles like R2P as a guideline for UN peace operations are based. On the one hand, they cannot bluntly revoke their commitment to the international community's responsibility to protect those whose basic human rights are at risk or even threatened by their own government. On the other hand, taking the commitment seriously would imply either constant frustration or open conflict within the Security Council. This chapter argues that what emerges from this is political coping in the form of giving official support to UN peace operations while practically undermining their ultimate peacebuilding effectiveness. The conceptual framework is a principal-agent model based on the assumption that, unlike what conventional theorizing suggests, principals of UN peace operations are interested both in failure and in ignorance about failure. Successful coping thus entails symbolic action creating and obscuring failure at the same time.

## UN Peace Operations as Modern Protectorates

As mentioned in the introduction to this volume, UN peace operations have undergone fundamental changes after the end of the Cold War. In the era of US and Soviet Union dominance, classic peacekeeping was the dominant pattern. It was based on the surveillance of peace agreements between conflicting parties, if necessary with military support through lightly armed troops, the typical "blue helmet" forces called after the color of their headgear. Traditional peace operations of this sort necessitated the consent of the conflicting parties. They were based on UN non-partisanship. The use of force was limited normally to self-protection of the deployed troops. In the insider jargon, these elements were ironically called the *Holy Trinity of Peacekeeping*.

This pattern changed from the early 1990s when the frequency of UN peace operations increased sharply while the Holy Trinity of Peacekeeping was gradually abandoned. One reason was the UN response to humanitarian disasters in the aftermaths of failing states and the dissolution of the state monopoly on the legitimate use of force. UN operations responding to situations characterized not only by the escalation of violence but also by the collapse of domestic governmental and administrative structures became known as "multidimensional," "integrated" or just "complex" peace operations.[3] Eight out of sixteen peace operations in 2008 fell into this category. Those sixteen UN missions represented a machinery of 110,000 people, the vast majority of whom, 90,000, were military troops.

Complex UN peace operations create a conglomerate of international interim administration resulting in the international performance of tasks of national government and public administration. The UN is thus often in charge of wholesale administrative structures ranging from rule-of-law institutions to

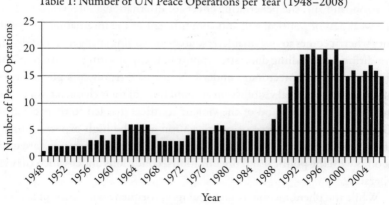

Table 1: Number of UN Peace Operations per Year (1948–2008)

Source: UN Department of Peacekeeping Operations, http://www.un.org/Depts/dpkolist/list.pdf, 2008, last access on March 19, 2009. Graph: own.

technical infrastructure, to de facto running of a modern type of protectorate. However, while the term *protectorate* has a negative connotation dating back to the League of Nations era—let alone its usage under the Nazi dictatorship[4]—there is good reason to acknowledge the merits of the modern protectorates erected under UN auspices. The victims of Rwanda and the Srebrenica genocide had been hoping for UN protection which the international community was not able or not willing to supply. The UN missions to Cambodia (UNTAC, 1992–93), Kosovo (UNMIK, since 1999), East Timor (UNTAET, 1999–2002), or Liberia (UNMIL, since 2003), by contrast, made a decisive contribution to peace and political stability and, presumably, saved many lives. Modern protectorates also exist outside the UN system. Prominent examples are the international administration of BiH, the American-led occupation of Iraq, and the international regime in Afghanistan where a UN mission does exist but only as a peripheral institution relative to the apparatuses of the International Security Assistance Force (ISAF) and the regional military administration it maintains in the form of so-called Provincial Reconstruction Teams or PRTs (since 2001).

However, modern protectorates under the auspices of UN peace operations face a series of fundamental contradictions and dilemmas. These relate to (i) the ideals of self-government and democracy versus the reality of foreign imposition of institutional settings and political will, (ii) the requirement of steadily functioning and enduring governmental institutions and public administration versus the more or less improvised erection of the transnational organizational structures with an *a priori* transitional character and a limited time horizon, and (iii) the penetrating effects of international intervention versus the weakness of political will and commitment of the international community when it comes to sustainable, resource-consuming engagement under the condition of dwindling domestic support in the sponsoring countries. Nonetheless, modern protectorates under UN mandate represent a phenomenon of prominent political visibility on account both of their character as a tool of international politics and of the violent conflicts that led to their creation. Consequently, the degree of politicization and the high expectations for effective performance connected to complex UN peace operations are quite at odds with the political and organizational conditions under which they are operating.

While the phenomenon as such and its consequences in terms of low performance and political hypocrisy are well known, the way UN member-states and their governments are coping with the multiple dilemmas described above has not attracted much scholarly attention so far. This chapter addresses the issue by tying together the geopolitical conditions of the emergence of UN peace operations in the form of modern protectorates with the perspectives of successful political coping with inevitable failure. This is based on the premise that success and failure of UN peace operations are above all a political issue in the sense that improvement of field level performance cannot compensate for lack of commitment of UN member states officially sponsoring a mission. The degree of commitment, however, is dependent on the very geopolitical factors that drove the emergence of the new protectorates in the first place.

Several theoretical approaches are helpful when it comes to the explanation of the emergence of the new protectorates under UN auspices after the end of the Cold War. From a liberal perspective,[5] the end of the Cold War is conceived as a fundamental reinforcement of Western democratic values, including human rights, as laid down in the UN Charter of 1945 in the first place as well as in the Convention on the Prevention and Punishment of the Crime of a Genocide (Genocide Convention), adopted by the UN General Assembly in 1948, in the Declaration of Human Rights, also adopted by the General Assembly in 1948, and in the Principle of a Responsibility to Protect, adopted by the General Assembly in 2005. UN involvement in the reconstruction of both failed states and civil society structures may then be interpreted as connected to the diffusion of democratic values and human rights.

From a neorealist perspective, by contrast, the emergence of modern protectorates as an integral part of UN peace operations may be interpreted as a response to declining hegemonic stability. This interpretation is particularly plausible when connected to the precursor of UN international interim administration which is the mandate system of the League of Nations between 1920 and 1939. League of Nations mandates represented international interim administrations in the form of protectorates erected as the transitional governments of former German colonies, detached territories of the German Reich, and of former territories of the bygone Ottoman Empire. Although the administration of those territories was de facto assumed by individual imperial states, France and Britain in particular, the legal status of an international administration was an important mechanism of legitimization in the post-World War I era since, by then, colonial administration had become less acceptable.[6] However, what the League of Nations mandates created were protectorates that compensated for the loss of hegemonic stability in the periphery previously supplied by the Great Powers vanquished in the war. Given the remarkable surge of complex UN peace operations after the end of the Cold War, modern protectorates under UN auspices may be seen as in the very same tradition. The collapse of a bipolar hegemonic order since 1989 created zones of instability in the periphery of the former Soviet Union and the communist states—with the Balkans as the most prominent example—which again made international transitional administration a politically acceptable mechanism of re-stabilization.

The liberal and the neorealist schools of thought imply different types of conclusion, though. In the liberal perspective, the end of the Cold War led to a convergence of the principles laid down in the UN Charter, the Declaration of Human Rights, and the Genocide Convention, on the one hand, and the values of Western democracy on the other hand, in a way that translated these values into UN operational activity, including decision-making at the UNSC. This seems to be corroborated by the increasing activity of the UN in the field of peace operations and the international administrations attached to those activities. In the realist perspective, by contrast, modern protectorates under UN auspices are a consequence of geopolitical change and as such remain geopolitically vulnerable, just as the League of Nations mandate system was vulnerable to the geopolitical frictions of the era.

### The Bureaucratic and the Political Logic of Modern Protectorates Under UN Auspices

Both the liberal and the neorealist perspective on modern protectorates under UN auspices are supported by empirical evidence which, however, affects different segments of the UN as an institutional hybrid. The UN is both a multilateral institution and an international bureaucracy. While the neorealist perspective is applicable to the UN as a multilateral institution, the liberal perspective makes sense when applied to the UN as an international bureaucracy.[7] As an international bureaucracy, the UN in the post-Cold War era turned out to be capable of learning and susceptible to new international norms. As a multilateral institution, however, the UN makes the implementation of norms and principles dependent on the diverging interests in the General Assembly and the Security Council. The bureaucratic and the political logics of modern protectorates under UN auspices are thus potentially divergent.

The apparatus of the United Nations in its capacity as an international bureaucracy—just as in any other huge administrative body—is both the locus of structural inertia and a forum of organizational learning and development of organizational doctrines, standard operational procedures and routines.

Table 2: UN Peace Operations Bureaucracy and its Environment(s)"

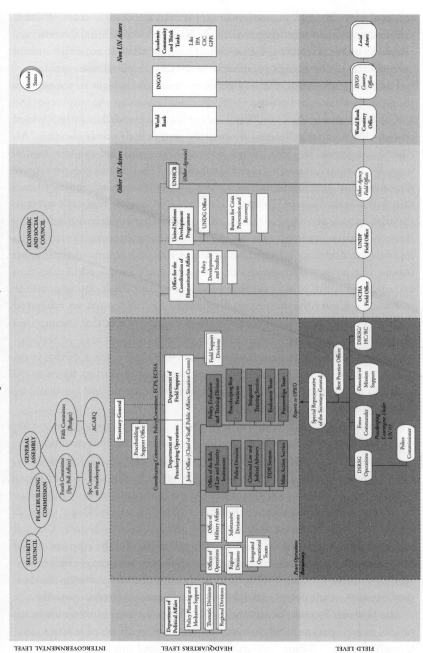

Source: Benner *et al.* 2008, p. 29.

It is here that the implementation of UNSC mandates takes place. There is good sense in acknowledging that the UN as an international bureaucracy proved to be apt at learning and capable of strategic adaptation, which indeed corroborates the optimistic perspective of the liberal school of thought.

From the early 1990s, the UN peace doctrine was subject to continuous progress. The enhanced prospects of peacebuilding under the auspices of the UN after the end of the Cold War were explicitly addressed in a paper issued by the UN Secretary-General Boutros Boutros-Ghali under the title "An Agenda for Peace" in 1992.[9] What Boutros-Ghali outlined as a new framework for the pursuit of the crucial goals of the UN Charter was preventive diplomacy and peacebuilding measures including, if necessary, the use of military force on the basis of Chapter VII of the UN Charter. Tragically enough, the first spectacular application of this new doctrine, pressed hard for by Boutros-Ghali himself, became the 1992 humanitarian intervention in Somalia with the decisive participation of US military forces. According to an insider narrative,[10] the Somalia fiasco made the Clinton administration extremely reluctant to take decisive measures against the looming genocide in Rwanda. Under the wary eyes of withdrawing UN troops, an estimated 800,000 people were slaughtered. Another tragic incident that traumatized the entire UN system was the overrunning of the UN "safe area" of Srebrenica by Serb and Bosnian Serb troops in July 1995. Again, the UN troops on the ground proved incapable of protecting the local population. Some 8,000 boys and men, almost exclusively Muslims, were deported and murdered by the Serbian military and militias.

The traumas encoded "Rwanda" and "Srebrenica" triggered a re-evaluation of the shape and conditions of UN peace operations. These efforts resulted in the report of the former Under-Secretary-General of the UN, Lakhdar Brahimi, known accordingly as the "Brahimi Report," which in the recent history of the UN went down as a key document of the latest generation of UN peace operations.[11] Based on the ideas of Boutros-Ghali's "Agenda for Peace" of 1992, the Brahimi Report advocated clear, credible and realistic UN Security Council mandates and the crafting of basic rules and techniques for the erection of civil transitional administration, including the overall improvement of crucial managerial functions in order to meet the requirements of coordination in the ramified network of the complex machinery that shapes UN peace operations.

The Brahimi Report focused primarily on the internal governance issues of UN peace operations while bypassing a crucial problem of international law which is the relationship between international intervention and state sovereignty. This is a particularly pressing issue when it comes to the use of force on the basis of Chapter VII of the UN Charter and the ensuing erection of a civil transitional administration assuming tasks that, under regular circumstances, fall under the jurisdiction of a national government and public administration. It was the International Commission on Intervention and State Sovereignty (ICISS) convened by the Canadian government that developed a formula designed to bridge the gap between international intervention and state sovereignty. The formula became known as the Principle of a Responsibility to Protect (R2P), which is based on two complementary principles. On the one hand, the point of reference is the responsibility of every state to protect its citizens against genocide, ethnic cleansing, war crimes, and crimes against humanity. On the other hand, R2P stipulates the right of the UN to assume the responsibility to protect the citizens of a given state against genocide, ethnic cleansing, war crimes, and crimes against humanity in cases where the originally responsible state is incapable of doing so. Accordingly, R2P is a formula that may justify an international intervention under UN mandate in territories whose governmental framework has ceased to exist and where, consequently, governmental institutions have become incapable of protecting the elementary rights of the people as stipulated in Article I(4) of the UN Charter.

The principle of a Responsibility to Protect was integrated into the final report of the High Level Panel on Threats, Challenges and Change (2004) commissioned by Secretary-General Kofi Annan.[12] Remarkably enough, it became part of the unanimously adopted outcome document of the UN General Assembly on the occasion of the 60th anniversary of the UN founding act in 2005.[13] In a way, this was a triumph of UN bureaucracy over the General Assembly. The Secretariat had managed to mobilize a network of independent experts, think tanks, and experienced practitioners—an epistemic community in the true sense[14]—whose contribution to the work of the ICISS and of the High Level Panel had a strong impact on the strategic statements of the Secretary-General on human rights protection[15] and on the General Assembly's outcome document. The traumatic disasters of Somalia, Rwanda and Srebrenica had finally led to a decisive shift in doctrine building whose pivotal expression was R2P. R2P as laid down in Kofi Annan's report "In Larger Freedom: Towards Development, Security and Human Rights for All"[16] and the outcome document of the General Assembly, made official what was de facto UN practice since the late 1990s in East Timor, Kosovo and Liberia. Representatives of the member states assembled in New York, much more concerned with

UN institutional reform than with issues of peacekeeping doctrine building, may not have realized the full meaning of R2P. However, the norm itself had been officially acknowledged and this was a decisive step on the way towards a discursive framework where human rights protection and state sovereignty could no longer be played off against each other.

A series of further reports and papers, written and issued on behalf of Secretary-General Annan, completed the process of peacekeeping doctrine building whose basic document remained the Brahimi Report of 2000. Crucial among those reports was a paper on the Integrated Mission Task Force (IMTF) as an instrument of effective coordination in the running of UN peace operations.[17] So far, turf wars and lack of coordination among the various UN sub-organizations already in place in regions where a UN peace operation was to be deployed were a notorious source of internal friction and organizational inefficiency. Since 2005, "integrated mission" stands for a concept according to which the SRSG in the field and the IMTF at UN headquarters in New York control all relevant UN activities on the ground. A Deputy Special Representative of the Secretary-General (DSRSG) for humanitarian affairs, acting at the same time as Resident Coordinator (RC) for the UN sub-units other than those directly connected to the relevant peace operation, and another DSRSG for rule of law and police together with the Force Commander (FC), are in charge of running all the civil and military components in a coordinated way.[18] To this author, this amounts to proof that the UN in its capacity as an international bureaucracy active in the field of peace operations has developed a coherent normative basis and a relatively consistent implementation structure at its disposal. This is clearly the result of the traumatic experiences with the failure of the traditional peacekeeping philosophy dating back to the era of the Cold War and the humanitarian disasters following it during the 1990s.

In its capacity as a multilateral institution the UN is dependent on UNSC consent when it comes to mandating, mobilization of resources, and political support of peace operations. The way these factors come to bear is shaped by the interests of UNSC member states, primarily by the veto-carrying P5. P5 behavior itself is shaped by both geopolitical interests and the domestic political support for the respective UN peace operation. Negotiations in the Security Council are subject to coalition building, bargaining, and the usual mechanisms of log-rolling and package deals that characterize any polyarchical system of decision-making.[19] Accordingly, decision-making in the UNSC is a classic example of the veto-player syndrome.[20] It is the attempt to avoid political deadlock that frequently leads to weak mandates, insufficient political support even of unanimously launched peace operations, and insufficient or unreliable resource mobilization.[21]

It is the concurrence of the bureaucratic and the multilateral aspects of the UN system that reveals a closing "window of opportunity" in the first decade of the twenty-first century with respect to UN peace operations and the learning effects of the 1990s. While the increasing relevance of modern protectorates under UN auspices may be ascribed to a convergence of the dominant political power and the dominant political values of Western democracies during the transitional period that followed the end of the Cold War, it is the volatility of decision making in the Security Council that renders the prospects of successful peace operations dim.

During the "long decade" from 1989 through 2001 the dominant interests and values of the international community, the re-stabilization of the geographical periphery, the promotion of democracy, human rights and, last but not least, "good governance," had seemed to be compatible with the UN's institutional mechanisms for the first time in its history. The adoption of R2P by the General Assembly in 2005 symbolized this. Since the turn of the millennium, however, this constellation began to change in two important respects. First, Russia and China as non-democratic great powers and veto-carrying members of the UN Security Council gained or regained considerable geopolitical influence. Furthermore, the US-led intervention in Iraq in 2003, prepared by means of deliberate distortion of facts, as well as the ensuing disaster of the US/UK occupation regime contributed to a general delegitimation of international intervention in the name of democratic values. This also weakened the political dominance of Western democracies and their political value as the driving force of doctrine development and organizational reform of UN peace operations. The compatibility of the dominant interests and values of the international community under democratic auspices and the institutional mechanisms of the United Nations, including the power relations within the Security Council, gradually vanished.

As a result, a growing distance between rhetoric and reality emerged in the period following the UN General Assembly of 2005, which evidently impacts on the operational level of UN peace operations. There are clear signs of non-decisions[22] as well as weakened support or outright obstruction of peace operations and the international administrations connected to them. These phenomena have been characterized as organized hypocrisy[23] in the sense of a UN lack of will in translating its own principles into operational policy. From an analytical perspective, however, organized hypocrisy is too broad a concept when it comes to the specific geopolitical changes that shape the reality of UN peace operations. These changes are primarily connected to the role of two authoritarian states as permanent members of the UNSC. The mere diagnosis of a rhetoric-versus-reality gap affecting UN peace operations does not give any hint how the international community is actually dealing with that gap. The remainder of this paper is devoted to a theoretical conceptualization of this problem and some empirical illustrations.

## The Responsibility to Protect: Rhetoric and Reality

There is no shortage of relevant cases for the application of R2P as it was adopted by the World Summit of 2005. Public debates in Western democracies focused, for instance, on a potential intervention in Myanmar when its government refused to accept foreign humanitarian aid after the disastrous hurricane of April 2008.[24] In February 2008, Desmond Tutu, former Anglican archbishop of Cape Town and Nobel Peace Prize laureate, pleaded for the application of the principle of R2P to the civil war-like conditions in Kenya and the ensuing humanitarian crisis.[25] The most prominent case, however, is the massive violence in Darfur with several hundreds of thousands people killed and more than two million displaced persons living in refugee camps. There can be no serious doubt that Darfur is a classic R2P case,[26] especially since the Sudanese head of state, Omar Al-Bashir, was indicted by the ICC in July 2008.[27]

However, the case of Darfur and the indictment of president Al-Bashir of Sudan make obvious the UN's failure to comply with its own principles. Decisive measures directed against the government of Sudan and its criminal activities have been blocked by Russia and China several times.[28] Both countries have strong economic ties to Sudan, but China's dependency on oil imports from the country is particularly important. Both Russia and China are in deliberate breach of the weapons embargo imposed on Sudan by the UNSC.[29] Time and again, the Sudanese government managed to avert any effective UN intervention through adeptly maneuvering the permanent members of the UNSC against each other. Sabotage of the Darfur Peace Agreement of July 2005 was used as a potential threat.[30] In early 2009, when the arrest warrant against Al-Bashir was issued, the US, the UK and France did not give their official commitment to R2P with respect to Darfur. UNAMID, the peace operation on the ground—a "hybrid mission" since it was sponsored by both the African

Union and the United Nations—remained largely ineffective because of the lack of commitment of the Western democracies.

This leads us to a question scarcely addressed in the relevant literature: How do actors in the UN system behave once they end up in a political deadlock that causes the failure of peace operations to which they remain officially committed? The UN and the humanitarian norms on which their activity is based provide a source of political legitimacy in their own right.[31] Abandoning the commitment to UN peace operations altogether might be as risky in terms of losing a constituency's support as wasting taxpayers' money for an ineffective international intervention. However, complex UN peace operations in the form of modern protectorates remain costly endeavors anyway and the irony is that the costs will increase as the operation succeeds in terms of long-term, sustainable political and economic reconstruction. Thus sponsoring states may develop an interest in low-cost, low-performance operations. However, purposely weakened peace operations do not cease to consume tax money (even if at a reduced level), nor can they be justified vis-à-vis the constituency. Theoretically, the dilemma may be solved if we assume that sponsoring states combine their presumed interest in low-cost, low-performance modern protectorates with an interest in ignorance about performance in the first place. Strange as it may sound, this assumption is well grounded in both theoretical and empirical terms.

## Institutionalized Ignorance and Successful Failure: A Modified Principal-Agent Model for Modern Protectorates Under UN Auspices

The above hypothesis may be translated into a modified principal-agent model that combines components of two rival strands of theorizing on human decision making: the "rational choice" versus the "bounded rationality" paradigm.[32] We may assume the key governing bodies of the United Nations—the Secretariat and the Security Council—as well as the UN member states behave as principals, unwilling to see their agents do what they are supposed to do. This obviously collides with the standard assumptions of the conventional principal agent theorem.[33] There are, however, sound theoretical reasons that shatter the assumption of principals being constantly performance-conscious as well as interested in reducing information asymmetries. Once we sustain the related assumption we obtain a matrix combining different types of principals with different types of failure and ignorance.[34] Prior to addressing the model, however, I will discuss its theoretical justification.

The assumption of purposeful organizational failure may be based on aspects of the seminal study *A Behavioural Theory of the Firm* by Richard Cyert and James March.[35] Cyert and March pointed to the fact that conflicting goals in a formal organization might be mitigated through structural differentiation. Goals that are temporarily or constantly not achievable but nonetheless belong to the official set of the organization's strategic objectives may be "delegated" to subunits whose failure may be deliberately taken into account. Under these circumstances, it is on the very failure of the organizational subunit that the success of the entire organization might hinge.

This style of "solving" problems that are basically unsolvable may create cynicism. How cynicism might be mitigated or eliminated becomes conceivable by means of the classic psychological theorem of cognitive dissonances.[36] In reality, managers of formal organizations will not openly declare their intention to have organizational subunits fail. Of course they may lie.[37] But they also may engage in self-denial. The tension between a behavioral norm and the actual behavior of individuals, according to Festinger, might be mitigated by an "unwillingness to know" and by self-legitimizing myths. Similarly, Timur Kuran puts forward the assumption that individuals conceal their actual preferences behind their revealed preferences in an attempt to avoid the adopted pressure of behavioral norms one is unable or unwilling to follow.

Furthermore, it is common knowledge among political scientists that political actors, under certain circumstances, are engaged in symbolic problem-solving and that solving problems merely symbolically may nonetheless contribute to the legitimization of political action.[38] The same holds for Bacharatz and Baratz's non-decisions theorem.[39] Non-decisions, in the Bacharatz and Baratz sense, are decisions that do not appear on the political agenda, a mechanism that may be instrumental in keeping unsolvable problems out of the process' operational policy where the insolvability of problems could create stress and even political crises. This, in turn, corresponds to John Kingdon's theory of the political entrepreneur who, just in accordance with opportunistic tactics, manages to couple politically relevant "streams" (problem streams, policy streams, politics streams), thus shaping the political agenda.[40] This also may allow for keeping issues off the political agenda that might be perceived as political insolvabilities with related risks of de-legitimization.

If we accept the above as sufficient theoretical reasons to assume principals to be interested in both the failure of agents and in the ignorance about the failure itself, what are the configurations of preferences, failure, and ignorance that can be hypothetically derived in the context of UN peace operations? The graph below delivers the matrix for some related assumptions and illustrations.

Table 3: Assumed Preferences of the UN and of the Member States in Successfully Failing Peace Operations

|  |  | Interest in Failure | Interest in Ignorance about Failure |
| --- | --- | --- | --- |
| UN | Secretariat | I | II |
|  | Security Council | III | IV |
| UN Member States | Government | V | VI |
|  | Parliament | VII | IIX |
|  | Public | IX | X |

"Principals" appear in the United Nations system in two versions: in the form of the UN as an international organization and in the form of its individual member states. The UN as an international organization has to be subdivided into the Secretariat and the UNSC. The UN member states cannot be conceptualized as unitary actors either. It is the government, parliament, and general public concerned that function as "principal." If we combine this spectrum of principals with the latter's assumed interest in the failure of their agents and the interest in ignorance about that failure, we obtain the matrix depicted in Table 3 in which the cells I through X stand for different variants of intended failure and intended ignorance. Some exemplary cases taken from the context of UN peace operations may be used in support of the hypothesis represented by the individual cells in the graph.

Cell III, for instance, stands for the assumption according to which members of the UN Security Council are interested in the failure of a peace operation, or of the international interim administration connected to it. This may occur for the very same reason that explains why the mandates issued by the Security Council for certain peace operations often remain vague and hard to operationalize precisely because they rely on a compromise in the UNSC.[41] Members of the UNSC who have accepted the mandate may be interested in the failure of the respective peace operation since success of the mission might prove them wrong, thus damaging the national prestige, national interests, or the interests of their allies. The UN transitional administration of Kosovo and the behavior of Russia may serve as an example. Although Russia as one of the

P5 should be interested in UNMIK's success, a transfer of ownership from the UN to the Albanian majority of Kosovo's population was obviously not what the Russian government was interested in—at least not as long as a quasi-independent Kosovo is perceived (or portrayed) as an encouragement for ethnic minorities in the periphery of the Russian Federation and their strife for political autonomy.[42]

The future status of Kosovo, in the meantime, had become a bargaining chip in the framework of complex package deals involving international problems whose solution was (and still is) in the interest of the Western democracies, the USA in particular. This affected the enforcement of UNSC resolutions designed to put a halt on the Iranian nuclear program[43] and the cooperation with Russia in the combat against terrorism, which might explain why Russia, meanwhile, had no interest in the successful termination of the UN transition administration in Kosovo and the fulfillment of the mandate.

Cell IV refers to a situation in which members of the UNSC have an interest in ignorance about the actual performance level of an UN peace operation. This might occur when information on mission performance would trigger a political demand for more resources and improvements that are likely to create secondary political costs. A tragic example is the failure of the UN mission in Rwanda in 1994. The governments of France and the US were not interested in precise information on the events in Rwanda that occurred under the wary eyes of the UNAMIR and a blue helmet contingent attached to it under the command of General Roméo Dallaire from Canada. Still under the shock of failure in Somalia when dead US soldiers had been dragged by the mob through the streets of Mogadishu, President Clinton was presumably not interested in another "quagmire," while France under President Mitterrand effectively supported the very Hutu militias that were chiefly responsible for the genocide of the Tutsi minority.[44] Precise knowledge on what happened in Rwanda would have increased both domestic political pressure in favor of an intervention and cognitive dissonances of Presidents Clinton and Mitterrand.[45] Similarly, the fate of the UN safe area [!] of Srebrenica led to serious questions about what members of the UNSC must have known and what, under the given circumstances, they were not willing to know. They were not willing to know when the threat of takeover by Serbian troops became apparent.[46]

Cell VIII refers to the assumption according to which members of national parliaments may display an interest in ignorance about the actual performance of a UN peace operation to which the parliament initially had given its consent. In a parliamentary system—for example, a democracy where the government is strictly dependent on the parliamentary majority—this affects primarily the majority parties. Majority Members of Parliament not only have to support the government in parliament, they also have to justify the UN peace operation (which may include national troops in accordance with Chapter VI or Chapter VII of the UN Charter) vis-à-vis their constituency. For those Members of Parliament, accurate knowledge about the actual performance of a peace operation officially supported by the government entails the risk of losing constituency support in case a weak performance has to be admitted. Accordingly, members of the governing coalition might be tempted to resort to legends and legitimizing myths, necessarily more or less concealing the actual state of affairs, in order not to be compromised by the failure of a peace operation supported by the coalition. However, the interest in ignorance about the actual performance of peace operations is not necessarily limited to the governing party or the governing coalition and parliament.

The German Bundestag delivers an example. Parliamentary control of the armed forces and of German forces deployed abroad is the sacred cow of the German political class. Accordingly, one should take as guaranteed a strict determination of the parliament to get as much information as possible regarding the activities of German troops deployed abroad. This, however, is a heroic assumption. It is common knowledge that the federal government, regardless of its composition, usually applies for more troops via-à-vis the parliament than are actually needed, in an attempt to maintain leeway in case a quick increase of troop strength is required due to a local crisis. The margin is such that it easily covers the deployment of special forces that are limited in number but highly effective in combat strength. As a consequence, the most sensitive part of military action gets the least control.[47] This might even appear plausible from a pragmatic point of view, but it is certainly the opposite of the mainstream political opinion the Bundestag will find acceptable. If Members of Parliament do nonetheless accept the status quo one may conclude that they are just not interested in knowing what precisely German special forces are doing. Institutional alternatives such as establishing a special subcommittee in charge of controlling the activity of German troops abroad—similar to the one already existing as institutional control of German intelligence services—could strengthen parliamentary control.[48] However, no parliamentary support for this kind of intensified control is in sight. Accordingly, parliamentary control of the politically most sensitive elements of the use of Germany's military force abroad is largely nonexistent. One may assume that more and precise knowledge on what German special forces do is precisely what Members of Parliament do not want to acquire, because it would just aggravate the tension between what they know and what they can openly discuss, let alone justify, with or vis-à-vis their constituency.

Cell X refers to a situation in which the overall public is interested in ignorance rather than in knowledge about the performance of a peace operation. There are, indeed, sad examples of what one might call, following Samantha Power, the collective bystander phenomenon[49]—the obvious willingness to ignore the failure of the international attempt to keep the peace, save lives and end massive human rights violations. Rwanda and Srebrenica are cases in point, as is Darfur—all of which are connected to the failure of the UN and its missions on the ground to fulfill their mandate. The Rwanda genocide could have been contained or even prevented if the public in a limited number of key states such as Belgium, France and the US had been willing to realize that the small UN contingent was doomed to fail and leave unprotected those who had invested hopes in the international community—a kind of knowledge that would have made it crystal-clear that only massive military intervention could prevent the imminent humanitarian disaster. No such "will to know" emerged in the Western democracies. Similarly, the overall public in the Western democracies was not willing to realize the imminent threat exerted by Serbian troops surrounding the UN "safe area" of Srebrenica in early July 1995. What attracted public attention in key nations such as France, Germany and the UK at least as much as the fate of the citizens of Srebrenica was an event at the far side of the world—the French nuclear tests on the Mururoa atoll, restarted by the newly elected president Jacques Chirac.[50]

## Conclusion

This chapter has argued that modern protectorates under UN auspices are subject to the tension between coherent doctrines and organizational principles that govern UN peace operations, on the one hand, and the erosion of its geopolitical preconditions, on the other. That tension is the result of the double nature of the UN as a multilateral institution and an international bureaucracy. As an international bureaucracy the UN can create various kinds of international administration as well as guidelines and doctrines, standard operation procedures, and implementation structures. As a multilateral institution, by contrast, the UN (and the UNSC in particular) is exposed to the divergent interests of the member states, with emphasis on the P5.

Rather than following mainstream criticism of bureaucracy in general and the UN bureaucratic machinery in particular, this chapter stresses the positive aspects of the UN as an international bureaucracy that, since the end of the Cold War, proved capable of learning and of effective doctrine building. The locus of learning and strategic planning is the Secretariat and the epistemic community surrounding it, consisting of think tanks and experts. The development of the R2P doctrine has been presented as a prominent example. By contrast, it is in the UNSC that the gains in terms of learning and doctrine development are crippled. The fate of R2P again is a telling example. Despite its unanimous adoption by the General Assembly World Summit of 2005, R2P has not even gained the full commitment of the Western democracies represented in the UNSC, let alone that of G77 countries. This lack of commitment cannot be sufficiently explained by the veto-player constellations in the UNSC or by endemic cynicism ("organized hypocrisy"). Rather it has to be contextualized in the wider frame of the loss of bipolar hegemonic stability that resulted from the end of the Cold War. Modern protectorates connected to peace operations under the auspices of the UN are as much mechanisms of regional stabilization as was the international interim administration under the auspices of the League of Nations mandate system. In both cases, the effectiveness of an administrative mechanism created by the international community was determined by the political will of the relevant key-players in international politics. Much as the League of Nations system collapsed owing to the colonial and revisionist efforts of Italy and Germany, the coherent guidelines and doctrines governing UN peace operations, R2P in particular, might be doomed to fail owing to the resistance of Russia and China as non-democratic members of the UNSC.

Under these circumstances, UN member states sponsoring modern protectorates connected to peace operations are bound to acknowledge humanitarian norms and the necessary failure to enforce them at the same time. They are thus facing the dilemma of losing constituency support through either ignoring the humanitarian norms or wasting tax money for virtually failing UN peace operations. The hypothesis presented here is that they cope with the dilemma by adopting an "as if" style of policy: the official commitment to UN peace operations is eclipsed by both the interest in low-cost, low-performance operations and the interest in ignorance about performance in the first place. The chapter presents both a theoretical model and empirical illustrations in support of that assumption. Plausible as they are, the empirical examples reveal a disturbing pathology of how the international community deals with the issue of peacebuilding and the "responsibility to protect" human rights. Accordingly, taking peacebuilding and human rights protection seriously implies more than well-intended normative appeals: that is, more vigorous research into the political and psychological mechanisms of intended failure and intended ignorance as far as modern protectorates connected to peace operations under UN auspices are concerned.

# 9

# THE NORMATIVE UNDERPINNINGS OF
# THE UN PEACEBUILDING COMMISSION

*Richard Caplan and Richard Ponzio*

International efforts to promote the consolidation of peace in the aftermath of violent conflict have expanded considerably in the past two decades. From 1989 to 2009, the United Nations alone initiated more than fifteen new multidimensional peacebuilding operations involving hundreds of thousands of military and civilian personnel. The large number of actors involved and the wide range of activities undertaken testify to the increased importance that states and international agencies attach to the need for more concerted action to establish a durable peace in states and territories emerging from war.

The creation of the United Nations Peacebuilding Commission (PBC) reflects this increased international concern. Established by the Security Council and the General Assembly in December 2005,[1] the PBC exists to help states emerging from civil war to avoid a relapse into violent conflict. The PBC is not the sole UN body concerned with post-conflict peacebuilding and, as an intergovernmental advisory body, it is arguably less consequential for practice than some of its sister entities, notably the Department of Peacekeeping Operations (DPKO), the Department of Political Affairs (DPA) and the UN Development Program (UNDP), all of which conduct actual field operations. The PBC's operational impact is also overshadowed by that of other multilateral organizations and agencies, such as the European Union and the World Bank, as well as by the bilateral efforts of the United States, Britain and other major donors and troop-contributing countries. However, as a focal point for peace-building activities at the United Nations, the PBC has influence as a generator and a disseminator of peacebuilding norms, both within the organization and in the wider international community, and is thus deserving of particular attention.[2]

This chapter is concerned with the normative underpinnings of the UN's peacebuilding architecture, with particular emphasis on the PBC. It examines the strategies and processes of engagement that the PBC has adopted for the four countries on its agenda to date—Burundi, Sierra Leone, Guinea-Bissau and the Central African Republic—for what these strategies and processes reveal about the premises on which the work of the PBC is based. We argue that the PBC's approach to peacebuilding reflects a combination of pragmatic considerations (the logic of expected consequences) and normative imperatives (the logic of appropriateness).[3] Drawing on the work of Roland Paris, we argue further that the normative imperatives predispose the PBC to adopt particular strategies and processes and to reject others, without regard necessarily for the effectiveness of a given approach. The sources of these normative imperatives are various. Some reflect entrenched norms that UN agencies feel constrained to respect; others reflect the various and at times even disparate orientations—humanitarian, security and developmental—of the different implementing agencies. We do not go as far as some observers, however, in arguing that the normative impulses that inform PBC peacebuilding are indicative of a larger hegemonic project on the part of dominant states within the UN system to remake war-torn states in order to serve their own interests.[4] Transformative though UN peacebuilding aspires to be, it does not represent a new form of hegemonic control or neo-imperialism. Nevertheless, some developing countries continue to express skepticism and even fear about the potential for UN peacebuilding to impose a new political order and corresponding values on fragile host countries. As the following essay shows, the PBC's consensus-making model of decision-making, North-South balance in terms of membership and other safeguards effectively preclude any such possibility.

## The Origins and Mandate of the PBC

The establishment of the PBC needs to be seen in the broader context of efforts to reform the United Nations in the early twenty-first century. Prompted principally by concerns about the seeming irrelevance of the United Nations in the face of the Iraq crisis, which fiercely divided member states and led a number of them to resort to unilateral action against the Saddam Hussein regime in 2003, UN Secretary-General Kofi Annan created a High-level Panel on Threats, Challenges and Change "to generate new ideas about the kinds of policies and institutions required for the UN to be effective in the twenty-first century."[5] Among the proposals put forward by the High-level Panel, and recommended by the Secretary-General in turn, was the creation of a new intergovernmental body that could assist states recovering from conflict.[6] There had been proposals earlier (notably in the 2000 Brahimi Report)[7] to strengthen the capacity of the United Nations to develop and implement peacebuilding strategies, and while the Iraq crisis may not have been symptomatic of weakness in this particular area, the opportunity for broad reflection gave renewed impetus to efforts to institutionalize peacebuilding in the United Nations.

The Secretary-General's proposal for the establishment of a Peacebuilding Commission reflected long-standing recognition of the fact that a stable peace often requires the cooperation and sustained engagement of a range of national and international actors over many years if not decades. The Security Council's and the General Assembly's inability to maintain support for conflict-affected societies, especially over the medium to long term, was thought to be one factor that explained the high incidence of conflict recurrence in the aftermath of civil wars.[8] A dedicated peacebuilding body would arguably help the Security Council, the General Assembly, multilateral agencies, donors and troop-contributing countries to coordinate their respective peacebuilding activities and to maintain international commitment to the rebuilding of war-ravaged states.

These expectations are reflected in the parallel resolutions adopted by the Security Council and the General Assembly in December 2005 that led to the establishment of the PBC. The resolutions identified three functions for the Commission:

(a) "To bring together all relevant actors to marshal resources and to advise on and propose integrated strategies for post-conflict peacebuilding and recovery;"

(b) "To focus attention on the reconstruction and institution-building efforts necessary for recovery from conflict and to support the development of integrated strategies in order to lay the foundation for sustainable development;"

(c) "To provide recommendations and information to improve the coordination of all relevant actors within and outside the United Nations, to develop best practices, to help to ensure predictable financing for early recovery activities and to extend the period of attention given by the international community to post-conflict recovery."[9]

UN member states were not equally enthusiastic about the prospects for the PBC. Developing countries in particular were somewhat circumspect even though the states most affected by civil strife, which therefore stood to benefit from the increased international attention, were developing countries. These states were concerned that the emphasis on peacebuilding at the United Nations would detract from development needs more broadly, especially at a time—in the wake of the terrorist attacks of 11 September 2001—when development assistance was becoming increasingly securitized. Developing countries were also concerned that the PBC could have the effect of "institutionalizing continuing interventions in the domestic affairs of the developing-country members of the UN," in the words of the former Indian foreign minister Muchkund Dubey.[10]

The PBC is only one pillar of the UN's new peacebuilding architecture. The other two pillars are the Peacebuilding Support Office (PBSO) and the Peacebuilding Fund (PBF). The PBSO is the PBC's Secretariat, providing administrative and analytical support to the PBC and liaising with other agencies in the UN system. It also functions as a knowledge center for lessons learned and good practices in peacebuilding. The PBF, administered by the UNDP, is meant to be a quick-disbursing facility "with the objective of ensuring the immediate release of resources needed to launch peacebuilding activities and the availability of appropriate financing for recovery."[11] As of 31 October 2009, with commitments to the fund totaling more than $300 million, the PBF had allocated US$162 million for 101 projects in ten countries.[12]

While the PBC functions strictly as an advisory body, it was thought that its unique composition would allow it to exert a major influence on peacebuilding activities within the United Nations and more widely. The PBC's 31-member Organizational Committee consists of seven members of the Security Council (including all the permanent members), seven members of the Economic and Social Council (ECOSOC), the five top providers of assessed and voluntary contributions to the United Nations, the five top providers of military personnel and civilian police to UN missions and seven additional members, giving due consideration to regional (or a balanced North/South) representation.[13] The breadth of the PBC's membership meant that if, as was expected, it could reach agreement on the approaches and strategies to be undertaken with regard to peacebuilding, then its recommendations would be difficult to ignore. As Amy Scott has observed, the key to success would not be the PBC's authority, which as an advisory body was inherently limited, but "the shared interest of its members"—many of them major states and key stakeholders—"in a more coherent approach to peacebuilding."[14] In addition to the legitimacy bestowed by its balanced North/South membership, the PBC derives its influence from the perceived merit of its policy recommendations, the relevance of the information it shares and its ability to generate additional resources for conflict-affected states whose importance on the international agenda has receded. The PBC also exerts influence through the articulation and affirmation of fundamental international norms that underpin peacebuilding strategies and processes, as we discuss in the following sections.

## The PBC's Strategies and Their Normative Underpinnings

Peacebuilding strategies are predicated in part on assumptions about the nature of conflict and the requirements for establishing a sustainable peace, in general terms and with respect to a given conflict situation. These assumptions inform the pragmatic considerations that govern mandate formation reflected in, for instance, the demilitarization of armed groups, the training of police forces, the promotion of the rule of law, the establishment of political institutions, the resumption and strengthening of public service delivery, and measures to stimulate economic growth, among numerous other peacebuilding activities. Pragmatic considerations are not the only factors that bear on the design and implementation of peacebuilding strategies, however. Normative considerations with regard to both what is desirable and what is appropriate are also important. These normative considerations are often not stated explicitly and are therefore rarely, if ever, debated; rather, they generally constitute an unspoken consensus or simply acquiescence in the preferences of particular stakeholders.[15]

Peacebuilding strategies over the past decade have sought to promote a broad range of political, economic and social norms. Representative of these normative commitments is the UN's Kosovo Standards Implementation Plan, adopted in March 2004, which seeks *inter alia* the establishment of a "truly multi-ethnic" Kosovo where public institutions are "representative and democratic"; where "all [national] communities are proportionately represented at all levels" of government; where "the interests of women are fully reflected in [government] policies and legislation"; and where "a functioning market economy is in place."[16] Similarly but more modestly, the Afghanistan Compact (January 2006) subscribes to "a democratic, peaceful, pluralistic and prosperous state based on the principles of Islam," increased "female participation in all Afghan governance institutions" and the elimination of the "immoral" narcotics trade, among numerous other norms-based objectives.[17]

The merits or demerits of these and other particular commitments are not what concern us here. Our interest is simply to observe that peacebuilding strategies often entail normative commitments that can be distinguished from pragmatic considerations, although the distinction between the pragmatic and the normative may not always be a hard and fast one. Take the commitment to a "truly multi-ethnic" Kosovo. Leaving aside the question, which the Kosovo Standards Implementation Plan does not answer, of what exactly should true multiethnicity mean for Kosovo. Whether this be the return of Kosovar Serbs to the territory; a fair representation of Serbs (and other minorities) on public bodies; peaceful coexistence between largely separate Serb and Albanian communities or integration of the two communities. It would appear that multi-ethnicity is as much a normative as a pragmatic imperative for the United Nations, if not more. While there is demonstrable evidence that ethnic representation on public bodies is important for the legitimacy and effectiveness of these bodies, it is not evident that integration—the maximalist goal—would necessarily generate greater mutual understanding leading to increased tolerance. Indeed, some have argued in favor of a de-mixing of diverse populations to eliminate flashpoints and thus mitigate conflict.[18] If it is not clear precisely what pragmatic considerations may underpin the UN's commitment to multiethnicity, it is clear that the UN has been reluctant to accept demographic shifts that, with Serbs concentrated in northern Kosovo, might facilitate a partition of Kosovo or encourage secession elsewhere (for example in neighboring Bosnia and Herzegovina and Macedonia) and, moreover, would appear to be tantamount to an admission of failure on the part of the UN to reverse ethnically motivated forced migration.[19] Multi-ethnicity is desirable then not only, or even primarily, for its contribution to a sustainable peace but also for its normative symbolic value and its broader political ramifications.

Informed by the experiences of Kosovo, Afghanistan and other similar frameworks for peacebuilding, such as the compacts with Iraq and Timor-Leste and the Common Assistance Framework for the Democratic Republic of Congo, the UN Peacebuilding Commission's strategies have expressed comparable normative commitments in the context of its efforts to assist states emerging from conflict. The PBC's integrated peacebuilding strategies are characterized by two over-arching sets of normative commitments in particular: to liberal democratic governance (the establishment or strengthening of inclusive, accountable and transparent political institutions, and the holding of periodic free and fair elections to these institutions, which should uphold the rule of law and protect the human rights and civil liberties of all citizens); and to a market-oriented economy (the establishment or strengthening of an economic regime that relies on the private sector as the chief engine for the generation of wealth and jobs, and ensures minimal government interference in the economy), although the PBC's policy objectives do not always reflect strict neo-liberal economic orthodoxy, as we will see below. In addition, the PBC's peacebuilding strategies often also contain commitments to various social norms such as gender mainstreaming, multi-ethnicity and reconciliation.

The promotion of liberal democracy and market-oriented economic reforms has been a centerpiece of the PBC's efforts both during the consultations for, and in the final drafting of, the Commission's integrated peacebuilding strategies (also known as Strategic Frameworks for Peacebuilding) in Burundi, the Central African Republic, Guinea-Bissau and Sierra Leone.[20] In addition to the PBC's strategic frameworks, liberal democratic governance and the market economy have been promoted through the Commission's Working Group on Lessons Learned (WGLL) and the Commission's Organizational Committee, in particular its Strategy and Policy Task Force on the Private Sector.[21]

In his article "Peacekeeping and the Constraints of Global Culture," Roland Paris observes that peacekeeping agencies and their member states "are predisposed to develop and implement strategies that conform with [prevailing] norms...and are disinclined to pursue strategies that deviate from these norms."[22] The prevailing norms, in Paris' view, are those generated by what he refers to as the "global culture," which comprises "the formal and informal rules of international social life."[23] Liberal democratic and free-market values, together with other broadly accepted norms, he observes further, are constitutive of this global culture.

Whether or not the notion of a "global culture" best explains the basis of these norms, Paris' findings are broadly consistent with what can be observed in the work of the United Nations generally and the Peacebuilding Commission specifically. The United Nations exhibits a predisposition towards particular normative prescriptions, to the exclusion of others, and without regard necessarily for the effectiveness of these prescriptions. A case in point is the UN's promotion of liberal democracy in the context of peacebuilding. While a credible claim can be made that there is an "emerging right" to democratic governance and even to suggest that democracy may already be a settled or entrenched norm,[24] states differ in their views as to the preferred characteristics of democracy. The United Nations has formally acknowledged these differences. In his *Agenda for Democratization* (1996), the then Secretary-General Boutros Boutros-Ghali wrote:

While democratization is a new force in world affairs, and while democracy can and should be assimilated by all cultures and traditions, it is not for the United Nations to offer a model of democratization or democracy or to promote democracy in a specific case. Indeed, to do so could be counter-productive to the process of democratization which, in order to take root and to flourish, must derive from the society itself. Each society must be able to choose the form, pace and character of its democratization process. Imposition of foreign models not only contravenes the Charter principle of non-intervention in internal affairs, it may also generate resentment among both the Government and the public, which may in turn feed internal forces inimical to democratization and to the idea of democracy.[25]

This formal commitment to pluralism (of sorts) notwithstanding, the United Nations often does promote democracy in specific cases and, when it does, it shows a clear preference for democracy of a Western-liberal orientation. UN operations, peacebuilding or otherwise, have never had a mandate to promote or establish autocratic forms of governance (although the UN's own transitional administrations have been criticized for their autocratic tendencies).[26]

In the context of post-conflict peacebuilding, it could be argued that the preference for liberal democracy represents a pragmatic choice, insofar as it has long been thought that liberal democratic regimes—those with well established norms of tolerance and peaceful dispute resolution mechanisms—are less likely to experience civil war.[27] The validity of this claim, however, is not beyond dispute. Some question the contribution that the degree of democracy actually makes to the consolidation of peace.[28] Based on their study of 68 post-conflict episodes, Collier, Hoeffler and Söderbom, for instance, observe: "Severe autocracy appears to be highly successful in maintaining the post-conflict peace...If the polity is highly autocratic, the risk [of reversion to conflict] is only 24.6 percent; whereas if it is not highly autocratic the risk more than doubles to 62 percent."[29] The authors conclude that liberal democratic development may be an intrinsically desirable objective but should not be viewed as a mechanism for increasing the durability of a post-conflict peace. It is easier to imagine the UN seeking to accommodate this inconvenient truth (if that is indeed what it is) than it is to imagine the organization favoring autocracy over democracy in its peacebuilding strategies; this underscores the normative commitment that lies at the heart of this approach.

Similarly, the orientation towards market-oriented recovery belies normative commitments as well as pragmatic considerations. The PBC works in support of the major international financial institutions (World Bank, IMF) that promote a mix of neoliberal prescriptions emphasizing monetarism, public expenditure restraint, privatization, deregulation and foreign direct investment in an effort to achieve macroeconomic stability and to stimulate economic growth. The PBC has sometimes departed from strict neoliberal orthodoxy, however: in the case of Burundi, for instance, it observed, "Economic reforms such as the privatization of public enterprises may cause a deterioration of social conditions and generate conflicts," and thus encouraged the adoption of "basic social protection" measures alongside economic reforms.[30] In his examination of peacebuilding operations launched between 1989 and 1999 (before the PBC was established), Roland Paris found that the dislocations and asymmetrical effects of economic liberalization often reproduced the very conditions—notably, enormous disparities of wealth—that generated unrest in these host countries in the first place.[31] Michael Pugh and Neil Cooper, in their analysis of post-war economic recovery strategies, are even harsher in their assessment of these strategies: "The [neoliberal economic] model emphasizes macroeconomic stability that is absolutely at odds with sustainable recovery," they conclude.[32] The PBC's sensitivity to the social ramifications of the neoliberal model is noteworthy. It also provides further evidence of the normative choices—conjoined with pragmatic considerations—that are embedded in its strategic planning.

Whatever the strengths or weaknesses of the PBC's peacebuilding strategies, our point is simply to observe that there are frequently normative commitments underpinning these strategies that can be distinguished from—and indeed may even be at odds with—pragmatic considerations regarding the measures required to achieve peacebuilding objectives. Because they are often not made explicit and rarely deliberated upon within the United Nations, these normative commitments are not always highly visible. And yet, integral though these norms are in UN peacebuilding, they do not necessarily enjoy universal validity. As Bhikhu Parekh reminds us, "the liberal principle of individuation and other liberal ideas are culturally and historically specific. As such a political system based on them cannot claim universal validity."[33] The need for greater deliberation, locally and internationally, about the normative foundations of peacebuilding strategies may be one conclusion that can be reasonably drawn from this analysis.

## The PBC's Processes of Engagement and Their Normative Underpinnings

The normative underpinnings of PBC peacebuilding can also be discerned from the Commission's processes of engagement with conflict-affected countries. Two norms receive particular emphasis: national ownership and mutual accountability. They owe their origins to a variety of UN and non-UN documents that predate the creation of the Peacebuilding Commission, including "An Agenda for Peace" (1992), the "United Nations Millennium Declaration" (2000) and the "Paris Declaration on Aid Effectiveness" (March 2005). These normative commitments also reflect the consensual nature of PBC engagement: prospective host countries must make a formal request to be considered for placement on the agenda of the Peacebuilding Commission. Normally this request is transmitted by a head of state to the UN Secretary-General, who then forwards it to the President of the Security Council if the Council is currently "seized" with the country in question—which it has been in every case to date—or otherwise to the General Assembly. The Security Council (or General Assembly) then issues a statement confirming the referral of a country to the PBC, and increasingly, as in the recent cases of Guinea-Bissau and the Central African Republic, the tendency is for the Security Council to prescribe specific issues to be focused on that may emanate from the original host country request. Once a country is formally confirmed by the thirty-one-member-state Organizational Committee of the PBC and it agrees on a chair of the new Country-Specific Configuration, an initial assessment or fact-finding mission is normally undertaken by the chair and PBSO. Their report helps to frame the initial agenda for subsequent Country-Specific Meetings, including work on an integrated peacebuilding strategy.

The use of the term "national ownership" has become something of a mantra within the PBC. As an extension of national sovereignty, arguably the foundational concept of the international system, national ownership within the PBC and the broader UN context has come to signify the central importance of indigenous institutional and human capacity-building, as well as nationally led (both state and non-state) strategies in the spheres of security sector reform, governance strengthening and socio-economic recovery. It is rare that a policy or even procedural dialogue takes place in a PBC-related forum without reference to national ownership or an associated term, such as "locally owned," "home-grown," "nationally driven" or "nationally led" peacebuilding. The commitment to national ownership is reflected in the General Assembly and Security Council resolutions establishing the PBC, which affirm "the primary responsibility of national and transitional governments…in identifying their priorities and strategies for post-conflict peacebuilding, with a view to ensuring national ownership."[34] As noted in the "Outcome of the PBC Strategy and Policy Task Force on the Private Sector" (December 2008): "The local government must make all efforts to maintain peace and stability, which is vital to sustain economic activity. In this regard, the international community needs to support the concerned host governments in enhancing their capacities and resources, in accordance with their identified national priorities and needs."[35]

The PBC's commitment to national ownership is more than mere rhetoric. Given that a PBC host country must willingly welcome the Peacebuilding Commission to focus attention (and expected new resources) on any peacebuilding challenges, and that the preparation of a PBC strategy provides an opportunity for the host country to exert leadership in a democratic consultative exercise, national ownership is practiced in a substantive manner, rather than being only drafted in the form of a commitment. Some analysts attribute the successful efforts of Burundi and Sierra Leone to steer the Peacebuilding Commission away from internally sensitive topics, such as corruption and national resource extraction, as evidence of the pervasive influence of national ownership in the PBC's deliberations.[36] Similarly, the need for land reform was a recurring theme in the PBC countries of Burundi, the Central African Republic and Guinea-Bissau, and objections from either developing countries serving on the PBC or the host countries themselves ensured that if land reform was dealt with at all, it was raised in a limited, non-threatening manner—often through references to how other conflict-affected countries have responded to tensions emerging over land issues.

The imperative of national ownership clashes regularly with the view, especially among leading Northern donor countries, that the PBC should serve as the driver of progressive policy and institutional reforms. This point is demonstrated, for example, in the constraints placed on effective monitoring of commitments made by PBC countries as part of the peacebuilding strategies. Despite initial attempts to introduce precise, time-bound and measurable benchmarks and accompanying indicators in the "Monitoring and Tracking Mechanisms" of Burundi and Sierra Leone—the first two countries on the agenda of the Commission—it soon became evident that there was little appetite among many PBC member states and the host countries alike to enforce the commitments made in PBC peacebuilding strategies. As argued earlier in this chapter, normative imperatives predispose the PBC to adopt particular strategies and processes and to reject others, without regard always for the effectiveness of a given approach. The subordination of effective monitoring to national ownership is another case in point.

An indication of this broad reluctance to engage in a rigorous and meaningful review of commitments endorsed in the PBC's peacebuilding strategies is the intentionally vague and limited assessments and recommendations articulated in the Burundi, Central African Republic, Guinea-Bissau and Sierra Leone biannual review progress reports. The first Burundi report calls for the National Parliament to "favor consultative approaches over confrontation to clear blockages" and for the UN, bilateral and other multilateral partners to "Pursue their multilateral support to the security sector."[37] Similarly, the inaugural Sierra Leone report calls for the government to "continue training and empowering local councils" and for the PBC to "broaden the donor support for the police and armed forces."[38] One result of these imprecise and unambitious targets for cooperation with a host government is a weakened ability on the part of the Peacebuilding Commission and the Peacebuilding Support Office to exert their coordination roles effectively within the UN system and the wider international community.

The other major normative commitment embedded in the PBC's processes of engagement is mutual accountability. Representing a commitment between donors and a host country to "jointly assess through existing and increasingly objective country level mechanisms mutual progress in implementing agreed commitments on aid effectiveness,"[39] mutual accountability has become, at least notionally, a bedrock principle. Unlike the case of national ownership, however—which as noted above has gained considerable traction and is reinforced through the deliberations of the Commission—the frequent use of the term mutual accountability across various PBC configurations should be characterized as little more than lip service. While the founding resolutions of the PBC established a support office within the UN Secretariat with a mandate and qualified staff to (i) gather and analyze relevant donor financial resources related data, and (ii) monitor progress of both host country and international partner towards meeting short and medium-term recovery goals,[40] the limited political and technical reach of those monitoring instruments, limited financial resources channeled to PBC countries,[41] and common over-use of mutual accountability in innumerable PBC documents suggest that either a genuine and comprehensive application of the concept is unachievable or, more cynically, that the concept is meant to divert attention away from the actual interests of an international actor within a conflict-affected society. Undoubtedly the PBC, as a transmitter of peacebuilding norms, has contributed significantly to an almost instinctive introduction of mutual accountability into diverse intergovernmental discussions. With the PBC mandate review in 2010, however, the opportunity awaits to revisit the sincerity of commitment by both a host country and international partners alike to match rhetoric with reality.

## Conclusion

The Peacebuilding Commission and the associated elements of the new UN peacebuilding architecture are still in their infancy. It remains to be seen to what extent they can or will make a significant contribution to the consolidation of peace in states emerging from civil war. Already, however, the PBC's impact can be observed with respect to its generation and dissemination of peacebuilding norms. This chapter has discussed four of the principal normative underpinnings of the work of the PBC: its commitment to liberal democratic governance, a (qualified) market-oriented economy, national ownership and mutual accountability. The fact that these normative commitments, or at least aspects of them, are often only implicit limits the scope for critical discussion of their appropriateness. It also conceals the extent to which there is a broad consensus in support of these norms.

As an intergovernmental advisory body based in New York, the Peacebuilding Commission has inherent limitations in terms of directly affecting field-based operations, particularly given the reluctance of its members to institute sanctions in response to failures of a host country or international partners to uphold commitments agreed within the PBC's chief instrument: the integrated peacebuilding strategy. The skepticism and fears expressed among some developing countries about the potential for UN peacebuilding to impose a new political order and corresponding values on a fragile host country are largely unfounded. Besides the PBC's cumbersome consensus-making model for decision-making and advising the Security Council and the General Assembly, the Commission's balanced membership between Northern and Southern countries, the lack of direct control of financial resources by the Peacebuilding Commission, the reluctance of member states to allow the Commission to address conflict prevention issues directly, and the relatively low-level rank of Assistant Secretary-General given to the head of the Peacebuilding Support

Office have dampened efforts by some (mainly Northern) countries to advance progressive policies in direct, operational terms. This is consistent with arguments made by Christopher Clapham elsewhere in this volume, where he contends that the reach of UN peacebuilding in Africa—despite the large number of missions—is limited compared to more intrusive (non-PBC supported) missions in other countries.

At the same time, as a locus for the sharing of peacebuilding experience and theoretical insights within the UN system, the Commission exhibits considerable promise in the capturing, consolidation and dissemination of norms essential for effective peacebuilding both in PBC countries and in the far more numerous non-PBC countries. Learning from its inaugural four country engagements and policy discussions in the Commission's apex body, the Organizational Committee, it remains to be seen whether member states and the UN Secretariat, with pressure from civil society and other external actors, will succeed in exploiting the full potential of the Peacebuilding Commission as a generator and disseminator of peacebuilding norms.

# 10

# POLICING THE NEO-IMPERIAL FRONTIER

## CIVPOL MISSIONS IN THE NEW PROTECTORATES

*Michael J. Boyle**

One of the fundamental challenges facing the international community in the new protectorates concerns the provision of basic public order in the context of real or potential challenges to its monopoly on the use of violence. In cases of preventive deployment, such as Eastern Slavonia (1995–98), the protectorate status is designed to forestall the use of violence or to prevent the spread of violence across borders. But in the cases where protectorate status follows sustained armed conflict (such as Bosnia, Kosovo and East Timor), international authorities often find themselves confronting a wide range of threats to public order, ranging from organized violence like targeted assassinations, reprisal killings and insurgencies to more ordinary forms of disorder such as street and organized crime. In these cases, the questions facing those administering the international protectorate are among the most essential: how does one re-establish the monopoly on the use of force within a territory of a weak or recently failed state? How can this be done in a way considered politically and

* The author is grateful for the helpful advice and comments of Philipp Rotmann, Ricardo Soares de Oliveira, and two anonymous reviewers. Parts of this chapter are drawn from Boyle (2004). All errors and omissions are his own.

morally legitimate? How can this assistance be rendered in a way that advances the democratic development of the state?

One way that the UN has approached this problem has been through the deployment of international police units, often in tandem with traditional military forces.[1] Unlike the military forces deployed as peacekeepers, UN Police units are composed of individual police officers from contributing nations.[2] These officers—usually currently-serving or recently retired officers in their own countries—are grouped together under a command structure sponsored by the UN or regional organizations and charged with restoring public order and with building local capacity for policing.[3] In cases where their deployment follows an armed conflict, police officers find themselves in an uneasy marriage with either a UN-backed peacekeeping force or a national military charged with restoring order (for example, Australia in East Timor). They also operate within a wider international political context dominated by a myriad international organizations and NGOs. UNPOL officers are functionally differentiated for a host of tasks, including control over borders, prisons, fixed infrastructure targets, and training of local police forces, and are charged with boosting local capacity for providing public order once the protectorate status has ended.

A number of scholars have pointed out that there is a distinctly imperial or colonial echo in the deployment of police officers, often under the command of officers from Western countries, to pacify or police a formerly restive territory.[4] But the deployment of UNPOL is not merely a repeat of previous cases of imperial policing. In contrast to the often brutal forms of policing that characterized colonial wars, the UN police forces are not formally charged with pacifying the country, as the so-called "hard security" tasks are delegated to the military forces. At the same time UN police forces are not relegated to training and advisory missions. The collapse or near-collapse of the governing authority that often follows armed conflict means that UNPOL forces are sometimes vested with "executive authority" to enforce basic law and order.[5] UNPOL forces are not an attempt to impose the UN's political will by *fiat*, but they are not entirely subservient to the will of local actors either; they exist in a political grey zone, retaining a modest degree of agency but constrained in their bargaining with international actors (such as the peacekeeping forces) and local agents. Their mission is then both functional—to restore basic law and order and to combat special kinds of crime, like organized crime and human trafficking—and political, as UNPOL is charged with inculcating the skills of democratic policing among the locals in order to boost support for the new political regime.[6] Although rarely noted as an official matter, this is in part an ideological task, as UNPOL forces are asked to serve as the midwife for the birth of a new liberal democratic state.[7] Thus UNPOL forces are tasked not only with statebuilding, but also with establishing, and then reinforcing, the political legitimacy of the protectorate within an international context where the liberal democratic state is considered the basic unit of political order.[8]

This new mission—in its objectives, strategy and organizational purpose— is beset by at least three internal contradictions. First, there are cross-cutting Weberian and Kantian dimensions to goals of the UNPOL mission, insofar as the establishment of control over the means of violence is coterminous with the establishment of a democratic state. These goals are at odds in some fundamental respects, and the tension between them leaves UNPOL forces uneasy with the exercise of brute force in the protectorate. Second, the strategy of civilian policing in new protectorates is quasi-imperial, but is done on behalf of a condominium of predominantly Western powers, rather than a single imperial power.[9] This collection of neo-imperial powers, often led by the United States, is uneasy about its mission and faces substantial coordination problems which render its multilateral strategy often less than the sum of its parts. Finally, the tactical and organizational dimensions of civilian policing are often at odds with one another, with the UNPOL commanders insisting on preserving local agency while facing organizational pressures that pull them towards greater centralization. The result is an UNPOL mission that is neither international nor local, but an inchoate mix of the two.

The purpose of this chapter is to discuss each of these contradictions in detail, with special reference to two executive authority missions, Kosovo and East Timor. In both cases, UNPOL forces were given the direct authority for the establishment of law and order after the state apparatus had collapsed but were paired up with UN-backed military peacekeeping forces.[10] In both cases the goals, strategies and organizational dimensions of the missions were marked by internal contradictions which undermined the effectiveness of their mission and left these new experiments in post-modern imperial policing with uncertain prospects.[11] Examining how these three contradictions within the contemporary UNPOL missions played themselves out within Kosovo and East Timor helps to identify the normative assumptions that underlie the administration of protectorates in the international system.

## The Evolution of International Policing

Until the nineteenth century, policing was seen almost solely as a domestic affair. In the mid-nineteenth century, initial moves were made to facilitate international police cooperation, particularly among European states.[12] The internationalization of policing occurred initially through the deployment of national police units outside the borders of their own state, usually on an exceptional basis.[13] Early international "police operations" included small-scale missions in Crete (1896–97), Saarland (1935) and Shanghai's International Settlements during the interwar years.[14] Police units were also deployed as part of counter-insurgency campaigns in colonial missions, including the South African Constabulary during the Anglo-Boer War (1899–1902) and the American-organized Garde d'Haiti (1916–34).[15]

Later developments in police cooperation revolved around cooperation through international or regional organizations such as INTERPOL and later EUROPOL.[16] A post-World War II boom in international police cooperation eventually led to the formation of national police advisory units, particularly under Western governments. These advisory units—often organized on functional grounds to deal with cross-national threats like organized crime and smuggling—began to cooperate within a wide range of international and regional organizations, including INTERPOL and the UN. The UN was a latecomer to the policing business, and when it began its deployments they were often limited in scope and size. In fact, these were properly considered peacekeeping missions with police functions performed by military officers (and thus not official UNPOL missions). For example, UN peacekeepers were responsible for the civil policing functions during the transfer of Port Said and Port Fuad from the British and French Expeditionary Forces in UNEF I (1956–57). Similarly, UN forces were used for policing functions during the withdrawal of Israeli forces from the Gaza Strip in 1957.[17]

The idea that the international organizations would field their own police forces—while popular in academic circles—gained relatively little traction until the early 1960s when the UN began to field its first deployments of UNPOL forces in so-called first generation peacekeeping missions.[18] Prior to 1989, the UN had deployed UNPOL contingents in only three missions: Congo (1960–64), West New Guinea (1962–63) and Cyprus (1964-present).[19] In West New Guinea, the purpose of UNPOL was primarily to train and advise existing police forces in support of a peace settlement. In the UN missions in Cyprus and the Congo, this mission blended into what is now called peace enforcement, with UNPOL forces fielded—like in Kosovo and

East Timor—in the wake of armed conflict. The most notorious case of peace enforcement concerned the Congo, in which UN Civilian Operations became embroiled in protecting the fledgling Congolese government against foreign predation and the secession of Katanga.[20] But even in Congo, the overriding emphasis of these missions was to restore the legal and political integrity of the existing state, even if the actual conditions of the state rendered claims about its full independence somewhat dubious.[21] The UN operations were seen as in support of existing legal entities; UNPOL was not seen as a tool for state creation so much as for propping up an existing, if weak and often dysfunctional, state.

After this brief experiment in the 1960s with active UNPOL deployments, the UN did not engage in substantial UNPOL deployments for the second half of the Cold War. This was in part due to heightened tensions: there was only a limited chance of getting the US and the Soviet Union to agree on where an UNPOL mission should be deployed. Although there were police monitors assigned to UN missions during the Cold War, nothing of the scale of the 1960s deployments of UNPOL reoccurred until after the collapse of the Soviet Union. Even in the immediate post-Cold War period, the UN did not deploy police officers with a mandate to use force against the local inhabitants but instead limited their mandate to advisory and training functions. For instance, UNPOL were deployed as part UN Transitional Assistance Group (UNTAG) to monitor the behavior of South African-trained local police in Namibia.[22]

During the 1990s, the deployment of UNPOL forces in the context of UN missions boomed, as the UN greatly expanded its reach and began a more aggressive deployment of police forces, often in a more than advisory capacity. Eleven of the sixteen peacekeeping missions operating in 2006 contained some UNPOL component.[23] In 1999, Chuck Call and Michael Barnett noted the rapid expansion of UNPOL in training and advisory capacity. "Numbering only 35 in 1988," they wrote, "UNPOL has increased a hundred-fold within four years and have been deployed in a dozen countries."[24] The numbers deployed per mission also increased significantly. By 1999, there were 1,500 UNPOL in Namibia, 3,600 in Cambodia, 900 in Haiti, and 1,800 in Bosnia. Yet still in these training and advisory missions, the objectives of UNPOL deployments were relatively modest, consisting largely of training local police forces in democratic standards and humane treatment of civilians. Most important, previous UNPOL missions had no "executive authority"—meaning the right to arrest suspects and use force—because official responsibility for policing remained with the local authorities. Until the end of the Cold War, as Harry

Broer and Michael Emery noted in 1998, "Neither [the local authorities] nor the UNPOL-contributing governments are inclined to accept that such responsibilities would be assumed by the United Nations; the costs would be prohibitive; and the risks of casualties and escalation would be great."[25]

As in many other respects (see the Introduction to this volume), the UN engagement in Bosnia was the watershed development leading to a rapid expansion in the size and mandate of UNPOL deployments. At the end of the war in 1995, the institutions of the Yugoslav state had withdrawn, leaving only rump police forces in each of the remaining ethnic entities. The new state of Bosnia and Herzegovina—consisting of the Federation of Bosnia and Herzegovina (FBiH) and the Republika Srbska (RS)—had three police forces, each organized along ethnic lines. Worse still, these three police forces included people who had been complicit in war atrocities, therefore rendering them unacceptable for policing duties. In the context of statebuilding objectives of the Dayton Peace Accords, the UN committed itself to the reform of the Bosnian police, through the creation of the International Police Task Force (IPTF). The initial IPTF mandate was only to assist and observe the BiH forces.[26] But following the lead of the Office of High Representative (OHR), IPTF forces began to assist in the restructuring of the forces to condense them into two police forces, organized along entity lines, in 1996.[27] In 1998, under encouragement from the OHR, the IPTF assumed responsibility for promoting democratic policing, which "emphasizes transforming the culture within the police and the citizens' perceptions of the police" so that the police are seen in the service of the people, not the state.[28]

By 2000, the IPTF had expanded its objectives beyond observing and advising the police and towards enforcing institutional change for the Bosnian police as part of a UN-sponsored statebuilding project. The UN monitoring of the Bosnian police mission was truly an extraordinary expansion of international authority into the operation of local police forces. Through the OHR, international authorities monitored the ethnic and gender composition of the police forces, in an attempt to foster reconciliation and cross-ethnic cooperation. The OHR also wielded its power to dismiss unresponsive police commissioners and to insist that the police become multiethnic and de-politicized, all in the name of democratic policing. Such a mission was an explicit effort at social engineering as police were hired, fired and disciplined as part of an effort to foster better inter-communal relations. While the effect of these programs remains debatable, the shift in objective was striking: UNPOL had become part of an international effort to reconstitute Bosnia as a liberal democratic state founded on principles of ethnic tolerance.[29]

Following the onset of the mission in Bosnia, two important conceptual developments transformed UNPOL's mission, leading to an expansion of its mandate for executive authority missions. The first innovation was the broad notion of security sector reform (SSR).[30] Security sector reform holds that the transition to a peaceful society extends beyond simply demobilizing the armed forces and reintegrating their members into civil society, and must also include transforming the nature of civil-military relations in the state. Advocates of SSR regard the job of international authorities in post-conflict states as not only breaking apart potentially dangerous standing armies or militias but also reforming the military culture of the security services and improving their institutional safeguards to prevent abuse. Instituting a culture of civilian control over the military in these societies is seen as an essential step in keeping the peace. For the most part, SSR advocates locate police reform as part of this program, although some critics have called for police reform to be de-linked from other SSR programs.[31] As international police deployments became agents of SSR in these countries, their mandates increased dramatically in scope and complexity.

The second key concept, "police-keeping," extends the logic of SSR by placing the police as the chief engine of the reform of the state.[32] This is inherently a long-term project, for police-keeping "begins in the immediate aftermath of hostilities and continues in diminishing measure until governance has been fully transferred to local authorities."[33] Operating under Chapter VI or Chapter VII UN authorization, the UNPOL forces would seek to integrate military assistance, rule of law, reform of domestic institutions, the improvement of the economy and the establishment of a civil society as part of a unified package in the society. Just as it did with SSR, UNPOL again acts as an instrument for reform, with a wider and more complex mandate than it had during the missions of the 1960s.[34] Together with the birth of SSR as a doctrine, the police-keeping concept marks the evolution of UNPOL's mandate from being reactive and advisory to being proactive and constitutive in shaping law and order in a post-conflict state. These conceptual innovations were acknowledged in the Brahimi Report, which called upon the UN to institute a standing pool of available UNPOL officers for rapid deployment in crises.[35]

The culmination of this trend towards greater authority for the Civillian Police (CIVPOL) came in the late 1990s with the appearance of executive authority missions. Within these missions, the goals were more ambitious: to establish a monopoly on the legitimate use of violence within an established territory, as well as to generate and sustain the political authority of the state.

In part, these missions are a nod to reality. In both Kosovo and East Timor, for instance, the collapse of all governmental authority on the territory left the UN with few options but to undertake a statebuilding mission. But it nevertheless represented a significant step forward for UNPOL, which found itself involved in the task of generating a state or at least its ability to maintain order, not simply propping up an existing one or reforming its institutions. As a result of this mission, the public order dimension of the UNPOL mission has become more pronounced and ambitious in the new protectorates of Kosovo and East Timor. The only question is whether this new dimension would be complementary or contradictory to the vast array of other objectives occurring under the rubric of democratic policing.

## Objectives at War

There are at least two distinct objectives to the UNPOL deployments in the new protectorates. The first is Weberian: the UNPOL force is charged with establishing a monopoly on the use of force within a territory.[36] This consists of isolating and destroying potential but illegitimate claimants to state power, disrupting criminal networks and establishing basic public order amidst widespread chaos and criminality. The objective also comprises bolstering the political authority of the so-called "internationals" administering the territory against any threat. In the absence of a government, the phalanx of international and regional institutions orchestrating the intervention takes its place and relies on UNPOL forces, often working in tandem with military peacekeepers, to ensure that there is no organized threat to their lives or authority. Of particular concern to IOs and NGOs working in post-conflict groups are armed groups that wish to challenge the formal or effective terms of the settlement.[37] For example, in Kosovo, NATO peacekeepers and UNPOL officers worked in tandem to restore public order but also to fend off attempts by the KLA to intimidate minorities and inhibit the relief operations of the UN, the OSCE and other regional organizations.[38]

The Weberian dimension to a UNPOL mission was particularly pronounced in the first few months of the new protectorates. In Kosovo and East Timor, effective government collapsed after the retreat of the Yugoslav Army from Kosovo and the Indonesian Army in East Timor. A security vacuum emerged in both cases and generated serious threats to public order. In Kosovo, when NATO peacekeeping forces entered the province on 12 June 1999, they confronted "a rising tide of violence and crime."[39] Thousands of refugees flooded back in what was described as "biggest refugee return in modern history and also the quickest role reversal."[40] In four months, the OSCE reported 348 murders, 116 kidnappings, 1,070 lootings, and 1,106 cases of arson.[41] They also confronted a number of rival claimants to state power. Within days of the end of the air war in Kosovo, an unauthorized KLA-backed provisional government assumed control over much of the territory. Allegations of reprisal violence against Serbs and Roma began to appear as approximately 100,000 of the 230,000 Serbs remaining in Kosovo fled to Serbia and surrounding states.[42] Porous borders opened up new opportunities for organized crime. Reports of Albanian on Albanian political violence became interwoven with stories of mafia gangs settling scores through killings, arsons and assaults.[43] The intelligence gap was so severe that many international officials lacked information even about the street names in Pristina and other major cities.[44] In the words of a long time observer, Kosovo had become a "frontier-style place."[45]

The NATO-led peacekeeping force, named KFOR, was charged with traditional military tasks—including ensuring the cessation of hostilities between the combatants, establishing control over the border with the Federal Republic of Yugoslavia, and disarming the remaining combatants on both sides— while CIVPOL would assume the basic tasks of providing law and order. Once KFOR had established effective control over the territory, starting with the cities and spreading out through the rural areas, it would assume the backup role in policing and turn primary responsibility for policing to CIVPOL. The original mandate for CIVPOL in both cases was to provide for temporary law and order and to fill the security gap that had emerged in the aftermath of the war. In Kosovo, the mandate of CIVPOL was: (1) to provide temporary law enforcement; and (2) to establish and develop a professional, impartial and independent local police, called the Kosovo Police Service (KPS). But in practice, the division of labor and transfer of power between international law enforcement agencies never happened in the neat and seamless way envisaged at the UN Secretariat in New York. Both KFOR and CIVPOL experienced problems with deployment, delaying their arrival in force and allowing violent crime to spread across the province. KFOR, which did not initially see policing as part of its mandate, had to rapidly adjust as CIVPOL forces did not arrive on time and Albanian extremist groups conducted murders and expulsions of Serb and Roma individuals. For the first two years of its operation, CIVPOL was understaffed.[46] Though designed to have at least 3,100 officers according to the terms of UNSCR 1244, CIVPOL fielded only 1,974 officers by the end of 1999 and 2,456 by the end of 2000.[47] While the level and diversity of serious crime in Kosovo far exceeded what is normally found in Western cities, the CIVPOL deployment did not provide the kind of basic force coverage common to those cities.[48] In most American and European cities, the police departments aim for a 20 person per police officer ratio.[49] Across Kosovo, there were 1,044 people for every CIVPOL officer in 1999; by 2000, there were roughly 869 people per CIVPOL officer.[50]

While understaffed, KFOR and CIVPOL needed to re-establish public order through the use of persuasion and force. KFOR and CIVPOL officers employed force to protect vulnerable Serb and Roma communities from reprisal killings, to push back mafia infiltration of the state and to stop the widespread looting and seizure of private property that took place after the withdrawal of Yugoslav forces. But their relative weakness due to understaffing and lack of needed personnel (like Special Police Units) meant that CIVPOL Officers occasionally needed to look the other way for some minor offences. They were also forced in some instances to rely on former KLA commanders, who had established control over most of the municipalities in the territory, to provide public order.[51] The first contingent of CIVPOL officers faced an acute dilemma in Kosovo: they needed to restore public order with the cooperation or acquiescence of the KLA, but did not want to ratify the KLA's illegal seizure of power. Through co-option and force, CIVPOL officers and KFOR peacekeepers were engaged in classically Weberian tasks: (1) to re-establish the monopoly of the legitimate use of force with the international authorities and (2) to punish or destroy those who would use violence without that legitimation.[52]

In East Timor, the situation was less chaotic and violent after the Indonesian forces retreated in September 1999.[53] The pro-independence Timorese umbrella group, the CNRT, assumed control and began to work with local tribal chiefs to restore public order.[54] There were scattered murders of those returning militias and a few anecdotal accounts of severe beatings and expulsions.[55] The most serious violent depredations in the country were directed against the East Timorese refugees trapped over the border in West Timor.[56] The Timorese trapped in camps in West Timor (specifically in Kupang and the Atumbua region, near the border with East Timor) were effectively kept as hostages by pro-Indonesian militia members, who used a combination of intimidation, violence and misinformation to convince them that they would be killed if they returned.[57] UNHCR staff who were responsible for humanitarian care and refugee returns were not immune to attacks, and after some effort resorted to a "snatch and grab" operation in order to return East Timorese to their homes. Although it sporadically cooperated with UNHCR, Indonesia did little to confront the predatory militia members who remained intermingled with the 70,000 refugees still trapped over the border.[58]

In East Timor, an Australian-led peacekeeping force (entitled INTERFET) was principally responsible for maintaining order. As was the case in Kosovo, UNPOL was also responsible for backing up INTERFET's efforts and for establishing responsibility for law and order once the peacekeeping force had withdrawn. Having learned lessons from Kosovo, the UN also gave the UNPOL in East Timor a more expansive mandate: (1) to provide security and maintain law and order throughout the territory of East Timor; (2) to establish an effective administration; (3) to assist in the development of civil and social services; (4) to ensure the coordination and delivery of humanitarian assistance, rehabilitation and development assistance; (5) to support capacity-building for self-government; and (6) to assist in the establishment of conditions for sustainable development.[59] The Special Representative of the Secretary General gave international peacekeeping forces robust rules of engagement and permitted them to pursue and fire upon militias that had infiltrated the country from Indonesian territory.[60] In East Timor, UNPOL had a less difficult time in re-establishing public order in this case, in part because many of those responsible for war crimes fled across the border into West Timor and in part because the CNRT worked co-operatively with UNPOL to re-establish order in the far-flung villages of the country. Crime was generally lower than it was in Kosovo, consisting of only a few scattered murders and assaults against Indonesian collaborators.

Neither mission, however, had the re-establishment of public order as the sole purpose of its deployment. In both Kosovo and East Timor, UNPOL forces were also given a second, Kantian goal: to instill the values of democratic policing in the local police forces as part of a transitional administration and state creation project. Part of this involves promoting human rights. Annika Hansen notes that "civilian police forces are now established actors in the human rights field and are deemed the single most effective agency when it comes to promoting human rights and assessing government compliance with human rights standards."[61] In Kosovo, the UNPOL forces were asked to be the agents of human rights reform, building local capacity among the police and training them in international standards of human rights.[62] Under the leadership of the OSCE, UNPOL forces were engaged in training the Kosovo Police Service (KPS), setting up a police academy in Vučitrn and using US-based training manuals for democratic policing.[63] This was perceived to be a long-term project in Kosovo, as the KPS officers were monitored by UNPOL for years after they began to deploy on their own. UNPOL also played a role in establishing the new legal code, resolving the dispute over which law was now applicable in the state.[64] These efforts were constitutive, not advisory, and in their departure UNPOL aimed to leave a fully-functioning democratic police force for a future Kosovo government.

A similarly ambitious agenda was given to the UNPOL forces in East Timor. When the Indonesian armed forces withdrew from the country, tens of thousands of Indonesians fled the country, most of them senior and mid-level bureaucrats. This led to the collapse of the police force and the need to re-establish public order. But UNTAET and later UNMISET established a Police Academy, designed to create a local police trained in the standards of democratic policing.[65] UNPOL forces were expected to work co-operatively with UN and CNRT political leaders to promote human rights in the country. UNPOL was also charged with supporting the Serious Crimes Unit (SCU) in its investigation of the violence inflicted by pro-Indonesian militias in 1999.[66] These long-term projects were among the efforts towards achieving a culture of "democratic policing" in East Timor.[67]

In both Kosovo and East Timor, the Weberian and Kantian objectives were compressed, linking state creation and democratization into a single package for the new protectorates. The Weberian dimension requires the judicious application of force to deal with ordinary criminality and threats to the authority of the state. The Kantian dimension was value-based and aimed at creating democratic police forces imbued with Western human rights standards, which would support whatever government emerged following the intervention. In European states, the trajectory of political development sequenced the Weberian and Kantian objectives, often across centuries; the state gradually established effective control over its territory—often through horrific violence—and then was eventually made legitimate by democratic election.[68] But in the new protectorates, these two objectives are simultaneous; indeed, they are imposed as part of a single package, as the creation of a functioning state and a liberal democracy were seen as coterminous. Just as the international community struggles when it tries to liberalize the politics of a state before establishing functioning institutions, efforts by UNPOL to foster democratic police forces founder in the absence of an effective, even ruthless, monopoly on the use of force in the territory.[69]

Yet the Weberian and Kantian order dimensions of UNPOL's mission are at odds in two important respects. First, the re-establishment of public order requires application of the coercive power of the state or supporting international authority in the service of destroying or criminalizing actors whose goals the international authorities do not share. This implies a subjective judgment about who is and is not a suitable interlocutor for the state. But UNPOL's Kantian dimension—which implies a liberal openness to political contestation by multiple and competing claimants to state power—suggests that international authorities should not pre-judge who is an authorized claimant to state power. Without any clear writ of legitimacy beyond the UN, or any elections to determine who is and is not a legitimate political player, international authorities should be reluctant to deal with any political actor for fear of enhancing that actor's legitimacy and altering the political landscape beyond the consent of the local population. In theory, UNPOL should adopt an attitude of studied neutrality towards all actors in the province. In Kosovo and East Timor, it therefore follows that UNPOL should be reluctant to make deals with the KLA or the CNRT commanders to re-establish public order. To do so would strengthen the armed wing of certain political actors, giving them a privileged position in the emerging political class of the state. Yet the basic necessity of re-establishing public order as a precondition of building a functioning state, coupled with its own staffing constraints, often leaves UNPOL with little option but to do a deal with those who have the guns, irrespective of their political legitimacy. In this respect, the practical needs of establishing political order work at cross purposes with the Kantian preference for free, fair and unbiased political contestation. The practical need for outsiders to establish public order may inadvertently undermine the legitimate foundations of the state they are trying to build.

Second, the lack of local legitimacy that UNPOL itself faces often undermines the application of force during the re-establishment of public order.[70] In most modern democratic states, the coercive power of the state is underwritten by its legitimacy. But in the new protectorates the legitimacy of the mission—if it exists at all—is provided by the UN mandate. Thus UNPOL is applying force against criminals and illicit challengers to state power (such as insurgents) without a formal writ of legitimacy from an election by the local population; in a sense, it has a Kantian deficit.[71] At the same time, it is charged with promoting human rights standards and the rule of law—the very hallmarks of legitimate domestic government—while facing its own distinct legitimacy gap. The gap between the questionable internal legitimacy of UNPOL forces and their insistence that any local police force be legitimate makes their mission objectives contradictory. It also makes UNPOL naturally reluctant to engage in the kind of application of brute force to pacify the country that was so common in the earlier protectorates. One can see this particularly in the halting and inconsistent way that force was applied in Kosovo and East Timor. The glaring gap in legitimacy makes the UNPOL forces—who remain inter-positioned between local actors, but apart from them—hesitant to employ violence that may be needed to achieve their Weberian objective, especially when dealing with spoilers or other armed challengers to the political order.

*An Uncertain Imperial Strategy*

Historically, trusteeship was seen as an enterprise for an imperial power which sought to extend its dominion for the purposes of power, profit or charity. Empire was rarely, if ever, established for a single, dominant motive; often greed and charity coexisted happily in the minds of those leading imperial missions. The British, for example, justified their colonial holdings in India as necessary for expanding commerce and increasing national wealth but also to bring development and good governance to the local population.[72] The infamous Congo Free State was established to "introduce civilization and trade into the centre of Africa," but under the stewardship of King Leopold of Belgium it descended into misrule and barbaric mistreatment of the local population.[73] Influenced by racism and notions of cultural superiority, many of those who advocated empire believed that they had a responsibility "to sacrifice themselves in order that their less-fortunate fellows may learn how to share in their blessings."[74] As Will Bain has pointed out in his chapter, a trusteeship relationship presumes inequality between the parties, as the dependent is looked after in a paternal-istic fashion by the imperial power. Imperial trusteeship was, however, not gen-erally seen as a shared task. Indeed, the very notion of duty that underpinned notions of trusteeship in the colonial era presumed that a single power was exclusively responsible for managing the affairs of a dependent colony or territory.

Despite echoes remaining, the days of imperial trusteeship are long gone.[75] In the new protectorates of Kosovo and East Timor, the responsibility for man-aging the affairs of the dependent territory is shared by a condominium of interested parties rather than a single state. This condominium of states is often referred to by the shorthand of the "international community," though it hardly reflects the diverse range of states present in the UN General Assembly. More-over, the representatives of the international community are not solely states. In the words of James Fearon and David Laitin, "in contrast to classic imperialism, in these new forms of rule subjects are governed by a hodgepodge of foreign powers, IOs and NGOs and domestic institutions, rather than by a single imperial or trust power asserting monopoly rights within its domain."[76] More recently, international trusteeships tend to be the wards of regional organizations dominated by Western powers (such as NATO in Kosovo) or the United Nations, often with the support of powerful regional states (such as Australia in East Timor).[77]

As pointed out in the introduction to this volume, the predominant problem that these condominiums of states face when managing a trusteeship is that of coordination. Trusteeship poses a classic collective action problem, in which the major players must find ways to come up with the necessary resources and manage their respective contributions in the absence of a supranational authority that can offer incentives or penalties for participation (or lack thereof).[78] Even when they agree that ongoing disorder in the trusteeship is not desirable, the "international community" often has problems overcoming its collective action problem in putting an end to even modest forms of criminality. Especially in cases where the international community overcomes its collective action problems and makes a formal commitment to oversee the development of a new protectorate, its multilateral approach is often beset by staffing, command and control and discipline problems. One of the many reasons why UNPOL missions are under-resourced, on short time horizons, and beset by internal infighting is that their state sponsors are reluctant to admit that they are engaged in what might be termed post-modern imperialism.[79] The anti-imperial sympathies of states engaged in UNPOL operations tend to undercut their strategic effectiveness, even while they often score tactical victories.

The uneasy imperialism of the condominiums of powers involved in trusteeships—and their difficulties in resolving collective action problems—can be seen in the deployments of police forces to restore public order. From the outset, collective action problems bedeviled the UN in Kosovo, as the UN Secretariat found itself unable to recruit and deploy CIVPOL in sufficient numbers on short notice, leaving KFOR responsible for law and order tasks beyond its mandate.[80] The slow speed of deployments had a direct impact on the UN's ability to achieve its Weberian task of reimposing order. Problems in the deployment and geographical spread of CIVPOL in Kosovo in late 1999 meant that Serbs, Roma and other minorities in distant rural regions could not rely on regular patrols to protect them from reprisal attacks by their neighbors.

In part because of the problems of recruitment, the UN deployment had skills gaps in what they were able to achieve early in the Kosovo mission.

CIVPOL had an abundance of officers trained in basic police tasks—traffic control and ordinary investigations, for example—but few with specialized skills (such as riot control) or knowledge (forensics). The CIVPOL forces in Kosovo—often derided by the locals as the "Rainbow Coalition" or the "Coca-Cola Cops"—featured significant variations in the level of skills, training and education across contributing nations, posing supervisory problems for the UN.[81] Moreover, the varying CIVPOL contingents have different standards for dealing with local interlocutors and employing force. In Kosovo, CIVPOL officers from countries with strong histories of community policing were accustomed to gathering intelligence from the local population, while those from countries with quasi-military traditions were less inclined to use language translators and to trust local intelligence. Similarly, varying standards in the use of force across CIVPOL contingents often undermined the notion that the UN had a single coherent strategy for policing Kosovo.[82] While there was a unified CIVPOL command, it had limited powers over the national units, which often saw themselves as reporting both to the UN and to their own home governments. Command and control over this multilateral police force were weak and exhibited little of the unity of effort that sometimes characterized imperial policing.[83]

A similar set of coordination problems undermined the UN strategy for maintaining law and order in East Timor. Like Kosovo, East Timor did not have an indigenous army or police force; during the Indonesian occupation, internal law and order were maintained (often brutally) by the Indonesian Army (TNI) and Indonesian National Police (POLRI).[84] Once the Indonesian forces withdrew in October 1999, the Australian-run peacekeeping force INTERFET was responsible for maintaining law and order until January 2000, when the UN deployed its UNPOL officers. Between 2000 and 2002, the UN deployed 1,600 UNPOL officers, headed by a UN Police Commissioner with executive authority for restoring law and order to the society.[85] As with UNPOL in Kosovo, the multinational character of UNPOL in East Timor multiplied its coordination problems. In the words of the UN SRSG Sérgio Vieira de Mello, "the mixing up of 40 different nationalities of police (and thus of training, backgrounds and competencies, policing philosophies and approaches) and the task of this hybrid with establishing an immediate and effective policing presence in a territory to which it is alien both linguistically and culturally is an approach which is inherently fraught with risk."[86]

The UNPOL mission in East Timor, while shorter-lived and arguably more immediately successful than the one in Kosovo, suffered from some of the organizational and political pathologies that afflict multilateral peacekeeping missions.[87] According to Ludovic Hood, UNPOL were "plagued by inadequate planning and deficient mission design arising from the death of institution-building expertise at UN headquarters."[88] The UNPOL command did not have a strategic plan for developing an indigenous police service and lacked qualified UNPOL officers for institution-building. Appointments to UNPOL leadership positions were often done on the basis of political considerations rather than expertise.[89] Some UNPOL officers lacked experience in community policing and respect for the local population, whilst others lacked the specialized skills for tasks such as riot control and training. Even fewer had any capacity with the local languages or familiarity with the Indonesian criminal code, which still applied.[90]

Because of the coordination problems for recruitment and resource management, UNPOL officers were forced to improvise on the basis of their previous policing experience. Karl Clark, a retired US police officer who spent five years in East Timor remarked that in the early days of the mission:

The UN was very slow in getting resources. We had no radios, no communications, no law and we were told make it up as you go along. We didn't have places to lock people up and if we arrested someone we took them to Dili, but weren't sure what happened after that. Most of the time we allowed the village system, that they had for centuries, come into play. And it worked. There was a court system in effect, and people did get arrested. Very early in the mission, there was no system in place and we had to make it up as we went along. So we fell back on our own methods of policing.[91]

The UNPOL mission depended upon the cooperation of the local population, the militias and the entrepreneurship of its officers. Yet its multinational character also meant that East Timor featured significant unevenness in policing standards and approaches, which led to serious difficulties when the transition to local policing authority got underway.[92]

As a multilateral organization, reflecting all of the positives and negatives that this concept implies, the UNPOL missions in Kosovo and East Timor were often less than the sum of their parts. They were akin to exercises in imperial policing but were not conducted by a single power. Rather, they were managed by a consortium of states and international and regional organizations, often with overlapping mandates and diffuse lines of control. Because maintaining a political balance between contributing members was important, the UNPOL missions were determined by what states offered rather than what the new protectorates needed. Such volunteerism stood at odds with some basic imperial tasks, including subduing armed actors who were willing to challenge international authorities with force. The political and operational problems experienced by UNPOL were in part of a function of this uncertain multilateral imperialism, which tended to undermine and put at cross-purposes the Weberian and Kantian objectives of the missions. Because of the uneven performance and coordination problems that UN multilateralism implies, in the words of one observer, for UNPOL "a successful UN mission happens by accident, not design."[93]

## Organizational Imperatives and Local Agency

One of the most common refrains in the implementation of peacekeeping missions is that the ultimate responsibility for the state needs to remain with the local population and that the mission should be sensitive to the needs and desires of local actors.[94] Reflecting this desire, UNPOL missions often strive to be both international and local, with the internationals concerned to keep agency with the local population and be sensitive to their needs. In each of the cases of trusteeship surveyed here, UN-backed UNPOL forces were charged with building and training a local police force. This goal is explicitly normative, as UNPOL forces are regularly asked to inculcate the skills of democratic policing among the indigenous forces.[95] This specific task for UNPOL is understood to support the overall transformative goals of the new protectorates.[96] To do this, the conventional wisdom holds, one must strike an appropriate balance between international control and local agency.

While this call for local agency has been a regular feature of most UNPOL deployments, achieving a perfect harmony between international tutelage and local control in the most recent international protectorates has remained elusive.[97] There are a number of reasons for this, not the least of which is that international actors tend to privilege their understandings of political order over those of the inhabitants of the new protectorate.[98] The explicit or unspoken bargain of trusteeships is that the international authorities will give way to the local authorities once the state is functioning and the local elites have become capable of governing. Yet this rarely, if ever, seems to happen; in fact, international deployment of peacekeepers tends generally to be the precursor for long-term military or policing deployments, as a shifting array of normative goals keeps international authorities invested in protectorates on a seemingly indefinite basis.[99] International peacekeeping missions begin but they rarely end decisively; the international stewardship of trusteeship societies tends to last long after news about a particular conflict falls out of the headlines. Bosnia is a perfect case in point; sixteen years after the end of its civil war, international officials, particularly a European Union-led police advisory mission, remain involved in the day-to-day affairs of the country. Kosovo and East Timor (both now independent) have residual UN missions which are seen as supporting their nascent democracies. More often, UN protectorates tend to fall into dependency for both administrative support and finances on their external partners.[100]

Key reasons for the duration of the new protectorates are their ambitions and organizational complexity. Far from being simply missions to restore order, trusteeships often come equipped with wide mandates for economic reform, civil administration, media management, humanitarian assistance, the resettlement of refugees and a host of other activities.[101] In Bosnia, the OHR retained the right to fire Bosnian civil servants and dismiss elected officials if it judged their behavior to be contrary to the letter or spirit of the Dayton Accords. In Kosovo, a range of international organizations (including the UN, EU and OSCE) divided responsibility for governing Kosovo and soon found themselves responsible for such diverse issues as issuing license plates, regulating radio broadcasts and ensuring fair property restitution for displaced people. Particularly in East Timor, the imperial dimension of the trusteeships was pronounced: the SRSG had nearly unlimited power "to enact new laws or to amend or repeal existing ones—powers that he immediately used to create a central fiscal authority, courts and a police system, defense force, even traffic rules."[102] The UN mandate in East Timor clearly carried an echo of imperial trusteeships, as some suspected the UN of paternalistic involvement in managing the affairs of the country.[103]

The growing complexity of the UN missions is mirrored by the growing complexity of the UNPOL missions. In contrast to the early UNPOL missions, which consisted largely of unarmed observers, the UNPOL missions in the new protectorates require police trained in complex tasks such as forensics investigations, riot control, VIP security, organized crime, as well as a host of administrative tasks. In Kosovo, for instance, UNPOL eventually assumed responsibility for running the prisons service and established a training academy to offer instruction to the new members of the Kosovo Police Service (KPS). The complexity of the UNPOL missions is reflected not only in the proliferation of their tasks, but also in their numbers. In July 2000, the three UNPOL missions in the new protectorates—UNMIBH (1,572 officers), UNMIK (3,954 officers) and UNTAET (1,303 officers)—were of an order of magnitude larger than other advisory UNPOL deployments.[104] Owing to their increased specialization and size, the UNPOL missions in the new trusteeships have larger institutional footprints than those with advisory roles.

This complexity has a distinct political implication for its ability to work with local partners. Complex organizations are rarely able to function without a strong centralized bureaucracy and a tight control over resources. Differentiation of constituent units of an organization often requires some degree of integration to manage collective action.[105] UNPOL missions in Kosovo and East Timor were no exception. As both UNPOL missions expanded their remits to include training and functional tasks related to promoting law and order, both developed hierarchical central command structures with sharp divisions of labor among constituent units. This centralization process concentrated decision-making power in the hands of the central command, often at the expense of the initiative of locally-based UNPOL units. It also led to efforts by UNPOL in both missions to generate standard operating procedures (SOPs) for their operations, in part to compensate for the institutional pathologies of having police officers assigned to UNPOL on a short-term basis.[106]

The growing centralization and professionalism of the UNPOL missions is for efficiency reasons. But it has generated a series of perverse incentives for international actors to husband resources at the expense of working with local actors. First, centralization tends to lend itself to institutional rigidity, which is inimical to the spirit of engaging local actors in a consultative process to understand their needs. The development of SOPs—itself a function of complexity—tends also to undermine local agency, by establishing set procedures for how UNPOL mission should operate irrespective of whether local actors found these methods appropriate. This raised the question of whether UNPOL missions were implementing so-called "international" standards of justice over more local forms of conflict resolution.[107] This was apparent in East Timor. UNPOL officials encountered a complex system of local justice, in which the tribal chief of each village would often judge the responsibility of those involved in violence during the Indonesian occupation and mete out punishments accordingly. The tribal system also determined whether someone would be able to return to a village once they had fled. But this informal system of justice—with its lack of a guarantee of a fair trial or even appropriate standards of evidence—would not be up to the formalized standards of Western courts or UNPOL manuals. During the early days of this mission, the understaffed UNPOL officers turned a blind eye to this system, in part because they lacked the resources and information to compete.[108] But growing centralization and command—and an insistence that agents within a complex organization follow standard operating procedures—tend to eliminate the flexibility and adaptation needed to be responsive to local agents who often have their own ways of doing things. It is unclear whether a much more fully staffed and professionalized UNPOL force later in the mission in East Timor would have been able to demonstrate the same level of flexibility in accommodating local justice as the early under-directed and under-staffed UNPOL did.

Second, the centralization of missions strengthened UNPOL as a political force within their host societies, generating a series of perverse incentives to keep control over resources even if that meant excluding local actors. Jarat Chopra, for instance, has chronicled how UNTAET resisted Timorese participation in the UN's work to "safeguard the UN's influence."[109] The same dynamic can be seen in the development of a local police force. UNTAET failed to engage with the local political leadership or civil society in the construction of a local police force; the police service was excluded from the power-sharing arrangements implemented by the UN for the first two years of the mission. Until East Timor achieved full independence, local PNTL officials reported directly to the UNPOL Commissioner and the UNTAET Deputy SRSG.[110] This process seriously undermined Timorese ownership of the PNTL and left a dysfunctional and often under-resourced local police force at the end of the transitional period.[111] Similar concerns were voiced in Kosovo, as UNMIK's heavy institutional and bureaucratic footprint was seen as standing in the way of the province's independence.[112] Prior to independence, local KPS officers had to report to CIVPOL commanders while on patrol in Kosovo, thus creating a police service which is local in character but international in command. This dual structure—international in leadership, local in legitimacy and execution—led to deep resentment among KPS officers who felt that they were disadvantaged in pay and treated as a second class police service in their own country. Further, this structure raised troubling questions about how sustainable the KPS would be once the "internationals" had left. The growing centralization of highly complex UNPOL missions generates a series of standard operating procedures which are necessary for the management of complex organizations, but they generate perverse incentives and may have untold costs for local agency over the long term.

## Conclusion

The use of UNPOL forces to restore law and order has become codified as a kind of standard practice for new protectorates and similar cases of civil disorder after war. Particularly after the bitter experience of policing in Iraq—in which UNPOL forces were not employed and internal disorder eventually metastasized into an insurgency—international officials in the UN and regional organizations will likely call again on UNPOL forces to restore order and promote democratic policing in other failed or failing states. Today, in both Iraq and Afghanistan, police officers, employed under a national flag or the bilateral programs such as the US-led ICITAP initiative, are called upon to support statebuilding efforts under harsher conditions than were present in Kosovo or East Timor. Operating without executive authority, these missions mark a return to the traditional capacity building and mentoring roles of international police. In some respects, the experience of Kosovo and East Timor may have led both national governments and the UN to scale down their ambitions for UNPOL and establish mandates more commensurate with their limited resources and capacities. Such a move away from the executive authority model towards a more advisory capacity may allow UNPOL to avoid or mitigate some of the dilemmas that arise from balancing the Weberian and Kantian aspects of statebuilding.

The employment of UN-led UNPOL forces or other police in statebuilding missions may ultimately be necessary because internal security is the precondition for political life and economic development. But this cannot come at the expense of paralyzing local actors who want to play a role in the future of their country. Michael Ignatieff aptly describes the challenge that international authorities in the new protectorates face:

Taking responsibility without confiscating it is the balance international administrators have to strike. The trick in nation-building is to force responsibility—for security, for co-existence—back onto local elites. This is not easy. The spectacle of disgruntled locals, sitting in cafes, watching earnest young internationals speeding around to important meetings in Toyota Land Cruisers has been repeated in every nation-building experiment of the 1990s. The most successful transitional administrations are the ones that try to do themselves out of a job.[113]

Yet too often in the new protectorates the impact of UNPOL deployment on this crucial balance between responsibility and local agency has been overlooked. UNPOL deployments are not merely blunt instruments that can be used to pacify a territory or to marginalize the issue of security so that political and economic developments may go forward. Rather, UNPOL deployments are inherently political activities authorized by the UN or a regional organization and conducted on behalf of a condominium of often competing states in the service of building a liberal democratic state in place of the war-torn territory.[114] More than just technocratic exercises, UNPOL deployments in the new trusteeships are themselves constitutive interventions in the attempted construction of a new polity.

The major difference from historical precedents is that the liberal paternalism which underlies policing in the new protectorates is now an uneasy one. These missions carry a distinct imperial echo but they lack the single-minded purposefulness or coherence of the imperial trusteeships or mandates system. This is not entirely a bad thing: that single-minded purposefulness about restoring order led to significant brutality against the colonial populations. But policing in the new protectorates is not unproblematic either. In their objectives, strategy and organizational makeup, they are instead beset by internal contradictions, as they try to strike that balance between restoring order (with the implicit threat of violence) and building a consensual democratic state. Their multilateral character and the tension between their organizational complexity and their need to preserve local agency often renders these police deployments less than the sum of their parts. Until international police deployments are acknowledged by the UN and other actors for what they are—ineluctably political acts in the service of constituting a new liberal democratic polity, deemed acceptable by external actors more than internal actors—these internal contradictions will remain irreducible.

# 11

# THE POLITICAL ECONOMY OF PROTECTORATES AND "POST-CONFLICT" INTERVENTION

*Mats Berdal and David Keen*

Throughout the post-Cold War era, Western-led statebuilding efforts in countries affected by war and violent conflict have been powerfully informed by what has been aptly described as a "mechanical metaphor" of state failure: a view of the social world and the challenges involved in statebuilding that treats failed states "like broken machines, [which] can be repaired by good mechanics."[1] Interventions have been conceived, and their record assessed, as grand projects in social engineering, with outsiders free to rebuild societies constrained only by the familiar problems of delivery: lack of donor coordination, bureaucratic turf battles among agencies, finite resources, poor sequencing and inadequate implementation of otherwise sound plans. One danger is that the societies on the receiving end are conceptualized as passive and inert. As Edward Said noted shortly before he died in September 2003: "It is quite common to hear high officials in Washington and elsewhere speak of changing the map of the Middle East, as if ancient societies and myriad peoples can be shaken up like so many peanuts in a jar."[2]

There are numerous difficulties with this understanding of the nature of the challenges posed by post-conflict peace- and statebuilding, not least the static, a-historical and culturally blind assumptions that underlie it. There is a further consideration of special interest to this chapter: the distinction between "us" and "them" implicit in the social engineering approach to peace- and state-building necessarily neglects the degree to which the policies and actions of outsiders feed back into, and themselves play, a critical role in shaping the character and dynamics of conflict-ridden societies.

Against these deficiencies, the chapter emphasizes the analytical value of a political economy approach to armed conflict, arguing that such an approach does much to explain why the record of outside involvement in war-torn societies, including in latter-day protectorates, is so mixed and uneven.[3] The chapter is especially concerned with the dominant economic policies and ideas promoted by outside actors and their effects on the political economy of conflict zones subject to external intervention. It proceeds in two parts.

The first part sets out what we understand by a political economy approach and the ways in which it challenges conventional approaches to state- and peacebuilding, most notably in the attention it draws to the functions of violence and the importance of informal power structures resting on patronage and coercion in post-conflict societies. The section also considers the effects of outside intervention on the political economy of conflict zones and, in particular, how and why the economic priorities of outsiders have often failed to transform predatory and exploitative political economies.

Drawing on this discussion, the second part examines two related sets of challenges that have increasingly come to preoccupy both policy-makers and scholars. The first is the so-called "spoiler problem," that is, how to deal with and manage actors determined to thwart the peace- and statebuilding activities promoted (in large part) by outsiders. The second, closely related, centers on how to think of, and how most effectively to address, the challenges posed by crime and the criminalization of post-conflict settings, including those that have often flourished in the new protectorates.

These are all large and complex issues to which a single chapter of limited length cannot possibly do justice. Our chief aim is to demonstrate—drawing on examples from Iraq, parts of Africa and the Balkans—how a political economy approach to armed conflict yields analytical insights of direct relevance to the study of protectorates and external involvement in "post-conflict" environments. By examining how economic, social and political agendas interact—recognizing that they do so in what will always be a historically and culturally distinct context—we suggest an approach to the understanding of conflict that draws attention not only to the importance of informal power structures and the networks of "privilege and patronage where real power lie,"[4] but also to their survival and continual adjustment to new post-war realities (including a large foreign presence or a particular set of policy priorities promoted by external actors). Highlighting the blurring of distinctions between "war" and "peace" and the emergence and reproduction of "alternative systems of power, profit and protection"[5] behind the façade of formal institutions within post-conflict environments, a political economy approach helps to explain why the actions of outsiders have frequently produced perverse and unintended consequences, including the entrenchment of illiberal, violent and exploitative actors. As such, it should also induce a certain caution about our use of labels and categories to capture and "explain" the drivers of any given conflict. Regarding "spoilers," for example, we stress how a political economy analysis should make us very skeptical about the definitions of spoilers that prevail at any point in time. Similarly, as James Cockayne has perceptively cautioned, "what is labeled 'organized crime' may at times manifest a deeper politico-economic system that satisfy the needs and interests of extensive communities straddling the state-society boundary."[6] In both cases, labels conceal a more complex reality on the ground, one that any outside intervener, however well intentioned, needs to understand better as it struggles to design policies aimed at building "sustainable peace" in societies fractured by war and violent conflict.

## The Political Economy of War and Peace[7]

The International Rescue Committee (IRC) has estimated that 5.4 million people died in the Democratic Republic of the Congo (DRC) in the decade from 1998 as a result of violence and humanitarian crisis.[8] The vast majority of deaths stemmed from malnutrition and preventable diseases rather than direct casualties from combat. Notwithstanding a large UN peacekeeping presence in the country for much of this period, the combination of repeated population displacements, reduced food security and the collapse of health services has taken a horrific toll.[9]

In such circumstances it is difficult to think of war as anything but a calamity for all involved, and much of the media attention given to the DRC over the past decade has concentrated, quite understandably, on the staggering and undoubted costs of continued violence. As with the portrayal of other post-Cold War conflicts, however, focusing exclusively on the costs of war—treating war merely as an irrational and catastrophic departure from "normal peacetime" conditions—frequently obscures the extent to which violence can also provide obvious benefits to many, both inside and outside the conflict zone itself. Indeed, the history of war and "peacebuilding" in the DRC highlights, with particular clarity, the functional utility of violence within politically fragmented, war-torn and economically fragile states. Here, for well over a decade, warring factions, neighboring powers, transnational corporations and actors have all employed and/or benefited from continued violence as a means of facilitating the exploitation of the country's vast and diverse mineral resources. The result has been a distinctive, though continually mutating, war economy with regional and global dimensions. In November 2009, the most recent in a series of reports by a UN-appointed Group of Experts on the DRC concluded that the illegal exploitation of natural resources—specifically of Congo's gold and cassiterite reserves—remains a major driver of conflict.[10] Indeed, so transparent has been the salience of economic agendas in the wars in the DRC and parts of West Africa in the 1990s that some commentators have reduced them to little more than "greed"-driven conflicts, initiated and sustained by predatory and loot-seeking rebels.[11]

This, the so-called "greed thesis" of civil war, should not however be confused with our understanding of a political economy approach to armed conflict and war-to-peace transitions. Though plunder and personal enrichment have undoubtedly played their part in many contemporary conflicts, they provide only one part of a far more complex picture. Economic agendas cannot be treated in isolation from a wider range of factors and motivations, including the key issues of power and identity, which have helped shape the character of individual war economies. As Karen Ballentine, basing her conclusions on the findings from a series of qualitative case studies, has perceptively argued "economic incentives and opportunities have not been the only or even the primary cause of these armed conflicts; rather, to varying degrees, they interacted with socio-economic and political grievances, interethnic disputes, and security dilemmas in triggering the outbreak of warfare."[12] While Ballentine and Sherman show that wars are often "economized,"[13] with purely economic incentives assuming a more prominent and critical role in sustaining violence over time, reducing wars and conflict simply to matters of greed fails to capture the complex interaction of economic and political agendas that translates into a distinctive political economy of war and peace. Even in the case of the DRC, as Stephen Jackson has persuasively argued, the wars that began in the eastern part of the country in the late 1990s were not grounded in "explicitly economic motives," though they "became successively more and more economic in ... scope, means and ends."[14] In short, unraveling the logic and dynamics of violence, including in the aftermath of war, requires a consideration of the many ways in which different agendas—overlapping, competing and complementary—are connected.

## Implications for Externally-Driven Peace- and Statebuilding Projects

The implications for the analysis of "post-conflict" peacebuilding, including trusteeships, are several. In the first instance, the political economy perspective makes it clear that war-to-peace transitions are much better understood as "a realignment of political interests and a readjustment of economic strategies rather than a clean break from violence to consent, from theft to production, or from repression to democracy."[15] As indicated above, the reason for this is that armed conflict and what is often loosely subsumed under the label of state "collapse" or state "failure" also involve the creation of new social and economic orders that reflect the exigencies and opportunities of war.[16] Such orders are often underpinned by a "perniciously symbiotic relationship between the economic activity and violence," which does not simply disappear with the formal end of conflict.[17] Understanding the political economy of any given conflict zone thus requires an appreciation of the way in which different actors—political and military elites, economic interest groups, external players (including neighboring states, firms and transnational corporations)—develop an interest and see functional utility in the continuation of violence and conflict. In addition, many ordinary people find ways of accommodating themselves to violent processes in the struggle to survive.

In an attempt to capture the multiplicity of interests among players in war and post-war settings, Stephen Jackson has usefully distinguished between three categories of actors: conflict "entrepreneurs," "opportunists" and "dependents."[18] The first of these refers to those for whom war, owing to the economic and other benefits it brings, including power and prestige, has become an end in itself. Such entrepreneurs, drawn from political, military and business elites, tend to form loose and highly pragmatic alliances among themselves and to develop symbiotic links to transnational and regional criminal networks. They also tend to have a vested interest in continued violence, whether direct or indirect. The second category covers those who profit in more opportunistic fashion from the apparent chaos that war offers. In terms of actors, there may be some overlap with the first category. Opportunistic actors will often include local officials and traders, middlemen, transnational corporations and other "actors who profiteer on the edges of the conflict."[19] Finally, to populations and citizens at the grass roots whose traditional livelihoods and entitlements have been destroyed by war, the functioning of the war economy will be primarily a matter of "coping."

Clearly, these are not are not hard and fast categories. Even so, while fluid, they provide a useful way of mapping the dynamics of conflict also in post-conflict settings (including many of the cases examined in the present volume), as they offer some sense of the processes by which alternative working systems emerge; processes that involve a criminalization of the economy, radical changes to "livelihood strategies" among ordinary populations, and a continual mutation of goals and objectives among parties to the conflict. A clearer sense of the multiple agendas held by actors also helps explain other distinctive features of many contemporary conflicts and their immediate post-war settings, including the tendency for apparent enemies to collaborate across ethnic and political fault-lines, avoiding direct and costly fighting in order to benefit more effectively from a continued state of war, violence and instability. Such alliances frequently survive into the post-war phase, when more indirect forms of violence and coercion are employed in response to changing realities on the ground. The central point is that actors adapt and realign their political and economic interests in response to changing circumstances and new opportunity structures. Importantly, as Timothy Raeymaekers has stressed, the very "process of adaptation and accommodation is likely to have an impact on the conflict environment itself, as well as on the future conception of social and political institutions."[20]

The political economy of a given conflict zone is likely to have crystallized over a long period of time and will reflect the differential impact of violence and conflict on local communities and within the wider region. Thus the political economy of war and peace in Afghanistan, as Barnett Rubin observed in 2000, "developed in response to the demands of warlords for resources and of the Afghan people for survival in a country devastated by over 20 years of war."[21] Over that period the war economy "sprea[d] internationally through a variety of social networks" and there emerged a political economy of war and peace with significant transnational, regional and global dimensions.[22] The transnational character of many war economies is another feature that political economy analysis has tended to bring into sharp relief. Indeed, the political economy of most contemporary armed conflicts is deeply embedded within more informal regional networks of a social, military and economic kind.[23] Such cross-border linkages among peoples and groups—making use of long-standing trade and commercial networks and benefiting from the lack of effective state control—are important to an understanding of the drivers of conflict and logic of violence, and therefore also to any peacebuilding effort that follows.[24]

## The Effects of External Intervention on the Political Economy of Conflict Zones

The political economy of conflict-affected societies, then, is never impervious to outside pressures and influences. In fact, the actions of outsiders—before, during and in the aftermath of wars—not only feed into but also shape and help define the political economy of a given conflict zone; a fact that the static and templated approach to peacebuilding promoted by donors and agencies has persistently underestimated. Indeed, outsiders have frequently ended up empowering rather than weakening those with an interest in continued violence; a striking example is provided by the highly ambiguous effects of economic sanctions and embargos imposed by the "international community" on both state and non-state actors since the early 1990s.[25]

A growing recognition of the often perverse and double-edged consequences of sanctions stems from the better understanding we now have of their impact on the political economy of Slobodan Milosević's Serbia and Saddam Hussein's Iraq in the 1990s. In both these cases, sanctions ended up strengthening rather than weakening the respective bases of power as the elites associated with regime stability were in a position, unlike the population at large, to benefit from a new opportunity structure given by the sanctions regime—a development with direct consequences for subsequent post-conflict developments in both countries (explored more fully below in the discussion of spoilers). This is particularly clear in the case of Iraq, where the rationing system set up by Saddam Hussein in response to the imposition of sanctions in the early 1990s became "one of the most coherent institutions of state power under sanctions... [tying] an increasingly impoverished population to the state, exacerbating their dependence on the ruling elite that sanctions were meant to coerce and societal pressure reform."[26]

Such perverse effects of externally imposed "control regimes" on the political economy of conflict zones are also evident in other cases. As Jackson has noted, "many policies for tackling the resource dimensions of armed conflict risk unintended negative consequences when they pay insufficient attention both to the damage they may inflict on the most vulnerable and to the perverse incentives they may offer for further rent seeking by conflict elites."[27] In

West, Central, and Southern Africa, for example, sanctions regimes imposed against non-state actors engaged in natural resource exploitation have also had unintended secondary effects by sometimes increasing levels of predation and violence against vulnerable civilian populations.[28]

The wider point here is a basic, though critical, one: the political economy of a conflict zone subject to outside intervention—whether the intervention assumes the form of sanctions, peacebuilding or even a trusteeship—is inseparable from the actual policies and actions taken by the outside intervener. Those actions have often reproduced systems whose internal logic runs counter to the stated goal of building self-sustaining peace on the foundations of accountable and properly functioning institutions, the rule of law and protection of human rights. While the social engineering perspective alluded to at the outset would tend to concern itself with how best to implement what are otherwise sound policies and noble objectives (and who, after all, does not want effective institutions, rule of law and protection of human rights?), a political economy analysis may conclude that the international presence itself is, or has become, part of the problem. As Timothy Raeymaekers has observed about the continuing failure of outsiders to address the crisis in Congo—what he calls "Congo's peacebuilding deadlock"—it is possible to see that "failure" as "a working system in which the reproduction of collapse and failure is consciously used as means to satisfy certain (political and economic) ends."[29]

## Economic Policies in Post-Conflict Societies and Protectorates

Graciana del Castillo has persuasively shown that external assistance aimed at aiding transitions from war to peace requires more than the "development as usual" approach traditionally favored by the Bretton Woods institutions, as well as by most donor countries and UN agencies.[30] Building lasting peace is a deeply political exercise and as such requires constant attention to "transitions" other than just the purely economic one. And yet, as Castillo notes, "the dogmatism and 'development as usual' approach to policymaking that the IMF has often preached have not contributed to national reconciliation, and have even endangered peace."[31]

Castillo's particular concern, first expressed in relation to her involvement with the peace process and post-conflict peace consolidation in El Salvador, was that the requirements of macroeconomic stability laid down by the IMF and donors, driven by neoliberal economic analysis and priorities, were often in direct and dangerous tension with the demands of the still-fragile and delicate transition to "self-sustaining peace."[32] The policies promoted by the IMF in El Salvador in the early 1990s reflected broadly what was known at the time as the "Washington consensus": that is, a neoliberal set of policy prescriptions emphasizing fiscal austerity (involving strict control of and cuts in public expenditure), rapid privatization, reliance on market mechanisms and the liberalization of capital and trade. In extreme form—entirely divorced from political, economic and social context—these policies amounted to a form of "market fundamentalism" resting on the ideological premise "that there is a market solution to any question about the nature of society."[33] That certainly was the belief that informed US policies in Iraq in 2003 and 2004 when the occupation authorities under Paul Bremer made radical economic transformation along neoliberal lines one of its chief objectives for post-Saddam Iraq.[34]

The case of Iraq may well represent, in the words of Ali Allawi, an extreme case of "raw and unfettered Darwinian capitalism" given free rein in a post-war setting.[35] It is nonetheless deeply instructive as it demonstrates how—in deeply fractured polities devastated by armed conflict—the application of neoliberal prescriptions can be politically destabilizing and economically counter-productive and yet fail to transform the underlying political economy of the country. The level of ambition exhibited by the Coalition Provisional Authority (CPA) was staggering, with a series of executive decisions made in 2003 that exposed Iraq's economy "to the most thoroughgoing form of neoliberal shock treatment of any country in the world."[36] The treatment included a privatization program for public sector companies, the elimination of all restrictions on foreign investment, a flat tax of 15 per cent for corporations and individuals, and "100 percent repatriation of profits, a 5 percent tax on most imports and 'national treatment' for foreign firms."[37] Because these ideologically-driven policies were implemented in willful ignorance of the political, socio-economic and historical context on the ground, the chances of success were always very remote, and indeed the aim of effecting a "radical restructuring and reduction of the state's role in the economy, has been an almost complete failure."[38] While the Ba'athist elites that supported Saddam's regime were removed by the occupation authorities, informal power and "shadow state" structures were able to capitalize on the opportunities for enrichment, theft and corruption created by the nature of outside intervention in Iraq's economy. Paradoxically, as Toby Dodge observes, the attempt to reform Iraq's political economy has not only been unsuccessful, it has run full circle, with the current regime—though it is clearly less brutal than that of Saddam— "ruling Iraq in a broadly similar way, using oil funded patronage and coercion to guarantee its survival."[39] In short, "the basis to Iraq's political economy, a rentier state fuelled by oil revenue striving to coercively dominate society, remains largely unchanged."[40]

The co-option or nullification of external economic policies and prescriptions by the "shadow state" is not unique to Iraq. In the case of Haiti, no fewer than seven international interventions since 1994 have failed to alter, in any fundamental sense, the country's underlying political economy. The reason, as James Cockayne has noted, is closely linked to the fact that those very interventions

> operated from an overly narrow, neoliberal conception of post-Cold War transformation. They divorced politics from political economy. In their attempts to reinforce the state's protection of its population and reform state-society relations, they focused excessively on democratization and reform of security institutions, failing to consider adequately the underlying need to transform Haiti's political economy.[41]

### Rethinking Policy? Conflict Sensitivity and the GEMAP Experiment in Liberia

It would be wrong to suggest that no lessons have been learned from these experiences. Both Haiti and, especially, Iraq do provide unusually clear-cut cases whereby the policies of external actors have served to reinforce the power of "shadow" structures, setting the conditions for their successful adaption to new post-war realities. Partly in response to the experiences in El Salvador, both donors and international financial institutions have come to recognize the dangers of too rigorous and inflexible application of economic policies in conflict-strewn and war-torn societies. Thus, in an evaluation of its own record in post-conflict reconstruction issued in 1998, the World Bank accepted that "immediate and widespread privatization may well not enhance the prospects for sustained, equitable development, and may even make them worse."[42] In light of such findings and to borrow the jargon, the policies of the World Bank have become more "conflict sensitive" with greater attention now paid to the sequencing and pacing of reform as well as to the use of instruments such as trust funds to provide grants rather than loans. There is also greater recognition than in the mid-1990s of "the need for increased flexibility in setting economic objectives and targets that allow for peace-related expenditure, including through access to some domestic financing, despite its potentially inflationary impact."[43] For all this, the IFIs (above all the IMF) have continued to emphasize the validity of neoliberal prescriptions as the dominant framework for post-conflict societies, and efforts to ensure greater conflict "sensitivity" have, in the view of some critics, been half-hearted and not sufficiently mainstreamed into the organizations. Writing in 2004, James Boyce still felt it necessary to urge IFIs not to "stick to the same policies they would follow if a country has never had a civil war."[44]

Since then, however, post-war Liberia has to come to provide a unique case of external intervention in the economic sphere of a sovereign state, and it now represents an unusually direct and intrusive attempt by donors to tackle the persistence of shadow structures and predatory war economies after war. For that reason it has attracted both interest and controversy. It merits special attention here also because it touches on many of the fundamental issues raised by the efforts of outsiders to support war-to-peace transitions, including how to effect the transformation of the political economy of societies emerging from protracted violence and state collapse.

The Comprehensive Peace Agreement for Liberia signed in August 2003 brought an end to years of brutal civil war; a war that had left the formal institutions of the state and the country's economic infrastructure in ruin. It soon became clear, however, that the peace accord—whose content and provisions reflected a power-sharing compromise between the principal military factions at the end of the war—had singularly failed to bring an end to the plundering of the country's resources that had been such a feature of the civil war period. During the two-year transition phase, members of the National Transitional Government of Liberia (NTGL) focused much, if not all, of their energies on enriching themselves.[45] To this end, the transitional period itself was viewed as an opportunity, perhaps the final such opportunity, "to continue to milk the traditional cash cows of the Liberian state such as the ports, the airports and the customs."[46]

It was against this background that Liberia's international "partners"—chief among the US, the EU and the Bretton Woods institutions—evinced growing concern about what was euphemistically described as "economic mismanagement" by the NTGL, specifically its evident inability to control revenue collection and expenditure. At the same time, many ordinary Liberians and civil society groups were also venting their anger and increasing frustration at the failure to bring the ingrained predatory practices of warlords-turned-politicians to an end. As a result, and following intense donor pressure, the transitional government and the International Contact Group for Liberia reached agreement in September 2005 on a Governance and Economic Management Assistance Program (GEMAP), initially for a three-year period.[47] The program is aimed at improving and closely monitoring the economic governance of the country, specifically to help "establish transparent financial management systems, train and build capacity of Liberian staff, and report openly on their operations, revenue and spending."[48] Uniquely, it has sought to do so by placing international officials or experts—appointed by the IMF and, crucially, given co-signing authority for all major decisions—inside key ministries, public corporations and parastatals, including *inter alia* the Central Bank, the National Port Authority, Roberts International Airport, the Forestry Development Agency, the Petroleum Refining Corporation and the Public Procurement and Concessions Commission.[49] It is above all the co-signatory powers of international officials for "all operational and financial matters" that distinguish GEMAP in its degree of intrusiveness from other technical assistance programs and that give the experiment, in the view of many, the character of economic trusteeship.[50] Additionally, overseeing the work and activities of GEMAP is an Economic Governance Steering Committee chaired by Liberia's President, Ellen Johnson-Sirleaf, though with the US ambassador acting as Co-Chair.

Designed to protect the country's revenue base by creating "transparent and accountable" systems and procedures for financial and budgeting management, GEMAP is an unprecedented attempt by outsiders to regulate the economic affairs of post-conflict states, and calls have already been made by donors (under increasing pressure at home to ensure that aid is not "wasted") for similarly intrusive programs to be adopted elsewhere.[51] A significant increase in government revenues since its adoption—by as much as fifty per cent from 2006–7 to 2007–8 according to GEMAP's own figures—appears to indicate progress and has further strengthened calls for extending the model to other weak and post-conflict states. There are reasons, however, for being cautious about drawing lessons too early from the "success" of the program, and in particular for seeing it as a model than can easily be replicated elsewhere.

In the first place, GEMAP's actual achievements to date have been questioned, notwithstanding the rise in government revenues since 2006. According to Bøås the "culture of patrimonial exchange [that] encompasses all aspects of life in Liberia" has not been broken, and "there is little to suggest that the level of corruption has been drastically reduced, making it questionable whether the system is working."[52] At the same time, "good governance" has become less of Liberian responsibility than a task for outsiders to tackle.[53] William Reno also notes how "reform programs such as GEMAP often just give bureaucrats new opportunities to abuse power" and argues that outsiders need instead to proceed from an understanding of the political economy inherited from the war and then "engage in the much more complex politics of weighing which elites are true obstacles to reform and which ones can be bargained with to preserve at least some elements of reform while ensuring that the war does not resume."[54]

Second, as noted above, GEMAP represents more than just a symbolic intrusion into the domestic jurisdiction of a sovereign state and, partly for this reason, it has been resisted by many Liberians (though plainly many economic elites have resisted it also because greater "transparency" threatens to undermine their continued ability to benefit from state failure and conflict). The reactions, especially to the initial ideas expressed by international donors, were highly critical, with members of Liberia's political class and many neighboring African states emphasizing the extent to which the proposals would amount to an unacceptable loss of sovereignty. GEMAP's eventual adoption was made possible by the unequal bargaining power between Liberia and its international donors who, through the US and EU in particular, were able to bring effective pressure to bear on the Liberian government. Since the election of President Johnson-Sirleaf in 2006, support for the program has been more robust, though so has resistance to it in many quarters.[55] Clearly, any government, not just that of Liberia, is unlikely to welcome this degree of intrusion into its external affairs for an indefinite period, however much it is presented as a partnership between the state in question and the international community. Unsurprisingly, other African countries have chosen to "see economic oversight programs in Liberia as a threatening precedent for eroding African sovereignty."[56] Similarly ambitious programs therefore, even if modified to take account of lessons learned from GEMAP, are bound to be resisted elsewhere. Added to this is the critical question of sustaining donor commitment over the long term, the lack of which is certain to undermine whatever achievements have been made.[57]

GEMAP on its own will not transform the political economy of Liberia; whether it has succeeded in assisting the process of transformation will only become clearer in the medium to long term. In spite of increased revenues flowing to the government, many GEMAP-monitored institutions remain deeply corrupt, indicating how difficult it is to transform "alternative systems" that have emerged against the backdrop of protracted state failure, war and violence. Understanding that system—not a templated vision of how states should be "rebuilt"—remains a fundamental starting point for considering the effects and likely success outside intervention.

## Spoilers and Crime in "Post-Conflict" Settings

In the context of peacebuilding exercises, it has become fairly routine to seek to identify peace "spoilers." The term goes back to Stephen Stedman's pioneering work.[58] Whilst this enterprise can be a helpful one, it carries certain dangers, particularly in a current context where, first, the identification of "spoilers" and "enemies" has at times been linked in a relatively crude manner to the "War on Terror" and, second, the fashion for UN integrated missions invites coordinated support for transitional governments and confrontation with non-governmental spoilers. A key problem is that discussion of "spoilers" has too often been divorced from a political economy analysis of conflict. Policy debates have tended to simplify the dynamics at work in conflict zones, in part by neglecting or ignoring "the complex interpenetration of the legitimate and the illegitimate, the state and crime, that is part of the lived experience of many populations in weak states and conflict-affected areas."[59] It is this "complex interpretation" to which a political economy perspective draws attention.

In circumstances where a spoiler is deemed to be a determined opponent of peace, the solution this routinely invites is the destruction—or at least the severe weakening—of the spoiler. Yet the "implacable" character of a particular spoiler may not be such a "given" as is claimed or implied. There are at least four reasons for this. First, a spoiler's violence may sometimes be sustained by violence against it; this is likely to apply particularly when relatively indiscriminate counterinsurgency has the predictable effect of radicalizing civilians and attracting support for the "spoiler."[60] Second, the spoiler's strength and determination has surprisingly often been boosted by covert support from elements of the coalition that claims or appears to be ranged against it.[61] Third, external support for the spoiler has often been a vital—and neglected—factor (as is evident in the support the Taliban have received from powerful groups in Pakistan), and this support may diminish (or increase) over time. Fourth, the spoiler's determination to derail a peace may lessen when circumstances (including economic incentives) change: today's implacable spoiler may be tomorrow's calculating pragmatist.[62] This possibility tends to be obscured when a particular group is labeled as a "total spoiler" (in Stedman's phrase).

Another consideration that should caution against an over-ready identification of spoilers, total spoilers and enemies more generally is that conflict resolution frequently demands a "re-think" on the commonly accepted "spoiler." This was certainly the case in Sierra Leone, where UK-led reforms of the government army contributed powerfully to peace (something that often gets forgotten when the British are hailed as having successfully defeated the RUF, a military confrontation that actually never took place).[63] In Colombia, President Alvaro Uribe successfully explored the possibility of negotiating with the paramilitaries. Whereas it had always been thought that paramilitary demobilization would follow the peace made with the insurgency, now there was a policy of negotiating with the paramilitaries for demobilization (negotiations that included the threat of prosecution).[64] The failure to see government troops as powerful spoilers has more recently been notable in the DRC.[65] In the passage below, we look in more detail at the case of Iraq, which illustrates some of the problems with the labeling of spoilers and shows, once again, the need to incorporate a political economy analysis.

## The Case of Iraq

After the US-led occupation of Iraq, it was commonly stated that the Iraqi insurgency was based in the so-called "Sunni triangle" bounded by Baghdad, Ramadi and Fallujah, and that Sunni Arab opposition to the Americans was underpinned by "the Sunnis'" close ties to the deposed tyrant Saddam Hussein. While this analysis was plainly not altogether without foundation, it represented a rather crude invocation of ethnicity-as-explanation and neglected important nuances in Iraq's political economy. Perhaps most important, the prevailing analysis misleadingly portrayed the hostility of many Sunnis as some kind of given. In reality, the "Sunnis" were not such an implacable "spoiler" as they were often made to appear. The attitude of Sunni Arabs to the coalition government was actually far more complicated. For one thing, the loyalty to Saddam was variable: in fact, most of the attempts to overthrow the President had come from Sunnis.[66] More generally, the nature and intensity of insurgency against the US-led coalition government requires an understanding of the winners and losers in the complex political economy prevailing under Saddam Hussein, including adaptation to international sanctions in the 1990s, as well as an understanding of the impact of misguided US-led policies in relation to the Ba'ath security apparatus, key aspects of which were the blanket de-Ba'athification policy embarked upon in mid-May 2003, followed shortly afterwards by the dissolution, in one fell swoop, of the Iraqi army. The de-Ba'athification policy involved purging from government jobs all those who had held Ba'ath party membership above a certain rank, something which, given the nature of the party and its relationship to society and the regime, meant that managers and professionals employed by government-run institutions of any kind (including, for example, school teachers and senior hospital staff ) were sacked. Dissolving the Iraq army resulted in some 400,000 men being made redundant, quite literally, overnight.[67] The subsequent "Anbar awakening" among the Sunni from late 2006—which saw traditional Sunni sheikhs throwing their power and influence behind the US-led coalition, and the Americans throwing their power behind the sheikhs—should serve as a reminder that what appears immutable and inevitable may actually be neither.[68]

The role of external action in turning potential allies into enemies—and potential enemies into allies—comes out rather clearly in Ahmed Hashim's impressive study of the Iraqi insurgency. The book includes an enlightening discussion of the insurgency in Fallujah, which was the focal point of rebellion in 2004, and Hashim observes, "… the idea that Fallujah was an intractable pro-Saddam and pro-Ba'thist bastion that was determined to fight in support of the former leader is belied by the reality on the ground."[69] Notably, many influential figures in Fallujah rejected Saddam's clandestine call to intensify the fight against the occupiers. A major factor in spurring Fallujah into outright rebellion was two US-led attacks on the city in April and November 2004, in which large numbers of civilians were killed.[70] Also feeding into rebellion in Fallujah were factors connected to Iraq's political economy, which had been profoundly shaped and distorted by international sanctions. Significantly, when UN sanctions were imposed on Iraq in the wake of Iraq's 1990 invasion of Kuwait, Fallujah became a focus of the smuggling trade across the borders with Syria and Jordan, and the trade involved an alliance between local tribes and local security service members.[71] This was part of a broader system— referred to above—under which large numbers of Ba'athist officials were able to exploit, manipulate and evade UN sanctions.[72] Crucially, the end of sanctions dealt a blow to this smuggling economy—without eliminating the beneficiaries as political, economic or potentially military actors. In Fallujah, there was a growing local resentment against the coalition among large sections of the local population who had come to rely on the smuggling economy. The fall of Saddam threatened to marginalize those who had gained preferential access to sanctions-evasion profits, and this seems to have been a powerful motive for insurgency. Compounding this situation was the fact that Allied reconstruction efforts failed to fill the vacuum: as Hashim put it, "all the propaganda about reconstruction notwithstanding, the United States was unable to provide an alternative source of gainful employment or income."[73]

Adding further to the economic problems in Fallujah and elsewhere was the hasty dissolution of the Iraqi armed forces—something that proved particularly devastating for a city so heavily reliant on military employment. Large numbers of men in Fallujah had joined both the armed forces and the security services, and dismissed officers and rank-and-file proved a fertile soil for the Iraqi insurgents. Whilst the combination of insurgency, organized crime and shifting ethnic allegiances in post-2003 Iraq at times seemed to defy understanding, a political economy analysis can help to make these phenomena more comprehensible. Again, it helps to put contemporary violence into the longer-term context of sanctions and a state that was sponsoring its own demise.

Another connection with the history of sanctions in Iraq was that networks previously used for smuggling goods under UN sanctions were used during the insurgency, first to smuggle fighters and funds into Iraq to support the insurgency and, second, to support various forms of organized crime.[74] Another connection with the past was the boost to organized crime—and disorder more generally—from the fact that the post-2003 regime "inherited" a governmental structure that had for some time been forfeiting its obligation to provide services and security, often delegating these to tribal structures, rather as the British had done in the 1920s.[75] Though formally rejecting tribalism as a remnant of colonialism, from the beginning Saddam Hussein used members of his own tribe for key security positions. He widened the circle of tribes that he relied on when the 1980s war with Iran thinned out the presence of loyal party officials in tribal areas; loyal tribes helped him put down the 1991 rebellion in southern Iraq. With sanctions also weakening the Iraqi state, Saddam Hussein even began to allow sheikhs to create their own private armies and to tax on behalf of the central government. Tribal authorities were now well placed to benefit from the smuggling that flourished under UN sanctions.[76] By 2003, as Andrew Rathmell put it, "Iraq's governing bureaucracies were hollowed out, its society was impoverished and fractured along lines of clan loyalties, and its physical infrastructures were often held together by the proverbial wire and string."[77]

It was this history of partial state collapse—so poorly understood by senior US officials who counted on taking control of a strong state—that set the context not only for large-scale insurgency and crime but also for some shifts in ethnic politics that seemed to defy understanding. In particular, from late 2006, the discourse of Sunni-as-spoiler changed rapidly into the discourse of Sunni-as-savior. At this time, the US and the Iraqi government stepped up efforts to harness tribal networks to fight "Al-Qaeda in Mesopotamia" (AQM), in particular the Anbar Salvation Council. This helped significantly in reducing levels of violence and it became something of a model for improving security elsewhere in Iraq. With the passing of time, many Sunni tribal leaders were beginning to see an advantage in engaging with the US-led political process.[78] Significantly, AQM was competing with the tribal authorities (essentially a dispute within the Sunni of Iraq) for control of revenue sources like banditry and smuggling. This seems to have prompted a major turning away from AQM, as tribal leaders allied with the beleaguered US forces, helping to turn around the security situation in Iraq. According to Hashim's study of the Sunni insurgency, a critical moment in the severing of relations between Sunni insurgent groups and AQM was reached when the latter started to "interfere in the funding operations of local insurgent groups by extorting money from local business and traders affiliated with or already paying protection money to local groups," and also began to "encroach on the lucrative smuggling activities of sheiks and local insurgent leaders."[79]

If the Sunni-as-spoiler discourse was misleading, so too is the discourse of Sunni-as-savior. The strategy of wooing tribal sheikhs—in large part a reinvention of Saddam's policy—is vulnerable to shifting calculations based, in large part, on economic and political self-interest. In particular, the loyalty of tribal sheikhs cannot be taken for granted, especially in the context of continued Al-Qaeda threats to these individuals. Meanwhile, arming tribal sheikhs carries major risks. The authority of the Iraqi state is being threatened by this turning back of history, and even democratization is in sharp tension with reinforcing the authority of tribal sheikhs.[80] Again, one is struck by important continuities in the governance of Iraq and by the difficulty of imposing an outsider's blueprint for a better society.

## Conclusion

More generally, a nuanced political economy analysis—whether of Iraq or other crisis-affected countries—is essential if we are to stand a chance of avoiding the pitfalls of reinforcing abusive elites, fuelling criminality, and encouraging violent backlashes by elites and others who are threatened by particular reforms. Assuming a *tabula rasa* would seem to be an invitation to thwarted idealism and the endless reproduction of violence. Nor can we assume that if a society and its political economy have been properly and thoroughly understood, we can then proceed in a rather mechanistic way to an appropriate solution. Every intervention—whether it is the imposition of sanctions, the liberalization of an economy, the dismissal of "rogue" officials, or some kind of military action—will generate a whole range of strategies from those who are trying to block, mitigate, adapt to, or simply take advantage of the relevant intervention. Unless these reactions are constantly tracked—and continuously fed into the design of policy—there is little chance that the intervention will improve security on the ground. A good doctor will try to anticipate the side-effects of his or her intervention, and will design the intervention accordingly. We should not be applying a lesser standard to interventions on a mass scale.

# 12

# CIVIL-MILITARY RELATIONS IN THE NEW PROTECTORATE

*K.J. Drewienkiewicz*

Multinationality guarantees respectability; it does not guarantee efficiency[1]

Civil-military relations in the new protectorates are complex interactions between the military and civil agencies ostensibly engaged in the same task. The military actors may be international or local, or a mix of both, and there will certainly be both international and local civil actors. The nature of the relationships will vary, but at its most uncomplicated, one international agency will be in charge of all the other actors. However, this model is not now standard, nor commonplace. In the last 20 years it has become more usual for each international actor to have its own separate mandate, which typically confers a degree of independence. There is also an increasing trend for defining extensive areas where the locals retain some autonomy. So the relationships can be a dynamic matrix rather than simple subordination of one by another.

Civil-military relations also encompass dedicated military staff branches, established inside deployed military headquarters, whose task is to be the link between the international military and the international and local civilian agencies in a theatre of operations. Some armed forces also include specialist units, designated Civil-Military Cooperation (CIMIC) units, which are established and deployed in order to assist with reconstruction in areas where such action can advance the success or enhance the standing of the international military mission.

It was not always so. Early in World War II it was realized that there would be a requirement to reconstruct German society once the war had been won. The formulation of doctrine for military government was begun as early as 1941, whilst in 1942 a School for Military Government was established in Virginia. In 1944 the first Civil Affairs detachment was set up on German soil four days after the first US troops had entered Germany and by May 1945 there was an Allied Civil Affairs detachment in each German town, each with the authority to replace uncooperative mayors and other officials. The occupation and rehabilitation of post-war Germany contains many instances of the benefits of the extensive preparation, at many levels, for the task of running Germany. People were appointed to locations in advance and arrived knowing the legislative and administrative framework under which they would be operating, even down to the relevant booklets having been prepared. The story was similar in Japan.[2] However, this commendable level of international preparation and application of resources to achieve an agreed outcome has not been seen since. Despite the creation of crowds of IOs and NGOs, so that there is a virtual "standing army" of professionals ready to assist with the reconstruction of states after conflict, the successes of the rehabilitation of Germany and Japan have not been repeated.

Modern international protectorates emerged as a result of the Balkan civil wars of the 1990s. Details of each varied, but in all of them there was a substantial international military presence. The conviction that military implementation could not be subordinated to a civilian head arose in 1995 from events in the Balkans when the senior UN civilian had the power of veto over military actions. As Wesley Clarke explained, "We had another difficult issue with the Europeans on the issue of civil-military relations. One key lesson [...] was the necessity for a clear military chain of command. We wanted no repeat of the UNPROFOR experience in which a diplomat could insert himself into the command chain and block military action."[3]

Fifteen years on, there has been little debate over this decision, which has become a fundamental ground rule of international interventions. Yet, as will be seen, this system of parallel mandates is extremely inefficient and relies on all the key actors agreeing to act in the best interests of one another. Unfortunately this happy state of affairs seldom occurs. This chapter will discuss some of the major issues that have arisen in the field of civil-military relations in the new protectorates, mostly on the basis of the author's personal experience in the Balkans since the mid-1990s.[4]

However mandated, the task of the international military presence is to enforce the military provisions of the peace settlement, and to provide a "safe and secure environment"[5] in which the other responsible agencies are able to pursue their objectives. Within this broad definition there has been considerable variation in the exact nature, command arrangements and mandates of the various protectorates. There is also an inverse correlation that the more sophisticated the military force, the more likely it is that its commander will have a separate mandate from the international civilian head. So while a military force may have a staggeringly wide range of military and technical means at his disposal, they are rarely at the disposal of the civilian head.

The nature of standing armed forces is that, when they are not engaged in an operation, they remain in being. They are organized in a hierarchy, trained and equipped, and are capable of administering themselves. They can be ordered to be ready to move at short notice, and held at short notice for considerable periods. They are therefore capable of arriving early in a post-conflict zone, and of having an immediate impact on a situation. So they are often among the first internationals to arrive[6] in a newly designated international protectorate. This was certainly the case in Eastern Slavonia, Kosovo and East Timor, although the reasons for the military forces being poised to arrive early varied from case to case. It was similar in BiH, although the Dayton Peace Accord did not bring with it international executive authority. However, the particular circumstances of BiH are relevant to any study of modern protectorates. The BiH Civilian High Representative (HiRep) will be examined, since although the HiRep started out with extremely limited powers, his powers were increased very substantially relatively early on. Before late 1997 the HiRep only had power to coordinate those areas of the international community and the local political structures that were prepared to be so coordinated, and he had absolutely no authority over the International Military Implementation Force. The former High Representative Carl Bildt described his impotence: "My problem in these discussions did not cut much ice in the hard political game over the future of Bosnia was that I did not really have much leverage [...] It was all dependent on a basic desire on their part to move the process forward [...] I had the moral authority of the international community behind me, but moral authority alone."[7]

At the annual review of progress in Bonn in December 1997 the powers of the HiRep were increased so that he could dismiss uncooperative local officials at every level and impose legislation if it was being blocked unreasonably. This gave BiH many of the characteristics of an international protectorate, and the experience in BiH influenced the thinking when the missions in Kosovo and East Timor were being designed and constructed.

In Eastern Slavonia in late 1995, there were military forces and international civilians and police officers already nearby as part of the UNPROFOR organization. When that operation in BiH was replaced by the NATO-led IFOR, most contingents transferred to it and remained in BiH. A substantial minority of former UNPROFOR military and civilian contingents, however, did not, and they moved by road to Eastern Slavonia and became the UNTAES, with a new UN mandate.[8] Both military and civilians were rapidly in place and although their mandate and military means were far less robust than that of IFOR, IFOR undertook to be prepared to back up UNTAES if its situation deteriorated. The mandate was limited in time and jurisdiction, and the Civilian Head of UNTAES had full authority over the military contingent, which he used energetically. The mission aimed to maintain a secure environment for twenty-four months while the Croatian Government prepared to assume full sovereign authority over the area. It did not attempt to change the eventual objective for the area, which was to be handed over to Croatian jurisdiction. The time under international control provided a "soft landing" for the Serbs resident in the area. Most Serbs left in advance of the Croatian Government taking over, but they were able to make the decision over months and to make arrangements to sell property, move possessions and transfer schools. UNTAES did not ensure that the area was restored to its pre-war multi-ethnic character, rather the UN presided over the orderly return of the Croatians who had been driven out in the war, while the Serbs left. The UN did, however, protect the departing Serbs from any repetition of the "massive and brutal ethnic cleansing of the Krajina in August 1995."[9] As a mission whose aim was to extract the UN from the area without triggering a catastrophe, it was a success. The strong personality of the UN SRSG Jacques Klein certainly helped the mission to succeed. That said, the fortuitous way that the resources were all already available was an enormous advantage and owed little to prudent planning.

In the case of Kosovo, the NATO military force had been deployed in Macedonia since before the start of the NATO air campaign in late March 1999, so it had had three months to prepare for the short drive into Kosovo when its mandate was confirmed in June 1999. There were extensive negotiations between KFOR and the Serbian Authorities to ensure that as the Serbian Military and Police withdrew in a phased operation, they were replaced by KFOR.

This worked militarily, but the Serbian police were not replaced by international police, and a very serious security vacuum ensued. This occurred because the UN was not ready to deploy its civilian contingent, despite having had the luxury of seventy-eight days, while NATO was bombing, in which to form and prepare its civilian contingent. The mandates for the International Military Force and for the UN Special Representative were kept completely separate, in a way very similar to the international presence in BiH. However, civilian implementation was structured more organizationally than in BiH, as is shown below in Table 1; this proved that some lessons had been learned, even if the UN operation lacked urgency in its arrival.

Table 1

Implementation Pillars 1999

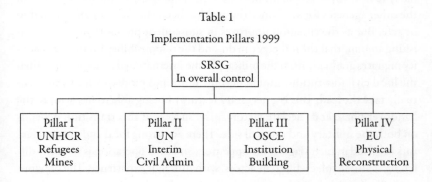

In East Timor, the initial deployment of international military was almost exclusively from the lead nation, Australia, and they were able to arrive by sea. This ensured that they were supported by forces afloat and were able to depend on logistics and communications assets at all stages of the operation. However, as in Kosovo, the international civilian presence was slow to arrive and by the time it had arrived the situation on the ground was less favorably inclined towards the international community than it had been earlier. The situation did not deteriorate into a security vacuum, mainly because the military contingent was under a unified command and was broadly able to act temporarily as police officers.

It is notable that there has been little redesign and rebalancing of military force structure in the "lessons learned" process that follows any operation. It can be argued that since the end of the Cold War the need for some military specialities, such as air defense artillery, has greatly diminished. One could ask, with some justification, whether such forces are still needed in their Cold War proportions. On the other hand, there has been a steep rise in the need for, and usefulness of, military police. This or similar transformations would make the forces more usable, as well as reducing the equipment cost as expensive missiles are replaced by inexpensive truncheons. But this blinding glimpse of the obvious has not yet registered with those who design forces, and cynics now refer to the reviews as "lessons ignored" rather than "lessons learned."

Peace Support Operations are generally seen as having three phases. These are: security, stabilization and institution building, followed by handover. The duration of these phases varies and one phase can overlap another, but the pattern is followed consistently. During the first phase, when security is being established, the lead rests unambiguously with the military. The military are likely to lead any deployment into the area of operations, and are likely to call the other agencies forward once the area has been checked out and proved to be safe. But as the situation improves in subsequent phases there is a diminishing amount that the military can do, and the responsibility for the lead activity migrates gradually from the military to the international civil agencies. Then the local civil institutions should become more and more involved and eventually take the lead. This is a necessary feature of being able to move on to the handover phase and "declare victory." The success of this transition depends on both the military and the civil side. There are strong local and cultural factors involved in each stage of the operation, and each operation is not only different, it also involves different actors, with different experience. The previous operation is rarely a good guide to the next one, but there is a marked tendency to draw heavily on previous experience, especially by those whose experience is limited to a single deployment.

*Security*

In the first phase leading to the establishment of the new protectorates, that of creating a safe and secure environment, the military had the greatest task, and were firmly in the lead. At this stage the military may have had a "can do" rather than a legalistic approach, although that could not in all cases be guaranteed. In the early stages of a mission many of the military were prepared for and often culturally sensitive to the conditions and circumstances of the indigenous people. In the first stage the military were also able to stop "bad things" from happening, often by threatening dire consequences for any perpetrator. Indeed, this exemplified the first phase. It was rarely possible at this stage to persuade people to do things that they were disinclined to do. Since the military and the civilian contingents were unlikely to be under a unified command, a very high premium was set on the relationships between the senior internationals. If they hit it off as people they were more likely to confer over problems and more likely to institutionalize regular consultation. In these circumstances, in theory, it is therefore likely that this practice of consultation would filter down to the lower levels of the organizations. At its best this translates into a shared approach to problem solving, often with the military sharing resources that it has and which the civilians lack, to the advantage of both parties. This goes beyond consultation into key areas such as intelligence, where the military commander will have access to means not available elsewhere. Other key areas include communications[10] and logistics.[11]

However, this only works if both sides invest effort in the process. Practice inevitably departs from theory. In most cases the backgrounds of the military and the civilian actors are likely to be radically different. While the military may have prepared for the particular mission, they are often on their first or second such mission. Many of the internationals will have taken part in many similar missions, and are likely to arrive at short notice, having been selected and deployed at short notice and with a small, hastily improvised team. Culturally the civilians may be better prepared by their previous experience, and may be mentally prepared to be pragmatic in their approach, while the military may have a specific detailed plan which they want to implement in a predetermined way. This difference in cultural backgrounds is significant, and is shown below in Table 2. While each of the attributes shown is easily capable of being overcome individually, they can represent a significant institutional barrier in aggregate. Another associated issue is that of tempo. The military are deployed for short periods and therefore look for short-term improvements that are rapidly visible. They tend to work "every hour God sends" while some of the civilians, who may expect to be there longer, tend to pace themselves more.[12] This can look like a lesser degree of commitment to the military, especially to the inexperienced ones deployed for the first time. The senior civilians may have a background as diplomats or as politicians. Each background leaves its mark on the approach that an individual adopts when elevated to a senior position. Broadly, the diplomats look for solutions that leave everyone content. The politicians have a better understanding of the way deals are done, and that every wish is rarely fulfilled. Both types have seldom had much experience of directing large staffs, but both types are very sensitive to the need to work with the media at every stage. Overall the ex-politicians have been more successful in charge of protectorates than the ex-diplomats. The bottom line is that relationships are absolutely fundamental to success between the military and the civilians, and that significant effort needs to be invested in them in order to nurture trust and mutual understanding, particularly at the highest levels.

Table 2: Military and civilian characteristics

| Military | Civilian |
|---|---|
| Male, older, hierarchical | Often female, younger, corner-cutting |
| Preformed into groups and teams | Act as empowered individuals |
| Long chains of command | Short chains of command |
| Short periods deployed, 4–12 months | Long periods deployed, 12–36 months |
| Resource rich | Resource limited |
| Expect short-term results | There for the long haul |
| Wary of media | Used to media |
| Used to planning | Allergic to planning |

Given the extent to which good personal relationships can oil the wheels of a mission, it is a pity that so little account is taken of the issue of turnover of senior staff. It was notable that relationships in BiH were affected by the changes of HiReps and military commanders. There it was an advantage that the overall military command remained in the hands of very senior US officers, who brought consistency and maturity to the military command. In the first, crucial years the US commanders were deployed for significant periods, and the civilian HiReps were similarly long in post. This allowed relationships and trust to grow. In Kosovo, on the other hand, the turnover of both military and civilian senior staff was uncoordinated and rapid. Within six months of the establishment of UNMIK and KFOR there had been a complete change of senior staff in both missions, and this set the tone for the way the two missions continued. The situation was made less easy by the agreement within NATO to rotate the nationality of the KFOR military commander and his senior staff periodically, in some instances at six-month intervals. The tenure of the various Heads of UNMIK was almost as brief, with the majority serving less than 12 months. The result in Kosovo has been that the international civilian and international military sides have kept themselves to themselves and have dealt separately with the locals, resulting in the locals viewing the military in a different light to the international civilians. The international community has lost sight of the need for alliance cohesion, which is often regarded as the core of any international mission. The principle of "divide and rule" has been applied by the locals to the international community, with considerable success.

These tensions tend to arise between agencies that are unfamiliar with one another. They are far less likely to occur when there are regular meetings and interaction. If agencies actually live and socialize together then many problems are overcome by routine interaction. Unfortunately the civilian agencies tend to be accommodated in civilian housing, among the local people they have been sent to look after, while the military tend to erect fortified bases, where all their needs are met. Movement in and out is strictly controlled, so the two sets of agencies tend not to meet except in programmed meetings. The international civilian agencies will also tend to employ locals as guards, drivers, interpreters and logistic personnel, and this will increase the exposure of the international civilians to the population that is their responsibility; while the military are able to spend months on end in their own company, without any interaction beyond that with interpreters. Add to this that much military information is classified and not normally made available to the civilian agencies, and there is a recipe for insularity and mistrust. The heads of the agencies may well be aware of these developments, and it is up to them to set the tone of cooperation that will reduce the mutual mistrust. One way of dealing collectively with problems is to bring the senior internationals together regularly, if need be several times a week, in order to ensure that action is coordinated and mutually supporting. This "Principals" meeting can be powerful, especially if actions are considered before the crisis strikes. At its best a secretariat can be established to circulate papers in advance and to keep track of decisions.

The issue of planning is illustrative. Planning in detail is part of military culture. The military will have a detailed "Campaign Plan," which has been written by planning specialists. In order to develop this level of detail, assumptions are made early on in the planning process. Any substantial change to the situation from that envisioned by the planners should lead to a review of the assumptions. This can be very time consuming.[13] However, it is not always the case that the planners who devised the plan actually accompany the force on deployment. In some cases they remain far away, monitoring the situation, and measuring success against the original parameters. Certainly the military force will be under more scrutiny from its superiors than a civilian presence will. A detailed plan can lead to a culture of expecting events to unfold in a certain way, and this can become a hindrance. Paddy Ashdown remarked that "the military may be the best planners, but they are the worst people to lead this planning process. For this is essentially a political process, not a military one."[14]

The civilians, on the other hand, have much broader objectives, not developed into a formal plan. The civilians are sometimes better placed to be opportunistic and flexible in their approach, and can exploit success wherever it is found. The two approaches are both valuable, but mixing them in this way can lead to the each side being frustrated by the other.

Remaining with the issue of the first phase, that of creating a "safe and secure environment," the military contingent will also contain a number of different national contingents, and they will vary in their ability to create the effect that they intend. At the heart of this is the uncomfortable fact that military forces are not uniformly capable. Some will be culturally more at ease with the situation that they find on the ground, some will have trained for the mission before deploying, while less helpfully, others may have been deployed at short notice after a political deal involving participating in the mission has been agreed. In contentious situations some contingents may "take sides," and this was certainly so in Kosovo in June 1999 when certain military contingents were noticeably biased against the Serb populations in their assigned areas. This may well have been a factor in the triggering of the Serb exodus of late June 1999. Even if a country has decided to participate with a particular force level, there may be domestic parliamentary debate over the nature of the contribution. It may be deemed more acceptable to deploy logistic or support troops rather than combat troops, even if they are not what is required militarily. Again, troops may be well or poorly equipped, which can affect the capability of the force. Some complicated technical equipment may not be appropriate, or may be relied on too much. There is a tendency to rely, for instance, on electronic intelligence gathering, at the expense of deploying personnel on the ground to gather "human intelligence," in other words to talk to the locals. Communications equipment is one area where there is a wide variety of capability. Some contingents have secure radio down to low level, while others may communicate by mobile phone. This can make it impossible to use a contingent in certain areas where secrecy of aspects of the mission is required. Another key area is night vision devices, and this can affect the willingness of a contingent to operate at night. Even if troops are equally capable, the government of a troop-contributing nation may impose limitations or caveats on the missions that their troops can undertake. These are known colloquially as "national red cards," and at the very least require the commander to consult with his capital before accepting a mission or an order. In all cases time is lost while consultation goes on. At worst this problem can compromise the entire mission, particularly if the proposed mission has been discussed over insecure communications means. Finally in this area, different contingents calculate the risk to their troops differently. This is often described as the "force protection" policy. A rigorous force protection policy can require that every move outside a fortified base is preceded by a conscious decision to make that move, and has to set out in advance the information that the operation will hope to generate. This makes it easy to justify each operation, but it can limit the accessibility of the military force to the local population. It may also require that the posture of the force is more aggressive than it needs to be; for instance, there is a difference in image between a force which operates in soft hats and light vehicles and one which operates in helmets, body armor and armored vehicles. Nonetheless nations set the conditions from afar, influenced by the likely public reaction at home to possible casualties.[15]

"Red cards" have multiplied with time. In UNTAES the mission was short and limited, and involved troops already deployed. Few red cards were evident, but the force limited its aims as well. In reality there was certainly a measure of deliberate self-limitation, as the UN could ill afford any more human disasters and/or bad publicity from the area. In BiH at the start of the IFOR Mission great emphasis was placed on cohesion of the force and the effort, and national caveats were a private affair. Nonetheless it was still felt necessary for the Force Commander to consult in advance to check that a contingent was willing to obey an order before the order was confirmed. These limitations on different contingents were not publicized, so it came as a surprise to the international civilians that they existed at all, and that this was a real limitation on what could be done by the military force. This was another potential source of misunderstanding and friction between the military and the civilians. In UNTAET the military force was dominated by one large contingent, which was also the lead nation for the force, and as a result "red cards" were not apparent. In Kosovo there were few limitations imposed by capitals at the start, however, within days the security situation had deteriorated dramatically. The departure of the only civilian police (who were Serbs) was not matched by the arrival of international civilian police. Consequently the military contingent was forced to deal with the law and order vacuum. This was within the capacity of some, but by no means all, of the military contingents, and some performed badly. This resulted in a very uneven standard of imposition of the rule of law for weeks, if not months, until the international civilian police force had been built up. Even when they did arrive, international civilians and international police officers were contracted and deployed individually, so that teams could not be formed, nor procedures agreed, until they arrived in the mission area. These individuals had to be introduced to the mission, and their skills assessed, before they were assigned to roles. It takes time to form teams and acquire local knowledge. Moreover, forming small teams from people with diverse backgrounds reduced the extent to which such people could work together from a cold start. Thus multinationality and diversity, while theoretically desirable, carried a significant price in terms of inefficiency. At times one might long for a slightly less respectable approach that gets results more quickly. This is most true for civilian police who represent a wide variety of policing traditions, but who have to act consistently.[16]

*Stabilization*

Once there is a safe and secure environment the operation evolves to the second phase, and the non-military agencies can begin to act in order to execute their mandates. These mandates are very diverse, and their owners are often loath to be directed where to concentrate on, and how quickly to act. The very act of pursuing some of these mandated actions can in itself be seen as a destabilizing force. An example is refugee return. The imposition of the original safe and secure environment consists, in effect, of creating an enforced truce, with everyone remaining in their current locations. Refugee return can involve helping people who have been driven from their homes, usually by different ethnic groups, to return home and repossess their property. These areas may have been "multiethnic" before the conflict, but they have been rendered mono-ethnic by the conflict, by "ethnic cleansing." The return of the refugees will be bound to pit the majority, who have remained and who may well have benefited from the process, against the returnees. The returnees will want their homes back; they may well be able to identify those who drove them out.

In extreme cases the original "ethnic cleansers" may be in positions of authority, such as mayor or police chief, if so the re-entry of returnees onto the scene can be highly destabilizing. There is then a risk that the international military force will clash with those seeking to assist refugee return, or property re-appropriation, as activities that may be destabilizing. In the early stages the international agencies will have been dealing with the local authorities and will be embarrassed when they find that they have been dealing with insalubrious people. In 1997 the Pope visited Sarajevo, and when this was first mooted the reaction of the military was to see all the risks rather than all the potential benefits. The Papal reconnaissance team was left in no doubt by the international military that the visit was far too risky, and that his safety could not be guaranteed.[17] Luckily for BiH the Pope was made of sterner stuff than the military. Even then the international military made their own security plan, which they were unwilling to share. At the insistence of the Papal team the local security authorities were included and a successful joint plan, in which international military and international police worked together with local civilian police, was made and executed. In retrospect this may have been a major achievement of the visit.

## Institution Building

The situation becomes more complicated as the mission matures into Phase 3, institution building. At the start a small number of international agencies share the mandate, but as the situation improves more players appear and wish to participate. In Phase 2 it is mainly the military and the international civilian agencies, but in Phase 3 the locals have to be allowed to participate. It is obvious that the international presence cannot depart until it has handed over authority to a functioning local civil and security apparatus, but this requires the internationals to give up power, and to accept this necessity even if the local successor institutions will be less capable than the international-run ones that they will replace. In Bosnia the HiRep once remarked that the proportion of corrupt Bosnian magistrates was about 70 per cent. A visiting dignitary expressed horror until it was explained that the proportion had been 95 per cent a few years before, so this was an indicator of real progress.[18] Here the more pragmatic approach of the international civilians can be more helpful than the military's cultural tendency to wish to control as much as possible. As the situation improved in Bosnia civilian control of the local armed forces was gradually established. It then became clear that when the local military did something offensive, it was often at the behest of local political leaders, who were not subject to the writ of the international military. On the other hand, the local politicians could be dealt with by the civilian HiRep, so the effective power of the international presence had shifted from the military to the civilian side.

CIMIC staff sections, consisting of military officers, exist inside military headquarters to facilitate interaction between the military and the international civilian agencies. These staff can become the main area of contact between the military and some civilian agencies, and the success of the contacts can be a real force multiplier. But liaison duties are not generally seen as being jobs for high flyers. General Sir Rupert Smith accurately identified the problem:

In our modern conflicts, dealing with the civilian population is directly associated with the objective and is a primary not a secondary activity. Furthermore it is also the nexus for cooperation with all other agencies and levers of power in theatre....yet they are frequently ill prepared for the task, drawn at random from other branches...and on short tours in theatres that often demand the establishment of trust and good relations with the people over time.[19]

When sensitively led these liaison staff can be a force multiplier. Typically they can share information and discuss frankly the obstacles to progress, and each party can assist the other. This however requires all parties to respect each other's mandates. Civilian agencies such as UNHCR may well have accumulated local knowledge of conditions in certain areas that helps the military to have a clearer picture of the situation, and this can help the military to identify areas of higher risk, to the advantage of all. Information exchange has to be just that, however, and an inexperienced CIMIC section can forfeit trust by asking civilian agencies for information and giving nothing back. As in other areas, familiarity and continuity are force multipliers. Shared nationality can also help, and there has been an increasing tendency for NGOs from a particular country or region to locate themselves inside the sector occupied by "their" military. This was especially effective in Central Bosnia where the Nordic Brigade became a magnet for Scandinavian charities, which had mutual benefits that extended far beyond the sauna.

As well as CIMIC staff sections, some countries include complete CIMIC units in their armed forces. These units exist to help "prime the pump" of reconstruction. They arrive early and can operate in areas not yet safe enough for international civilians. They are often made up of reservists and part-time military, who can also have civilian jobs and skill sets that make them especially useful. They can be directed to areas and projects that support the immediate aims of the military commander. This can give him a powerful extra tool to reward good behavior by the locals. It does however, need the early military-led reconstruction to be dovetailed with the later civilian-led reconstruction, since the aims of the military are likely to be short-term, and those of the civilian agencies to be long-term. As an example, the locals in an area may have a vested interest in not allowing refugee return, but the refugees may be in a separate country, and so do not impinge upon the security situation in the protectorate. At their best, CIMIC units can help the civilian agencies to be more effective. In Bosnia in early 1997, the rate-limiting factor for the UNHCR was that their staff were able to provide security surveys of areas for refugee return at a rate that would have taken up to 24 months to complete countrywide.

A CIMIC unit was assigned to assist the UNHCR staff and this enabled UNHCR to produce the surveys for the priority areas in three months, and to survey the whole country in six months. The other side of the coin is that all CIMIC units come from one country, and there is a risk that they can be directed nationally to work in areas beneficial to one troop provider to the detriment of the overall mission.

Military units carry the flag, policies and values of their government in a way that the main international agencies do not. This is a mixed blessing. It is a source of national pride that a unit is assisting in a humanitarian situation, but a setback for the unit can be seen domestically as a setback for the nation. The US experience in Somalia in 1993 was a most unhelpful factor in setting highly restrictive conditions for the US deployment into Bosnia. The Dutch experience at Srebrenica eventually brought the Dutch Government down. The intervention in Kosovo was relatively easy to sell to the international (predominantly Western) public as a response to Serbian Government brutality, but the ease of deployment was not matched by ease of execution when the internationals realized the extent to which underlying Kosovar Albanian criminal networks were interwoven with the Kosovar Albanian liberation movement. It was discovered that the Kosovars were delighted to be liberated but reluctant to drop their ways and generally converge with what outsiders thought of as acceptable behavior. The policy of one international contingent to be robust in the execution of the mandate may not be reflected across the international military force, and other contingents, possibly with issues at home that resemble the situation on the mission, may instruct their contingents to stay strictly inside their mandates and to avoid "mission creep."

The problem of "mission creep"—whether to allow it or not—can be seen in the assistance given over elections in BiH. The international civilian community was determined to hold elections as soon as it was feasible, and the task was assigned to the OSCE. The OSCE arrived and established itself, but had understandable difficulty in attracting to Bosnia the right sort of election experts. This led to delay in voter registration. The planning got to a point where there was just too much for the OSCE, with its limited manpower and logistic resources, to achieve in the available time. In order to save the reputation of the international community the military placed itself at the disposal of the OSCE. Roads to remote polling stations were improved by military engineers; temporary buildings were transported by helicopter to hilltops; ballot boxes and voter papers were delivered in military vehicles with military escorts. International police monitored the actions of local police to ensure that they did their jobs. In the end the elections were held on the appointed day and were a technical success, thanks in part to the "aid to the civil community" rendered by the international military. In the early stages the task was seen as completely outside the military mandate, but the need for the international effort as a whole to succeed led to the view that it was appropriate activity. Even Javier Solana, the civilian head of NATO, saw military success and civilian success as separate issues rather than two sides of the same issue.[20] The fact that the military were not always responsive was commented on by Richard Holbrooke, the chief US negotiator of the Dayton Agreement, when referring to a military interlocutor: "On the military goals....he was fine; his plans for separating the forces ...and protecting his forces were first-rate. But he was hostile to any suggestion that IFOR help implement the non-military portion of the agreement. This, he said repeatedly, was not his job."[21]

There are many examples where the international military have consciously limited their effort, for instance in mine clearing, only to those areas where it was considered vital for military operations, even if by so doing access was denied to the international civilian agencies: "Generals have to realize that... as soon as the fighting is over, they are acting...'in aid of the civil power' and that means in support of the civilian administrators, not in charge of them."[22]

In a situation where each actor preserves his independence, most attention is devoted to areas which are exclusive to one party. This leaves gaps in areas where there are tasks to be done but no lead agency. Education is one such, and the provision of educational facilities can be denied to an area so as to become a barrier, for example, to refugee return. This happened in both Bosnia and Kosovo, where locals used segregated education as the cement of ethnic cleansing. It also allowed little room for maneuver in areas that arose after the mandate had been issued. The most complicated mandate in this regard was the Dayton Peace Accord, which assigned each international agency its own separate mandate. These mandates varied in specificity. The least successful areas were those where an issue was identified but not assigned exclusively to one particular agency. These "orphan areas" included property rights and religious and cultural monuments. Without a responsible international lead property return was stalemated and this became a major factor limiting refugee return. When this blockage was recognized, the HiRep had to recruit new staff and take the issue forward by himself. The issue of religious and cultural structures had unforeseen consequences. It was intended to ensure that the reconstruction of structures that had been destroyed during ethnic cleansing operations could not be blocked at local level. What actually happened was that in the early stages of implementation many new structures were built in areas where there had been none before, to define the "turf" of a particular ethnic group.[23]

## Conclusion

The ideal situation for protectorates is that both military and civilian components of the international presence should be under one overall head, but this is increasingly not the case. The norm has now become two parallel organizations, with heads who are enjoined to cooperate but have separate mandates and widely different resources. It is remarkable that the principle of separate mandates was not seriously challenged during the period covered in this volume, given the evidence against it that had been amassed. As an alternative, overall control by one agency, legally mandated and sensitively exercised, with broadly compatible people would be a preferable construct than the current situation, where it is left to chance whether senior people "hit it off" and choose to cooperate. Separate mandates lead to stop/go implementation, with progress at full speed only when all the international actors are prepared to act in concert for the overall benefit of the mission. Otherwise those opposed to progress tend to resort to delaying tactics, in the expectation that the effective internationals will soon move on, and will probably be replaced by less effective ones.

The military have most to do in the early stages, and arrive well equipped to achieve their primary objective. However, the military are culturally unused to working in areas where they do not have the lead, and find it difficult to operate in support of civilian objectives. As the security situation improves the military start to work themselves out of a job and the civilian side has much more to do. The civilian component has historically been slow to set itself up, particularly with police officers, and this has damaged the credibility and effectiveness of certain missions. As the security situation has improved the civilian agencies have increased their authority and their ability to influence events, while the military have been more marginalized. In all circumstances the lack of formal subordination of one international component to another has placed a great premium upon the personal relationships at the head of the components. This is most effective when individuals are in post for extended periods. Rapid changes of key personalities make it very difficult to build up mutual confidence and trust, and this can lead to a siege mentality wherein each agency concerns itself exclusively with its own mandate. It is high time to challenge the perceived wisdom and start a new debate.

# 13

# STRUGGLING FOR GOVERNMENT LEADERSHIP

## THE RELATIONSHIP BETWEEN AFGHAN AND INTERNATIONAL ACTORS IN POST-2001 AFGHANISTAN

*Clare Lockhart*

This chapter explores the relationship between the Afghan authorities—the Interim Administration, the Transitional Islamic State of Afghanistan and the Islamic Republic of Afghanistan—and various components of the international presence between 2001 and 2006.[1] It describes the strategies, frameworks, policies and systems that the Afghan authorities and international actors adapted or invented to manage their relationship, analyzing the impact of those initiatives on the effectiveness of domestic and donor policy as well as the drivers and constraints on this effectiveness.

It should be noted from the start that the status of Afghanistan was not one of a formal international protectorate: it was clearly agreed during the Bonn negotiations of November 2001 that the Afghan Government would retain sovereignty, and the UN would be present to assist where requested. Under the political settlement, the development approach as described by the National Development Framework, and the military assistance project agreed by ISAF (the International Security Assistance Force), the objective of this "light footprint" international presence would be to assist Afghan institutions in acquiring legitimacy and capability and therefore de facto sovereignty. In some ways this sets it apart from other cases discussed in this book where sovereignty was formally assumed by another actor, whether the UN (Kosovo, East Timor) or the US (Iraq). That said, this phase could be considered akin to a protectorate by contrast with subsequent phases of engagement in Afghanistan.

## Afghanistan and the Geopolitical Context

The character of international engagement with Afghanistan has varied dramatically over the last few decades, and will be analyzed with reference to four distinctive phases. The first two phases describe the broad patterns of aid between the Soviet invasion and the fall of the Taliban, while the subsequent phases describe distinctive periods in the aid relationship between the fall of the Taliban and 2006.

Afghanistan has been at war more or less continuously since 1979, following the invasion of Afghanistan by the former Soviet Union and the resulting resistance movement. From this period until 1989, when Soviet forces withdrew, foreign financial assistance was channeled to the country through two main mechanisms. First, the Soviet Union invested up to $10 billion in Afghanistan (in today's value). Approximately $2 billion was invested in major physical infrastructure projects, including highways, power stations and tramlines, with the remainder taking the form of "military assistance." At the same time Western powers, mainly the US, channeled considerable resources to the Mujahedeen, much of this through humanitarian assistance to refugee communities based in Pakistan. Even after the withdrawal of Russian forces in 1989, aid continued to various actors in the country.

Between 1992 and 1996, whilst the parties attempting to share power increasingly turned their energies against one other, a number of NGOs channeling support to the Northern Alliance during the resistance continued to be active; together with UN agencies they attempted to sustain basic services for the population. A small number of NGOs gained specialized skills in particular areas and consolidated a network of service delivery organizations, including the Swedish Committee which sustained large numbers of schools across the country, Dacaar which managed water supplies, and UN Habitat which established a network of community fora across six major urban areas.

In 1997, after the establishment of Taliban rule, a group of donors under the leadership of the UN Office for the Coordination of Humanitarian Affairs (OCHA) established the "Strategic Framework," which sought to establish protocols to ensure the coherence of humanitarian assistance under a UN umbrella. The political arm of the UN—the United Nations Special Mission to Afghanistan (UNSMA)—took a different view, urging some coordination with government structures. Little distinction was made between the political arm of the government, the Taliban, and the administration—professional civil servants in technical domains. During this time the World Bank kept a "Watching Brief" on Afghanistan, which involved monitoring aspects of the situation from a distance, but maintained no on-the-ground presence or programs. After the overthrow of the Taliban in November 2001, leaders of developed nations pledged to "rebuild Afghanistan." This pledge took different forms of assistance, characterized here as military, political, developmental and humanitarian.

Military assistance was deployed in three major forms; (i) the Coalition, which focused on the elimination of terrorism and particularly the capture of Osama bin Laden; (ii) ISAF and Provincial Reconstruction Teams (PRTs), which carried out two major functions, safeguarding the political settlement by deterring coups, and developmental work; and (iii) assistance from a variety of agencies from various countries geared to establishing the Afghan National Army and reforming the police force, border control and secret services. At the time of the 2004 Berlin Conference, the Government of Afghanistan estimated that the cost of the military presence since the Bonn Agreement was roughly $30 billion; during the same period, it estimated $3 billion had been disbursed through the aid system.

Political assistance was undertaken, most importantly through the UN's facilitation of the Bonn Agreement, which set out a political framework, and its sustained diplomatic attention to the implementation of that agreement from 2001 to 2004. Development assistance was pledged in the form of support to recurrent and capital expenditures in order to restore services. Humanitarian assistance was pledged in the form of fund-raising for UN agencies and NGOs to implement projects in a variety of domains, including food distribution and refugee assistance.

The speed and effectiveness with which a government can assume the functions of governance determines the rate at which assistance can "exit," handing over any function temporarily assumed. In terms of military and security assistance, the extent to which the government is dependent on the presence of foreign forces is linked to the pace at which a reliable domestic security service can be established, and the extent to which the national government can maintain its legitimacy in the eyes of the population. At the end of 2004, a National Army of 20,000 had been built, and forces previously incorporated into the Ministry of Defense had been disbanded. However, the police had received no serious attention, and were reputed to be at the center of criminal networks, drugs-running, money-laundering and arms-trafficking.[2] "Illegal armed groups" existed across the country, plaguing the population, while non-governmental militia forces, at times funded by Western powers, continued to control the border posts.[3] The viability of the national government required the ongoing presence of ISAF to underwrite its stability and prevent coups d'état.

Between the presidential elections in 2004, which formally ended the Bonn Process, and the beginning of 2005 when the new Government was formed, the government became less dependent on and responsive to political facilitation. The role of the UN and of the United Nations Assistance Mission to Afghanistan (UNAMA), in particular, shifted from its earlier focus on co-producing the political process to replacing the World Bank and IMF as coordinators of the economic effort, through the Joint Coordination Monitoring Board. In the 2001–03 period, international actors backed a multiplicity of objectives, ranging from the War on Terror to humanitarian assistance to poverty reduction, but did not view these within an integrated framework.[4] Most donors did not officially endorse a statebuilding framework until the Berlin meeting of 31 March and 1 April 2004. While they increasingly shifted to adopt the rhetoric of statebuilding, in practice parallel initiatives existed.

ISAF played a key role, with its mandate expanding from a peacekeeping mission confined to Kabul to the oversight of a number of PRTs, initially in the North and West, extending to the South and finally the East. ISAF came under NATO command in 2003, and NATO took control of the PRTs in 2006–07. With the resurgence of the Taliban threat in 2005, the mandate of ISAF evolved to a mixture of peacekeeping, reconstruction and counter-insurgency work.

Large amounts of bilateral aid have continued, increasingly in stated support of the Government's policy frameworks, with increasing amounts of finance channeled through the Government's Trust Funds. This said, given the reluctance of some significant donors to utilize these mechanisms, the balance of aid through and outside government channels has remained fairly consistent.[5]

In early 2005, the Government decided to dismantle or diminish emphasis on an integrated management system through National Programs that had, from 2001 to 2004, supported a nationally-led development strategy through joint donor implementation mechanisms. When these programs were abandoned, supporting donors reverted to a dominant approach of direct financing of UN agencies and NGO and private sector implementation mechanisms.[6]

This period coincided with two key trends. The first, described by many commentators as the consolidation of the "narco-mafia state," was defined by a rapidly criminalizing economy, increased narcotics production and a government increasingly influenced by these interests.[7] The second, and perhaps related phenomenon is the resurgence of the Taliban.[8] One underlying factor in the further deterioration in governance might be the resignation of the "core economic team" who designed and implemented the governance and National Program agenda, but resigned in late 2004 as a result of the "Cairo memo"[9] and the failure of key international partners to allow for revenue collection and sufficient financial support to legitimate institutions, and the failure of the Government to agree to take steps to tackle narco-mafia interests, corruption and revenue leakage.

### Internal Versus External Resources

Afghanistan's Government is dependent on foreign resources for its operations. As Table 1 below indicates, Afghanistan's operational expenditure in 2003 was approximately $500 million. Of this approximately $235 million was funded by external actors through the ARTF, the World Bank administered trust fund through which donors contribute to the Government's budgetary needs and its priority investment projects.[10] The balance was met through domestic revenue collection and customs receipts. Table 2 sets out the revenue collection streams in more detail. Separate trust funds were established to fund the army, the police and the demobilization process.[11] Donor financing meets a small proportion of Afghanistan's capital budget; the reconstruction window of the Trust Fund received a total of $1,272 million from 2002 to 2006. Other contributions were made to pay off many of Afghanistan's arrears so that it could commence borrowing from the IFIs. Further contributions were made to financing donor-designed and managed projects. Only a small amount was provided to the Afghan budget directly. In 2002, $3 million was provided by Oman, while India and Pakistan provided $5 million each.

Despite the Afghan Government's current dependence on external resources, there is significant opportunity for financial independence. The potential for economic growth is often overlooked in donor analyses, which have tended to see Afghanistan as a "charity case." The publication of the US Geological Survey made evident the extent of Afghanistan's mineral wealth. Potential revenue exists through leasing or selling mining rights; agriculture, land leases and sales and textiles also represent significant opportunity. Further, given the increase in trade flows since 2001[12] potential customs revenue available for the domestic revenue base is notable.[13] The IMF agreed targets with the government for the mid-range future, projecting an incremental increase in revenue collection, but probably underestimated the amount of revenue potentially available.

Table 1: Afghanistan's recurrent budget and proportion met externally

| In millions of US dollars | Est 2003/04 (1,382) | Est 2004/05 (1,383) | Est 2005/06 (1,384) | Proj. 2/2006/07 (1,385) |
|---|---|---|---|---|
| Donor assistance grants (to operating budget) | 235 | 350 | 384 | 312 |
| ARTF (recurrent window) | 191 | 288 | 309 | 241 |
| LOTFA | 44 | 60 | 75 | 72 |
| Operating expenditure | 518 | 624 | 764 | 865 |
| Wages and salaries | 343 | 442 | 477 | 544 |
| Purchase of goods and services | 109 | 98 | 150 | 167 |
| Transfers and Subsidies | 15 | 18 | 48 | 56 |
| Pensions | 4 | 21 | 38 | 40 |
| Capital expenditure | 47 | 46 | 42 | 49 |
| Interest | | | 9 | 9 |
| Grants as a % of operating budget | 45% | 56% | 50% | 36% |

Note: For 2006–07, the exchange rate for 2005–06 was used.

Much external and policy discussion is focused on the mobilization of aid resources rather than on increasing domestic revenue collection and strengthening the financial base of the state. Bucking this trend, between 2002 and 2004 some external actors—notably the IMF, the World Bank and the Government of Canada—focused much of their policy dialogue on revenue collection. A mid-range goal of total revenue self-sufficiency and an end to aid dependency is something that neither donors nor governments commonly adopt. Yet this goal is critical to the establishment of sustainable state institutions.

Table 2: Revenue collection

| In millions of US dollars | Est 2003/04 (1,382) | Est 2004/05 (1,383) | Proj. 2/2005/06 (1,384) | Proj. 2/2006/07 (1,385) |
|---|---|---|---|---|
| Domestic revenue | 238 | 299 | 427 | 588 |
| Tax revenues | 146 | 223 | 289 | 449 |
| Taxes on income, profits and capital gains | 8 | 23 | 40 | 76 |
| Taxes on international trade and transactions | 125 | 169 | 212 | 326 |
| Other taxes | 12 | 30 | 37 | 46 |
| Non tax revenues | 91 | 76 | 138 | 140 |

Funds could have been generated through customs revenue. For the national government to deploy customs officers without fear of the militia forces who maintained control of the border areas would have required support from ISAF or the Coalition. It was not possible to obtain such support until the end of 2004. The underlying dynamic militating against revenue collection lay in alliances made between factions in the Afghan Government, regional power-brokers or "warlords" and US forces supporting the power-brokers to maintain militias and pursue the security goals of tracking Al-Qaeda and Taliban operatives.

There are now significant flows of aid money into the country but most circumvent government systems, passing through parallel organizations. The Government estimated that only 10–20 per cent of donor financing flowed through its systems in 2002–04.[14] In early 2007, Afghanistan's Ambassador to the United States, H.E. Said Jawad, stated that out of "the entire financial assistance that's been given to Afghanistan, only 5 percent has been given to the Afghan government; 12 percent has been given to the Afghan Reconstruction Trust Fund. The remaining 82 or 83 percent has been spent outside the budget and control of the Afghan government."[15]

The political impact of a project-based aid system, where individual donor representatives negotiate with individual ministers, department heads, and even governors to win projects, can have highly fragmentary effects; the budget process, and Afghan legal systems in general, quickly became meaningless. This stands in marked contrast to a rules-based aid system, where resources would only be channeled through the budget, and donors could not negotiate with individual ministries or departments. It is telling that in the 1970s, if a governor visited Kabul, he was obliged to report to the Ministry of Interior, who would manage his schedule of meetings with foreign dignitaries; but now, governors openly lobby hundreds of agencies for resources. This pattern of bypassing and actively undermining through importing other legal regimes is common to aid efforts in many parts of the world, but can have a particularly damaging effect in an environment of weak institutions.

## The Domestic Political System

The central task of the Bonn Agreement was to transform a pariah state—Taliban Afghanistan had only been formally recognized by three other nations—into a legitimate state. The Bonn Agreement, itself endorsed through the UNSC, recognized and pledged to support a process of legitimization, by offering assistance to the Afghan authorities in rebuilding their governance institutions. Thus the Afghan Government became the entity that international actors were, under international law, obliged to support. Yet in practice, international actors varied tremendously in the degree to which their actions matched these legal obligations.

The journey from the unrepresentative group who met at Bonn towards a legitimate government demanded a process that would enfranchise a broader group of stakeholders, endorsed through traditional gatherings. The leadership of the Interim and Transitional Administration was composed of wide-ranging skills and experience. The team had been chosen by the Bonn participants with the facilitation of the SRSG Lakhdar Brahimi. They included former leaders of the *jihad*, members of the former King's court, and people with professional skills and experience from both inside and outside Afghanistan. This team was recognized to lack the requisite legitimacy to lead a country in the long term, and was accordingly tasked with managing the interim period while a series of Loya Jirga and Commissions would select a Transitional Administration, and draft a constitution for the long term. Although this interim team was not representative, the mechanism had been recognized and endorsed by the international community as legitimate, and sovereignty was therefore vested in the Interim and Transitional Administrations.

The Transitional Administration team added to their ranks, appointing a number of technocrats who had served inside and outside the country. These actors partnered with their Cabinet colleagues to form a unified team, at the same time seeking to attract cadres of deputies, directors and managers with the personal integrity needed to reinvigorate Afghanistan's public institutions. The presence of these technocrats in government was one factor that led to the establishment of relationships of trust between international and national actors.

Contrary to the assertions of many commentators who suggest that Afghanistan was a blank slate devoid of domestic institutions in 2001, a capable civil service had proved quite resilient through the years of war.[16] Payroll estimates show approximately 250,000 civil servants in place at the end of 2001.[17] Most of these professionals had served since the 1970s through the successive regimes of the King, the Soviets, Najibullah, seven-party rule and the Taliban. There is sometimes a misperception that these civil servants had exclusively known a state-controlled economic management system, or that ministries were rebuilt from scratch. Many had served in the pre-1979 government and were familiar with the practices of the 1950s–1970s style of governance. A government systems audit conducted in 2002 by the author demonstrated considerable capacity in most ministries.

The Government asserted that these civil servants represented a great asset in terms of knowledge, institutional memory, and skills for the future administration of the country, and requested that the World Bank and the Afghanistan Research and Evaluation Unit (AREU) conduct a study of this administrative resource.[18] When this study confirmed the Government's view in 2003, donors responded by asserting that aid should be channeled through government systems.[19]

As critical as the presence of a competent team of ministers to the establishment of trust are institutional mechanisms, including a policy process managed by sets of rules that are predictable, transparent and reliable. These included regularization of key governance processes such as the budget, reporting mechanisms, unification of the treasury account, and reform of the customs procedures. The process was epitomized by the report, "Progress against Promises."[20] Key to the process was the use of "National Programs" as the means to establish systemic capability within ministries at the same time as delivering country-wide reach.

## Misallocation of Forces and Resources

Many donors came to place their trust in the Government, entering into a partnership with a long-term goal to institutionalize key government functions. Nevertheless, it is arguable that if support for a genuine statebuilding agenda ever really arrived it amounted to too little, too late. In early 2002, donors initially pledged $20 million to the ARTF, to cover annual operational and capital expenditure of the Government including the payroll for 240,000 public servants, while they provided $1.8 billion to UN agencies and NGOs through the first consolidated appeals process. Other donors focused their attention on building parallel systems, particularly UN agencies and US and Japanese aid actors. This course of action tended to be justified with reference to corruption and "lack" of government capacity. These alternative systems often involved complex layers of contracting arrangements managed from afar by Western firms incapable of operating in the Afghan security environment. It is not entirely clear that this alternative constituted a better value proposition. While the Bonn Agreement had requested the presence of ISAF in key cities and roads across the country, this force was initially confined to Kabul. NATO/ISAF only assumed command of the country in the autumn of 2006. The legitimate government in Afghanistan was therefore initially equipped with $20 million and an international force confined to the capital.

In 2003, donors refused to finance the Government's district outreach program. In 2004, the Government requested $200m in emergency support to the ARTF to meet basic salary payments for frontline civil servants; this was refused, which arguably hastened the collapse of governance. By 2006 it was claimed that the new front line in the War on Terror resided in the quality of district and provincial administration and its ability to deliver services.[21] Had the Government been backed by $200m and countrywide international military support from early 2002, it seems plausible to imagine the situation might have unfolded differently, particularly in terms of the ability of the Government to assert its authority over the "warlords" and to provide administrators and police officers capable of collecting customs revenue from 2002.

## Policy Process and Content

The Afghan authorities moved quickly in 2002 to assert their leadership of the reconstruction agenda. The government used five main approaches: agenda-setting, legislation, creation of coordination mechanisms, establishment of implementation mechanisms and pursuit of an institution-building agenda.

### Agenda setting

The Interim Administration, at the pledging conference in Tokyo in January 2002, set out its vision based on extensive consultation with the people. The vision laid out a plan for the establishment of a prosperous, stable Afghanistan, rebuilding systems of governance through six National Programs. This vision was articulated in the Government's strategy document, the *National Development Framework*, and presented in April 2002 at Afghanistan's first donor meeting, chaired by the government in Kabul. The Programs were further developed in the National Budget presented at a subsequent donor meeting in September 2002, and at meetings of the Afghanistan Development Forum, in March of each year.

In the autumn of 2001, donors jointly prepared a "needs assessment" mostly written in Islamabad and Manila, without consultation with the Afghan Government—until January 2002, when the assessment was nearly complete, there were two days of ad hoc consultation with some Cabinet members. To prepare a plan better aligned to the realities of the country, the Government launched a consultative process with a steering committee including the IMF, World Bank, UNDP and Asian Development Bank and dozens of sector experts seconded by the government, steering committee members, and other agencies. This process led to "Securing Afghanistan's Future" which set out Afghanistan's three-, seven- and twelve-year fiscal and reform programs. A financing requirement of $27.5 billion was presented to sixty of the world's finance, development and foreign ministers at Berlin in March 2004. The figure of $27.5bn was endorsed, and $8.2bn was pledged for the next three years. At the same time, the Government committed itself to the implementation of a medium term (three year) reform program with concrete benchmarks, and to a revenue compact in which Afghanistan would increasingly assume responsibility for its recurrent and capital expenditure.

This agreement set out the goal of statebuilding as the central objective of the Afghan Government, the international community and the people of Afghanistan, where institution building would be implemented by the Government in a series of benchmarked phases monitored by the international community. This formed the "double compact" between the Government and the people, and the Government and international community, cemented in President Karzai's election manifesto and further elaborated in the Afghanistan Compact, presented in London in January 2006, which set out a role for the UN in the post-Bonn phase. "Securing Afghanistan's Future" was known colloquially as the "re-costing" exercise, because of its primary intention of producing a plan that was more accurate and appropriate to context than the needs assessment, which had not been tailored to context (as the foregoing analysis should make clear), and had radically underestimated the cost of reconstruction.[22]

Legislation

The Government established a set of *principles and rules* for donor interaction with its various agencies. These included:

a. That the national budget should be the instrument of policy-making, and that any off-budget aid would be illegal;

b. That any donor could only operate in a maximum of three sectors, unless at least $30m was allocated to each sector;

c. That financing should be channeled to the government through budget support or through one of the Trust Funds, or to a program account, in order of preference;

d. That where possible, donors should indicate their financing commitments for the medium to long term;

e. That donors were required to provide information on allocations and disbursements on a timely basis to the government;

f. That any entity through which funds were directed was obliged to issue full, accurate and timely reports to the Afghan public. These reports functioned as the basis for comparative analysis of the value of a dollar of aid in real terms, in order to take account of the reduction in value created by multiple contracting layers.

In practice, where donors refused to abide by such rules and laws some negotiation tended to take place. Enforcement was incentivized through peer pressure: working groups were established under the Consultative Group mechanism, rules were designed by donors themselves in a participatory manner and donors then mutually reinforced each other to adhere to the rules. In some cases, the minister of finance refused to accept aid altogether. USAID and Japan were the two significant entities that provided large amounts of off-budget aid and preferred not to put money through the Trust Funds. The US entered into a constructive dialogue with the ministry of Finance on how to allocate their funding appropriately, but was constrained by its interpretation of the rules of Congress in not being able to fund either the Trust Funds or the National Programs—the key vehicles of Afghanistan's strategy and policy.

Coordination Mechanisms

A number of mechanisms for managing donors were established:

a. The Afghanistan Development Forum (ADF) was established as the annual meeting between donors and government, to be chaired and hosted by the Afghan Government;

b. The Consultative Group (CG) process was established as the means of inter-action between the donors and the government. Donors could participate in as many sectoral CGs as they wished, and each sectoral CG would be chaired by the relevant ministry. The overarching CG group would meet at least monthly, and was chaired by a committee of the four policy ministries;

c. Mechanisms for ensuring regional cooperation were developed. Major donors and regional trading partners, such as Pakistan, India and Iran, were incorporated into the CG process, but a range of further multilateral and bilateral fora were developed to increase cooperation on trade and invest-ment. These included frequent meetings with Iran and Pakistan, and a regional trade meeting that was established to remove constraints to cross-border trade;

d. Regular conference calls with a small group of donors providing budget and support to the ARTF were held, with the facilitation of Under-Secretaries John Taylor (US Treasury) and Alan Larson (US State Department).

A coalition of the political representation of the UN (through UNAMA), the multilateral organizations, diplomatic representations, government, and NGOs was built around a common financing and implementation agenda and embedded in a series of rules and processes, including legislation and regula-tions for donor financing, meetings, and modalities of financing.

Consultative processes ensured community input and consultation. For example, technical sectoral work managed by Afghans was combined with the policy of the nascent Cabinet, through a series of interviews and focus groups conducted up to January 2002, similar efforts linked delegates from across the country through interaction with the Emergency Loya Jirga and Constitu-tional Loya Jirga.

## Implementation Mechanisms

A number of mechanisms were established to ensure accountability, transpar-ency and effectiveness of expenditure. The ARTF was designed as the mecha-nism to pool donor financing behind a single set of policies and implementation mechanisms, creating cost-effectiveness and policy coherence. International procurement, financial management and audit agents were contracted by the government to manage the flow of donor resources to key programs, through the ARTF. Sectoral policies were prepared, based on in-depth analysis by Afghan teams of the context and needs of their country, and of new policy approaches and technologies. National Program teams were established to manage programs that were national and even-handed in scope. To this end, specific laws and procedures were designed, including steering committees that included key donors. These mechanisms ensured that in both policy design and implementation the government moved to establish itself with a high degree of credibility. The National Solidarity Program and National Emergency Employment Program were two of the programs earning the most credibility for effectiveness in disbursement and reconstruction terms, and establishing institutional processes that gained the confidence of Afghans.

The AACA (Afghanistan Assistance Coordination Authority) functioned as a catalytic organization to support the writing of key policy documents, establish aid coordination modalities, establish the skeletal structures and design of key National Programs, and put in place implementation mechanisms such as international procurement and audit agents to provide capacity and competence in core management of programs.

## Pursuit of an Institution-Building Agenda

The government began to implement a statebuilding agenda, declaring that the task of building key institutions, including revenue collection, would be central to stability and ought to be privileged as the common policy goal of both the government and the international community. This was reflected in a number of instruments, benchmarks, national programs and policy agreements with the World Bank, IMF and Asian Development Bank, which formed a mutually reinforcing web of agreements. It was complemented by an agenda for regional stability and partnership with each of Afghanistan's key neighbors, in the security, political and economic domain. These will not be documented here in detail for reasons of space.

Three sets of reforms were fundamental to the process. The first were fiscal, involving reforms in currency, banking, budget, treasury, customs and taxation. The second, in the security sector, involved the creation of a national army, police force and secret service. Thirdly, the administrative domain was reformed through three complementary programs at the village, district and provincial level. The reforms were built on stakeholder analysis which revealed the overwhelming desire of Afghans for a fair and predictable civilian authority that was responsive to their needs. Contrary to donor pressures to "deliver the peace dividend" in the form of "quick impact projects," there were clear signs that the citizenry understood that reconstruction of large infrastructure and public institutions would take years, if not decades.

Some commentators have noticed an apparent decline from late 2004 in the government's ability to manage strategy and policy, maintain law and order, regional and international consensus, and the trust and moral authority to govern. The causes of the decline will need to be examined by historians in future years. One factor may lie in the resignation of a core team of approximately 20 Afghans, in place across government, who were responsible for strategy, budget and program planning and implementation in early January 2005. This team had been systematically recruited and trained from October 2001; many were from Afghan NGOs and had experience in building and managing teams of Afghans within Afghanistan. They collectively adhered to a common vision of building state institutions through Afghan leadership via the national programs (which were beginning to yield development results across the country). Following the departure of this team, the individuals who took over formal authority decided to start strategy planning *ab initio*. This meant strategic redesign of the development process, dismantling the National Programs and many of the policies that underpinned these programs—in effect setting back the clock from January 2005 to January 2002.

## The Foreign and Donor Relations Process: Two Mental Models

### The Donor Response to Government Leadership

There were, on this reading, two divergent policy and budgeting processes, set in motion by the needs assessment, that diverged into two parallel processes.

*Model one* is that designed, articulated and legislated by the government and backed by the World Bank, other IFIs, and like-minded donors. The key objective was to gear efforts under government leadership, create functioning institutions, from a National Army and police and a justice system through to education, health and agriculture services. Its characteristics can be summarized as follows:

a. Pooling of financing to the budget, either directly or through trust fund or common programming mechanisms;

b. Alignment behind the government's strategy and policy agenda, most notably through adoption of the National Development Framework and the budget as the policy basis;

c. Program implementation through government-managed national projects and programs, tendered through transparent mechanisms to the most effective organization for the job, whether private sector, NGO or international organization;

d. Investment in Afghan human capital to staff the required Afghan functions and organizations;

e. Reporting on implementation of the budget through a single annual report that is shared with the population, Parliament, media and international community.

*Model two* is a project-based, donor-managed approach. Its key characteristics include:

a. Financing flows directly from each donor agency to the respective implementation agency, and does not flow through the government of Afghanistan;

b. Strategy and policy for the financing program is determined by the donor in question, usually in national or international headquarters, and is not included in the Afghanistan budget process;[23]

c. Implementation (procurement, accounting, management) takes place through projects managed by international staff and project units outside the Afghan government;

d. Staffing is largely derived through "technical assistance" contracts with firms to provide foreign personnel;

e. Reporting takes place from implementing agency to donor agency and is not incorporated in the national annual report.

Donor behavior in Afghanistan between 2001 and 2006 could be seen to fall more or less into the following three categories.

### Statebuilding Agenda and Alignment Behind Government Systems

*Model one*. A number of international organizations and donors aligned behind this approach. The multilateral development banks (World Bank and IMF) did this by agreeing to subsume the needs assessment within the government's visioning and strategy process, with the IMF also rapidly establishing a Staff Monitored Program, a mechanism for dialogue between IMF staff and the government. The European Commission's early country strategy document, endorsed in February 2003, stated that it did not need to prepare its own strategy as it endorsed the government's own strategy (European Commission 2003). A number of bilateral donors also pledged all, or most, of their support through the Afghanistan Reconstruction Trust Fund, and endorsed the government devised implementation vehicle: National Programs. These bilateral donors included the agencies of Canada, the Netherlands, the United Kingdom and Norway. The UN's political arm also aligned behind this approach, supporting the government's efforts to prepare a budget and embark on a reform program that would harness the population's energies behind a positive agenda. Pakistan and India moved early to provide direct budget support and, together with Iran, supported some large infrastructure and investment projects requested by the government.

## Hedging Bets: Hybrid Model One and Two

A number of donors provided some of their assistance through the government's preferred modalities, but continued to finance a significant proportion of their assistance through parallel mechanisms. These included Germany, Italy and Sweden.

## Building Parallel Systems: Model Two

Another category of actors adopted the second model. The first category was made up of the large bilateral donors, such as the US and Japan. Each of these initially prepared their own strategies, policies and projects, with little consultation, and largely contracted implementation to domestic contractors. Both Japan and the US subsequently began to shift towards cooperation with Afghan authorities in terms of priorities for expenditure, but implementation of their projects remained substantially with foreign organizations that functioned outside government policy and government implementation frameworks.

The second group is composed of the United Nations agencies and humanitarian funding system, including funding mechanisms such as the European Commission's Humanitarian Office (ECHO) and USAID's Office of Transition Initiatives (OTI), which argued that money should not flow through the World Bank-managed ARTF, but rather through UN agencies. In early 2002, UN agencies conducted a survey of Afghanistan and issued an appeal for $1.8 billion, followed by a second appeal for $900 million in 2003. Each appeal contained hundreds of projects, to be administered by international or national UN or NGO staff, and implemented through organizations that would be established for the purpose. Such a large UN agency field presence ran directly counter to the UNAMA/UN Secretariat view that a "light footprint" would be the key to stability.

Analysis shows that such expenditure often did not result in implementation of the promised projects, and, if they did materialize, they were often not conducted in a cost-effective manner. This had a serious negative impact on the capacity of the state, effectively undermining the functionality of state institutions, and the trust of the population in the state (examined below). The consequences of such a decision on the prospects for Afghanistan's stability additionally warrant consideration and further study.

It must be recognized that some humanitarian aid was necessary in the post-2001 period. In particular de-mining and refugee assistance required urgent attention, and both were transitional in nature and provided no obvious rationale for building up state capacity. Furthermore, the agencies and the government both recognized the necessity of maintaining some flexible capability within the humanitarian system, in case of either political turmoil or humanitarian disasters.

The volume and modality of the assistance earmarked as "humanitarian" warrants consideration: while some food assistance may have been necessary, it is questionable whether the amounts and methods of delivery were appropriate. Food—mainly wheat—was shipped from the US through prescribed companies, mainly paid for by the European Commission, instead of being purchased internally from the Afghan market or in the region, where the price would have been considerably cheaper and transport costs reduced or avoided. It has been suggested that as a result of the volume of food imported the domestic wheat market collapsed, with farmers across the country destroying their crops rather than harvesting them; the product was not worth the cost of labor.[24] A connection between the collapse in wheat market prices and the growth in opium production requires further validation.

## Impact of Donor Behavior on Government Systems

### Model One

Where donors adopted financing along the lines of model one, several impacts on government systems were observable. First, a collective approach to conditionality ensured a policy dialogue that was coherent across donors and government ministries, allowing focus on carefully sequenced reforms. Second, regular system audits would highlight attention to constraints in the system and allow an orderly approach to fixing problems. Third, diplomatic pressure was aligned to the cause of bringing fiscal discipline and coherence to a hitherto highly fragmented field of financial flows, which had contributed to past conflict. Fourth, concentrating leadership and management capability on the most significant programs, such as the National Solidarity Program, the National Emergency and Employment Program and the National Accounting and Audit Program created efficiencies and impact.

Model Two: Effectiveness of Expenditure

The value proposition of model two financing is quite poor. It could be postulated that between 40 and 90 per cent of a project cost is spent abroad in overheads. Given the long contractual chain of many donor-managed projects, the resources that were available for a project on the ground would often be a fraction of the overall project allocation. The cost-effectiveness of the USAID-managed school and clinic building program has now been well documented by a range of reviews and investigative reports. It is now estimated that $600 million per year is spent on technical assistance to the government, which outweighs the cost of maintaining the entire civil service of 260,000 people (Stephens and Ottaway 2005a, Stephens and Ottaway 2005b).

Harm to State Institutions

The impact of building organizations in chains to implement projects across the country outside government structures warrants analysis. Whereas $20m was initially pledged from the donors to the government for 250,000 civil servants, $1.8bn was requested for UN agencies which had seven staff in the country at the time, to implement hundreds of small projects. Large numbers of international staff were deployed to the country, each requiring drivers, translators, secretaries, and guards who were paid in the region of $600 per month. This attractive salary, which the government could not match, saw large numbers recruited away from the civil service where they had served as teachers, doctors and managers. It is arguable that much of the aid given had—and continues to have—a damaging impact on state institutions, capacity and policy coherence. In effect the international agencies drew their staff from government positions to support an aid bureaucracy that could not operate outside Kabul in a declining security environment. The impact of the decision to circumvent the ARTF support for core government staff and functions and build parallel UN and NGO organizations has yet to be seriously studied. However, it is a source of much tension and resentment among the Afghan population

The hundreds of different projects each came with specific internal rules for procurement, managing, and reporting. This mess of rules undermined the coherence of the laws and procedures of the country. Where there was a conflict between Afghan law and donor regulations, in virtually every case donor regulations trumped Afghan law, even in "rule of law" projects.

Perhaps even more harmful was the concomitant impact of the private security firms hired to protect international contractors, particularly in more remote provinces. These private security firms either attract existing police or army personnel away from Afghan national institutions, or train new personnel in the use of firearms and then hire them on short-term contracts. The potential dangers of such practices, involving tens of thousands of people, do not need to be spelled out.

Lastly, establishing hundreds of projects, each run through different sets of procedures, had the effect of deflecting the attention of the national authorities from formulating and implementing a national policy agenda to dealing with the minutiae of each project and its delegation. Further, it could be argued that such projects undermined the accountability of the government. Given that little information was supplied about their implementation, the government was unable to report on the implementation of the budget, despite many requests from the population and their elected delegates, including through the two Loya Jirga. In sum, it was quickly evident that a humanitarian and developmental agenda conducted without sensitivity to institutional realities would be destructive of state functionality.

## Conclusions

There are many implications and lessons that can be drawn from the Afghanistan case study.

First, the case underscores the need to gear short-term strategies and policies more sensitively to a medium to long-term agenda of the creation, bolstering or protection of institutional capability of the country concerned to manage its own affairs. Afghanistan has served as a catalyst for learning about new instruments and partnership modalities, particularly in terms of long-term financing mechanisms; linking financing to long-term reform programs; the use of multi-donor trust funds; the use of national programs as cost-effective implementation mechanisms that promote national ownership and catalyze capacity-building; and the importance of the use of the budget as the instrument of policy-making. The Afghanistan model applied from 2001 to 2005 has already served as a source of learning, innovation and adaptation for a number of initiatives, including the Good Donorship in Fragile States initiative, and country processes elsewhere.

Second, the role of national leaders and managers to craft strategies and laws within their own policy frameworks is shown to be key. All too often, Afghanistan included, leadership is crowded out or marginalized by overwhelming international presence. Those countries that have transformed successfully in the recent past did so when the leadership team of a country cohered around and drove an agenda that they had crafted.

Third, the Afghanistan case sounds a cautionary note about the appropriateness of using foreign-based private contractors, UN agencies and NGOs, designed for short-term interventions, for building up parallel mechanisms that then cannot fulfill their promises of delivering services to entire populations, and on the dangers of imposing conflicting policy priorities on a fledgling government.

Fourth, the case points towards the difficulty, even where a coherent leadership team articulates a sound vision and a UN mandate provides legitimacy, of corralling donors, who insist on dancing to their own tune. To keep even a limited number of donors behind a coherent agenda frequently required the direct intervention of the minister of Finance, and huge investments of time, resources and energy. For example, to try to limit the negative impact of one parallel process working in direct competition against the national budget, the eight senior managers of the AACA were required to work for six weeks during budget preparation time to review the $1.8 billion projects already prepared by the UN agencies, instead of using their time to prepare and implement the national budget. Sixty per cent of these projects were then rejected, on the basis of World Bank QAG rules. The failure to align donors robustly behind an institution-building and fiscal accountability agenda in the 2001–05 period arguably set the stage for the stark deterioration in governance standards and trust post-2005.

The case also suggests that even where a recipient government has adequate frameworks, policies and systems in place for managing aid, a substantial number of donors choose not to use them, thus deliberately bypassing and undermining them. Many donors consistently flouted the country's rules and laws for aid management, despite their own rhetoric about "rule of law." This is most likely a combination of the use of standard operating procedures for humanitarian disasters; a trust gap towards Afghan institutions which resulted in an inclination to bypass rather than help build mutual accountability; and the bureaucratic-financial imperative for agencies, particularly UN agencies and NGOs, to use crisis to mobilize funding to pay for their own running costs. It is interesting to note that while the ARTF system provided international procurement, financial management and audit firms, and comprehensive, audited annual reports, many donors elected not to use this system on the basis that they did not consider it transparent, accountable or effective enough. UN agencies were financed, although by 2004 they had yet to provide a financial report on more than $3 billion of expenditure. Comparison of benchmarks and standards of transparency, effectiveness and accountability could be a useful exercise.

Fifth, where budget support is used as a mechanism in itself it is not sufficient; other supporting mechanisms are required to deliver the institutional effectiveness necessary to ensure implementation. In the case of Afghanistan this supporting mechanism was the National Programs, which ensured a high degree of accountability, transparency and effectiveness in implementation across the country, across levels of governance—village, district, province, municipality and center—and across functions of governance. A second mechanism is to maintain a single procurement unit, with efforts to ensure that appropriate rules, procedures and personnel are in place to manage the process.

Sixth, the degree of collapse of accountability and trust post-2004 retrospectively points to the need for building robust accountability mechanisms for use of resources, both domestic and foreign-donated. Such mechanisms might have included World Bank-IMF accountability-related conditionality, and/or a more robust, sequenced roadmap of conditions attached to the ARTF. In the author's opinion, the decision made in 2006 to transfer "coordination" authority from the World Bank to the UN was damaging to accountability; the World Bank through the ARTF was in a stronger position to produce accountability than the UN. The UN has relative strengths in management of political process; the World Bank is stronger at economic and financial management. A division of labor between the two institutions worked comparatively well in 2001–04, whereby the UN led on the political process and the World Bank led the economic process.

Finally, there is the need to tailor approaches to a specific context, time and place. Where mechanisms have been copied from Afghanistan to other contexts, they have not worked well, because they were designed with particular features of the context in mind. Equally, when mechanisms developed in Afghanistan for one point in time are applied at a different point in time, they will not serve their purpose.

# 14

# THE NEW PROTECTORATES

## STATEBUILDING AND LEGITIMACY

*Dominik Zaum*

The last fifteen years have seen increased involvement of donor countries and international organizations in the governance and development of post-conflict countries, to assist with the creation of representative political institutions, build governance capacity, promote judicial reform, and reform economic structures. Their efforts at institutional and societal transformation have attempted to change the underlying structures and dynamics that are thought to have fuelled a conflict, and build institutions to enable societies to resolve conflicts between political factions without violence. This has encompassed interventions ranging from highly intrusive efforts of international transitional administration, temporarily taking over the government of a territory, to complex peace operations with state- and peacebuilding mandates, and more limited assistance missions to governments in post-conflict countries.

In light of the intrusive character of many of these new protectorates, the authority that they exercise, and the contested situations within with they operate, this kind of intervention has received increasing attention over the last few years, and has faced a range of legitimacy challenges. Thus, interveners' exercise of political authority over post-conflict territories seems to be at odds with contemporary conceptions of legitimate government. While the legitimacy of governments is rooted in notions of self-determination and (more controversially) democracy,[1] many of the new protectorates, at least temporarily, seem to deny both to the people whom they govern.[2] As William Bain has slightly polemically argued in his discussion of the normative dilemmas posed by international administration: "a zeal for emancipating the oppressed, ... affirming their freedom of thought and freedom of expression, leads to the temporary suspension of their freedom to think and to express for themselves."[3]

Furthermore, the states over which the new protectorates have been established tend to face unique legitimacy problems themselves. Their legitimacy might be challenged by political factions contesting a state's authority, questioning its borders, and the character of the political community over which it has authority. What Kalevi Holsti has described as the "horizontal" legitimacy of the state[4] has been challenged in particular in cases of communal violence and ethnically-based civil war, as in Bosnia and Herzegovina for example. Legitimacy might also be undermined by a state's inability to provide security and public services such as education, healthcare, electricity, or clean water, and by other actors filling the spaces vacated by the state and challenging its authority, often with violence. The implicit social contract between the state and the political community breaks down, and with it what Holsti has described as the state's "vertical" legitimacy.[5] As David Keen highlights in his discussion of the war in Sierra Leone, support for the RUF rebels was originally fuelled by the failure of the Freetown government to fulfill the basic expectations of many Sierra Leonean citizens and a concomitant decline in its legitimacy.[6]

The new protectorates can be seen as an attempt to address the legitimacy deficits of such weak states affected by conflict and violence. Many Western donor governments and international organizations have increasingly considered "liberal statebuilding"—encompassing the establishment of democratic political institutions and a liberal market economy, the promotion of human rights, and building state capacity—as the best path to a legitimate post-conflict order and sustainable peace.[7] However, the legitimacy of liberal statebuilding has been questioned by critics who argue that such efforts reflect the normative preferences of the international statebuilders rather than those of the affected societies, whose values and traditions are marginalized in the process. While some have denounced the whole enterprise of liberal statebuilding as thinly disguised Western imperialism,[8] others have been more concerned about the consequences of absent or limited legitimacy for the sustainability of newly established institutions.[9] In Bosnia, for example, the limited local legitimacy of the selection criteria for senior civil servants undermined the effectiveness of the international efforts to reform the civil service, a key element of the strategy to enhance the capacity of the central state.[10] In East Timor, the limited legitimacy of the judicial system established by the UN Transitional Administration (UNTAET), which did not take account of traditional understandings of authority and justice, meant that many Timorese, particularly in rural areas, avoided the courts and instead continued to rely on traditional authorities to find justice.[11] The legitimacy problems that the new protectorates have faced therefore pertain to both aspects of what Joel Beauvais has called their "dual mandate": first government, and second, statebuilding.[12]

This chapter aims to unpack the legitimacy challenges faced by the new protectorates. Rather than making a general argument about their legitimacy or illegitimacy, it aims to provide a framework for thinking about the specific problems that different instances of international governance face in light of their specific structures, mandates, resources, and operational environments. To that end, the next section will very briefly discuss why the question of legitimacy is important for the new protectorates. It will then unpack the concept of legitimacy, and identify its four dimensions, which can help to shed light on the different challenges that the new protectorates face: procedural legitimacy, legitimacy based on the congruence of values, output legitimacy, and structural legitimacy. It is followed by a more detailed examination of each of these four dimensions, exploring how they are reflected in different legitimation practices and how these claims have been challenged. The discussion in these sections draws predominantly (but not exclusively) on the cases of Bosnia, Kosovo, and East Timor, as the highly intrusive interventions there have posed some of the most protracted legitimacy challenges faced by the new protectorates. The chapter concludes with a short discussion of the implications of these findings for the politics of international efforts at building liberal states.

## The Importance of Legitimacy for the New Protectorates

The literature on legitimacy highlights several arguments for legitimacy's importance for institutions, focusing especially on the contribution that legitimacy makes to compliance[13] and on the association between legitimacy and institutional stability.[14] With regard to the new protectorates, legitimacy can be argued to be important for three reasons in particular.

First, legitimacy strengthens the international support for the new protectorates. An enterprise of post-conflict reconstruction by foreigners that is seen as legitimate by donor governments and international society more generally will find it easier to obtain financial and military resources. The fate of the US-led occupation in Iraq illustrates this point. The war that led to the occupation was fought without express authorization by the UNSC, and many states viewed it as illegitimate. To the extent that states associated the occupation with an illegitimate war, this made it more difficult for the US and its allies to share the military and financial burden of reconstruction with other states.[15]

Second, legitimacy can strengthen local support for the objectives and policies of a new protectorate, and can strengthen the stability of the political order the protectorate aims to establish. An order that is perceived as legitimate by the local population will face less (violent) opposition as the community generally considers it as promoting shared objectives. Legitimacy is therefore likely to reduce the amount of coercion necessary to uphold new political institutions. Legitimacy supports the governance efforts of the new protectorates as well as newly established local political institutions.

The final, and related, reason for the importance of legitimacy is sustainability. If the institutions established by the new protectorates are not considered legitimate, they are unlikely to outlast the international presence which sustains them with money (and if necessary force) for long, once that presence has gone.

### Legitimacy and Legitimation

How then should one understand legitimacy in the context of the new protectorates? Legitimacy, in Ian Hurd's words, is "an actor's normative belief that a rule or institution ought to be obeyed."[16] This understanding of legitimacy emphasizes the social character of legitimacy: legitimacy cannot be unilaterally declared, but must be recognized by others.[17] It is a quality that is attributed to institutions or rules and can, as Buchanan and Keohane suggest, have both a normative and a sociological meaning.[18] The normative understanding ascribes legitimacy to an institution if its structure and actions fulfill particular normative criteria, such as being based on some expression of consent, institutional integrity, and the promotion of justice.[19] The sociological understanding examines the relationship between societal beliefs and an institution's character and practices, ascribing legitimacy on the basis of the congruence of the institution with the beliefs, values and expectations that provide a justification for its power.[20] Both meanings, however, are inextricably intertwined. The criteria against which normative legitimacy is judged are not objective and universal but those held by a particular audience making a normative judgment on an institution's legitimacy. At the same time, those making a judgment on the congruence of their beliefs with an institution's structures and practices do so on the basis of certain normative suppositions. Therefore one cannot be understood without the other.

Legitimacy, however, not only needs to be recognized, but also claimed and sustained. It is not just an attribute, but a social practice, legitimation, that can be practiced by both rulers and the ruled.[21] Legitimation can be both a bottom up practice exercised by those subject to an institution's or actor's authority (for example the process of democratic validation of the legitimation claims of office holders through the act of voting); and one exercised from above, by the actors claiming legitimacy. From this perspective, legitimation is, in the words of Rodney Barker, "an action or series of actions—speech, writing, ritual, display—whereby people justify to themselves or others the actions they are taking and the identities they are expressing or claiming."[22] In other words, it is a process of self-legitimation, where institutions communicate their claims sideways (to other institutions) or downwards (towards the subjects of their authority). This latter form of legitimation will be at the center of the discussion below. It is reflected, for example, in the practices of new protectorates, in their public statements defending their authority, and in the language they use in their decisions and resolutions.

Different actors make legitimation claims with reference to a range of different dimensions of legitimacy. With regard to the new protectorates, four of these dimensions are discussed in more detail below. The first is procedural legitimacy, which is claimed with regard both to the processes by which the new protectorates are established and to the character of their decision-making processes.[23] The second relates to the congruence of the goals and practices of the new protectorate with shared values, and the extent to which its core principles can be justified in terms of these norms.[24] The third source of legitimacy is what Mark Sutchman has called the "structural legitimacy" of an institution. In Sutchman's words, "[t]he structurally legitimate organization becomes a repository of public confidence because it is 'the right organization for the job'"[25] it is perceived as particularly suited to address a particular challenge, or it has access to particular resources or expertise. Arguments that root the legitimacy of the UN in its multilateral character and its universal membership, for example, fall into this category, as do claims to legitimacy by the

World Bank or UNDP, who produce extensive expert research and claim specific expertise on development issues. The final dimension of legitimacy discussed here is what Fritz Scharpf has called "output legitimacy,"[26] the effectiveness of the new protectorates in addressing the problems they have been established to solve. •

## Procedural Legitimacy

Decision-makers in the new protectorates have invoked the processes by which they were established and authorized, as well as their specific decision-making practices, when justifying their authority. In their legitimation efforts, the new protectorates have relied on well-established international practices of establishing such institutions, with strong sociological legitimacy. Some, such as UNMIK in Kosovo or UNTAET in East Timor, have emphasized their authorization by the UN Security Council under Chapter VII of the Charter.[27] Others, such as the Office of the High Representative (OHR) in Bosnia, have relied on the consent of the host governments to their establishment.[28] Mostly, these processes have been uncontroversial. Instances where the authorization process has been challenged, however, highlight the importance of procedural legitimacy for the new protectorates. The successor missions to UNMIK in Kosovo, the EU-led rule of law mission EULEX and the International Civilian Office (ICO), are good examples of the legitimacy problems that can arise. The divisions in the UNSC over Kosovo's unilateral declaration of independence meant that there was no agreement on the closure of UNMIK and on authorizing EULEX and ICO to succeed it, leading to uncertainty about the authority of the new missions and their relationship with UNMIK. This uncertainty not only delayed the full deployment of the missions for over a year, but severely limited the cooperation of the Serb government and the Kosovo-Serb community with EULEX and the ICO, as well as that of other international organizations in Kosovo, such as the OSCE. The lack of procedural legitimacy has clearly undermined the effectiveness of these operations.[29]

Claims of procedural legitimacy have also been made with regard to the way in which the new protectorates take their decisions. They have focused in particular on local accountability, the transparency of their decisions, and the involvement of local actors, especially local political elites, in decision-making processes. Often the new protectorates have deliberately sought to legitimize themselves with regard to the local population by involving local political elites in consultation and co-decision mechanisms. The resolution establishing

UNTAET in East Timor, for example, emphasizes the need for UNTAET to cooperate and consult with the Timorese in its efforts to fulfill its mandate,[30] while Security Council Resolution 1483, recognizing the authority of the US and Britain as occupying powers in Iraq, also asks them to form a transitional Iraqi authority and cooperate in the governance of the country until a representative government can be established.[31] The memoirs and statements of many senior international officials involved in different new protectorates highlight their own unease with what they perceived as the democratic deficit of these operations, but also their desire to share the responsibility for government with local politicians.[32] In East Timor, the SRSG, Sérgio Vieira de Mello, quickly set up the National Consultative Council (NCC) to advise him on the administration of the territory. While it was formally only a consultative body without any formal authority, in practice de Mello only issued resolutions that the whole NCC supported.[33] Similarly, Bernard Kouchner, head of UNMIK in 1999 and 2000, who convened the advisory Kosovo Transitional Council (KTC), reflected after his departure from Kosovo that:

"I wanted to implicate the Kosovars, all the ethnic groups—Albanians and Serbs, Bosniacs and Roma, Ashkali, Turks, and the others—in the ensemble of decisions that concerned them or had bearing on the future of Kosovo... The sharing of competences would allow them to become players but also responsible actors—that is equally accountable with the international community: partners in success as well as in failure."[34]

These concerns for local participation not only reflected the awareness of these international officials of the need to ensure local legitimacy, but also informed the relatively rapid devolution of authority to local institutions in both Kosovo and East Timor, well before these institutions had the capacity for effective self-government.[35]

However, both local elites and international observers have regularly criticized the character of ITA governance and decision making. In East Timor, political elites complained about the perfunctory nature of their involvement in decision making. Timorese ministers, for example, threatened to resign over what they considered the insufficient local involvement in the UNTAET-led transitional authority, arguing that "[t]he Timorese Cabinet Members are caricatures of ministers in a government of a banana republic. They have no power, no duties, nor resources to function adequately."[36] In Kosovo, the UN-appointed Ombudsperson commented on the undemocratic nature of UNMIK decision-making, arguing that "UNMIK is not structured according to democratic principles... The people of Kosovo are therefore deprived of protection of their basic rights and freedoms...";[37] while the Council of Europe, in a report on Bosnia's prospects for integration into Europe, remarked that the High Representative's powers and impositions of laws were incompatible with Bosnian membership in the Council of Europe, as there was insufficient local ownership of the decisions.[38]

A range of scholars have highlighted the rather limited accountability of ITAs, in particular towards the local community.[39] The Ombudsperson in Kosovo, for example, could investigate violations of human rights by the Kosovo institutions, but not by UNMIK itself, or by the NATO-led KFOR troops.[40] International personnel of the new protectorates, both military and civilian, generally enjoy immunity from prosecution by local courts.[41] The existing accountability mechanisms for the new protectorates are predominantly international, such as regular reports on the operations to the UNSC (or, in the case of the OHR in Bosnia, to the European Parliament), or supervision of legal decisions by the Office of the Legal Adviser in the UN Secretariat. While the latter's supervision has at times been very extensive,[42] the former has generally not been particularly significant as an oversight mechanism and has rarely affected specific actions of such operations.[43]

## Legitimacy and the Congruence of Values

In their legitimation efforts, the new protectorates have regularly emphasized their promotion of shared values, in particular relating to human rights and democracy. References to human rights norms permeate the mandates and statements of many of these operations, committing them to their promotion and protection.[44] While the universality of such values is often alleged, beyond a rather limited canon of human rights such claims are vigorously contested by many states.[45] In an international society characterized by value pluralism, the new protectorates therefore face a difficult challenge. An institution is legitimate in the eyes of a particular community to the extent that its objectives reflect the normative beliefs and expectations of that community's members. The new protectorates, however, need to address two distinct communities with their legitimacy claims: first, the local population over which they exercise governmental authority and on whose cooperation they rely to implement their statebuilding mandate; and second, the international community of states, international organizations, and donor agencies which authorize, fund and staff them. The relevant normative structures within which each of these communities judges the legitimacy claims of the new protectorates can differ substantially, reflecting different conceptions of morality, order, and justice.[46] The problem of having to deal with diverging values and interests is not a new one, but is familiar to students of colonialism. It is at the core of what Kenneth Robinson identified as the dilemma of trusteeship: "Was it not unlikely that, taking the sphere of colonial government as a whole, the interests of the colonial power should be *identical* with those of the natives? [...] How, again, could a balance be struck between the social changes that any economic development must bring and native satisfactions with their own social order?"[47] These different demands from new protectorate audiences of the legitimacy claims at time, contradict each other and require different priorities.[48]

The case of Kosovo's status highlights the problem this poses for the legitimacy of international efforts at creating liberal states.[49] In the aftermath of NATO's 1999 war against Yugoslavia, it was important for the legitimacy of UNMIK that it did not endorse or promote the secession of Kosovo. Not only did Western states not want to concede independence to Kosovo as the consequence of a war they had argued was fought for humanitarian purposes, but Russia and China would have vetoed any resolution that did not assert Yugoslav sovereignty over the territory. As China argued in the UNSC meeting establishing UNMIK on 10 June 1999, "[I]n view of the fact that...the draft resolution has reaffirmed ... the commitment of all Member States to the sovereignty and territorial integrity of the Federal Republic of Yugoslavia, the Chinese delegation will not block the adoption of this draft resolution."[50] For the Kosovo Albanians, on the other hand, any return to Serb rule was inconceivable, and international administration was only seen as a stepping stone to independence.

As UNMIK, the Contact Group, and the Security Council remained unwilling to address the status question, the local legitimacy of UNMIK deteriorated, the process culminating in the riots against the Serb minority and UNMIK in March 2004. This increased the pressure on UNMIK and the UN to resolve the status question. Western states which previously feared that attempts to address Kosovo's status would destabilize the region, and lead to renewed calls for separatism in Bosnia and Macedonia, now viewed a delay in resolving the issue as a source of instability (a view unsurprisingly supported by the vast majority of Kosovo Albanians); while Russia and Serbia continued to argue that independence for Kosovo would be a breach of international law and a threat to core principles of international order. Both sides had contradictory expectations towards UNMIK, which could not be resolved and ultimately undermined the legitimacy of the operation in the eyes of both after

Kosovo unilaterally declared its independence on 17 February 2008. While Serbia and Russia demanded that UNMIK should denounce the declaration as illegal and take steps to reverse it,[51] Kosovo Albanians and Western states pushed for the closure of the mission and the transition to the envisaged successors, EULEX and the ICO, with the European Commission withdrawing the funding for the economic reconstruction pillar of UNMIK (Pillar IV), which ceased to operate in June 2008.

Not only the legitimacy of a new protectorate, but also that of the political institutions that it establishes and supports, depend on the degree to which they reflect local values, contributing to the stability and sustainability of these institutions. However, as a range of authors have shown, the statebuilding efforts of foreigners have been shaped predominantly by liberal norms, and emphasized the establishment of democratic institutions and a free market, the promotion of the rule of law and human rights, and the establishment of effective government,[52] reflecting the normative preferences of the statebuilders. While these norms might significantly overlap with those of the affected society, at times their application has undermined the legitimacy of particular institutions. Graciana Del Castillo, for example, argues that the decision of the CPA in Iraq to privatize the oil industry ignored the strong historical opposition of Iraqis to foreign ownership of their assets (in particular in the oil sector). This not only forced the CPA to back-track on its privatization proposal but also undermined the CPA's legitimacy in the eyes of the Iraqi population.[53]

The problem of conflicting local and international normative frameworks has been particularly acute with regard to the rule of law—one of the most important elements of statebuilding, but also one of the most difficult ones.[54] The provision of justice is different from other public services, such as healthcare or public administration. Rule of law promotion is not susceptible to technocratic solutions that can be applied, with minor variations, in the same way to institutions across the world, independent of their social, cultural and historic context. Instead, it is deeply rooted in existing local customs, traditions and values, and needs to reflect those to be effective. Conceptions of justice can differ, in particular in societies characterized by traditional authority structures, be they tribal or religious, often emphasizing mediation and reconciliation to ensure the welfare of the community over individual rights. While there is now a greater recognition of the importance of traditional law, and the challenge of reconciling it with the authority of formal state institutions, this has proved to be difficult terrain for international actors,[55] and consequently it has been an area where local and international conceptions of legitimacy have clashed frequently, especially in traditional societies such as East Timor or Afghanistan.

In East Timor, the strength of traditional local conceptions of justice and authority, prevalent in particular in rural areas, undermined the effectiveness and legitimacy of the formal judicial system established by UNTAET after 1999.[56] Little attempt was made by UNTAET to try to reconcile these different conceptions of justice, mostly because traditional law was largely seen as incompatible with international human rights standards. This has contributed to the continued weakness of the judiciary in East Timor, the legitimacy of which has remained contested. The limited attention to local traditions, values and conceptions of authority thus undermined the statebuilding efforts.[57]

*Structural Legitimacy*

The third dimension of legitimacy and the legitimation claims of the new protectorates discussed here concerns their structural legitimacy, or claims that they are perceived as particularly suited to address the challenges posed by weak institutions and the political culture of the countries they are deployed in, and have access to particular resources or expertise that help them in this task. In general, the structural legitimacy claims take two different forms. On the one hand, they are based on their "international" and multilateral character: they are neutral in disputes over the sovereignty of a territory, making them acceptable as an interlocutor to all sides in a dispute.[58] On the other hand, they are based on claims to be able to muster international resources and expertise to address the capacity problems of weak post-conflict states.

Neither legitimacy claim is unproblematic. Oliver Richmond and Jason Franks, for example, suggest that UNMIK in Kosovo was not neutral, that the "liberal peacebuilding" policies it pursued structurally favored the Albanian majority.[59] More generally, as Mats Berdal and Richard Caplan have argued, unlike traditional peacekeeping operations such efforts are deeply political enterprises, which need to make deeply political choices that affect the identities of actors in post-conflict territories as well as the distribution of power and access to resources.[60] While their relative ability to muster military and financial resources might be high, this needs to be seen in the context of the overall size of the territories within which they operate. The substantial financial and human resources that some of the new protectorates can deploy, as indicated by high per capita figures of aid and of soldiers or police personnel per thousand inhabitants—highlighted for example in studies by the RAND Corporation—are also due to the fact that these operations took place in small territories with relatively small populations.[61] Furthermore, as the discussion of output legitimacy claims below indicates, the new protectorates have often faced problems of recruiting the right personnel in a timely fashion, raising further questions about their structural legitimacy.

## Output Legitimacy

The fourth and final dimension of the new protectorates' legitimacy claims focuses on their output legitimacy, their ability to effectively provide security, basic public services, and economic development—and do it better than a local government could without international assistance or guidance. Most territories where protectorates have been established have experienced a previous collapse of government, because of a lack of functioning institutions in the wake of conflict, or because of ongoing divisions and mistrust between former conflict parties. In Kosovo and East Timor, UNMIK and UNTAET were explicitly tasked to provide for interim or transitional administration in the light of such capacity problems. Both operations have emphasized the need to provide effective government in the absence of functioning local institutions, and the need for authority to fulfill their mandates, in particular the building of political institutions to which authority could be transferred.[62]

The limited effectiveness of the governance and statebuilding efforts by foreigners has been noted by a range of observers, and has been associated, *inter alia*, with their understanding of development,[63] the structure and staffing of the missions,[64] the lack of local participation,[65] and poor and ad-hoc planning of the operations which often had to be established on the hoof in the wake of a peace agreement.[66] The problems have had two consequences for the new protectorates.

First, planning and staffing problems meant that it took missions many months to establish their presence across the territory. As James Dobbins and his co-authors recount, in Iraq the CPA's staff turnover was rapid, and most of the time only half of the notional staff of around 2,000 were in the country;[67] this seriously undermined its governance capacity, and severely limited its presence beyond Baghdad's Green Zone. In East Timor, UNTAET personnel were mostly recruited not by the mission but by the DPKO in New York, and it took about six months to staff the mission's governance structures, before UNTAET could start to address the creation of a Timorese administration.[68]

The issue was not helped by disagreements between the DPKO and the UN Department of Political Affairs over who should be responsible for the mission.[69] In the absence of an effective international administrative presence, the previous clandestine structures of the former resistance movement CNRT that spread into every village in East Timor assumed administrative functions on the village level, distributing aid, providing reconciliation and justice, and providing a range of other administrative services.[70] Similar problems plagued the mission in Kosovo. Three months after it had been established, UNMIK personnel were only deployed to 18 of Kosovo's 29 municipalities.[71] The existing power vacuum had been filled by the unrecognized "Provisional Government of Kosova," led by the Kosovo Liberation Army (KLA), which appointed mayors and established a parallel governmental structure.[72] These "mayors" collected taxes, issued license plates, and often appointed managers of socially owned enterprises in the municipalities—all supposed to be prerogatives of UNMIK.[73]

Second, the new protectorates have often been characterized by a limited understanding of local conditions, customs and circumstances, compromising their ability to develop and implement public policy. Often staff recruited to these operations neither speak local languages nor have detailed knowledge of the countries' history and customs. In addition, the operations lack the epistemic capacities to effectively develop public policy. In Kosovo, limited understanding of potential ownership claims against socially owned enterprises first delayed the privatization process, and later led to its temporary suspension.[74] In Bosnia and Herzegovina, where more than half of the population lives in the countryside engaging predominantly in subsistence agriculture, the OHR for over a decade did not develop a rural development strategy,[75] which it itself conceded to be central to Bosnia's economic and political stability.[76] The detailed agricultural statistics necessary to develop such a policy were lacking. In contrast to neighboring countries with similar structural problems, like Bulgaria or Romania, which with EU support developed extensive rural development plans, the OHR's efforts by 2005 had culminated in a public information campaign with television and radio broadcasts, and a 50-page booklet on how to make profits in agriculture, rather than a comprehensive development effort.[77]

Not only has the governance record of the new protectorates been sketchy, but their statebuilding achievements have arguably been problematic, too. In East Timor public order collapsed almost exactly four years after UNTAET's departure, and a new peacekeeping operation had to be deployed to the country.

In Kosovo, post-independence institutions are weak and closely associated with the illicit economy,[78] and the territory is effectively divided along the river Ibar into a Serb North and a predominantly Albanian South. Ashraf Ghani and Claire Lockhart argue that the problems that international organizations and donor governments have faced in their statebuilding efforts is systemic, a consequence of the structure of international and non-governmental organizations that has developed to manage the reconstruction of post-conflict countries.[79] By the development of an internationalized parallel bureaucracy to channel aid and manage aid projects, the capacity of local institutions to develop and implement policy is (in Michael Ignatieff's words) "sucked out"[80] of the state rather than being built. Not only is the state deprived of funds; international organizations can also attract the most capable officials, who leave public service and work as drivers and interpreters for the much higher salaries that international agencies pay. As local organizations and companies are often effectively frozen out of the implementation of aid projects, the benefits to the local economy are limited, and barely contribute to the development of the local private sector.

However, despite these valid criticisms, one should not overstate the failure of the statebuilding efforts of the new protectorates. As Ian King and Whit Mason argue with respect to UNMIK, such criticisms at times seem to resemble the Judean complaint in the Monty Python's *Life of Brian*: "What have the Romans ever done for us?"[81] Through their institution-building activities, they have established and/or legitimized institutions through which societal conflicts can be managed, and which have stabilized post-conflict environments in places such as Macedonia, Namibia and Sierra Leone. In Kosovo, the legitimacy of the new state institutions has been questioned by Serbia and by large parts of the Serb minority in the territory, but they have the support of the vast majority of Albanians. In East Timor, these institutions failed during the collapse of public order in April/May 2006, following a mutiny by a third of the East Timor Defense Force; importantly, though, the violence in 2006 did not question the legitimacy of the institutions as such, but focused instead on the failings of the political leadership.[82] The 2007 elections broke the hold of FRETILIN over the post-independence institutions, and this might help to restore the legitimacy of the still weak Timorese state.

## Conclusion

As this chapter highlights, legitimacy is important both for the new protectorates themselves and for the governmental institutions they aim to establish.

However, the character and practices of building of liberal states also raises a range of legitimacy questions. The preceding discussion does not examine whether the idea of new protectorates fundamentally supports or contradicts certain conceptions of global order that would make the whole enterprise legitimate or illegitimate. Instead, by unpacking the concept of legitimacy and examining how some of its different dimensions relate to the practices and structures of the new protectorates, it has highlighted a range of legitimacy challenges that different operations face in their specific contexts.

Two issues with important implications for the politics of the new protectorates stand out. First, the chapter highlights the very limited political space available to these operations, squeezed as they are between the values and priorities of the international community, on the one hand, and those of the local population on the other. If these two audiences are further divided—as the international community has been over Kosovo, or local communities have been in a range of ethnically defined conflicts in particular—this space shrinks even more. In the worst case, this can mean that the policies of certain new protectorates merely reflect the lowest common denominator, which might leave all sides dissatisfied. The difficulties that UNMIK and the UN faced over the resolution of Kosovo's status, and the dissatisfaction about the process among all sides, speak to this problem. Second, the character of legitimacy challenges to the foreign attempts at building sustainable institutions changes over time. In the immediate post-conflict phase, differences in normative preferences between international interveners and the local population are unlikely to be a major issue, as addressing humanitarian emergencies and basic law and order issues are shared priorities. However, they will become significantly more important once local institutions have been established through which alternative conceptions of order can be voiced, and once statebuilding policies with wider ranging societal implications are pursued. Ultimately, questions about the legitimacy of the new protectorates are questions of degree, and legitimacy judgments will be shaped both by the specific practices of particular operations and by the contexts within which they operate. Understanding the different dimensions of the legitimacy challenges that the new protectorates face should help to better understand the constraints on such operations, and help to identify priorities for action.

# NOTES

## INTRODUCTION

1. Ruggie (1998).
2. Metcalf (1997).
3. Of a growing literature, Caplan (2005), Chesterman (2004), Wilde (2009), Zaum (2007), Fearon and Laitin (2004) and Paris and Sisk (2009) are particularly valuable.
4. There is an extensive literature on late twentieth-century globalization, e.g., Appadurai (1996) and Scholte (2004).
5. Clark (1997).
6. Mayall (2007: 26).
7. Duffield notes that this period saw a widespread "fear of underdevelopment as the source of conflict, criminalised activity and international instability" (2001: 7).
8. Ruggie (1998: 199).
9. Fukuyama (1989).
10. Influential "pessimist" writings include Huntington (1993), Kaplan (2000), Gray (1998), and Mearsheimer (2000).
11. Commenting on American foreign policy in the first half of the twentieth century, Kennan had noted "the lack of any accepted, enduring doctrine for relating military strength to political policy, and a persistent tendency to fashion our policy towards others with a view to feeding a pleasing view of ourselves rather than achieving real, and desperately needed, results in our relations with others" (1984: viii).
12. On "rogue" states, see Litwak (2000). Litwak notes that the Clinton Administration's rogue-state policy, by lumping together states as different as North Korea, Cuba, Iraq and Iran, created a "generic strategy of comprehensive containment despite significant differences in US objectives toward and political circumstances within the disparate group of rogue states." See Litwak (2007: 31).
13. Ikenberry (2001) and (2006).

14. Anthony Lake, "From Containment to Enlargement," address delivered at the Johns Hopkins University School of Advanced International Studies, Washington, DC 21 September 1993.

15. Russian critics think differently. They do think this is a true strategic vision: a sort of global Monroe doctrine by the US to extend its sphere of domination.

16. Chollet and Goldgeier (2008).

17. For an early treatment see Mayall (1996).

18. See Urquhart (1988: 248 ff.) for a classic statement of "first generation" peacekeeping by its foremost practitioner.

19. Power (2008: 92).

20. The record was not uniformly negative. Despite the UN's failure to provide a secure environment, the population nonetheless turned out in impressively large numbers in the election. As a result the prospects of democratization as a template for post conflict reconstruction seemed more promising than they turned out to be in practice.

21. See Boutros-Ghali (1992).

22. Quoted in Hippel (1999: 64).

23. Fortna and Howard (2008: 287–8).

24. See Simms (2001) for a searing study of British non-interventionism during the Bosnian war.

25. Paris and Sisk (2008: 6–7).

26. Caplan (2005: 2).

27. The US's impatience towards the UN in general, and the Russians specifically, led it to use NATO as the legitimating framework for the intervention in Kosovo. In the case of Iraq, the US deferred to Britain in trying to secure UNSC backing, but when that ultimately failed the US raised a "coalition of the willing," bypassing the UN altogether.

28. Finnemore (2003: 137).

29. Finnemore (2003: 74).

30. John Ruggie notes that "the fact of *American* hegemony was every bit as important as the fact of American *hegemony* in shaping the post-WW II international order." This is accurate in regard to the post-Cold War era as well (1998: 14).

31. While one should bear in mind the specifically Western roots of liberal interventionism, International Organizations (IOs) are important agents in their own right and in no way fig leaves for Western intentions.

32. From the opposite end of the spectrum, there are commentators who roll up all instances of intervention into a Western "liberal imperialist" project, their goal being that of denouncing it wholesale. Needless to say, this is no substitute for serious comparative analysis.

33. Fortna and Howard (2008: 293).

34. Mandelbaum (1996).

35. See Boot (2002) for a work skeptical about exogenous state building but enthusiastic about "small wars" as a way of coping with instability on the frontier. The case of piracy in contemporary Somalia and the international decision to aggressively patrol coastal waters shows that a language of repression and containment shorn of any claims to "save" and "state-build" can still be deployed in the context of failed and unstable states. So far these efforts have failed to contain the problem, despite the participation of several maritime Asian states in addition to the Western powers. The pirates have been driven further out to sea and while the cost of freight has risen, the insurance companies have mostly been prepared to pay up. The solution, if there is one, presumably lies onshore, a conclusion that points to the possibility that direct administration may yet recommend itself. If so, it would be as revealing of the inclination of those who make the decision as of the character of the problem itself.

36. Mark Blyth quoted in Ruggie (1998: 19).

37. Mayall and Srinavasan (2009).

38. Finnemore (2003).

39. At this stage in the 1990s, US policy-makers still distinguished between failed states, which were supposed to be a danger to themselves (and thus perceived through the lenses of charity rather that threat), and rogue states with malevolent intentions. This hard and fast distinction collapsed in the following decade with the realization that failed states and ungoverned regions (Afghanistan, Yemen, Somalia, the Af-Pak border etc.) could act as havens for terrorist activity.

40. Duffield (2001: 37).

41. For a critique, see Barnett et al. (2007); the foundational work on democratic/liberal theory is Doyle (1983a) and (1983b). Paris (2004) is an influential discussion of the impact of the liberal peace agenda on UN peacekeeping missions in the first decade after the Cold War.

42. Quoted in Duffield (2001: 4).

43. Cooper (2005: 30).

44. The US has its own imperialist record, both formal (Philippines) and informal (Central America), but its self-image is strongly anti-imperialist and not, like that of Britain or France, steeped in memories of colonial rule. On the US experience in the Philippines see, e.g., Karnow (1989).

45. Mazower (2009: 11).

46. Bain (2004).

47. The standard of civilization studied in Gong (1984) was, during the imperial heyday, an "explicit legal principle and an integral part of international law prevailing at the time" (p. 14) which disappeared with decolonization.

48. Pomeranz terms these efforts "western developmental imperialism" (2005: 41).

49. On a night plane to CPA-ruled Iraq in 2003, the constitutional adviser Noah Feldman noted the reading matter of his fellow passengers: "Not one seemed to need

a refresher on Iraq or the Gulf region. Without exception, they were reading new books on the American occupation and reconstruction of Germany and Japan" (Feldman, 2004: 1).

50. Bain in this volume.

51. Influential works in this vein include Ferguson (2004) and Ignatieff (2002).

52. See Mayall in this volume.

53. Mayall and Srinivasan (2009: 70). In his brief history of empire, Pagden (2001: 174–6) also notes the obvious linkages between current ideas of law, individual rights and liberal democracy as "universal" and the impulse that some of the key values "'we' treasure are in some larger sense the obvious and necessary values of humankind."

54. The UN has obviously run many missions in Africa since (Sierra Leone, DRC, Darfur, etc) but these are better categorized as (occasionally ambitious) peace-building missions without the ambitions and degree of external political control of the new protectorates. Partial exceptions with some statebuilding aspirations may include the missions in Liberia and South Sudan.

55. Clapham in this volume.

56. See Mayall (2009). Western strategy, for the most part enthusiastically endorsed by African states in general and South Africa in particular, has been to build up African capacity to support the self-help *Pax Africana* that has been the African goal ever since the establishment of the OAU in 1963. The Charter of its successor organization, the African Union (AU), deliberately included good governance criteria and a provision for the AU to intervene directly in failing African states, in an attempt to provide some insurance against any attempt to reintroduce Western style protectorates or trusteeships. Whether in the long run this strategy will prove effective, or whether, once again, liberal values will wither on the African vine remains to be seen.

57. In a useful study of Russian skepticism vis-à-vis the humanitarian agenda Baranovsky (2001: 3–4) notes that "most Russian analysts see numerous inconsistencies in the idea of humanitarian intervention, point to its conceptual weakness, warn about the dangerous practical implications and blame its supporters for deliberately promoting this approach with biased political purposes." See also MacFarlane (2002: 60ff.).

58. Although neither matches the combative stance of India, Brazil and South Africa seem to prioritize their status as developing world countries, as opposed to their status as democracies, in their UN voting on such divisive issues, and are not consistent stakeholders in Western-led statebuilding agendas. See G. Rachman, "America is losing the free world," *Financial Times*, 4 January 2010.

59. Mayall (2007: 31)

60. "For the sovereignty-conscious developing world, [Kofi] Annan's [post-sovereignty] agenda was like a red flag for a bull, but the NAM could do very little to

counter the new debate on humanitarian intervention. The issue was no longer whether to intervene but when and how to do so." See Mohan (2002: 45).

61. On 22 July 2010, the ICJ issued the non-binding advisory opinion that had been requested by the General Assembly on the basis of a resolution tabled by Serbia in October 2008. By a majority of 8 to 4 the Court took the view that there was nothing in international law to prohibit a unilateral declaration of independence. The final impact of this opinion, which fell short of ruling on whether Kosovo's independence itself was legitimate, is not clear. The Russian judge was one of those who dissented, and the Russian government indicated that it would continue to oppose recognition and to support "a diplomatic solution." Their current position suggests that they are unlikely to be swayed, even if those in favor command a majority in the General Assembly, until and unless they are offered a *quid pro quo* in the form of recognition of South Ossetia and Abkhazia.

62. Michael Wines, "China Willing to Spend Big on Afghan Commerce," *New York Times*, 30 December 2009. Commentators have hinted at the fact that China is "free-riding on the public good [the US offers]"; Robert Kaplan, "Beijing's Afghan Gamble," *New York Times*, 7 October 2009.

63. This was UN Resolution 1244 for Kosovo and UN Resolution 1483 for Iraq.

64. Chesterman (2004: 55).

65. Berdal (2009).

66. Berdal (2009: 150, 167).

67. The insurgents targeted the UN compound in August 2003, killing the SRSG Sérgio Vieira de Mello and twenty other staff members.

68. Drewienkiewicz in this volume.

69. Although turf conflicts between UN agencies are recurrent, the UNHCR attracted some hostility from other agencies in the 1990s for seeking to raise its profile by crowding out competitors. The UNHCR's ultimate goal of becoming a "lead agency" for humanitarian intervention was anyway unsustainable in view of the character of the UN system.

70. Caplan (2005: 34.)

71. Barnett *et al.* (2007).

72. This is one area where the study of colonialism could inspire scholars of exogenous statebuilding in the post-Cold War world. Balandier (2002) wrote that colonialism had "a common language (the civilizing mission) enveloping particular languages and particular interests-bureaucratic, missionary and economic [etc]." The worldviews and routines of colonial officials, businessmen, soldiers and missionaries have been intensely studied, and there is a general understanding that they were differentiated and often antagonistic. We lack a similarly clear assessment of the plural characters of the internationals in present-day protectorates.

73. This argument is put forward in Autesserre (2010), especially on the basis of the peacebuilding bias for the macro-political and national, and corresponding neglect

of the micro-political and local, foundations of conflict. Peacebuilders indeed share many assumptions of a general nature. This introduction argues that these assumptions have seldom materialized as a consistent and operative project on the ground.

74. On coordination, Weiss adds that "everyone is for it, although no one wishes to be coordinated if it implies any loss of autonomy." See Weiss (1998: 57, 66).

75. King and Mason (2006: 4).

76. Slaughter (2009). Slaughter insists that the logic of networks goes beyond that of mere outsourcing, which still presupposes "an established hierarchy": in a proper network "hierarchy and control lose out to community, collaboration and self-organization."

77. Duffield (2001: 34).

78. In this regard, David Rieff's (2001) anxieties about a "servile state humanitarianism" seem mostly unwarranted.

79. Gordenker (1998: 1).

80. Report of the Panel on the United Nations Peace Operations A/55/305-S/2000/809. On the attempts to reform UN peacebuilding since the 1990s see Wolfgang Seibel's chapter in this volume.

81. Weiss (1998: 5). Weiss's article, which charts the frustrating (and failed) attempts to enhance UN system coordination in the 1990s, mostly fits the non-reform dynamics of the subsequent decade as well. The pathologies of the networked approach are arguably more damning in contexts where the goal was not just running humanitarian relief operations, but the building of liberal states.

82. The organizational assumptions of the new protectorate are historically unprecedented. Pre-modern states routinely farmed out (or discharged, in Weber's term) important dimensions of statehood such as taxation. But such options were pursued under the state's command and initiative: at least in theory, its pre-eminence was never questioned. Colonial states, while essentially different creatures from metropolitan states, shared with them a set of assumptions about state prerogatives. And present-day industrial states, despite the dominance for the past thirty years of neo-classical economics and a penchant for deregulation and privatization, remain identifiably Weberian constructs with strong institutions, credible fiscal administrations, and a monopoly of violence.

83. It is true that even within the governments of the Western democracies similar methods of decentralized and networked decision making have increasingly replaced strategic decision-making, which these days tends to be called "the comprehensive approach." The results have been almost equally disastrous.

84. This has become a staple of writings on the early US occupation of Iraq. For shocking examples see Chandrasekaram (2007), Packer (2005) and William Langewiesche, "Welcome to the Green Zone," *The Atlantic Monthly*, November 2004.

85. Mark Ward, "An Afghan Aid Disconnect," *Washington Post*, 26 December 2008.

Ward, a former USAID official, complained that "[Washington] Post correspondents appeared to have more access to our projects than we did."

86. Scott (1998).
87. Benner, Mergenthaler and Rotmann (2011).
88. Seibel in this volume.
89. Bensahel (2007). Even at the level of individual Western states, the building of this expertise, drawing as it does on the assumption that such deployments will extend into the long term, is the subject of constant politicization.
90. Chandrasekaram (2007: 35). There are precedents for this. When putting together his Occupation team for post-war Japan, General MacArthur made sure to marginalize "old Japan hands," for whom the prospect of a democratic revolution in Tokyo was "absurd." See Dower (1996: 74, 217–24). The results of misapprehending the local context in Iraq were less fortunate.
91. The 2005 replacement of Ashdown by Christian Schwartz-Schilling, who had a diametrically opposed view of the role of OHR and pointedly refused to intervene, further underlines the importance of individuals in this context.
92. See Knaus and Martin (2003) for a widely read indictment of the international role in BiH.
93. Of many examples, see Chopra (2002) on East Timor and Chandler (2000) on BiH.
94. Compare Stewart (2006) and Etherington (2005) with the memoirs of the American viceroy (Bremer, 2006).
95. Chesterman (2004).
96. This structure is "inadequate" in its own terms, i.e. from the viewpoint of the implementation of the transformative agenda of the interveners.
97. Cramer (2006: 245ff.).
98. Castillo (2008) derides this as the "development as usual" approach that fails to gauge the specificity of post-conflict environments.
99. On the subject of the political economy of peacebuilding see Berdal and Zaum (2011) and Castillo (2008).
100. Chandrasekaram (2007: 128–38).
101. Boyce (2002: 1042).
102. Pouligny (2004).
103. Lockhart in this volume.
104. In the event, economic growth in the new protectorates is related to their natural resource endowment (essentially oil) rather than economic reconstruction policies.
105. The failure of the internationals in providing for apparently straightforward public goods played a key role in diminishing popular respect towards them. See Cramer (2006: 274–5).
106. Le Billon (2008: 345).

107. Bruno Waterfield, "EU and UN abandon inquiry into missing £60 million in Kosovo," *Daily Telegraph*, 6 May 2009.
108. Berdal and Keen in this volume.
109. On Iraq, see Arato (2009).
110. Neil MacDonald, "Sovereignty chafes at outside supervision," *Financial Times*, 8 June 2010.
111. See Tilly (1985) for a famous interpretation of statebuilding in early modern Europe that puts the deployment of violence and the accumulation of capital at the center of the process.
112. Huntington (1968).
113. Mayall (2007: 43). As noted above, this book is primarily concerned with the interveners rather than the locals. Moreover, the comments in this subsection pertain to the role of local elites rather than the populations of the new protectorates. This is a matter of focus and not willful neglect of a vital subject. Overall, the literature concerning the domestic dimensions of international peacebuilding is small. See Pouligny (2005) and Autesserre (2010) for two of the most important contributions.
114. Commenting on Bentham's liberal internationalist views, Michael Howard (2008: 26, 74) noted that "Bentham in fact wanted to turn everyone into Englishmen. His recipe for perpetual peace could be effective only if a degree of cultural and political homogeneity could be established which did not as yet exist and which many people considered highly undesirable [...] That was the trouble: so very few people, outside Britain, Scandinavia and the United States, *were* liberal 'in the British sense of the word'" (italics in the original).
115. In his remarkable work on intelligence in the British Raj, Bayly (2000) showed the roles that local elites can play in the construction of knowledge in colonial situations. In a new protectorate characterized by the occupiers' lack of knowledge, unwillingness to coerce, and absence of political will to implement the liberal project, the traction of local empowered political actors is correspondingly much higher.
116. A case in point is the different discourses on the US role in Afghanistan. The polemical cover of *Time* magazine on 9 August 2010 portrayed an 18-year-old Afghan woman named Aisha whose nose and ears had been cut off by a vengeful husband with the approval of the Taliban. This illustrated a story titled "What happens if we leave Afghanistan." References to Taliban barbarism are recurrent in discussions of the country, especially in regard to the plight of women. President Obama, however, has restated that the US presence in Afghanistan owes to the 9/11 attacks and only rarely, if ever, refers to a rights agenda.
117. Alex de Waal, "Afghanistan: The Natural State," *Times Literary Supplement*, 4 November 2009.
118. Mayall (2009: 15).

119. See Paris (2004) for a critique of the compatibility of simultaneous market reforms and democratization in a peacebuilding context.
120. While the emergence of the modern state in early modern Europe came about as a series of pragmatic adjustments by rulers rather than through the implementation of a previously existing plan, the subsequent experience of statebuilding, as Anderson (1991) underlined, owed much to the conscious emulation of successful (mostly Western) precedents.
121. The problem of "end state certainty" in places such as Kosovo doubtless complicated the process, but even a comparatively clearer mandate in East Timor was not a magic formula for success.
122. Cramer (2006: 254).
123. Chesterman (2004).
124. Paris and Sisk (2008).
125. "Responsibility to Protect: An idea whose time has come—and gone?," *The Economist*, 23 July 2009.
126. For a case-study of Angola, see Soares de Oliveira (2011). Weinstein (2005) makes a case for "autonomous recovery" of post-war societies but is insufficiently critical of the character of such reconstruction agendas and the leading domestic actors that articulate them.
127. Dodge (2009). Prime Minister Maliki's government rolled back many of the CPA's high profile (if at the time unimplemented) economic reform efforts. This was part of a broader "de-Americanization" of post-CPA Iraq. Many of these measures were certainly inappropriate, but such an extensive rollback further underlines the ephemeral and unsustainable character of much "enlightened" policy-making in the new protectorates.
128. Winter (2006: 205).

## 1. PROTECTORATES NEW AND OLD: A CONCEPTUAL CRITIQUE

1. National Security Strategy of the United States of America, September 2002, 1 (available at www.georgewbush-whitehouse.archives.gov/nsc/nss/2002/nss.pdf).
2. Cooper (2002: 16–19).
3. Chesterman (2004: 6).
4. Protocol No. 1—Meeting of November 15, 1884, Protocols and General Act of the West African Conference, *Parliamentary Papers*, 1885 LV127 mf 91.435, 9.
5. Nkrumah (1962: xvi).
6. Philips (1977: 1405).
7. Charles Grant, "Observations on the State of Society Among the Asiatic Subjects of Great Britain," *Parliamentary Papers*, 1812–13 (282) x.31, mf 14.63–64, 45, 73.
8. Burton (2002: 234).
9. Brailsford (1971: 32), Morel (1906: 180).

10. Thornton (1965: 99).
11. Fearon and Laitin (2004: 12–13).
12. See Bain (2003), especially chapters 2–3.
13. See Oxfam, "Increase in Forced Labour, Rape and Harassment in Eastern Congo, says Oxfam," Oxfam Press Release, 13 November 2008 (available at http://www.oxfam.org.uk/applications/blogs/pressoffice); and J. Whitehead, "The Rev. J. Whitehead to Governor-General of the Congo State, July 28, 1903" and "The Rev. J. Whitehead to Governor-General of the Congo State, September 7, 1903," Cmd. 1933 lxii (1904), 65–69. The most famous account of conditions in the Congo Free State is found in Roger Casement, "Mr. Casement to the Marquess of Lansdowne—(Received December 12), December 11, 1903)," *Parliamentary Papers*, Cmd. 1933 lxii (1904), 23–52.
14. Chamberlain (1897: 117–28).
15. Carroll (2007: 100).
16. See Butterfield (1965).
17. For an elaboration of this argument see Bain (2007: 513–30).
18. See Long (1995).
19. See Lugard (1929), chapters 10–11.
20. Knaus and Martin (2003: 73).
21. Philips (1977: 1287) and Paddy Ashdown, "Inaugural Speech by Paddy Ashdown, the New High Representative for Bosnia and Herzegovina," Office of the High Representative Press Office, 27 May 2002.
22. Lebow (2003: 122).
23. Lebow (2003: 314–16).
24. See Pagden (1995: 11–14).
25. Ikenberry (2002: 45); and Krauthammer (2002/3: 17).
26. Abdullah Gul, "An Appeal for Leadership: Why Hasn't the World's Lone Superpower Stopped This Tragedy?" *The Washington Post*, 3 August 2006, A27. Gul is currently Turkey's President, although at the time of writing he was the country's foreign minister.
27. See Deng, Kimaro, Lyons, Rothchild, and Zartman. (1996: 2–3).
28. Kofi Annan, "Two Concepts of Sovereignty," *The Economist*, 18 September 1999.
29. See ICISS, *The Responsibility to Protect*, (Ottawa: International Development Research Centre, 2001).
30. This thought is adapted from Norbert Elias, "The Retreat of Sociologists," *The Norbert Elias Reader*, Goudsblom and Mennell (1998: 175–85).
31. See d'Entreves (1967: 1–3); and Oakeshott, "The Authority of Governments and the Obligations of Subjects (1)," *Lecture in the History of Political Thought*, Nardin and O'Sullivan (2006: 428–29).
32. Tierney (1963: 378, 382–6).
33. Tierney (1963: 385). On the Austinian theory of legislative sovereignty see Campbell (1920).

34. Tierney (1963: 394–5).
35. Tierney (1963: 390).
36. Max Boot, "Pirates, Terrorism and Failed States," *The Wall Street Journal*, 9 December 2008 (available at www.online.wsj.com).
37. Ibid.
38. Max Boot, "We Should Pay to Plan for Nation Building," *Los Angeles Times*, 16 November 2005 (available at articles.latimes.com).
39. For a defense of liberalism in an international context see Charvet and Kaczynska-Nay (2008), esp. Pt. I. A critique may be had in Geuss (2005: 11–28).
40. Laslett (1999: 306).
41. Mill (1991: 13–15, 85–6) and Mill, "A Few Words on Non-Intervention," *Essays on Politics and Culture*, Gertrude Himmelfarb (1973: 377).
42. Daniel Pipes, "The Middle East's Tribal Affliction," *Jerusalem Post*, 24 January 2008.
43. Daniel Pipes, "A Democratic Islam?" *Jerusalem Post*, 17 April 2008 [emphasis in original].
44. James Mill, *The History of British India*, Thomas (University of Chicago Press, 1975), p.76.
45. UN General Assembly Official Records, 929th Plenary Meeting, A/PV 929, 1047.
46. See Perham (1961: 26).
47. Brownlie (1992: 29).
48. Article 4(1), Charter of the United Nations.
49. Warner (1993: 136).
50. Lord Hailey (1943: 62); and Fukuyama (1992: 338).
51. Robinson (1965: 93).
52. Helman and Ratner (1992–93: 12).
53. Paris (2004: 186–8. 209).
54. Stephen (1883: 558).
55. Quoted in Perham (1967: 103).
56. Stephen (1883).
57. Max Boot, "The End of Appeasement: Bush's Opportunity to Redeem America's Past Failures in the Middle East," *The Weekly Standard*, 8, 21 (2003): 1 (available at www.weeklystandard.com).
58. Ibid.
59. Philips (1977: 1412).

## 2. THE EUROPEAN EMPIRES AND INTERNATIONAL ORDER: MODEL OR TRAP?

1. The speech was delivered on 6 September 1943 after the University had awarded him an honorary degree.
2. For background, see Maxwell (1971).

3. Laslett (1999: Chapter 1).
4. Hamilton (1953).
5. For a discussion of Moroccan irredentism see Mayall (1990).
6. Smith (2008).
7. One example is Kafiristan, now the Afghan province of Nuristan, which was only finally subdued and converted to Islam by Emir Abdul Rahman in 1895/96. Visited briefly by a British official, Sir George Robertson, three years previously, the province served as the model for Rudyard Kipling's story *The Man Who Would Be King* (1888).
8. See, for example, Van den Boogert (2005); and Curtin (1987).
9. See Trivkovic (2010).
10. Kerr (2000).
11. Onley (2007).
12. Mazower (2009).
13. Mazower (2009: 45–46, 50–51).
14. Mayall (1990).
15. Mazower (2009: 27).
16. US National Archives, "Towards a New World Order; Address to a Joint Session of Congress and the Nation, 11 September 1990" (available at www.sweetliberty. org/issues/war/bushsr/htm).
17. It is not my intention to denigrate these debates, which correctly identify the difficulty of generalization across time and space. For an excellent review of the issues involved, see Hopkins (2007: 395–404).
18. Bass (2008).
19. Mazower (2009: 11–12).
20. Schnabel and Thakur (2000).
21. The famous prophecy is contained in the final paragraphs of *Democracy in America*, Volume 1. Part 2. The book was first published in 1835.
22. Mayall and Srinivasan (2009).
23. Lewis and Mayall (2008).
24. Lewis and Mayall (2008: "Introduction").
25. Lord Hailey (1938: 52).
26. There was, it is true, a much wider consensus in Western society in the nineteenth century that "uncivilized" states and societies should not be admitted to international society since they could not meet the legal obligations that went with membership and therefore should not enjoy its rights. But this was not a problem for political conservatives, whose beliefs were grounded in respect for social hierarchy and the realities of power politics. Liberals, who professed to believe in human freedom, required a further justification. Gong (1984).
27. Chapter 1 above.
28. The classic text on this subject is Stokes (1959). See also Cell, "Colonial Rule" in Louis and Low (2009).

29. Ramesh (1999: 3532–3544).
30. For a nineteenth century account of this contrast see Burton (1851), republished, with an Introduction by Dane Kennedy (Berkeley: University of California Press, 1991).
31. Gellner (1983).
32. Castells (2009).
33. The principle of trusteeship was written into Article 22 of the League of Nations Covenant, with reference to the former German colonies and Ottoman territories that were to be administered by the victorious European imperial powers under the League's Mandate system. But the concept had its origins in British colonial policy. Robinson (1965).
34. Kedourie (1974: 1–152).
35. White (2008: 219–43).
36. Khan (2010).

## 3. AFRICA AND TRUSTEESHIP IN THE MODERN GLOBAL ORDER

1. See Pakenham (1991: Chapter 14). Brown (2006) draws attention to the similarities between the agenda of the British Government's recent Commission for Africa and the ideals at least ostensibly adopted by the Berlin Conference of 1884/85.
2. Jackson (1990).
3. See Clapham (1996: Chapter 4).
4. See Clapham (1996: Chapter 6).
5. See, for example Milliken (2003) and Rotberg (2004).
6. See Clarke and Herbst (1997).
7. There is now a large literature on China's renewed relations with Africa; see in particular Alden, Soares de Oliveira and Large (2008).
8. See, for example, Ellis (1999); Francis (2007); Richards (1996).
9. See Herbst (2000).
10. See Harris (2006: 375–95) and Kandeh (2003: 189–216); see also Kandeh (2008: 603–35).
11. ICG (2004).

## 4. PATERNAL AUTHORITY, CIVILIZED STATE: CHINA'S EVOLVING ATTITUDE TOWARDS INTERNATIONAL TRUSTEESHIPS

1. Wheeler (2000).
2. Gurtov and Van Ness (2005: 7).
3. Gong (1984); Zhang (1991: 3–16); Suzuki (2009).
4. Kim (1998: 73).
5. Bull and Watson (1984). This has at times paradoxically resulted in the phenomenon of "quasi-states" where states that have ceased to effectively govern a given ter-

ritorial space continue to exist, propped up by the sovereignty norm. See Jackson (1990).

6. Simpson (2004: 68).

7. Ibid.

8. In order to obtain a snapshot of the viewpoints of the Chinese political elite, I have relied extensively on works by Chinese International Relations (IR) scholars and interviews with analysts of leading Chinese think tanks. While the most important decisions pertaining to foreign policy remain the privilege of the Politburo, the growing complexity of China's external relations means that the Chinese political decision-makers are increasingly reliant on and actively seek the opinions of IR specialists. This gives the latter opportunities to influence and shape Beijing's foreign policy, even though the degree to which they can do so does often depends on the personal and institutional relations they enjoy with the top decision-making elite. For a detailed explanation, see Glaser and Saunders (2002: 597–616).

9. This is modified from Chesterman (2004: 153). Chesterman's definition incorporates the criterion of military intervention, but to my mind international trusteeships can also take place in the absence of prior military conflict on the part of the international administrators, as the case of Cambodia demonstrates.

10. Chesterman (2004: 153).

11. Paris (2002). Similarly, Martin Indyk uncritically suggests the construction of a Palestinian state along liberal democratic lines under a trusteeship arrangement. See Indyk (2003: 51–66).

12. For historically-informed discussion of the Eurocentrism and the paternalistic treatment of non-European peoples, see Hobson (2004).

13. Article 76 (b), Chapter XII, Charter of the United Nations.

14. Luzhi and Tiecheng (1993: 345).

15. Bain (2003: 134).

16. A typical example can be found in Hobson (1968). Hobson laid down strict conditions that imperialism had to fulfill specific conditions to be deemed legitimate: first, imperialism had to be directed primarily to advance civilization, rather than serving the interests of the imperialist power; second, the subjugated peoples had to experience "improvement and elevation of [their] character"; lastly, the above two conditions had to be deemed to have been fulfilled by the civilized international community. (Hobson (1968: 232)) Hobson himself was extremely critical of imperialism by the European powers, as he considered them to have not fulfilled these conditions. Furthermore, he showed considerable sensitivity to the colonized peoples, claiming that the imperial powers paid scant attention to their local traditions.

17. Bain (2003: 139).

18. UN (1988: 5). While China's general tendency to refuse to support the Soviet

Union until the early 1980s can be explained in the context of the Sino-Soviet split, this seems unlikely in the context of this meeting, as the two states were already moving towards rapprochement by 1988.

19. Report of the Trusteeship Council to the Security Council on the Trust Territory of the Pacific Islands, UN Document S/1994/346, 22 December 1992–18 January 1993, p. 13.

20. This aspect of China's behavior in the UN has been documented in detail by Kim (1979).

21. Nie Ligang, for instance, notes that the League of Nations Mandates system and the UN Trusteeship system share very close origins. Nie, however, argues (somewhat erroneously) that "the two have fundamental differences, the most important [with regard to the UN Trusteeships] being the goals set towards the self-governance of the territories under trusteeship." See Ligang (2001: 43). Also see Luzhi and Tiecheng (1993: 343).

22. Report of the Trusteeship Council to the Security Council on the Trust Territory of the Pacific Islands, UN Document S/1994/346, 22 December 1992–18 January 1993, p. 13.

23. Luzhi and Tiecheng (1993: 342). It should be noted that earlier forms of trusteeships shared (at least in theory) the same goal, and in this sense we can see a historical continuity in the institution of trusteeships. See Bain (2003).

24. For a detailed explanation of China and its quest for international status, see Harris (1998); Suzuki (2008: 45–63), and Deng (2008).

25. Robinson and Shambaugh (1994: 311–16); Dittmer and Kim (1993: 212–14).

26. Rotberg (2002: 85–87). Also see Gros (1996: 455–71); Mallaby (2002: 2–3).

27. See for instance Matthews (1989: 162–77) for an early exposition of this view. The seminal discussion of human security remains UNDP (1994).

28. "Note by President of the Security Council concerning the Responsibility of the Security Council in the Maintenance of International Peace and Security," UN Document S/23500, 31 January 1992, p. 3.

29. One of the best texts on the issue of "humanitarian intervention" remains Wheeler (2000).

30. Boutros Boutros-Ghali, "An Agenda for Peace," UN Document A/47/277, 17 June 1992, p. 17.

31. Bellamy (2005: 40).

32. This thinking can be seen in the UN's special adviser on R2P, Edward Luck's statement to the UNSC Working Group on Conflict Resolution and Prevention in Africa (available at www.responsibilitytoprotect.org/index.php/eupdate/1965, accessed on 18 June 2009). I am grateful to the anonymous reviewers for alerting me to this point. Also see UN Secretary-General Ban Ki-moon's report "Implementing the Responsibility to Protect," UN document A/63/677, 12 January 2009.

33. UN document A/63/677, p. 15.

34. Fukuyama (1989: 3–18) Also see Bowden (2004: 43–68) and Bain (2003: 155–6).

35. See Paris (2002). A recent expression of this policy can be found in United States Government, *The National Security Strategy of the United States of America* (September 2002).

36. Bain (2003: 169).

37. Clark (2005: 175). See also Clark (2001: 237–255); Krasner (2004).

38. Gong (1984); Donnelly (1998); Fidler (2001: 137–57).

39. Booth and Dunne (2002: 35).

40. Mallaby writes: "The best hope of grappling with failed states lies in institutionalising [a] mix of U.S. leadership and international legitimacy. Fortunately, one does not have to look far to see how this could be accomplished. The World Band and the International Monetary Fund...already embody the same hybrid formula: both institutions reflect American thinking and priorities yet are simultaneously multinational." Mallaby (2002: 7).

41. The document merely states that the international community would "commit ourselves, as necessary and appropriate, to helping States build capacity to protect their populations from genocide, war crimes, ethnic cleansing and crimes against humanity and to assisting those which are under stress before crises and conflicts break out." See paragraph 139 of "Resolution adopted by the General Assembly: 60/1. 2005 World Summit Outcome," UN Document A/RES/60/1, 24 October 2005, p. 30.

42. See for instance, Broome (2010).

43. Fravel (1996: 1116).

44. Zhigang (2000: 66–7).

45. Zhigang (2000: 67).

46. UN Security Council Resolution 1511 UN Document S/RES/1511, 16 October 2003, p. 2

47. Ibid.

48. Minutes of the 4844th meeting of UNSC, UN Document S/PV.4844, 16 October 2003, p. 5.

49. Gill and Huang (2009: 3).

50. Interview, Chinese Institute of Contemporary International Relations, 19 April 2007, China Foundation for International Strategic Studies, 23 April 2007.

51. Qing (2002: 3). Similar views can be found in Bin (2002: 48) and Tao (2006: 83–7).

52. Qing (2002: 3).

53. Yugang and Jianhua (2004: 271).

54. This point was made to me in my interview at the China Foundation for Interna-

tional Strategic Studies, 23 April 2007. The interviewee stated that a conference was held in Beijing in March 2007, with US practitioners invited to speak on the issue, and that "[t]he issue of peacebuilding and state reconstruction is very new for Chinese scholars, experts and the government; we still need to learn about it."

55. Dexing and Jinqi (2007: 35).

56. Wei and Shaoxian (2004: 13).

57. This view was also confirmed by my interview at the China Institute of Contemporary International Relations, Beijing, 19 April 2007.

58. Dongxiao et al. (2004: 201).

59. This point was made in an interview when I posed the question of how China would square practical needs of regional stability with Western neo-imperialism. Interview, China Foundation for International Strategic Studies, Beijing, 23 April 2007.

60. Dexing and Jinqi (2007: 35).

61. Honghua and Haili (2004: 10). Men is based at the Central Party School which trains CCP cadres, and this is a good indication of the debates on state reconstruction taking place at the highest political/academic circles.

62. See Roy (2002: 511–21). China's concern for ethnic insurgencies in Central Asia has also been one of its key motivations for establishing the Shanghai Cooperation Organization (SCO), which explicitly states that the Organization "strongly fights and constrains 'three evil forces'—terrorism, separatism and extremism." See the SCO website (available at www.sectsco.org/html/00035.html, accessed on 10 May 2007), as well as Zhang and Azizian (1998). It should be noted however, that some Chinese analysts are fairly sanguine about the prospects of Islamic terrorism in China, and believe that this problem can adequately be dealt with within Chinese borders. Interview, China Institute of Contemporary International Relations, Beijing, 19 April 2007. See also Martin I. Wayne, "Al-Qaeda's China Problem," *Asia Times Online*, 27 February 2007 (available at www.atimes.com/atimes/China/IB27Ad01.html, accessed 16 May 2007).

63. Meili (1998: 126).

64. Interview, Chinese Institute of Contemporary International Relations, 19 April 2007.

65. Chengxu and Miaofa (2001: 144). Wang's observations are based on his observation that non-state actors are increasingly taking over the authority traditionally enjoyed by states. For a similar point of view, see Yuchun, (2003: 46–7) and Lingliang (1998: 109–120).

66. Interview, China Foundation for International Strategic Studies, 23 April 2007.

67. This can be seen from China's participation in international human rights regimes, where it is required to regularly submit reports on the conditions of its human rights for international scrutiny. See Kent (1999).

68. See "Position Paper of the People's Republic of China on the United Nations

Reforms" (available at www.fmprc.gov.cn/eng/zxxx/t199318.ht>, accessed 18 June 2009). For a detailed discussion on how the Chinese political elite came to accept this view, see Carlson (2005: 146–83). Also see Sarah Teitt, "China and the Responsibility to Protect," Asia-Pacific Centre for the Responsibility to Protect, 19 December 2008, p. 8 (available at www.r2pasiapacific.org/images/stories/food/china_and_r2p.pdf, accessed 18 June 2009).

69. I owe this point to Sarah Teitt, "China and the Responsibility to Protect," p. 8.

70. Wenzong (1999: 40).

71. For a detailed analysis on China and the Kosovo crisis, see Gill and Reilly (2000: 46–8).

72. Ambassador Shen Guofang's statement at the 4011th UNSC meeting, UN Document S/PV.4011, 10 June 1999, p. 8.

73. Welsh (2004: 48).

74. International Crisis Group, "China's Growing Role in UN Peacekeeping," *Asia Report*, no. 166, 17 April 2009, p. 10, fn 91.

75. There is no evidence, for instance, of China opposing the Cambodian Transitional Authority's report which stressed (based on the advice of international financial institutions) "the importance of *market-based reforms* in Cambodia." See UN Documents A/47/285 and S/24183, 25 June 1992; and A/RES/47/209, 24 March 1993. This point was confirmed by my interview at the Chinese Institute of International Studies, Beijing, 23 April 2007.

76. One Chinese analyst pointed out that the case of Iraq clearly demonstrated the failure of these policies. Interview, China Foundation for International Strategic Studies and Chinese Institute of International Studies, Beijing, 23 April 2007.

77. Interview, China Institute of Contemporary International Relations, 19 April 2007.

78. Zhuang Liwei, "Shibai guojia," in Chen Yugang and Yuan Jianhua (eds), *Chaoyue weisitefaliya?*, p. 275.

79. Ibid., p. 279.

80. Interviews, China Institute of Contemporary International Relations, Beijing, 19 April 2007; China Foundation for International Strategic Studies and Chinese Institute of International Studies, and Chinese Institute of International Studies, Beijing, 23 April 2007.

81. Interview, China Institute of Contemporary International Relations, Beijing, 19 April 2007.

82. Zhongying (2005: 98).

83. I have explored the disjuncture between China's self-image as a "great power" and the international views of the PRC's status as a legitimate great power in greater detail in Suzuki, "Seeking 'Legitimate' Great Power Status in Post-Cold War International Society."

84. Zhang (2001: 252).

85. See for example Bernstein and Munro (1997: 18–32); Roy (1996: 758–71).
86. Johnston and Ross (2006: 200).
87. This conceptualization of a "status quo" power is based on Johnston (2003: 5–56), particularly p. 11.
88. A Chinese analyst at the China Institute of International Studies, which is closely linked to the Ministry of Foreign Affairs, noted that the Five Principles of Peaceful Coexistence, the ten-point declaration of the Bandung Conference, and the UN Charter are the principal international norms Beijing considers necessary to uphold. Interview, Beijing, 23 April 2007.
89. Interview, Chinese Institute of International Studies, Beijing, 23 April 2007; Interview, China Foundation for International Strategic Studies, 23 April 2007. For one of the most recent discussions for the role foreign policy plays in the cultivation of Chinese soft power, see Gill and Huang (2006: 21–23).
90. Xinbo (2001: 293).
91. For instance, Beijing invoked its "developing state" status in order to avoid the implementation of certain rules of the WTO. When it found itself isolated from international society, the PRC has also invoked its "Third World state" identity in order to garner the moral support of other developing states and escape its alienation.
92. This assertion is based on my interview at the Chinese Institute of Contemporary International Relations, Beijing, 19 April 2007. The analyst noted: "situations of "long-term trusteeship" (*changqi guoguan zhuangtai*) must be avoided, as paternalism annoys people in the long run. We need to have a clear entrance and exit strategy (*jintui you du*)."
93. See Carlson (2004: 9–27), p. 21 and Men Honghua and Huang Haili (2004: 12).
94. Interview, China Institute of Contemporary International Relations, Beijing, 19 April 2007.
95. Men Honghua and Huang Haili (2004: 27).
96. Ibid., p. 22
97. Ibid.
98. Yongsheng (2002: 41).
99. Suzuki (2008: 56). Chinese analysts have also noted that great powers are becoming increasingly active in PKO since the end of the Cold War. See for instance Tan Yonglei, "Cong weichi heping dao qiangzhi heping—lun lengzhan hou lianheguo weihe xingdong de bianhua," *Lanzhou xuekan*, 80, 1994, p. 51. Tan claims that during the Cold War both the US and the Soviet Union refrained from involvement in UNPKO, for fear of upsetting the balance of power.
100. Suzuki (2008: 56).
101. Interview, China Foundation for International Strategic Studies, Beijing, 23 April 2007.

102. This problem is discussed in detail in Bain (2003).

103. Robinson and Shambaugh (1994: 311–316); Dittmer and Kim (1993: 212–14).

104. Interview, Chinese Institute of International Studies, Beijing, 23 April 2007

105. Ibid.

106. Interview, Chinese Institute of Contemporary International Relations, Beijing, 19 April 2007.

107. This term is used metaphorically, and by no means describes the mental state of the Chinese elite in the late nineteenth century.

108. A fascinating discussion of this point can be found in Nyíri (2006: 83–106).

109. Gill and Huang (2006: 20).

110. James Mann, "A shining model of wealth without liberty," *Washington Post*, 20 May 2007 (available at www.washingtonpost.com/wp-dyn/content/article/2007/05/18/AR2007051801640_pf.html, accessed 26 May 2007), and Kurlantzick (2007). Also see Suzuki (2009: 779–93).


5. INDIA AND THE CHALLENGE OF THE NEW PROTECTORATES

1. See for example, Philip Gasper, "Afghanistan, the CIA, bin Laden and the Taliban," *International Socialist Review*, November-December 2001.

2. See Brecher (1958).

3. Ibid.

4. I have discussed in detail this aspect of the post-Cold War world in Ray (2004).

5. See Chandran and Chari (2008).

6. See Jansen (1966).

7. See Rajan (1990) and also Mates (1982).

8. Particularly useful and innovative have been the training for sportspersons and cultural activities, both including women. India's experience in these fields has made the programs both professionally attractive and rewarding for the target groups. An Indian diplomat in Kabul, with some experience in wrestling, is promoting this as a sport to draw the country's physically well-endowed youth away from self-destructive violence with some success; similarly, a few cricket and soccer teams, and screening of some Bollywood films, have aroused interest in sections of the Afghan youth. But the full potentials of such measures as a foil against the attractions of sectarian violence remains inadequately explored.

9. Pankaj Mishra, "Afghanistan: The India and Kashmir Connection," *New York Review of Books* 57, 1, 14 January 2010.

10. *Times of India*, 21 March 2007.

11. Ibid., 12 June 2008.

12. Ibid., 14 June 2008.

13. Ibid., 12 June 2008.

14. *The Hindu*, 16 June 2008.

15. See M.L. Rasgotra, in *The Tribune* (Chandigarh), 24 September 2005.
16. See P.R. Chari's "Overview" in Chandran and Chari (2008).
17. He quotes from the *Foreign Affairs* "failed states index" to include all other South Asian states, except India and Maldives, among the first sixty "failed states," with Afghanistan (8), Pakistan (12), Bangladesh (16), Nepal (21) and Bhutan (47), and Afghanistan and Pakistan designated by the Index as being "most critical."
18. Ibid.
19. *Times of India*, 4 September 2005.
20. Email circular of the International Relations Centre, Goa, 17 May 2008.
21. *Times of India*, 18 May 2008.
22. *The Hindu*, 16 June 2008.
23. P.R. Chari, op. cit., n.14.

## 6. THE EUROPEAN "PULL" IN THE BALKANS

1. See Todorova (1997): "Where is the adversarial group that has not been decried as "Balkan" and "balkanizing" by its opponents? Where the accused have not hurled back the branding reproach of "balkanism"?," p. 3.
2. Hill and Smith ( 2005: 367–87).
3. Zielonka (2006: 44–5).
4. Grabbe (2006).
5. Italy and Greece, Austria and Hungary.
6. Containment, it could be argued, best defines EU policy towards the Balkans between 1991 and 1995 when the regional situation, and hence the EU's foreign policy agenda, were dominated by the wars of Yugoslavia's succession culminating in the Dayton Accords. Conditionality, arguably, best captures the period from 2000 onwards in which the EU's policies towards the region have focused on issues beyond basic economic development and transition and moved into stability assistance and contractual arrangements drawing the region and especially the Western Balkans closer into the EU's orbit.
7. The region broadly defined would include existing and future EU/NATO members: Greece and Italy; then Austria, then Hungary. Then later Romania and Bulgaria.
8. This is just as true in 1991–92 with the secession of Slovenia and Croatia as it was with keeping Bosnia and Herzegovina together in 1995 (hence the absurdity of a single state divided into two entities under the Dayton Accords) as it was with Kosovo, Montenegro and the FYROM.
9. White (2001: 106).
10. Gow (1997: 328).
11. Gow (1997: 327).
12. UNSCR 1244 officially brought to an end the conflict in Kosovo in 1999 and set up, under UN authority, the military and civilian instruments to ensure stability

in Kosovo. It also reaffirmed the sovereign rights of Yugoslavia over Kosovo, while proposing a large degree of autonomy for the province until a final settlement could be reached. For more detail see Berdal and Economides (2007: 238–9).

13. The Ohrid Framework Agreement was signed on 13 August 2001 after talks between the Government and Albanian representatives. Its main points related to the maintenance of a single, multi-ethnic, multi-cultural state, in which, following the necessary constitutional reform, there would be a substantial degree of decentralization and local government autonomy. The ethnic and linguistic identity of the Albanian population would be guaranteed and the renunciation of violence as a means of resolving tension was a key feature of the agreement. Effectively, the Government conceded rights to the Albanian population in return for the maintenance of a single state.

14. As with the debate about deaths and casualties during the Yugoslav wars, the debates about the level of refugees and refugee returns is at times heated. The most reliable and often quoted figures are those of the Office of United Nations High Commissioner for Refugees (UNHCR). These can be found in the UNHCR's Annual Statistical Yearbook (available at www.unhcr.org/statistics.html). The EU also provides useful data on refugee returns, which as mentioned often form part of its political conditionality and is always addressed in the European Commission's regular Progress Reports on states in the region. For example, the most recent report on Croatia tackles the issue of refugee returns on p. 15. See, "Croatia 2009 Progress Report," 6 November 2007 (available at www.ec.europa.eu/enlargement/pdf/key_documents/2009/hr_rapport_2009_en.pdf). The issue of the level of deaths during the wars in Yugoslavia, and especially Bosnia, is much more acrimonious and subject to wild discrepancies between opposing sides that use the figures as a propaganda tool. The most useful scholarly analysis of this issue with respect to Bosnia, from credible sources, is Tabeau and Bijak (2005: 187–215).

15. See for example, Select Committee on the European Union, "Responding to the Balkan Challenge: The Role of EU Aid," House of Lords, Session 2001–02, 20th report. The official website of DG Enlargement of the Commission is a valuable resource for this particular issue. An important document in terms of the regional cooperation element inherent in EU assistance programs, the "CARDS Assistance Program to the western Balkans: Regional Strategy Paper 2002–2006" (available at www.ec.europa.eu/enlargement/pdf/financial_assistance/cards/publications/regional_strategy_paper_en.pdf). The CARDs program has been succeeded by the Instrument for Preaccession Assistance (IPA). Regionalism and regional cooperation are fundamental features of this mechanism as well (available at www.ec.europa.eu/enlargement/financial_assistance/ipa/index_en.htm).

16. For the best economic analysis of this question of regional integration see Vladimir Gligorov, "Regional Co-operation with Multiple Equilibria," Global Development Network-SEE Occasional Paper, WIIW Balkan Observatory, 2004 (avail-

able at www.wiiw.ac.at/balkan/files/GDN_EU_IBEU_RegionalCooperation.
pdf). See also Liebscher (2005) and Wim van Meurs (2003).

17. For a more detailed analysis of the political and political economy dimension of
regional cooperation and its place in the EU/SEE relationship, see Othon Anastasakis and Vesna Bojicic-Dzelilovic, "Balkan Regional Co-operation and European Integration," Hellenic Observatory Policy Paper No2 (Hellenic Observatory: LSE, July 2002) (available at www.lse.ac.uk/collections/hellenicObservatory/
pdf/DiscussionPapers/brie.pdf). See also Delevic (2007); Bechev (2006: 27–43);
and "The Road to Thessaloniki: Cohesion and the Western Balkans," European
Stability Initiative, Berlin, 12 March 2003 (available at www.esiweb.org/pdf/esi_
document_id_44.pdf).

18. A comparison could be drawn between the EU's physical and ideational containment of the Balkan crises and the ideological and military containment of the
Soviet Union by the US during the Cold War.

19. Huntington (1996: 268–72). The author devotes some space to looking at Southeastern Europe through the prism of the Bosnian conflict and in terms of "civilizational identities."

20. Or as one critic stated of the CFSP, "[it] is an acronym without empirical content." Richard Rosencrance, "The European Union: A New Type of International
Actor," in Jan Zielonka (ed.), *Paradoxes of European Foreign Policy*, p. 15.

21. This is reflected in the literature which often uses EU policy towards Central and
Eastern Europe as a case of the power of conditionality as a foreign policy tool.
See for example; Grabbe (2006); Pridham (2007: 446–71); Schimmelfennig and
Sedelmeier (2005); and Smith (2004).

22. Smith (2004: 44).

23. Smith (2004: 139).

24. See the next sub-section for more on ICTY and EU conditionality.

25. http://ec.europa.eu/enlargement/index_en.htm.

26. Linklater (2005: 375).

27. Apart from the monitoring missions, both EU and WEU, in place to observe the
adherence to cease-fires and the enforcement of UN sponsored sanctions regimes.

28. In the context of Kosovo, again EU members resorted to the use of force through
the vehicle of NATO in the humanitarian intervention of 1999. And as with SFOR
in Bosnia, so too KFOR in Kosovo comprised significant EU national contingents during the respective multi-year deployments.

29. Opinion polls suggest that the level of satisfaction with the EU in the Western
Balkans is on a downward trend, albeit starting from a very high level. Of course
this is particularly true in countries nearing accession such as Croatia. More interestingly, polling suggests that in Bosnia, the level of international involvement—
including the EU—is viewed with a great degree of skepticism, while in the
FYROM differences between ethnic groups also come to light. See "Perceptions

of the EU in the Western Balkans," *Gallup Balkan Monitor*, 2, June 2009 (available at http://www.balkan-monitor.eu/files/Gallup_Balkan_Monitor-Focus_On_EU_Perceptions.pdf).
30. See Zielonka (2006).
31. Knaus and Martin (2003: 60–74).

## 7. US FOREIGN POLICY AND THE NEW PROTECTORATES IN HISTORICAL PERSPECTIVE

1. Gelb (2009: 16).
2. Boot (2002: 102).
3. Gelb (2009: 40).
4. Boot (2002: 104–105).
5. Ferguson (2004: 50).
6. Boot (2002: 106–111); Rudyard Kipling, "The White Man's Burden," *McClure's Magazine*, 12 February 1899. Kipling subtitled his poem "The United States and the Philippine Islands."
7. Thomas (2002: 550).
8. Thomas (2002: 558).
9. Boot (2002: 132). The administration's greatest coup was Walter Reed's mosquito eradication campaign, eliminating yellow fever and curtailing malaria infections.
10. Boot (2002: 132–3).
11. Grob and Billias (1992: 164).
12. Boot (2002: 137).
13. Boot (2002: 138–142).
14. Ryan (1977: 10).
15. Ryan (1977: 14). President Obadiah's expression of gratitude in 1909 is often overlooked by historians who portrayed the Canal concession as naked aggression, but it is clear Panamanian leaders needed US assistance to achieve independence and the Canal Zone was a small price to pay for their new found freedom, although Secretary of State John Hay confided that Panama "came out on the short end" of the treaty terms.
16. Ryan (1977: 15–24). Title III of the 1903 Treaty bestowed "all the rights, power, and authority...which the United States would possess if it were the sovereign...to the entire exclusion of the exercise by the Republic of Panama of any such sovereign rights, power and authority." It looked like a settler colony as the inhabitants only spoke English, avoided Panamanian taxes and laws, and lived in a "little America." Panamanians, as guest workers in the Canal Zone, earned less than their "Yanqui" counterparts and the government received none of the toll revenues.
17. Ferguson (2004: 59).
18. Ibid.

19. Boot (2002: 132).
20. Cohen (1987: Chapter 1).
21. Cohen (1987: Chapter 3).
22. Ferguson (2004: 58).
23. Logan (1928: 429).
24. McDougall (1997: 150); Buchanan (1999: 243–5), Buchanan argues that the Good Neighbor policy originated in the Hoover years after a ten-nation tour of the region where Hoover pledged benign neglect. Hoover's Mexico and Brazil policy may bear this out but the US Marine landings in the Caribbean and Central America during Hoover's presidency belie this interpretation. Although the rhetoric may be Hoover's the actions were not.
25. Ferguson (2004: 58).
26. McDougall (1997: 150–51).
27. McDougall (1997: 177).
28. Bacevich (2002: 60).
29. McDougall (1997: 153).
30. McDougall (1997: 164–6).
31. Stafford (1949: 47–55). The American commitment to internationalize the administration of these precarious states ebbed as planners perceived weak governance as an entry point for Soviet influence. In the Italian ex-colonies, the Soviets adopted the American initial position in favor of United Nations trusteeship and the Americans shifted in favor of independence or colonial trusteeship. The jostling for position is even more obvious as the Soviet initial position in favor of colonies being returned to Italian trusteeship changed after the Italian Communists lost the 1948 elections. The Americans sought the least bad option as the Soviets pushed for the administration most vulnerable to communist influence.
32. Weeks (2002: 97).
33. Ibid.
34. Stebbins (1952: 15).
35. Ferguson (2004: 101).
36. McDougall (1997: 197).
37. Tucker and Hendrickson (1992: 53).
38. Gaddis (2005: 372).
39. Kennedy (1987: 538).
40. Fukuyama further argued that the West's Cold War victory represented "the end point of mankind's ideological evolution and the universalization of Western liberal democracy as the final form of human government." Fukuyama (1989).
41. Nye (1990: 153ff.).
42. Charles Krauthammer, "Democratic Realism: An American Foreign Policy for a Unipolar World" Irving Kristol Lecture, American Enterprise Institution, 20 November 2004.

43. Bacevich (2002: 57). Baker's diplomacy succeeded in denuclearizing the former Soviet satellites, and building a coalition to oust Saddam Hussein from Kuwait.

44. George H.W. Bush, "Address to Nation on Panama Invasion" 20 December 1989.

45. Gelb (2009: 62–3).

46. Michael Wines, "Mission to Somalia; Bush Declares Goal in Somalia to 'Save Thousands'" New York Times, 5 December 1992.

47. Bacevich (2002: 143).

48. Lapaix (2002: Introduction).

49. Freedom House, 2006 Country Report: Haiti (available at www.freedomhouse. org/uploads/WoW/2006/Haiti2006.pdf ); Transparency International Corruption Index, 2006 (available at www.transparency.org).

50. Bacevich (2002: 148).

51. Art Pines, "Clinton to Unilaterally Fund Bosnia Force—Military: President backs rapid-reaction plan with $95 million from emergency account" New York Times, 30 June 1995.

52. Bacevich (2002: 164).

53. "Bosnia and Herzegovina," CIA World Factbook, 1996.

54. Associated Press, "U.S. troops mark end of mission in Bosnia," Washington Post, 25 November 2004, A19.

55. Michael O'Hanlon, "Bosnia Option for Iraq," The American Interest, November–December 2006.

56. Transcript of President Clinton's speech on Bosnia, 27 November 1995.

57. Tom Delay quoted by John Nichols, "Victory Means Exit Strategy," The Nation, 23 September 2005.

58. Robert Kagan, "Kosovo and the Republican Future," The Weekly Standard, 5 April 1999.

59. Boot (2002: 130–34).

60. Zuercher (2006).

## 8. PEACE OPERATIONS AND MODERN PROTECTORATES: THE LOGIC OF SUCCESSFUL FAILURE

1. I am indebted to Elisabeth Schöndorf for completing sources and editing the manuscript.

2. See Benner, Mergenthaler and Rotmann (2011) for a notable exception.

3. Cf. Doyle and Sambanis (2006); Eide, Kaspersen, Kent and von Hippel (2005); Howard (2008).

4. This refers to the infamous "Protectorate Bohemia and Moravia" imposed by Nazi Germany in the Czech part of the Czecho-Slovak Republic in March 1939.

5. Fukuyama (1992); Keohane and Nye (1989); Keohane (1993).

6. Pedersen (2006: 560–82).

7. Barnett and Finnemore (2004).

8. Benner, Mergenthaler and Rotmann (2007: 29).

9. UN Secretary-General, "An Agenda for Peace," UN Document A/47/277-S/24111, 17 June 1992.

10. Barnett and Finnemore (2004: 121–55).

11. Durch, Holt, Earle and Shanahan (2003).

12. "A More Secure World: Our Shared Responsibility—Report of the Secretary-General's High-Level Panel on Threats, Challenges and Change," United Nations 2004.

13. UN General Assembly, "Responsibility to Protect Populations from Genocide, War Crimes, Ethnic Cleansing and Crimes against Humanity," para. 138–140. Evans (2008) provides a comprehensive account on the emergence of the principle of the Responsibility to Protect and its political background.

14. Haas (1992: 1–35).

15. UN Secretary-General, "In Larger Freedom: Towards Development, Security and Human Rights for All," UN Document A/59/2005, 21 March 2005.

16. Ibid.

17. Eide *et al.* (2008).

18. Weaknesses and inconsistencies remain, though. While the SRSG is formally in charge of the entirety of UN activity on the ground, he or she is not entitled to give direct orders to units outside the jurisdiction of the DPKO at UN headquarters.

19. Dahl and Lindblom (1953).

20. Tsebelis (2002).

21. Wesley (1997); Lipson (2007: 79–97).

22. Bacharatz and Baratz (1963).

23. Lipson (2007).

24. Madeleine Albright, "The End of Intervention," *New York Times*, 11 June 2008; "Sollen wir einen Krieg ins Zyklon-Gebiet tragen?" ["Should We Wage a War in a Hurricane Area?"], An Interview with Edward C. Luck, *Frankfurter Allgemeine Zeitung*], 15 May 2008. Edward Luck is Special Advisor to the UN Secretary-General for the Responsibility to Protect.

25. Desmond Tutu, "Taking the responsibility to protect," *International Herald Tribune*, 19 June 2008.

26. Piiparinen (2007: 365–90).

27. In early March 2009, the ICC issued an arrest warrant for Al-Bashir for war crimes and crimes against humanity. Al-Bashir, according to the ICC, "is suspected of being criminally responsible, as an indirect (co) perpetrator, for intentionally directing attacks against an important part of the civilian population of Darfur, Sudan, murdering, exterminating, raping, torturing, and forcibly transferring large numbers of civilians, and pillaging their property." International Criminal Court, Press Release, The Hague, 4 March 2009.

28. Williams and Bellamy (2005: 27–47); Security Council Report, "Report on Dar-

fur" (available at www.amnesty.org/en/library/info/AFR54/019/2007, accessed 13 July 2009). (Available at www.securitycouncilreport.org/site/c.glKWLeTIsG/b.1138997/k.19E7/November_2005brDARFUR.htm, 2005, accessed 19 March 2009); Security Council Report, "Report on Darfur" (available at www.security-councilreport.org/site/c.glKWLeMTIsG/b.2620623/k.3B7E/April_2007BR DarfurSudan.htm, 2007, accessed 19 March 2009).

29. This refers to UN Security Resolutions 1591 of 2005 and 1665 of 2006 and the UN Security Council Reports of 30 January, 19 April and 31 July 2006. See also Amnesty International, "Sudan: Arms Continuing to Fuel Serious Human Rights Violations in Darfur" (available at www.amnestyusa.org/document.php?id= ENGAFR540192007&lang=e, 8 May 2007, accessed 7 July 2009).

30. United Nations Office for the Coordination of Humanitarian Affairs, "Sudan: 'Anything is possible' If ICC Indicts President" (available at www.reliefweb.int/rw/rwb.nsf/db900sid/MCOT-7NJHY2?OpenDocument&query =comprehensive%20peace%20agreement%20sudan, 2009, accessed19 March 2009); International Crisis Group (November 2007).

31. Barnett and Finnemore (2004); Welsh (2004); Wheeler (2000).

32. Seibel (1996: 1011–24).

33. Fama (1980: 288–307); Ross (1973: 134–9).

34. Cf. infra.

35. Cyert and March (1963).

36. Festinger (1957).

37. Cf. Kuran (1995); cf. infra.

38. Edelman (1964).

39. Bacharatz and Baratz (1963: 632–42).

40. Kingdon (1995).

41. Wesley (1997).

42. In February 2007, the former Finnish President Martti Ahtisaari in his capacity as a Special Envoy of the United Nations presented a plan according to which Kosovo should have become an independently administered political unit under the supervision of the European Union. The plan entailed extensive and detailed stipulations designed to protect the Serbian minority, the civil rights, housing areas, and cultural sites. Nonetheless, Russia blocked the adoption of the Ahtisaari Plan several times in the UN Security Council through announcing its veto in case the plan would be put on the agenda. The political logic of Russia's stance on Kosovo and the Ahtisaari plan was nicely characterized by Richard Holbrooke, "Russia's test in Kosovo," *Washington Post*, 13 March 2007.

43. UN Security Council, "Non-Proliferation," UN Document S/2006/1696, 31 July 2006.

44. National Security Archive, "The US and the Genocide in Rwanda 1994: Evidence of Inaction" (available at www.gwu.edu/~nsarchiv/NSAEBB/NSAEBB53/index. html,accessed 3 March 2009). See Barnett (2002) and Des Forges (1999).

45. President Clinton made a personal apology when he visited Rwanda in March 1998. See "Clinton in Africa: the overview," *New York Times*, 28 March 1998.
46. Nederlands Instituut voor Oorlogsdocumentatie (2002).
47. Noetzel and Schreer (2007).
48. This is what Noetzel and Schreer (2007) propose.
49. Samantha Power, "Bystanders to Genocide," *The Atlantic Monthly*, 288, 2, pp. 84–108, 2001 and Power (2002).
50. There is a sad irony in the fact that Mururoa is the geographical antipode of Mecca, since it attracted so much interest among the Christian dominated public in the Western democracies while, at the very same time, some 8,000 Muslims were being slaughtered at the European Christian nations' doorstep. A highly influential agenda-setter in the campaign against French nuclear test series that deflected public attention to the Mururoa atoll was the non-governmental organization Greenpeace. As far as the present author can see, no critical account has been given by Greenpeace, so far, of its role as a public agenda-setter in July 1995 and its consequences for the attention being paid to the fate of the "safe area" Srebrenica and its inhabitants. A similar pattern of grotesquely asymmetric attention could be observed among those protesting against the G8 Summit of June 2007. While environmental issues were at the top of the agenda, the genocide in Darfur was not mentioned at all—an ignorance the protesters shared with the German G8 presidency and the rest of the participating governments. Only the newly appointed French Minister of Foreign Affairs, Bernard Kouchner, himself the founder of the Médecins sans Frontières organization and an ardent supporter of the "responsibility to protect" principle, requested addressing of the mass killings in Darfur and effective counter-measures at the summit. To no avail, though. Cf. *Tageszeitung*, 31 March 2007.

## 9. THE NORMATIVE UNDERPINNINGS OF THE UN PEACEBUILDING COMMISSION

1. Security Council Resolution 1645, 20 December 2005 and General Assembly Resolution 60/180, 30 December 2005.
2. Jenkins also discusses this function of the PBC but in a more limited sense, chiefly with regard to reaffirming the norm of state sovereignty. See Jenkins (2008).
3. March and Olsen (1998: 943–969).
4. Representative of this view is Chandler (2006).
5. High-level Panel on Threats, Challenges and Change, "A More Secure World: Our Shared Responsibility" (New York: United Nations, 2004), Executive Summary, p. 1.
6. "In Larger Freedom: Towards Development, Security and Human Rights for All: Report of the Secretary-General," UN Document A/59/2005, 21 March 2005. The High-level Panel envisaged that the PBC would also assist "countries which are under

stress and risk sliding towards State collapse," but this more preventive function was not included in the Commission's mandate. See *A More Secure World*, p. 264.

7. Report of the Panel on United Nations Peace Operations, UN Document A/55/305—S/2000/809 21 August 2000.

8. Collier, Hoeffler and Söderbom have found a 40 per cent risk of conflict recurrence within the first 10 years following the cessation of hostilities. See Collier, Hoeffler and Söderbom (2008: 465).

9. S/Res/1645 and A/Res60/180 (2005).

10. Cited in Berdal (2009: 150).

11. S/Res/1645 and A/Res60/180 (2005).

12. "Peacebuilding Fund: Allocations and Projects Approved as of 31 October 2009" (available at www.unpbf.org/index.shtml, accessed 9 November 2009).

13. With hopes for Security Council reform dashed at the UN World Summit in September 2005, the PBC—with its diverse, balanced membership from the global North and South—was viewed, in part, as a substitute for Security Council expansion.

14. Scott (2008: 9).

15. There are other factors that have an influence on mandate formation as well, bearing in mind that mandate formation, like politics, represents the art of the possible among stakeholders with divergent views and interests and levels of resources.

16. Kosovo Standards Implementation Plan (finalized on 31 March 2004) by the Kosovo Provisional Institutions of Self-Government and the United Nations.

17. Afghanistan Compact (agreed to on 31 January 2006) by the Government of Afghanistan, the United Nations, and the sixty countries and international organizations participating in the International Conference on Afghanistan 31 January-1 February 2006.

18. Kaufmann (1996: 136–75).

19. Caplan (2005: 80–85).

20. See Strategic Framework for Peacebuilding in Burundi, PBC/1/BDI/4, 30 July 2007; Strategic Framework for Peacebuilding in the Central African Republic 2009–2011, PBC/3/CAF/7, 9 June 2009; Strategic Framework for Peacebuilding in Guinea-Bissau, PBC/3/GNB/3, 2 October 2008; Sierra Leone Peacebuilding Cooperation Framework, PBC/2/SLE/1, 3 December 2007.

21. See, for instance, Peacebuilding Commission Working Group on Lessons Learned, Meeting on Elections in Sierra Leone, Summary Note of the Chair, 20 February 2007 and Outcome of the PBC Strategy and Policy Task Force on the Private Sector, 15 December 2008.

22. Paris (2003: 443).

23. Paris (2003: 442).

24. See Franck (1992: 46–91), and Newman and Rich (2004: 3–31).

25. Boutros-Ghali (1996: 10).

26. See, for instance, Chopra (2000: 27–39). Sérgio Vieira de Mello, the former UN transitional administrator of Kosovo and East Timor, was known to have likened his position to that of a "benevolent despot."
27. Paris (2004: chapter 2).
28. See Mansfield and Snyder (1995: 5–38), and Zartman (1995: chapter 15). Based on an analysis of the period 1816–1992, one study concluded that semi-democracies (regimes intermediate between a democracy and an autocracy) are more conflict-prone than autocracies, which in turn are less stable than established democracies. Hegre (2001: 17–33).
29. Collier, Hoeffler and Söderbom (2008: 470).
30. Strategic Framework for Peacebuilding in Burundi, PBC/1/BDI/4, 22 June 2007, p. 39, 36.
31. Paris (2004: 151, 212).
32. Pugh and Cooper (with Goodhand) (2004: 200).
33. Held (1996: 169).
34. S/Res/1645 20 December 2005 and GAR 60/180 (30 December 2005).
35. Outcome of the PBC Strategy and Policy Task Force on the Private Sector, 15 December 2008.
36. Jenkins (2008: 16).
37. UN General Assembly and Security Council, "Review of Progress in the Implementation of the Strategic Framework for Peacebuilding in Burundi," PBC/2/BDI/10, 9 July 2008, pp. 16, 18.
38. UN General Assembly and Security Council, "Progress Report on the Implementation of the Sierra Leone Peacebuilding Cooperation Framework," PBC/2/SLE/9, 23 June 2008, pp. 18, 25.
39. Paris High Level Forum, "Paris Declaration on Aid Effectiveness," 2 March 2009, p. 8.
40. S/Res/1645 and A/Res60/180 (2005).
41. For example, while pledges at the May 2007 Donors Roundtable in Burundi were encouraging, the actual delivery on pledges has fallen short of expectation, as was noted repeatedly by Burundian government officials during the May 2008 PBC delegation visit to Bujumbura. Moreover, concerns have been raised by the views expressed by some donors that the Peacebuilding Fund should operate as the key resource mobilization function of the Peacebuilding Commission. See Center on International Cooperation and International Peace Institute, "Taking Stock, Looking Forward: A Strategic Review of the Peacebuilding Commission," April 2008, p. 5.

## 10. POLICING THE NEO-IMPERIAL FRONTIER: CIVPOL MISSIONS IN THE NEW PROTECTORATES

1. These forces are called by a variety of names in different missions. In Kosovo, for instance, the UN police were called Civilian Police (CIVPOL). In East Timor and other missions, they have been called UN Police (UNPOL). This chapter will employ the term UNPOL, as it has now been officially adopted by the United Nations.

2. Some of these forces are sent on a volunteer basis, while others are ordered by their national government.

3. In the cases examined in this chapter, UNPOL deployments are grouped together under a UN-sponsored command structure. But UNPOL have also been deployed by multilateral and regional organizations. The OSCE, for example, was responsible for UNPOL units in Croatia and Eastern Slavonia. See particularly Hesztera (1998: 243–8).

4. See, in particular, Bain (2003), Ignatieff (2003), Chesterman (2004), Richmond (2005) and Williams (2006).

5. Executive authority missions have been the exception rather than the rule with UNPOL deployments. Most UNPOL missions have been for supervisory or training purposes. For an overview, see Oakley, Dziedzic and Goldberg (2002). On executive authority missions, see Dwan (2002); Holm and Eide (1999: 210–20).

6. See Nield (2001: 21–42).

7. This point has been recognized by a number of scholars and policymakers. See, for instance, Marenin (1998: 159–77), Bayley (2005: 206–215), and Bayley (1997: 59–64).

8. This is in part the argument of Fukuyama (1993). For critiques, see in particular Duffield (2001) and Richmond (2005).

9. See Ignatieff (2003).

10. It is important to acknowledge that not all post-conflict states feature ungoverned spaces after a war. Many post-conflict states feature a victorious government or an uneasy power-sharing arrangement that still counts as a government. Kosovo and East Timor are unique in so far as they lack a government, and therefore had a greater need for direct intervention to restore order. This chapter focuses primarily on the dilemmas in these "executive authority" cases, some of which may be less applicable to other cases.

11. The term "post-modern imperialism" comes from Fearon and Laitin (2004: 7). See also Cooper (2003).

12. Gerspacher (2008: 169–84). Interestingly the US was an outlier in this respect, accepting international cooperation much less than comparable European states.

13. See Nadelmann (1993: 15–102).

14. Sismandis (1997: 1).

15. Sismandis (1997: 2).
16. For a summary, see Gerspacher (2005: 413–34). See also Deflem (2005).
17. Sismandis (1997: 2).
18. Interestingly, whether the UN would ever be able to mounts its own standing police force was a concern of some classical realists. See, for instance, Morgenthau (1963: 393–403).
19. Decker (2006: 503). See also Hansen (2002).
20. Republic of Congo, ONUC Background (available at www.un.org/depts/DPKO/Missions/onucB.htm, accessed 4 June 2008). At its peak this mission involved over 20,000 UN personnel. For a full discussion of this mission, and the controversies associated with its mission creep, see James (1994: 44–58).
21. In this instance UNPOL propped up the formal institutions of a state whose material inequalities were stark and capacity for self-government dubious. See the discussion of "tolerated inequalities" of states in Simpson (2004: 56–61).
22. Hesztera (1998: 245). See also Schmidl (1998).
23. Statistic quoted in Decker (2006: 503).
24. Call and Barnett (1999: 43).
25. Oakley, Dziedzic, and Goldberg (1998).
26. See the helpful summary in Osland (2004: 548–9).
27. Even today, the reconstruction continues, as Bosnian officials only agreed in 2008 to create a single unified police force for the Federation and the RS. For a recent summary of the OHR's attempt to abolish the entity police forces and create a single Bosnian police, see International Crisis Group, "Bosnia's Stalled Police Reform: No Progress, No EU," Europe Report No. 164, 6 September 2005.
28. Osland (2004: 548).
29. For a critical overview, see Celador (2005: 364–76).
30. For a full discussion, see Chanaa (2002).
31. For a critical view, see Mani (1999: 11–12).
32. The concept of police-keeping also links the development of police to statebuilding, not just the immediate peacekeeping activities. See, for instance, Peake and Brown (2005: 520–32).
33. Day and Freeman (2005: 139–47).
34. Hartz (1999: 27–42).
35. See the executive summary of the Brahimi Report (2000) (available at: http://www.un.org/peace/reports/peace_operations/).
36. A similar line of argument, though focused more on Hobbes' insights on the nature of civil and international disorder, is advanced by Jackson in Bain (2006: 15–36). See also the discussion of the Weberian dimension of peace enforcement in Chesterman (2004: 99–125).
37. Stedman (1997: 5–53).
38. International Crisis Group, "What Happened to the KLA?," Report No. 88, 2000.

39. International Crisis Group, "Violence in Kosovo: Who's Killing Whom?," ICG Balkans Report N78, 2 November 1999, p. 3.
40. See Judah (2000: 286–312).
41. Quoted in Schmidt and Schroeder (2001: 114).
42. See Boyle (2004).
43. International Crisis Group, "What Happened to the KLA?." Report No. 88 (2000).
44. Interview with D. Christopher Decker, Chief, Law Enforcement, OSCE Mission, Pristina, Kosovo, 28 June 2002.
45. Interview with Paul King, Chief, Internal Investigations, UNMIK UNPOL, UNPOL Headquarters, Pristina, Kosovo, 20 March 2003.
46. Decker (2006: 504).
47. http://www.UNPOL.org/unmik/strength.htm, downloaded 11 November 2002 and UNPOL SITREP, 31 December 1999.
48. Dijkzeul and Beigbeder (2003: 262).
49. Interview with Paul King, Chief, Internal Investigations, UNMIK UNPOL, UNPOL Headquarters, Pristina, Kosovo, 20 March 2003.
50. UNPOL deployment statistics collected by author. Calculations based on an assumption of a population of two million.
51. International Crisis Group, "What Happened to the KLA?." Report No. 88 (2000).
52. This is not to say that UNPOL was fully successful in destroying claimants to state power. The KLA, for instance, survived well into the post-war period. See the International Crisis Group, "What Happened to the KLA?" Europe Report No. 88, 3 March 2000.
53. For a discussion of why the two post-conflict environments were significantly different, see Boyle (2009).
54. Interview with Major General Mike Smith, deputy commander of UN forces in East Timor. See Smith (2003: 86).
55. Interview with General Mike Smith.
56. See Human Rights Watch, "Indonesia/East Timor: Forced Expulsions to West Timor and the Refugee Crisis," 11, 7, December 1999 (available at www.hrw.org/reports/1999/wtimor/).
57. Human Rights Watch, "Indonesia/East Timor: Forced Expulsions to West Timor and the Refugee Crisis." See also Londey (2004: 249).
58. See Human Rights Watch, "Indonesia/East Timor: Forced Expulsions to West Timor and the Refugee Crisis."
59. UNTAET Mandate, UN Security Council 1272 (1999), 25 October 1999 (available at www.un.org/peace/etimor/UntaetM.htm, accessed 22 December 2008).
60. Paris (2004: 220).
61. Hansen (2002: 45).
62. Decker (2006: 508).

63. Perito (2008: 59–60).

64. Decker (2006: 505).

65. Interview with Brad Coulter and Grant Schultz, Australian Federal Police, PNTL Academy, Dili, 26 April 2005.

66. See for instance UN Policy on Justice and Return Proedures in East Timor (available at www.un.org/peace/etimor/DB/procedures.pdf, accessed 3 January 2008).

67. See Bayley (2005).

68. This is the argument of much of the sociological literature on the formation of states. See, for instance, Cohen, Brown and Organski (1981: 901–910), Evans, Rueschemeter and Skocpol (1985) and Mazower (2002: 1158–78). However, as Tilly points out, many post-colonial states never had the experience of a violent creation of borders and were left with intact, often colonial, borders. There is no *prima facie* reason to assume that they must follow the same violent trajectory that European states followed. The claim here is only that international efforts to build states often compress two very different imperatives into an extremely short time period.

69. This point draws an obvious parallel with Roland Paris' Institutionalization before Liberalization (IBL) thesis. See particularly Paris (2004).

70. One of the problems that UNPOL faces is that it may not have moral agency in the same way that states do. See Lang (2002: 189–190).

71. This is not to say that UNPOL forces did not have the goodwill of the local population, or that the local population was entirely unsupportive of efforts to apprehend criminal actors. It is only to say that they lacked a formal mandate, through an election of some kind.

72. Bain (2003: 27–74).

73. Quoted in Bain (2003: 68). See also Hochschild (2006).

74. P.H. Kerr (1916), quoted in Bain (2006: 198).

75. See the Introduction to this volume and also Newman and Richmond (2001: 101–118).

76. Fearon and Laitin (2004: 7).

77. In the words of former Deputy Secretary of State Strobe Talbott, Kosovo "goes about the business of rebuilding itself under the day-in, day-out protection and supervision of a consortium of global and regional organizations." Quoted in Bain (2006: 199).

78. Fearon and Laitin (2004: 13).

79. Another possible explanation is that UN peacekeeping might be subject to organized hypocrisy, in which competing external and internal pressures lead the organization to make commitments which it cannot hope to meet. See Lipson (2007: 5–34).

80. Much of what the UN Secretariat got from member states was token deployment of a few CIVPOL officers. By 31 December 1999, 68 nations had sent CIVPOL

forces to Kosovo, though the vast majority of contributions comprised only a few officers. The largest contributors in 1999 were the USA (434), Germany (208), Russia (124) India (87), Canada (85), France (78), Pakistan (65) and the United Kingdom (60). See Internal UN Document, "Monthly Military and Civilian Police Contributions," 31 December 1999. By late 2000, there were 52 countries contributing police offers to CIVPOL. The largest contributors in 2000 were: USA (608), India (535), Jordan (463), Germany (342), Pakistan (240), Ukraine (148), Nigeria (144) and the United Kingdom (135). See UNMIK UNPOL website, "Facts and Figures: Police Strength" (available at www.UNPOL.org/unmik/strength.html, accessed 18 January 2001).

81. Interview with Paul King, Chief, Internal Investigations, UNMIK UNPOL, UNPOL Headquarters, Pristina, Kosovo, 20 March 2003.

82. Interview with D. Chris Decker, OSCE Law Enforcement Division, OSCE, Pristina, Kosovo, 28 June 2002.

83. Not all efforts at imperial policing had high levels of what would today be called unity of effort. In some cases, imperial forces relied on local actors who had their own preferences. As Ignatieff points out, this strategy of indirect imperial rule, so favoured by the British, has been repeated by the American government in Afghanistan. See Ignatieff (2003: 98).

84. Hood (2006: 62).

85. Report of the UN Secretary-General on the Situation in East Timor, UN Document S/1999/1024.

86. De Mello (2003), quoted in Howard (2007: 282).

87. For a positive account of UNPOL's effectiveness, see Howard (2007: 281–3).

88. Hood (2006: 68).

89. Hood (2006: 69).

90. Durch (2006: 444–5).

91. Interview with Karl Clark, ICITAP/UNPOL officer, Dili, East Timor, 24 April 2005.

92. See in particular Hood (2006).

93. Interview with Karl Clark, ICITAP/UNPOL officer, Dili, East Timor, 24 April 2005.

94. See Chesterman (2004: 126–53). See also Caplan (2005: 195–211).

95. See Bayley (2005).

96. Richmond (2005: 175).

97. There has been less concern for local agency in UNPOL missions devoted primarily to monitoring, such as the mission in Cyprus (UNFICYP) established in 1963–64. See Schmidl (1998).

98. Richmond (2005: 174).

99. For the point on peacekeeping as a precursor to permanent military deployments, see Kissinger (2001: 18).

100. Caplan (2002).
101. Richmond (2005: 174).
102. Paris (2004: 220).
103. Chopra (2000: 27–39).
104. Statistics from the Office of the Police Advisor, July 2000, quoted in Dijkzeul and Beigbeder (2003: 265).
105. Dijkzeul and Beigbeder (2003: 31420).
106. Benner, Mergenthaler, and Rotmann (2007).
107. Oakley, Dziedzic and Goldberg (1998).
108. Interview with Karl Clark, ICITAP/UNPOL officer, Dili, East Timor, 24 April 2005.
109. Chopra (2000: 30–31).
110. Hood (2006: 69).
111. Hood (2006: 70).
112. See Durch (2006: 374). For more on why an exit from a mission like Kosovo is difficult, see Fearon and Laitin (2004: 40–41).
113. Holzgrefe and Keohane (2003: 321).
114. For an interesting debate on whether IOs/NGOs have the kind of agency needed to participate in the politics of state creation, see Lang (2002: 189–90).

## 11. THE POLITICAL ECONOMY OF PROTECTORATES AND "POST-CONFLICT" INTERVENTION

1. Ellis (2005: 6).
2. Edward Said, "A window on the world," *Guardian*, 2 August 2003.
3. By highlighting what we call the political economy perspective we do little more, at one level, than draw attention to a simple but vitally important fact. In the words of John Kay: "economic systems are embedded in a social and political context; so there is no escaping political economy." Although it seems obvious, it is surprising how often this reality has been ignored, including by outsiders charged with making policy to support post-conflict recovery and the economic reconstruction in war-torn states. Kay (2003: 307).
4. Tripp (2002: 26).
5. Berdal and Keen (1997: 797).
6. Cockayne and Lupel (2009: 153).
7. The themes explored in this section are developed more fully in Berdal (2009: 77–94), and Keen (1996).
8. International Rescue Committee, "Mortality in the Democratic Republic of Congo: An Ongoing Crisis" (New York, January, 2008).
9. With some 17,000 peacekeepers deployed, MONUC is currently the largest UN field operation.

10. See "Final Report of the Group of Experts on the DRC," S/2009/603, 23 November 2009 (available at www.un.org/sc/committees/1533/egroup.shtml).
11. Berdal and Malone (2000).
12. Ballentine and Sherman (2000: 260).
13. Stephen Jackson describes the process of "economization" as one in which "conflicts progressively reorient from their original goals towards profit, and conflict actors capitalize ever increasingly on the economic opportunities that war has opened up." Jackson (2002: 528).
14. Jackson (2002: 528).
15. Keen (1996: 32).
16. Berdal and Keen (1997: 797).
17. Jackson (2002: 527).
18. See Ballentine and Nitzschke (2005: 160–5).
19. Jonathan Goodhand, "Frontiers and Wars: the Opium Economy in Afghanistan," paper for conference on the "Transformation of War Economies after Conflict," University of Plymouth.
20. Raeymaekers (2006: 192).
21. Rubin (2000: 1790).
22. Rubin (2000: 1798).
23. This is the central focus of Pugh and Cooper with Goodhand (2003).
24. Karen Ballentine, "Programme on Economic Agendas in Civil Wars—Final Report," IPA, April 2004, p. 6.
25. For the unprecedented use of sanctions since 1990, see Lowe, Roberts, Welsh and Zaum (2008).
26. Dodge (2009: 6).
27. Ballentine and Nitzschke (2005: 153–54).
28. See, for example, Messiant (2004).
29. Timothy Raeymaekers, "Who calls the Congo? A Response to Jeffrey Herbst and Greg Mills," 10 August 2009 (available at www.rubeneberlein.wordpress.com/2009/08/10/who-calls-the-congo-a-response-to-herbst-and-mills/).
30. Del Castillo (2008).
31. Del Castillo (2008: 70–71).
32. Del Castillo and De Soto (1994).
33. Kay (2003: 364).
34. Dodge (2009: 11).
35. Allawi (2007: 198).
36. Allawi (2007: 12). For the ideological roots of the policy, see also Chandrasekaran (2007: 128).
37. Dodge (2009: 12).
38. Ibid.
39. Dodge (2009: 12).

40. Dodge (2009: 3).
41. Cockayne (2009: 82).
42. Quoted in James K. Boyce, "The International Financial Institutions: Postconflict Reconstruction and Peacebuilding Capacities," Paper prepared for CIC, New York, seminar on "Strengthening the UN's Capacity on Civilian Crisis Management," Copenhagen, 8–9 June 2004.
43. Castillo (2008: 74).
44. Boyce (2004: 7).
45. Bøås (2009: 1335); "Report of the Panel of Experts concerning Liberia," S/2006/976, 15 December 2006.
46. Bøås (2009: 1335).
47. For brief history of the immediate origins of GEMAP and politically delicate discussions between international donors and Liberian authorities leading up to agreement in September 2005, see Dwan and Bailey (2006).
48. Governance and Economic Management Program (GEMAP), www.gemapliberia.org
49. GEMAP advisers have served in 13 "key institutions," Roberts International Airport and the Ministry of Lands, Mines and Finance.
50. Bøås (2009: 1330).
51. For an early and necessarily tentative discussion of GEMAP as a model for other post-conflict interventions in the sphere of economic governance, see Dwan and Bailey (2006: 19–24).
52. Dwan and Bailey (2006: 1338).
53. Ibid.
54. Reno (2008).
55. President Johnson-Sirleaf (formerly a World Bank official) is herself sensitive to criticism of the program and the manner in which its intrusiveness effectively curtail and qualify Liberia's sovereignty. She was openly critical of the initial plans presented by donors before assuming office in 2006. See Bøås (2009: 1336).
56. Call (2008: 341); Bøås (2009: 1337).
57. In the view of Bøås, the chances that the "scheme will remain sustainable when donor interest shifts elsewhere is almost zero." Bøås (2009: 1339). See also Reno (2008: 398).
58. Stedman (1997: 5–53).
59. Cockayne and Pfister (2008: 7).
60. See, notably, Kalyvas (2004: 97–138); Keen (2006).
61. See, for example, Keen (2005); Autesserre (2007: 423–41).
62. See, notably, Greenhill and Major (2006/07: 7–40).
63. An example of analysis that exaggerates Britain's military confrontation with the RUF is Paul Collier's *Wars, Guns and Votes*. For assessment of British role, stress-

ing the importance of a longer-term commitment to security sector reform, see Berdal (2009: 103–107).

64. See Theidon (2009: 1–34).
65. See Vlassenroot and Raeymaekers (2009: 1–10).
66. Ahmed Hashim, *Insurgency and Counter-Insurgency in Iraq* (London: Hurst & Co.), p. 21.
67. For details of these policies and their highly destabilizing impact see Ricks (2006: 158–66); and Dodge (2009: 8, 12).
68. For a more extensive elaboration of this turn-around in US policy, see Berdal and Ucko (2009).
69. Hashim (2006: 24).
70. Ibid., see also Jonathan Steele and Dahr Jamail, "This is our Guernica," *Guardian*, 27 April 2005.
71. Hashim (2006: 25).
72. See, notably, Andreas (2005: 353–356); also Coalition for International Justice, Washington, "Sources of Revenue for Saddam and Sons: A Primer on the Financial Underpinnings of the Regime in Baghdad," September 2002.
73. Hashim (2006: 26).
74. Ibid. p. 373; Andreas (2005: 355).
75. Rathmell (2005: 1013–1038).
76. Long (2008: 75).
77. Rathmell (2005: 1024).
78. Long (2008).
79. Hashim (2009: 59–60). See also Williams (2009: 122). For a detailed account of how the situation developed on the ground, see also Kilcullen (2009: 115–83).
80. Long (2008: 87–8).

## 12. CIVIL-MILITARY RELATIONS IN THE NEW PROTECTORATE

1. This sentence, which aptly summarizes the author's thinking on the subject of this chapter, was first uttered in a discussion he had with General William W. Crouch (Commander of IFOR and SFOR) on why there were 15 generals and 48 colonels in a Headquarters that had previously had six generals and 20 colonels. It was subsequently used in verbal reports he made periodically to the OSCE Permanent Council during the period of October 1998 to March 1999.
2. See, e.g., Dower (1996).
3. Clarke (2001: 63).
4. The chapter also makes use of the memoirs of several politicians and military officers who have served in important positions in the new protectorates.
5. A "safe and secure environment" has never been properly defined.

6. Other agencies, notably major organizations such as UNHCR and less weighty non-governmental organizations, as well as the international media, are likely to have a presence before the military arrive, by virtue of dealing with the conflict that led to the creation of the protectorate.

7. Bildt (1998: 202–3).

8. Under UN arrangements each contingent was remunerated by the UN for their military contribution. The NATO IFOR continent was funded by the contributing nations, with costs falling where they lay. This may have been a factor for some countries when the decision was made whether to offer their contingents to NATO.

9. Bildt (1998: 80).

10. In 1996 the IFOR understood the need to be able to communicate with the HiRep over a secure line and embedded a small communications detachment in the HiRep's offices.

11. In the early stages this may be a need for space on military aircraft, or military escorts for civilian road deployments, particularly if the airports are being run by the military. There is also a need for mapping, and for weather related issues such as deciding which routes are to be demined, which bridges should be rebuilt first, and which should be kept clear of snow and ice.

12. This is a point about the short-term military tours of duty: as discussed in the Introduction to this volume, the civilian presence is often not long-term either.

13. Wesley Clarke remembers: "I then briefed the results of our planning. We had about a dozen plans completed or underway at this point." Clarke (2001: 137).

14. Ashdown (2008: 142).

15. In Bosnia in 1996 the US force protection policy was set very rigidly. Local commanders had no flexibility to vary the requirements. This was due to the strong US concern to avoid casualties. This risk-averse attitude stemmed from the public reaction to US casualties in Somalia in 1993. The heavy handed approach was the necessary price to pay in order to get US participation in IFOR, and guaranteed that the US provided a very strong, well resourced contingent. That said, the US posture was seen in some quarters as overcautious.

16. See Michael Boyle's chapter on policing in this volume.

17. "Trying to think the problem to its conclusions in military terms always drove one to 'worst case' analysis...... While it was well to see the risks, some of the risks would have to be discounted by common sense." Clarke (2001: 169).

18. Personal observation.

19. Smith (2005: 387 and 388).

20. Addressing Wesley Clarke, Solana stated: "[...] Understand that NATO cannot succeed with its mission if the international mission as a whole is not successful... You must actively help the civilians succeed. You have to stay within the limits of

the military mission you have been given... but you are going to have to do more to help the overall...implementation succeed." Quoted in Clarke (2001: 80).

21. Richard Holbrooke on Admiral Smith, quoted in Holbrooke (1999: 328).

22. Ashdown (2008: 143).

23. New mosques appeared where there had been none before. The skyline of Sarajevo contained many new minarets, demonstrating that the city had become a far less diverse place. Other cultural icons were built elsewhere. In Mostar, a hill overlooking the city had been the site of a Croatian cannon that persistently shelled Muslim areas of the city. In 1996 the gun was replace by a huge cross, illuminated at night, which implied that the area was entirely Christian. Elsewhere attempts to rebuild mediaeval mosques that had been destroyed were met by organized riots of Orthodox Christian Serbs. All the ethnic groups behaved in this manner. The issue was so sensitive that for years the internationals felt unable to intervene. Action was eventually taken in 2005 when Sarajevo International Airport was renamed after Alija Izobegovic, the President of the Federation during the 1992–95 war, and regarded as a war criminal by Serbs and Croats. The HiRep stepped in and annulled the renaming, using his Bonn Powers.

13. STRUGGLING FOR GOVERNMENT LEADERSHIP: THE RELATIONSHIP BETWEEN AFGHAN AND INTERNATIONAL ACTORS IN POST-2001 AFGHANISTAN

1. This paper was originally commissioned by the Global Economic Governance program at Oxford University in 2007. The author wishes to thank this program for commissioning that work and their permission to publish an updated and revised version here.

2. Delasgues and Torabi (2007: 21), International Crisis Group (2005: 24), Evans *et al.* (2004: 17–19).

3. This issue emerged privately in discussions in Kabul in 2002 and 2003.

4. The author conducted a review of key donor policy statements made between 2001 and 2006 which makes clear the multiplicity of objectives.

5. The World Bank-administered Afghanistan Reconstruction Trust Fund (ARTF) website provides a breakdown of contributions by country. This breakdown demonstrates the general increase in financing passing through the ARTF, as well as the unwillingness of certain donors to contribute significantly (Japan has chosen not to support the ARTF), or in proportion to their spending through other channels (the USA).

6. Interviews with key personnel working on Government programming, including representatives from UNAMA, UNDP, GoA and World Bank, 2006.

7. Ward and Byrd (2004). As finance minister, Ashraf Ghani warned of the possibility of Afghanistan becoming a "narco-mafia" state in 2003.

8. Radio Free Europe maintains a chronology of suicide bombings in Afghanistan which emphasizes this trend. (Available at www.rferl.org/featuresarticle/2006/01/9ac36a59-d683-4189-a2b9-94fe5fbf32ad.html).

9. The "Cairo Memo" was the basis of a meeting in Cairo in July 2004 between US Ambassador Zal Khalilzad, Finance minister Ashraf Ghani, Former Special Representative Lakhdar Brahimi and the then Special Representative Jean Arnault.

10. The majority of the funds going through the ARTF are allocated to the national budget; the salaries of approximately 250,000 civil servants including teachers, health-workers and engineers, and operations and maintenance costs.

11. The Law and Order Trust Fund for Afghanistan.

12. Recorded trade flows with Pakistan increased from $20 million in 2001 to at least $700 million by May 2004.

13. Afzal Khan, "Political and Economic Relations between Afghanistan and Pakistan Improve and Expand," *Eurasia Daily Monitor* 1, 52, 15 July 2004 (available at www.jamestown.org/publications_details.php?volume_id=401&issue_id=3017&article_id=2368257).

14. Rubin, Hamidzada and Stoddard (2003).

15. Robert McMahon interviewing Said Jawad, *Capital Interview: Kabul Lacks Capacity to Govern* (New York: Council on Foreign Relations, 28 February 2007). http://www.cfr.org/publication/12739/afghanistan_lacks_capacity_to_govern.html.

16. Manning (2004: 7).

17. To address the question of "ghost workers," exercises were undertaken to verify the payroll.

18. Manning *et al.* (2003), Manning (2004), Evans *et al.* (2004).

19. The World Bank-AREU study observed that in 2002 the government had a considerable capacity, in the form of at least 250,000 civil servants (Evans *et al.* 2004: 38), with representation in all 32 provinces, a fairly robust and resilient legal system, and knowledge of the rules. The report recommended that unless resources were channeled through government systems, it would not be possible to begin to make the systemic changes necessary to improve quality.

20. Referencing promises President Karzai made in his Tokyo speech, January 2002, and to the National Development Framework

21. Statement, General Karl Eikenberry, Commander Coalition Forces Afghanistan, July 2005.

22. The original World Bank-Asian Development Bank-UNDP assessment estimated that the Kabul-Kandahar road segment would cost $35m. It eventually cost $270 million (USAID 2003).

23. In April 2003 the UN wrote to the Government of Afghanistan, asking it not to run a process whereby Afghan ministers would prioritize their own projects (i.e. the budget process), as this might prejudice the UN's ability to raise money for its projects.

24. Interviews with Afghan farmers, 2002 and 2003, undertaken by the ministry of Finance.

## 14. THE NEW PROTECTORATES: STATEBUILDING AND LEGITIMACY

1. Fox (1992); Franck (1992).
2. See for example Chandler (1999).
3. See William Bain's chapter in this volume as well as Bain (2006: 536).
4. Holsti (1996: 87–90).
5. Holsti (1996: 91–7).
6. Keen (2005).
7. Paris (2004); Richmond (2005); Zaum (2007).
8. See for example Chandler (2006); Chopra (2000: 27–40; Duffield (2007); Jahn (2007: 87–106, 211–29).
9. See, e.g., Del Castillo (2008).
10. Zaum (2003: 102–20).
11. Hohe and Nixon (2003).
12. Beauvais (2001: 1101–78).
13. See for example Franck (1990).
14. Clark (2005: 15–17); Holsti (1996).
15. Morris and Wheeler (2007: 214–31).
16. See Hurd (2007: 7). See also Simmons (1999: 739–71).
17. For more on the social context of legitimacy, see Reus-Smit (2007: 157–74).
18. Buchanan and Keohane (2006: 405).
19. See for example Buchanan and Keohane (2006: 405–37); Buchanan (2004).
20. David Beetham (1991: 11).
21. Barker (2001: 22–5).
22. Craig and Rawlings (2003: 163–4).
23. Franck (1990).
24. Beetham (1991: 17–18).
25. Suchman (1995: 581).
26. Scharpf (1990).
27. SC Res. 1244 of 10 June 1999, SC Res. 1272 of 25 Oct. 1999.
28. General Framework Agreement for Peace in Bosnia and Herzegovina, 14 December 1995.
29. For a detailed discussion, see Zaum (2009).
30. SC Res. 1272 of 25 Oct. 1999, para. 8.
31. SC Res. 1483 of 22 May 2003, para. 9.
32. See Brand (2003).
33. Power (2008: 307).
34. Cited in Caplan (2005: 115).

35. See Zaum (2009: 189–208).
36. Cited in Chesterman (2004: 140).
37. Ombudsperson Institution in Kosovo, *Second Annual Report 2001–2002*, Pristina, 10 July 2002.
38. Parliamentary Assembly of the Council of Europe, *Honouring of Obligations and Commitments of Bosnia and Herzegovina*, Strasbourg, 4 June 2004, Para.102.
39. For a detailed discussion, see Rawski (2002: 103–32); and Caplan (2005: 463–76).
40. UNMIK Regulation 2000/38, On the Establishment of an Ombudsperson Institution in Kosovo, 30 June 2000.
41. Rawski (2002).
42. For the involvement of the OLA in the drafting and reviewing of privatization legislation in Kosovo, see Zaum (2007: 153–63).
43. Lowe, Roberts, Welsh, and Zaum (2008: 572–6).
44. Zaum (2006: 463–5).
45. See chapters by Aswini Ray and Shogo Suzuki, in this volume.
46. Hurrell (2005: 24), special issue on Force and Legitimacy in World Politics.
47. Robinson (1965: 68). The assumption that the interests and values of interveners and of people subjected to intervention coincide was central to Lord Lugard's famous notion of the "dual mandate," arguing that Europe was in Africa for "the mutual benefit of her own industrial classes, and of the native races in their progress to a higher plane." See Lugard (1926: 617).
48. Call and Wyeth (2008: 26).
49. For a detailed discussion of the status process, see Weller (2008a: 659–81) and Weller (2008b: 1223–43).
50. UN document S/PV.4011 of 10 June 1999, p. 9.
51. UN document S/PV.5839 of 18 Feburary 2008, pp. 5–6.
52. Paris (2004); Zaum (2007).
53. Del Castillo (2008: 207–8).
54. For the importance attached to the rule of law in statebuilding, see Report of the Panel on United Nations Peace Operations (The Brahimi Report), UN document S/2001/42, 21 August 2000, Paras. 79–83. Report of the High Level Panel on Threats, Challenges and Change, "A More Secure World: Our Shared Responsibility," UN document A/59/565 of 2 December 2004, Paras. 239–40.
55. There has been a growing literature on the relationship between traditional and formal judicial institutions in the context of intervention in societies with traditional authority structures, such as Afghanistan and East Timor. See for example Chopra and Hohe (2005: 289–306); Barfield (2003).
56. Hohe and Nixon (2003).
57. See Richmond and Franks (2008: 185–200).
58. See Wilde (2008: 193–203). On the legitimacy of multilateral interventions, see also Finnemore (2003: 136–7).

59. Franks and Richmond (2008: 81–103).

60. Berdal and Caplan (2004: 1–5). See also Berdal (2009).

61. See for example Dobbins, Jones, Crane, Rathmell, Steele, Teltschick, and Timilsina (2005).

62. UNMIK, Regulation 1999/1, On the Authority of the Interim Administration in Kosovo, 25 July 1999; UNTAET, Regulation 1999/1, On the Authority of the Transitional Administration in East Timor, 27 Nov.1999.

63. Del Castillo (2008).

64. Suhrke (2001: 1–20).

65. See for example Ghani and Lockhart (2007).

66. CSDG (Conflict Security and Development Group), *A Review of Peace Operations: A Case for Change—East Timor Study* (London: King's College, 2003); CSDG, *A Review of Peace Operations: A Case for Change—Kosovo Study* (London: King's College, 2003); Rohland and Cliffe (2002).

67. Dobbins, Jones, Runkle and Mohandas (2009: xvi).

68. Interview with World Bank official, Washington, 14 April 2003.

69. Suhrke (2001: 6).

70. Hohe and Nixon (2003: 32).

71. Report of the Secretary General on the United Nations Interim Administration Mission in Kosovo, UN Document S/1999/987 of 16 September 1999, Para.16.

72. ICG, *Waiting for UNMIK—Local Administration in Kosovo* (Pristina: ICG, 1999), pp. 2–3.

73. ESI/LLA (2002: 11–13).

74. See Zaum (2007: 153–66).

75. Knaus and Cox (2005: 50).

76. Opening Remarks by Principal Deputy HR Donald Hays at a Bosnia and Herzegovina Agricultural Conference, Sarajevo, 10 November 2005. Available at www.ohr.int (accessed 13 Feb. 2009)

77. OHR, *Agriculture and Profit*, 31 October 2003. (Available at www.ohr.int/ohr-dept/rrtf/pics/agriculture-campaign/, accessed 13 February 2009).

78. Strazzari (2008: 155–70).

79. Ghani and Lockhart (2007: 85–112).

80. Cited in Fukuyama (2004: 139).

81. King and Mason (2006).

82. See Lowe, Roberts, Welsh, and Zaum (2008: 365–7).

# BIBLIOGRAPHY

Alden, Chris, Ricardo Soares de Oliveira and Daniel Large (eds), *China Returns to Africa: a Continent and a Rising Power Embrace* (London: Hurst, 2008).

Allawi, Ali A., *The Occupation of Iraq—Winning the War, Losing the Peace* (New Haven: Yale University Press, 2007).

Anastasakis, Othon and Vesna Bojicic-Dzelilovic, *Balkan Regional Co-operation and European Integration*, Hellenic Observatory Policy Paper No. 2 (Hellenic Observatory: LSE, July 2002).

Anderson, Benedict, *Imagined Communities* (London: Verso, 1991).

Andreas, Peter, "Criminalizing Consequences of Sanctions," *International Studies Quarterly* 49 (2005), pp. 353–6.

Appadurai, Arjun, *Modernity at Large: Cultural Dimensions in Globalization* (Minneapolis: University of Minnesota Press, 1996).

Arato, Andrew, *Constitution Making Under Occupation: The Politics of Imposed Revolution in Iraq* (New York: Columbia University Press, 2009).

Ashdown, Paddy, "Inaugural Speech by Paddy Ashdown, the New High Representative for Bosnia and Herzegovina," Office of the High Representative Press Office, 27 May 2002.

——— *Swords and Ploughshares—Bringing Peace to the 21ˢᵗ Century* (London: Orion Books, 2008).

Austin, John, *Lectures on Jurisprudence or the Philosophy of Positive Law* (London: John Murray, 1920).

Autesserre, Séverine, "DR Congo: Explaining Peace Building Failures, 2003–2006," *Review of African Political Economy* 34, 113 (2007), pp. 423–41.

Bacevich, Andrew, *American Empire—The Realities and Consequences of U.S. Diplomacy* (Cambridge, MA: Harvard University Press, 2002).

Bacharatz, Peter and Morton S. Baratz, "Decisions and Non-Decisions: An Analytical Framework," *The American Political Science Review* 57, 3 (1963), pp. 632–42.

Bain, William, "Are There Any Lessons of History? The English School and the Activity of Being a Historian," *International Politics* 44, 5 (2007), pp. 513–30.

——— *Between Anarchy and Society: Trusteeship and the Obligations of Power* (Oxford: Oxford University Press, 2003).

———— "In Praise of Folly: International Administration and the Corruption of Humanity," *International Affairs* 82, 3 (2006), pp. 525–38.

Bain, William (ed.), *The Empire of Security and the Safety of the People* (New York: Routledge, 2006).

Balandier, Georges, "La situation coloniale: ancien concept, nouvelles réalités", French Politics, Culture and Society, 20 (2), (2002), pp. 4–10.

Ballentine, Karen, "Programme on Economic Agendas in Civil Wars—Final Report" (IPA: April 2004)

Ballentine, Karen and Heiko Nitzschke (eds), *Profiting from Peace: Managing the Resource Dimensions of Civil War* (Boulder, CO: Lynne Rienner, 2005).

Ballentine, Karen and Jake Sherman (eds), *The Political Economy of Armed Conflict: Beyond Greed and Grievance* (Boulder, CO: Lynne Rienner, 2000).

Baranovsky, Vladimir, "Humanitarian Intervention: Russian Perspectives," *Pugwash Occasional Papers* 2, 1 (2001), pp. 12–38.

Barfield, Thomas, *Afghan Customary Law and Its Relationship to Formal Judicial Institutions* (Boston University for the United States Institute for Peace: 2003).

Barker, Rodney, *Legitimating Identities: The Self-Presentations of Rulers and Subjects* (Cambridge: Cambridge University Press, 2001).

Barnett, Michael, *Eyewitness to a Genocide: The United Nations and Rwanda* (Ithaca, NY: Cornell University Press, 2002).

Barnett, Michael and Martha Finnemore, *Rules for the World: International Organizations in Global Politics* (Ithaca, NY: Cornell University Press, 2004).

Barnett, Michael, Hunjoon Kim, Madalene O'Donnell and Laura Sitea, "Peacebuilding: what is in a Name?," *Global Governance* 13 (2007), pp. 35–58.

Bass, Gary, *Freedom's Battle: The Origins of Humanitarian Intervention* (New York: Random House, 2008).

Bayley, David H., *Changing the Guard: Developing Democratic Police Abroad* (Oxford: Oxford University Press, 2005).

———— "Police Reform as Foreign Policy," *Australian and New Zealand Journal of Criminology* 32, 8 (August 2005), pp. 206–215.

Bayly, Christopher, *Empire and Information: Intelligence Gathering and Social Communication in India, 1780–1870* (Cambridge: Cambridge University Press, 2000).

Beauvais, Joel, "Benevolent Despotism: A Critique of U.N. State-Building in East Timor," *New York University Journal of International Law and Politics* 33, 4 (2001), pp. 1101–78.

Bechev, Dimitar, "Carrots, Sticks and Norms: the EU and Regional Cooperation in SEE," *Journal of Southern Europe and the Balkans* 8, 1 (2006), pp. 27–43.

Beetham, David, *The Legitimation of Power* (London: Macmillan, 1991).

Bellamy, Alex J., "Responsibility to Protect or Trojan Horse? The Crisis in Darfur and Humanitarian Intervention after Iraq," *Ethics and International Affairs* 19, 2 (2005), pp. 31–54.

Benner, Thorsten, Stephan Mergenthaler and Philipp Rotmann, "Learning to Build Peace? United Nations Peacebuilding and Organizational Learning: Developing a Research Framework," *DSF-Forschung* 9 (2007).

Benner, Thorsten, Stephan Mergenhaler and Philipp Rotmann, "Doctrine Development and the UN Peacebuilding Apparatus: The Case of the Constabulatory Police 1999–2006," Paper Presented at the ISA Convention, San Francisco, 29 March 2007.

Benner, Thorsten, Stephan Mergenthaler and Philipp Rotmann (eds) *Learning to Build Peace?* (Oxford: Oxford University Press, 2011).

Bensahel, Nora, "Organising for Nation Building," *Survival* 49, 2 (2007), pp. 43–76.

Berdal, Mats, *Building Peace After War* (London: Routledge, 2009).

Berdal, Mats and David Keen, "Violence and Economic Agendas in Civil Wars: Some Policy Implications," *Millennium: Journal of International Studies* 26, 3 (1997), pp. 795–818.

Berdal, Mats and David Malone (eds), *Greed and Grievance: Economic Agendas in Civil War* (Boulder, CO: Lynne Rienner, 2000).

Berdal, Mats and David H. Ucko (eds), *Reintegrating Armed Groups After Conflict: politics, violence and transition,* (London: Routledge, 2009).

Berdal, Mats and Richard Caplan, "The Politics of International Administration," *Global Governance* 10, 1 (2004), pp. 1–5.

Berdal, Mats and Spyros Economides, *United Nations Interventionism, 1991–2004* (Cambridge: Cambridge University Press, 2007).

Bernstein, Richard and Ross H. Munro, "The Coming Conflict with America," *Foreign Affairs* 76, 2 (1997), pp. 18–32.

Bildt, Carl, *Peace Journey* (London: Weidenfeld and Nicholson, 1998).

Bin, Liu, "'Shibai guojia lun' he 'xin diguo zhuyi lun': xin shiji de baquan lilun," *Guoji guancha* 5 (2002), pp. 46–50.

Bøås, Morten, "Making Plans for Liberia—A Trusteeship Approach to Good Governance?," *Third World Quarterly* 30, 7 (2009), pp. 1329–41.

Boot, Max, *The Savages Wars of Peace: Small Wars and the Rise of American Power* (New York: Basic Books, 2002).

Booth, Ken and Tim Dunne (eds), *Worlds in Collision: Terror and the Future of Global Order* (Basingstoke: Palgrave Macmillan, 2002).

Boutros-Ghali, Boutros, *An Agenda for Democratization*, United Nations, 1996.

Bowden, Brett, "In the Name of Progress and Peace: The 'Standard of Civilization' and the Universalizing Project," *Alternatives* 29, 1 (January-February 2004), pp. 43–68.

Boyce, James K., "The International Financial Institutions: Postconflict Reconstruction and Peacebuilding Capacities," Paper prepared for CIC, New York, seminar on *"Strengthening the UN's Capacity on Civilian Crisis Management,"* Copenhagen, 8–9 June 2004.

Boyle, Michael J., "The Prevention and Management of Reprisal Violence in Post-Conflict States," PhD Dissertation (University of Cambridge, 2004).

Boyle, Michael J., "Explaining Strategic Violence After Wars," *Studies in Conflict and Terrorism* (March 2009), pp. 209–236.

Brailsford, Henry, *The War of Steel and Gold: A Study of Armed Peace* (New York: Garland Publishing, 1971).

Brand, Marcus, *The Development of Kosovo Institutions and the Transition of Authority from UNMIK to Local Self-Government* (Geneva: CASIN, 2003).

Brecher, Michael, *India's Foreign Policy* (Oxford: Oxford University Press, 1958).

Bremer, L. Paul, *My Year in Iraq: The Struggle to Build a Future of Hope* (New York: Simon and Schuster, 2006).

Broome, André, *The Currency of Power: The IMF and Monetary Reform in Frontier Economies* (Basingstoke: Palgrave Macmillan, 2010).

Brown, Michael E., Sean M. Lynn-Jones and Steven E. Miller, *Debating the Democratic Peace* (Cambridge, MA: MIT Press, 1996).

Brown, William, "The Commission for Africa: Results and Prospects for the West's Africa Policy," *Journal of Modern African Studies* 44, 3 (March 2006), pp. 349–74.

Brownlie, Ian (ed.), *Basic Documents on Human Rights* (Oxford: Clarendon Press, 1992).

Buchanan, Allen, *Justice, Legitimacy, and Self-Determination: Moral Foundations for International Law* (Oxford: Oxford University Press, 2004).

Buchanan, Allen and Robert Keohane, "The Legitimacy of Global Governance Institutions," *Ethics and International Affairs* 20, 4 (2006), pp. 405–37.

Buchanan, Patrick, *A Republic, Not an Empire* (Washington: Regnery Publishing, 1999).

Bull, Hedley and Adam Watson (eds), *The Expansion of International Society* (Oxford: Clarendon Press, 1984).

Burton, Antoinette (ed.), *Through the Dark Continent (1879)—Politics and Empire in Victorian Britain* (Basingstoke: Palgrave, 2002).

Burton, Sir Richard Francis, *Goa and the Blue Mountains, or, Six Months of Sick Leave,* republished with an Introduction by Dane Kennedy (Berkeley: University of California Press, 1991).

Butterfield, Herbert, *The Whig Interpretation of History* (New York: W.W. Norton, 1965).

Call, Charles T., *Building States to Build Peace* (Boulder: Lynne Rienner, 2008).

Call, Charles T., with Vanessa Wyeth (eds), *Building States to Build Peace* (Boulder, CO: Lynne Rienner, 2008).

Call, Chuck and Michael Barnett, "Looking for a Few Good Cops: Peacekeeping, Peacebuilding and UNPOL," *International Peacekeeping* (1999), pp. 43–68.

Caplan, Richard, *A New Trusteeship? The International Administration of War Torn Territories* (Adelphi Papers, 2002).

——— *International Governance of War-Torn Territories* (Oxford: Oxford University Press, 2005).

——— "Who Guards the Guardians? International Accountability and Bosnia-Herzegovina," *International Peacekeeping* 12, 3 (2005), pp. 463–76.

Carlson, Allen, "Helping to Keep the Peace (Albeit Reluctantly): China's Recent Stance on Sovereignty and Multilateral Intervention," *Pacific Affairs* 77, 1 (Spring 2004), pp. 9–27.

Carlson, Allen, *Unifying China, Integrating with the World: Securing Chinese Sovereignty in the Reform Era* (Stanford: Stanford University Press, 2005).

Carroll, Lewis, *Alice's Adventures in Wonderland* (New York: McLoughlin Brothers/ DSI Digital Reproduction, 2007).

# BIBLIOGRAPHY

Casement, Roger, "Mr. Casement to the Marquess of Landsdowne—(Received December 12), December 11, 1903)," *Parliamentary Papers*, Cmd. 1933 lxii (1904), pp. 23–52.

Castells, Manuel, *The Information Age, Economy, Society and Culture—The Rise of the Network Society*, Volume 1, 2nd edn (Oxford: Blackwell Wiley, 2009).

Castillo, Graziana Del, *Rebuilding War-Torn States: The Challenge of Post-Conflict Economic Reconstruction* (Oxford: Oxford University Press, 2008).

Celador, Gemma C., "Police Reform: Peacebuilding through 'Democratic Policing,'" *International Peacekeeping* 12, 3 (2005), pp. 364–76.

Center on International Cooperation and International Peace Institute, "*Taking Stock, Looking Forward: A Strategic Review of the Peacebuilding Commission*," April 2008.

Chamberlain, Joseph, *Foreign and Colonial Speeches* (London: George Routledge & Sons, 1897).

Chanaa, Jane, *Security Sector Reforms: Issues, Challenges and Prospects* (Adelphi Papers 344, 2002).

Chandler, David, *Bosnia: Faking Democracy After Dayton* (London: Pluto Press, 2000).

——— *Empire in Denial: The Politics of State-Building* (London: Pluto Press, 2006).

Chandran, D.S. and P.R.Chari (eds), *Armed Conflicts in South Asia* (London: Routledge, 2008).

Chandrasekaram, Rajiv, *Imperial Life in the Emerald City: Inside Baghdad's Green Zone* (London: Bloomsbury, 2007).

Charvet, John and Elisa Kaczynska-Nay, *The Liberal Project and Human Rights: The Theory and Practice of a New World Order* (Cambridge: Cambridge University Press: 2008).

Chengxu, Yang and Wu Miaofa (eds), *Xintiaozhai: guoji guanxi zhong de "rendao zhuyi ganyu"* (Beijing: Zhongguo qingnian chubanshe, 2001).

Chesterman, Simon, *You the People: The United Nations, Transitional Administration, and Statebuilding* (Oxford: Oxford University Press, 2004).

Chollet, Derek and James M. Goldgeier, *America Between the Wars: From 11/9 to 9/11—The Misunderstood Decade Between the End of the Cold War and the Start of the War on Terror* (New York: Public Affairs, 2008).

Chopra, Jarat, "Building State Failure in East Timor," *Development and Change* 33, 5 (2002), pp. 979–1000.

——— "The UN's Kingdom in East Timor," *Survival* 42, 3 (2000), pp. 27–40.

Chopra, Jarat and Tanja Hohe, "Participatory Intervention," *Global Governance* 10, 3 (2005), pp. 289–306.

Clapham, Christopher, *Africa and the International System* (Cambridge: Cambridge University Press, 1996).

Clark, Ian, "Another 'Double Movement': the Great Transformation after the Cold War?," *Review of International Studies* 27, special issue (2001), pp. 237–55.

Clark, Ian, *Globalization and Fragmentation: International Relations in the Twentieth Century* (Oxford: Oxford University Press, 1997).

——— *Legitimacy in International Society* (Oxford: Oxford University Press, 2005).

Clarke, General Wesley K., *Waging Modern War* (New York: Public Affairs, 2001).

Clarke, Walter and Jeffrey Herbst (eds), *Learning from Somalia: the Lessons of Armed Humanitarian Intervention* (Boulder, CO: Westview, 1997).

Coalition for International Justice, Washington, *Sources of Revenue for Saddam and Sons: A Primer on the Financial Underpinnings of the Regime in Baghdad*, September 2002.

Cockayne, James, "Winning Haiti's Protection Competition: Organised Crime and Peace Operations Pats, Present and Future," *International Peacekeeping* 16, 1 (2009), pp. 77–99.

Cockayne, James and Adam Lupel, "From Iron Fist to Invisible Hand—Peace Operations, Organised Crime and Intelligent Law Enforcement," *International Peacekeeping* 16, 1 (2009), pp. 151–68.

Cockayne, James and Daniel Pfister, "Peace Operations and Organised Crime," *GCSP/ IPI Report*, 2008.

Cohen, Warren, *Empire without Tears: America's Foreign Relations, 1921–1933*, (Philadelphia: Temple University Press, 1987).

Cohen, Youssef, Brian Brown and A.F.K. Organski, "The Paradoxical Nature of State-Making: The Violent Creation of Order," *American Political Science Review* 75, 4 (1981), pp. 901–910.

Collier, Paul, Anke Hoeffler and Måns Söderbom, "Post-Conflict Risks," *Journal of Peace Research* 45, 4 (2008), pp. 461–78.

Cooper, Fred, *Colonialism in Question: Theory, Knowledge, History* (Berkeley: University of California Press, 2005).

Cooper, Robert, *The Breaking of Nations: Order and Chaos in the Twenty-First Century* (New York: Grove Press, 2003).

Craig, P. and R. Rawlings (eds), *Law and Administration in Europe: Essays in Honour of Carol Harlow* (Oxford: Oxford University Press, 2003).

Cramer, Christopher, *Civil War is Not a Stupid Thing: Accounting for Violence in Developing Countries* (London: Hurst, 2006).

Conflict Security and Development Group, *A Review of Peace Operations: A Case for Change—East Timor Study* (London: King's College, 2003).

Conflict Security and Development Group, *A Review of Peace Operations: A Case for Change—Kosovo Study* (London: King's College, 2003).

Curtin, Philip D., *Cross-Cultural Trade in World History* (Cambridge: Cambridge University Press, 1987).

Cyert, Richard M. and James G. March, *A Behavioral Theory of the Firm* (Englewood Cliffs, New Jersey: Prentice-Hall, 1963).

Dahl, Robert and Charles E. Lindblom, *Politics, Economics and Welfare: Planning and Politico-Economic Systems Resolved into Basic Social Processes* (New York: Harper, 1953).

Day, Graham and Christopher Freeman, "Operationalizing the Responsibility to Protect—the Policekeeping Approach," *Global Governance* 11, 2 (April-June 2005), pp. 139–47.

Decker, Christopher, "Enforcing Human Rights: The Role of the UN Civilian Police in Kosovo," *International Peacekeeping* 13, 4 (2006), pp. 502–516.

Deflem, Matthew, *Policing World Society: Historical Foundations of International Police Cooperation* (Oxford: Oxford University Press, 2005).

Del Castillo, Graciana, *Rebuilding War-Torn States: The Challenge of Post-Conflict Economic Reconstruction* (Oxford: Oxford University Press, 2008).

Del Castillo, Graciana and Alvaro de Soto, "Obstacles to Peacebuilding," *Foreign Policy* 94 (Spring 1994), pp. 69–83.

Delasgues, Lorenzo, and Yama Torabi, *Reconstruction National Integrity SystemSurvey: Afghanistan 2007*. London: Tiri. http://www.tiri.org/dmdocuments/RNISS% 20Afghanistan.pdf (2007).

Delevic, Milica, *Regional Cooperation in the Western Balkans*, Chaillot Paper, No 104 (Paris: European Union Institute for Security Studies, 2007).

Deng, Francis, Sadikiel Kimaro, Terrence Lyons, Donald Rothchild and I. William Zartman, *Sovereignty as Responsibility: Conflict Management in Africa* (Washington, DC: Brookings Institute, 1996).

Deng, Yong, *China's Struggle for Status: The Realignment of International Relations* (Cambridge: Cambridge University Press, 2008).

D'Entreves, A.P., *The Notion of the State* (Oxford: Clarendon Press, 1967).

Des Forges, Alison, *Leave None to Tell the Story: Genocide in Rwanda* (New York: Human Rights Watch, 1999).

Dexing, Song and Liu Jinqi, "Guoji tixizhong de 'shibai guojia' xilun," *Xiandai guoji guanxi* 2 (2007), pp. 28–35.

Dijkzeul, Dennis and Yves Beigbeder, *Rethinking International Organizations: Pathology and Promise* (New York: Berghahn Books, 2003).

Dittmer, Lowell and Samuel S. Kim (eds), *China's Quest for National Identity* (Ithaca, NY: Cornell University Press, 1993).

Dobbins, James, Seth Jones, Keith Crane, Andrew Rathmell, Brett Steele, Richard Teltschick and Anga Timilsina, *The UN's Role in Nation-Building: From the Congo to Iraq* (Santa Monica: RAND, 2005).

Dobbins, James, Seth G. Jones, Benjamin Runkle, and Siddhart Mohandas, *Occupying Iraq: A History of the Coalition Provisional Authority* (Santa Monica: RAND, 2009).

Dodge, Toby, "The Changing Political Economy of Iraq: Sanctions, Invasion, Regime Change, Civil War and beyond," paper delivered at the conference 'Power after Peace: The Political Economy of Post-Conflict State Building,' held at King's College London, 10 December 2009.

Dongxiao, Chen *et al.*, *Lianheguo: xin yicheng he xin tiaozhan* (Beijing: Shishi chubanshe, 2004).

Donnelly, Jack, "Human Rights: a New Standard of Civilization?," *International Affairs* 74, 1 (1998), pp. 1–24.

Dower, John, *Embracing Defeat: Japan in the Aftermath of World War II* (London: Penguin, 1999).

Doyle, Michael W, "Kant, Liberal Legacies, and Foreign Affairs", *Philosophy and Public Affairs*, 12, 3, (1983a), pp. 205–235.

———, "Kant, Liberal Legacies, and Foreign Affairs, Part 2". *Philosophy and Public Affairs*, 12, 4, (1983b), pp. 323–353.

Doyle, Michael and Nicholas Sambanis, *Making War and Building Peace: United Nations Peace Operations* (Princeton: Princeton University Press, 2006).

Duffield, Mark, *Development, Security, and Unending War* (London: Polity, 2007).

—— *Global Governance and the New Wars* (London: Zed Books, 2001).

Durch, William J. (ed.), *Twenty-First Century Peace Operations* (Washington, DC: USIP, 2006).

Durch, William J., Victoria K. Holt, Caroline R. Earle and Moira K. Shanahan, *The Brahimi Report and the Future of UN Peace Operations* (Washington, DC: The Henry L. Stimson Center, 2003).

Dwan, Renata (ed.), *Executive Policing: Enforcing the Law in Peace Operations. SIPRI Research Report No. 16* (Oxford: Oxford University Press, 2002).

Dwan, Renata and Laura Bailey, *Liberia's Governance and Economic Management Assistance Programme: A Joint Review by DPKO Best Practices Section and the World Bank's Fragile States Group* (May 2006, DPKO).

Edelman, Murray, *The Symbolic Uses of Politics* (Urbana, IL: University of Illinois Press, 1964).

Eide, Barth, Anja Therese Kaspersen, Randolph Kent and Karin von Hippel, *Report on Integrated Missions: Practical Perspectives and Recommendations (Independent Study for the Expanded UN ECHA Core Group)* (Oslo: Norwegian Institute of International Affairs, 2005).

Eide, Barth et al., *Report on Integrated Missions; UN Department of Peace Keeping Operations/UN Department of Field Support, Peacekeeping Operations Principles and Guidelines (Capstone Doctrine)* (New York: United Nations, 2008).

Ellis, Stephen, "How to Rebuild Africa," *Foreign Affairs* 84 (September/October 2005), pp. 135–148.

—— *The Mask of Anarchy: the Destruction of Liberia and the Religious Dimension of an African Civil War* (London: Hurst, 1999).

ESI/LLA, *The Ottoman Dilemma: Power and Property Relations under the United Nations Mission in Kosovo* (Pristina: European Stability Initiative, 2002).

Etherington, Mark, *Revolt on the Tigris: The Al-Sadr Uprising and the Governing of Iraq* (London: Hurst, 2005).

Evans, Gareth, *The Responsibility to Protect: Ending Mass Atrocity Crimes Once and for All* (Washington, DC: The Brookings Institution, 2008).

Evans, Peter B., Dietrich Rueschemeter and Theda Skocpol, *Bringing the State Back In* (Cambridge: Cambridge University Press, 1985).

Evans, Anne, Nick Manning, Yasmin Osmani, Anne Tully and Andrew Wilder, *A Guide to Government in Afghanistan*. Washington:World Bank/AREU. http://www.areu.org.af/index.php?option=com_docman&task=doc_view&gid=250 (2004).

Fama, Eugene F., "Agency Problems and the Theory of the Firm," *Journal of Political Economy* 80, 2 (1980), pp. 288–307.

Fearon, James and David Laitin (2004), "Neotrusteeship and the Problem of Weak States," *International Security*, 28, 4 (Spring 2004), pp. 5–43.

Ferguson, Niall, *Colossus: The Rise and Fall of the American Empire* (London: Penguin, 2004).

# BIBLIOGRAPHY

Festinger, Leon, *A Theory of Cognitive Dissonance* (Stanford: Stanford University Press, 1957).

Fidler, David P., "The Return of the Standard of Civilization," *Chicago Journal of International Law* 2, 1 (2001), pp. 137–57.

Finnemore, Martha, *The Purpose of Intervention: Changing Beliefs about the Nature of Force* (Ithaca, NY: Cornell University Press, 2004).

Fortna, Virginia Page, and Lise Morje Howard, "Pitfalls and Prospects in the Peacekeeping Literature," *Annual Review of Political Science* 11 (2008), pp. 283–301.

Fox, Gregory H., "The Right to Political Participation in International Law," *Yale Journal of International Law*, 17, 2 (1992), pp. 539–607.

Francis, David J., *Child Soldiers in Africa: Challenges and Opportunities for Social Reintegration* (London: Zed Books, 2007).

Franck, Thomas, "The Emerging Right to Democratic Governance," *American Journal of International Law* 86, 1 (1992), pp. 46–91.

——— *The Power of Legitimacy Among Nations* (Oxford: Oxford University Press, 1990).

Franks, Jason and Oliver Richmond, "Coopting Liberal Peace-building: Untying the Gordian Knot in Kosovo," *Cooperation and Conflict* 43, 1 (2008), pp. 81–103.

Fravel, M. Taylor, "China's Attitude toward U.N. Peacekeeping Operations since 1989," *Asian Survey* 36, 11 (November 1996), pp. 1102–1121.

Fukuyama, Francis, *State Building: Governance and World Order in the Twenty-First Century* (London: Profile Books, 2005).

——— *The End of History and the Last Man* (New York: Avon Books, 1992).

——— "The End of History?," *The National Interest* 16 (1989), pp. 3–18.

Gaddis, John L., *Strategies of Containment* (Oxford: Oxford University Press, 2005).

Gelb, Leslie, *Power Rules* (London: HarperCollins, 2009).

Gellner, Ernest, *Nations and Nationalism* (Cornell University Press, 1983).

Gerspacher, Nadia, "History of International Police Cooperation: A 150 Year Evolution in Trends and Approaches" *Global Crime* 9: Issues 1–2 (May 2008), pp. 169–84.

——— "The Roles of International Police Cooperation Organizations: Beyond Mandates, Towards Unintended Roles," *European Journal of Crime, Criminal Law and Criminal Justice* 13, 3 (2005), pp. 413–34.

Geuss, Raymond, "Liberalism and its Discontents," *Outside Ethics* (Princeton: Princeton University Press: 2005), pp. 11–28.

Ghani, Ashraf and Claire Lockhart, *Fixing Failed States: A Framework for Rebuilding A Fractured World* (Oxford: Oxford University Press, 2007).

Gill, Bates and Chin-Hao Huang, "China's Expanding Peacekeeping Role: its Significance and the Policy Implications," *SIPRI Policy Brief* (February 2009).

Gill, Bates and James Reilly, "Sovereignty, Intervention and Peacekeeping: The View from Beijing," *Survival* 42, 3 (2000), pp. 41–59.

Gill, Bates and Yanzhong Huang, "Sources and Limits of Chinese "Soft Power"," *Survival* 48, 2 (Summer 2006), pp. 17–36.

Glaser, Bonnie S. and Phillip C. Saunders, "Chinese Civilian Foreign Policy Research Institutes: Evolving Roles and Increasing Influence," *China Quarterly* 171 (September 2002), pp. 597–616.

Gong, Gerrit W., *The Standard of Civilization in International Society* (Oxford: Clarendon Press, 1984).

Goodhand, Jonathan, "Frontiers and Wars: the Opium Economy in Afghanistan," paper for conference on the "Transformation of War Economies after Conflict," University of Plymouth.

Goudsblom, J. and S. Mennell (eds), *The Norbert Elias Reader* (Oxford: Blackwell, 1998).

Gow, James, *The Triumph of Lack of Will: International Diplomacy and the Yugoslav War* (London: Hurst, 1997).

Grabbe, Heather, *The EU's Transformative Power: Europeanization through Conditionality in Central and Eastern Europe* (Basingstoke: Palgrave, 2006).

Grant, Charles, "Observations on the State of Society Among the Asiatic Subjects of Great Britain," *Parliamentary Papers*, 1812–13 (282) x.31, mf 14.63–64, 45, 73.

Gray, John, *False Dawn: The Delusions of Global Capitalism* (London: Granta, 1998).

Greenhill, Kelly and Solomon Major, "The Perils of Profiling: Civil War Spoilers and the Collapse of Intrastate Peace Accords," *International Security* 31, 3 (Winter 2006/07), pp. 7–40.

Grob, Gerald and George Athan Billias, "American Imperialism: Altruism or Aggression?," *Interpretations of American History* (New York, 1992), pp. 163–74.

Gros, Jean-Germain, "Towards a Taxonomy of Failed States in the New World Order: Decaying Somalia, Liberia, Rwanda and Haiti," *Third World Quarterly* 17, 3 (1996), pp. 455–71.

Gurtov, Mel and Peter Van Ness, *Confronting the Bush Doctrine: Critical Views from the Asia-Pacific* (London: RoutledgeCurzon, 2005).

Haas, Peter M., "Epistemic Communities and International Policy Coordination," *International Organization* 46, 1 (1992), pp. 1–35.

Hailey, Lord, *An African Survey: A Study of Problems arising South of the Sahara* (Oxford: Oxford University Press for the Royal Institute of International Affairs, 1938).

Hailey, Lord, *The Future of Colonial Peoples* (Oxford: Oxford University Press, 1943).

Hansen, Annika, *From Congo to Kosovo: Civilian Police in Police Operations*, Adelphi Paper 343 (Oxford University Press, 2002).

Harris, David, "Liberia 2005: an Unusual African Post-conflict Election," *Journal of Modern African Studies* 44, 3 (2006), pp. 375–95.

Harris, Stuart, "The PRC's Quest for Great Power Status: A Long and Winding Road," *Working Paper* (no. 1998/4, Department of International Relations, Research School of Pacific and Asian Studies, Australian National Realations, 1998).

Hartley, L.P., *The Go Between* (London: Hamish Hamilton, 1953).

Hartz, Halvor, "UNPOL: The UN Instrument for Police Reform," *International Peacekeeping* 6, 4 (1999), pp. 27–42.

Hashim, Ahmed, *Insurgency and Counter-Insurgency in Iraq* (London: Hurst, 2006)
——— *Iraq's Sunni Insurgency*, Adelphi Paper 402 (Routledge, 2009).

Hegre, Havard *et al.*, "Towards a Democratic Civil Peace? Democracy, Political Change, and Civil War, 1816–1992," *American Political Science Review* 95, 1 (2001), pp. 17–33.

Held, David (ed.) *Prospects for Democracy: North, South, East, West* (Cambridge: Polity Press, 1996).

Helman, Gerald and Steven Ratner, "Saving Failed States," *Foreign Policy* (1992–93), pp. 3–20.

Herbst, Jeffrey, *States and Power in Africa: Comparative Lessons in Authority and Control* (Princeton: Princeton University Press, 2000).

Hesztera, Gerald, "The Future of the Civilian Police Within the OSCE Framework" *OSCE Yearbook* (1998).

Hill, Christopher and Michael Smith (eds), *International Relations and the European Union* (Oxford: Oxford University Press, 2005).

Himmelfarb, Gertrude (ed.), *Essays on Politics and Culture* (Gloucester, MA: Peter Smith, 1973).

Hippel, Karin von, *Democracy by Force: US Military Intervention in the Post-Cold War World* (Cambridge: Cambridge University Press, 1999).

Hobson, John A., *Imperialism: A Study* (London: George Allen & Unwin, 1968).

Hobson, John M., *The Eastern Origins of Western Civilisation* (Cambridge: Cambridge University Press, 2004).

Hochschild, Adam, *King Leopold's Ghost* (London: Pan General Non-Fiction, 2006).

Hohe, Tanja and Rod Nixon, *Reconciling Justice: "Traditional" Law and State Judiciary in East Timor* (Washington, DC: USIP, 2003).

Holbrooke, Richard, *To End a War* (New York: The Modern Library, 1999).

Holm, Tor Tanke and Espen Barth Eide, "Post-script: Towards Executive Authority Policing?: The Lesson of Kosovo," *International Peacekeeping* 6 (Winter 1999), pp. 210–20.

Holsti, Kalevi J., *The State, War, and the State of War* (Cambridge: Cambridge University Press, 1996).

Holzgrefe, J.L. and Robert O. Keohane, *Humanitarian Intervention: Ethical, Legal and Political Dilemmas* (Cambridge: Cambridge University Press, 2003).

Honghua, Men and Huang Haili, "Yingdui guojia shibai de bujiu cuoshi: jian lun Zhongmei anquan hezuo de zhanlüexing," *Meiguo yanjiu* 1 (2004), pp. 7–32.

Hood, Ludovic, "Security Sector Reform in East Timor 1999–2004," *International Peacekeeping* 13, 1 (March 2006), pp. 60–77.

Hopkins, A.G., "Comparing British and American Empires: a Review Article of Charles S. Maier, 'Among Empires: American Ascendancy and its Predecessors,' and Bernard Porter, 'Empire and Superempire: Britain, America and the World'", *Journal of Global History* (2007), pp. 395–404.

Howard, Lise Morjé, *UN Peacekeeping in Civil Wars* (Cambridge: Cambridge University Press, 2008).

Howard, Michael, *War and the Liberal Conscience* (London: Hurst, 2008).

Huntington, Samuel P., *Political Order in Changing Societies* (New Haven: Yale University Press, 1968).

——— "The Clash of Civilizations?," *Foreign Affairs* 72, 3 (Summer 1993), pp. 22–49.

——— *The Clash of Civilisations and the Remaking of World Order* (New York: Touchstone, 1996).

Hurd, Ian, *After Anarchy: Legitimacy and Power in the United Nations Security Council* (Princeton: Princeton University Press, 2007).

Hurrell, Andrew, "Legitimacy and the Use of Force: Can the Circle be Squared?," *Review of International Studies*, 31 (2005), pp. 15–32.

ICISS, *The Responsibility to Protect* (Ottawa: International Development Research Centre, 2001).

International Crisis Group, *Liberia and Sierra Leone: Rebuilding Failed States*, Africa Report No. 87, 8 December 2004.

——— "China's Growing Role in UN Peacekeeping," *Asia Report* No. 166, 17 April 2009, p. 10, fn 91.

——— "Bosnia's Stalled Police Reform: No Progress, No EU" Europe Report No. 164 (6 September 2005).

——— *What Happened to the KLA?* Report No. 88 (2000).

——— *Violence in Kosovo: Who's Killing Whom?* ICG Balkans Report N78 (2 November 1999).

——— *Waiting for UNMIK—Local Administration in Kosovo* (Pristina: ICG, 1999).

International Rescue Committee, "Mortality in the Democratic Republic of Congo: An Ongoing Crisis" (New York: January, 2008).

Ignatieff, Michael, *Empire Lite: Nation-Building in Bosnia, Kosovo, Afghanistan* (London: Vintage, 2003).

Ikenberry, G. John, *After Victory: Institutions, Strategic Restraint, and the Rebuilding of Order after Major Wars* (Princeton: Princeton University Press, 2000).

——— "America's Imperial Strategy," *Foreign Affairs* 81, 5 (2002).

——— *Liberal Order and Imperial Ambition: Essays on American Power and World Politics* (Cambridge: Polity Press, 2006).

Indyk, Martin, "A Trusteeship for Palestine?," *Foreign Affairs* 82, 3 (2003), pp. 51–66.

Jackson, Robert H., *Quasi-States: Sovereignty, International Relations and the Third World* (Cambridge: Cambridge University Press, 1990).

Jackson, Stephen, "Making a Killing: Criminality and Coping in the Kivu War Economy," *Review of African Political Economy* 29, 93/94 (2002), pp. 517–36.

Jahn, Beate, "The Tragedy of Liberal Diplomacy: Democratization, Intervention, and Statebuilding (Parts I and II)," *Journal of Intervention and Statebuilding* 1, 1&2 (2007), pp. 87–106 and pp. 211–29.

James, Alan, "The Congo Controversies," *International Peacekeeping* 1, 1 (1994), pp. 44–58.

Jansen, G.H., *Nonalignment and the Afro-Asian States* (New York: Praeger, 1966).

Jenkins, Rob, "The UN Peacebuilding Commission and the Dissemination of International Norms," *Working Paper 38* (Crisis States Research Centre, London School of Economics, June 2008).

Johnston, Alastair I., "Is China a Status Quo Power?," *International Security* 27, 4 (Spring 2003), pp. 5–56.

Johnston, Alastair I. and Robert S. Ross (eds), *New Directions in the Study of China's Foreign Policy* (Stanford: Stanford University Press, 2006).

Judah, Timothy, *Kosovo: War and Revenge* (New Haven: Yale University Press, 2000).

Kalyvas, Stathis, "The Paradox of Terrorism in Civil War," *Journal of Ethics* 8, 1 (2004), pp. 97–138.

Kandeh, Jimmy D., "Sierra Leone's Post-Conflict Elections of 2002," *Journal of Modern African Studies* 41, 3 (2003), pp. 189–216.

———— "Rogue Incumbents, Donor Assistance and Siera Leone's Second Post-Conflict Elections of 2007," *Journal of Modern African Studies* 46, 4 (2008), pp. 603–635.

Kaplan, Robert, *The Coming Anarchy: Shattering the Dreams of the Post-Cold War* (New York: Random House, 2000).

Karnow, Stanley, *In Our Image: America's Empire in the Philippines* (New York: Random House, 1989).

Kaufmann, Chaim, "Possible and Impossible Solutions to Ethnic Civil Wars," *International Security* 20, 2 (1996), pp. 136–75.

Kay, John, *The Truth about Markets* (London: Penguin Books, 2003).

Kedourie, Elie (ed.), *Nationalism in Asia and Africa* (Abingdon: Frank Cass, 1974).

Keen, David, *Conflict and Collusion in Sierra Leone* (Oxford: James Currey, 2005).

———— *Endless War: Hidden Functions of the "War on Terror"* (London: Pluto Press, 2006).

———— *The Economic Functions of Violence in Civil Wars* (Oxford: Oxford University Press, 1996).

Kennan, George, *American Diplomacy* (Chicago: University of Chicago Press, 1984).

Kennedy, Paul, *The Rise and Fall of the Great Powers: Economic Change and Military Conflict from 1500 to 2000* (New York: Random House, 1987).

Kent, Ann, *China, the United Nations, and Human Rights* (Philadelphia: University of Pennsylvania Press, 1999).

Keohane, Robert O., *After the Cold War: International Institutions and State Strategies in Europe 1989–1991* (Cambridge, MA: Harvard University Press, 1993).

Keohane, Robert O. and Joseph S. Nye, *Power and Interdependence* (Glenview, IL: Scott & Foresman, 1989).

Kerr, George H., *Okinawa, The History of an Island People*, Revised Edition (Boston: Tuttle Publishing—Periplus Editions (HK)Ltd, 2000).

Khan, Ayesha, *Conceptualising AfPak: The Prospects and Perils*, London, Chatham House Programme Paper, January 2010.

Kilcullen, David, *The Accidental Guerrilla: Fighting Small Wars in the Midst of a Big One* (London: Hurst, 2006).

Kim, Samuel S., *China, the United Nations, and World Order* (Princeton: Princeton University Press, 1979).

Kim, Samuel S. (ed.), *China and the World: Chinese Foreign Policy Faces the New Millennium* (Boulder, CO: Westview Press, 1998).

King, Iain and Whit Mason, *Peace at Any Price: How the World Failed Kosovo* (London: Hurst, 2006).

Kingdon, John, *Agendas, Alternatives and Public Policies* (New York: HarperCollins, 1995).

Kissinger, Henry, *Does America Still Need a Foreign Policy* (London: Simon and Schuster, 2001).

Knaus, Gerald and Felix Martin, "Travails of the European Raj," *Journal of Democracy* 14, 3 (2003), pp. 60–74.

Knaus, Gerald and Marcus Cox, "Building Democracy after Conflict: The Helsinki Moment in Southeastern Europe," *Journal of Democracy* 16, 1 (2005), pp. 39–53.

Krasner, Stephen, "Sharing Sovereignty: New Institutions for Collapsed and Failing States," *International Security* 29, 2 (2004), pp. 85–120.

Krauthammer, Charles, "Democratic Realism: An American Foreign Policy for a Unipolar World," *Irving Kristol Lecture* (American Enterprise Institution, November 20, 2004).

———— "The Unipolar Moment Revisited," *The National Interest* 70, (2002/2003), pp. 5–20.

Kuran, Timur, *Private Truth and Public Lies: The Social Consequences of Preference Falsification* (Cambridge, MA: Harvard University Press, 1995).

Kurlantzick, Joshua, *Charm Offensive: How China's Soft Power Is Transforming the World* (New Haven: Yale University Press, 2007).

Lang, Anthony F., *Agency and Ethics: The Politics of Military Intervention* (Albany: State University of New York Press, 2002).

Lapaix, Mario, *US. Intervention in Haiti: An Assessment of the International Police Monitoring Program 1994–1995 and Beyond* (Navy War College, 2002).

Laslett, Peter (ed.), (Cambridge: Cambridge University Press, 1999).

Le Billon, Philippe, "Corrupting Peace? Peacebuilding and Post-Conflict Corruption," *International Peacekeeping*, 15, 3 (2008), pp. 344–61.

Lebow, Richard N., *The Tragic Vision of Politics: Ethics, Interests and Orders* (Cambridge: Cambridge University Press, 2003).

Leonard, Mark, *Re-Ordering the World* (London: The Foreign Policy Centre, 2002).

Liebscher, Klaus (ed.), European *Economic Integration and South-East Europe: Challenges and Prospects* (Cheltenham: Edward Elgar, 2005).

Ligang, Nie, "Lianheguo feizhiminhuajizhi qianxi," *Guoji luntan* 3, 3 (June 2001), pp. 42–7.

Lingliang, Zeng, "Lun lengzhan hou shidai de guojia zhuquan," *Zhongguo faxue* 1, (1998), pp. 109–120.

Lipson, Michael, "A Garbage Can Model of UN Peacekeeping," *Global Governance* 13, 1 (2007), pp. 79–97.

———— "Peacekeeping: Organized Hypocrisy," *European Journal of International Relations* 13, 1 (2007), pp. 5–34.

Litwak, Robert S., *Regime Change: US Strategy Through the Prism of 9/11* (Washington, DC: Woodrow Wilson Center Press, 2007).

———— *Rogue States and US Foreign Policy: Containment After the Cold War* (Washington, DC: Woodrow Wilson Center Press, 2000).

Logan, Rayford, "The Operation of the Mandate System in Africa," *Journal of Negro History* 13, 4 (October 1928), pp. 423–77.

Londey, Peter, *Other People's Wars* (Crows Nest, New South Wales: Allen and Unwin, 2004).

Long, Austin, "The Anbar Awakening," *Survival* 50, 2 (April/May 2008), pp. 67–94.

Long, Roger (ed.), *The Man On the Spot: Essays on British Empire History* (Westport: Greenwood Publishing, 1995).

Louis, William R. and Alaine Low (eds), *The Oxford History of the British Empire*, Volume 2, 6th Edition (Oxford: Oxford University Press, 2009).

Lowe, Vaughan, Adam Roberts, Jennifer Welsh and Dominik Zaum (eds), *The Security Council and War: The Evolution of Thought and Practice since 1945* (Oxford: Oxford University Press, 2008).

Lugard, Frederick D., *The Dual Mandate in British Tropical Africa*, 3rd Edition (Edinburgh and London: William Blackwood and Sons, 1926).

Luzhi, Chen and Li Tiecheng (eds), *Lianheguo yu shijie zhixu* (Beijing: Beijing yuyan xueyuan chubanshe, 1993).

MacFarlane, S. Neil, *Intervention in Contemporary Politics* (London: Routledge, 2005).

Mallaby, Sebastian, "The Reluctant Imperialist: Terrorism, Failed States, and the Case for American Empire," *Foreign Affairs* 81, 2 (2002), pp. 2–7.

Mandelbaum, Michael, "Foreign Policy as Social Work," *Foreign Affairs*, Jan./Feb. 1996.

Mani, Rama, "Contextualizing Police Reform: Security, the Rule of Law, and Post-Conflict Peacebuilding," *International Peacekeeping* 6, 4 (1999), pp. 11–12.

Manning, Nick, William Byrd, Andrew Wilder and Anne Evans. *Assessing Subnational Administration in Afghanistan: Early Observations andRecommendations for Action.* Working Draft. Afghanistan Research and Evaluation Unit and World Bank (2003).

Manning, Nicholas (Task Leader), *Afghanistan: Subnational Administration in Afghanistan (In Two Volumes) Volume I.* Afghanistan Research and Evaluation Unit, and the Poverty Reduction and Economic Management Sector Unit South Asia Region (2004).

Mansfield, Edward D. and Jack Snyder, "Democratization and the Danger of War," *International Security* 20, 1 (1995), pp. 5–38.

March, James G. and Johan P. Olsen, "The Institutional Dynamics of International Political Orders," *International Organisation* 52, 4 (1998), pp. 943–69.

Marenin, Otwin, "The Goal of Democracy in International Police Assistance Programs," *Policing* 21, 1 (1998), pp. 159–77.

Mates, Leo, *Es begann in Belgrad* (Augsburg: R.S. Schulz, 1982).

Matthews, Jessica T., "Redefining Security," *Foreign Affairs* 68, 2 (Spring 1989), pp. 162–77.

Maxwell, Neville, *India's China War* (New York: Pantheon Books, 1971).

Mayall, James, *Nationalism and International Society* (Cambridge: Cambridge University Press, 1990).

——— "Introduction," in Mats Berdal and Spyros Economides (eds), *United Nations Interventionism, 1991–2004* (Cambridge: Cambridge University Press, 2007).

Mayall, James (ed.), *The New Interventionism* (Cambridge: Cambridge University Press, 1996).

Mayall, James and Krishnan Srinavasan, *Toward the New Horizon: World Order in the Twenty-First Century* (New Delhi: Terminus Books, 2009).

Mazower, Mark, *No Enchanted Palace: The End of Empire and the Ideological Origins of the United Nations* (Princeton: Princeton University Press, 2009).

Mazower, Mark, "Violence and the State in the Twentieth Century," *American Historical Review* 107, 4 (2002), pp. 1158–78.

McDougall, Walter, *Promised Land, Crusader State: The American Encounter with the World since 1776* (Boston: Mariner Books, 1998).

McMahon, Robert, interviewing Said Jawad Capital Interview: Kabul Lacks Capacity to Govern. Council on Foreign Relations. http://www.cfr.org/publication/12739/afghanistan_lacks_capacity_to_govern.html (28 February 2007).

Mearsheimer, John, *The Tragedy of Great Power Politics* (New York: Norton, 2001).

Meili, Wang, "Guojia zhuquan yuanze shizhong shi guojifa he guoji guanxi de jichu," *Xiandai faxue* 1 (1998), pp. 124–6.

Metcalf, Thomas R., *Ideologies of the Raj* (Cambridge: Cambridge University Press, 1997).

Mill, James, *The History of British India* (Chicago: University of Chicago Press, 1975).

Mill, John S., *Considerations on Representative Government* (Amherst, NY: Prometheus Books, 1991).

Milliken, Jennifer (ed.), *State Failure, Collapse & Reconstruction* (Oxford: Blackwell, 2003).

Mishra, Pankaj, "Afghanistan: The India and Kashmir Connection," *New York Review of Books* 57, 1, 14 January 2010.

Morel, E.D., *Red Rubber* (London: T. Fisher Unwin, 1906).

Morgenthau, Hans, "The Political Conditions for an International Police Force," *International Organization* 17, 2 (Spring 1963), pp. 393–403.

Morris, Justin and Nicholas J. Wheeler, "The Security Council's Crisis of Legitimacy and the Use of Force," *International Politics* 44, 2&3 (March/May 2007), pp. 214–31.

Nadelmann, Ethan A., *Cops Across Borders: The Internationalization of U.S. Criminal Law Enforcement* (University Park: The Pennsylvania State University Press, 1993).

Nardin, Terry and Luke O'Sullivan (eds), *Lecture in the History of Political Thought* (Exeter: Imprint Academic, 2006).

Nederlands Instituut voor Oorlogsdocumentatie, *Srebrenica, A "Safe" Area. Reconstruction, Background, Consequences and Analyses of the Fall of a Safe Area*, (Amsterdam: NIOD, 2002).

Newman, Edward and Oliver P. Richmond (eds), *The United Nations and Human Security* (London: Palgrave, 2001).

Nield, Rachel, "Democratic Police Reforms in War-Torn Societies," *Conflict, Security and Development* 1:1 (2001).

Nkrumah, Kwame, *Towards Colonial Freedom: Africa and the Struggle Agsinst World Imperialism* (London: Heinemann, 1962).

Noetzel, Timo and Benjamin Schreer, *Spezialkräfte der Bundeswehr. Strukturerfordernisse für den Auslandseinsatz* (Berlin: Stiftung Wissenschaft und Politik, 2007).

Nye Jr., Joseph S., "Soft Power," *Foreign Policy* 80, Twentieth Anniversary (Autumn 1990), pp. 153–71.

Nyíri, Pál, "The Yellow Man's Burden: Chinese Migrants on a Civilizing Mission," *The China Journal* 56 (2006), pp. 83–106.

Oakley, Robert B., Michael J. Dziedzic and Eliot M. Goldberg (eds), *Policing the New World Disorder* (Washington, DC: National Defence University, 1998).

Oakley, Robert B., Michael J. Dziedzic and Eliot M. Goldberg, *Policing the New World Disorder* (Washington, DC: National Defense University, 2002).

O'Hanlon, Michael E. and Edward P. Joseph, "Toolbox: A Bosnia Option for Iraq," *The American Interest* (November/December 2006).

Ombudsperson Institution in Kosovo, *Second Annual Report 2001–2002*, Pristina, 10 July 2002.

Onley, James, *The Arabian Frontier of the Raj, Merchants, Rulers and the British in the Nineteenth Century Gulf* (Oxford: Oxford University Press, 2007).

Osland, Kari M., "The EU Police Mission in Bosnia and Herzegovina," *International Peacekeeping* (2004), pp. 544–60.

Packer, George, *The Assassin's Gate: America in Iraq* (New York: Farrar, Straus and Giroux, 2005).

Pagden, Anthony, *Lords of All the World: Ideologies of Empire in Spain, Britain and France, c.1500-c.1800* (New Haven: Yale University Press, 1995).

Pagden, Anthony, *Peoples and Empires* (London: Phoenix Press, 2001).

Pakenham, Thomas, *The Scramble for Africa* (London: Abacus, 1991).

Paris High Level Forum, "Paris Declaration on Aid Effectiveness," 2 March 2009.

Paris, Roland, "International Peacebuilding and the 'Mission civilisatrice,'" *Review of International Studies* 28, 4 (2002), pp. 637–656.

——— "Peacekeeping and the Constraints of Global Culture," *European Journal of International Relations* 9, 3 (2003), pp. 441–73.

——— *At War's End: Building Peace after Civil Conflict* (Cambridge: Cambridge University Press, 2004).

Paris, Roland, and Timothy D. Sisk (eds), *The Dilemmas of Statebuilding* (London: Routledge, 2008).

Parliamentary Assembly of the Council of Europe, *Honouring of Obligations and Commitments of Bosnia and Herzegovina* (Strasbourg: 4 June 2004).

PBC/1/BDI/4, Strategic Framework for Peacebuilding in Burundi, 22 June 2007.

PBC/1/BDI/4, Strategic Framework for Peacebuilding in Burundi, 30 July 2007.

PBC/2/SLE/9, UN General Assembly and Security Council, "Progress Report on the Implementation of the Sierra Leone Peacebuilding Cooperation Framework," 23 June 2008.

PBC/2/BDI/10, UN General Assembly and Security Council, "Review of Progress in the Implementation of the Strategic Framework for Peacebuilding in Burundi," 9 July 2008.

PBC/2/SLE/1, Sierra Leone Peacebuilding Cooperation Framework, 3 December 2007.

PBC/3/CAF/7, Strategic Framework for Peacebuilding in the Central African Republic 2009–2011, 9 June 2009.

PBC/3/GNB/3, Strategic Framework for Peacebuilding in Guinea-Bissau, 2 October 2008.

Peake, Gordon and Kaysie Studdard Brown, "Policebuilding: The International Deployment Group in the Solomon Islands," *International Peacekeeping* 12, 4 (2005), pp. 520–32.

Pedersen, Susan, "The Meaning of the Mandates System: An Argument," *Geschichte und Gesellschaft* 32, 4 (2006), pp. 560–82.

Perham, Margery, *Some Problems of Indirect Rule: Colonial Sequence, 1930 to 1949* (London: Methuen, 1967).

——— *The Colonial Reckoning* (London: Collins, 1961).

Perito, Robert M., "Police in Peace and Stability Operations: Evolving US Policy and Practice," *International Peacekeeping* 15, 1 (2008), pp. 59–60.

Philips, C.H. (ed.), *The Correspondence of Lord William Cavendish Bentinck*, (Oxford: Oxford University Press, 1977).

Piiparinen, Touko, "The Lessons of Darfur for the Future of Humanitarian Intervention," *Global Governance* 13, 3 (2007), pp. 365–90.

Pomeranz, Kenneth, "Imperialism, Development, and 'Civilizing' Missions, Past and Present," Daedalus, 134 (2), (2005), pp. 34–45.

Pouligny, Béatrice, "Civil Society and Post-Conflict Peace Building: Ambiguities of International Programs Aimed at Building 'New Societies'", *Security Dialogue*, 36, 4, (2005), pp. 447–462.

——— *Peace Operations Seen from Below: UN Missions and Local People* (London: Hurst, 2006).

Power, Samantha, *A Problem from Hell: America and the Age of Genocide* (New York: Perennial, 2002).

——— "Bystanders to Genocide," *The Atlantic Monthly* 288, 2 (2001), pp. 84–108.

Power, Samantha, *Chasing the Flame: Sérgio Vieira de Mello and the Fight to Save the World* (London: Allen Lane, 2008).

Pridham, Geoffrey, "Change and Continuity in the European Union's Political Conditionality: Aims, Approaches and Priorities," *Democratization* 14, 3 (2007), pp. 446–71.

Pugh, Michael, Neil Cooper with Jonathan Goodhand, *War Economies in a Regional Context: Challenges of Transformation* (Boulder, CO: Lynne Rienner, 2004).

Qing, Huang, "Qiangquan zhengshi de zaoshi zhi lun," *Renmin Ribao* (18 April 2002), p. 3.

Raeymaekers, Timothy, "The Power of Protection: Governance and Transborder Trade on the Congo-Ugandan Frontier" (PhD Dissertation: University of Ghent, 2006).

Rajan, Mannaraswamighala S., *Nonalignment and the Nonaligned Movement* (New Delhi: Vikas, 1990).

Ramesh, Jairam, "'Yankee Go Home and Take Me with you': Yet Another Perspective on Indo-American relations," *Economic and Political Weekly* 34, 50 (December 1999), pp. 3532–44.

Rathmell, Andrew, "Planning Post-Conflict Reconstruction in Iraq: What Can we Learn?," *International Affairs* 81 (2005), pp. 1013–1038.

Rawski, Frederick, "To Waive or not to Waive? Immunity and Accountability in U.N. Peacekeeping Operations," *Connecticut Journal of International Law* 18, 1 (2002), pp. 103–32.

Ray, Aswini K., *Western Realism and International Relations: a Non-Western View* (New Delhi, 2004).

# BIBLIOGRAPHY

Reno, William, "Anti-corruption efforts in Liberia: Are they Aimed at the Right Targets?," *International Peacekeeping* 15, 3 (2008), pp. 387–404.

Reus-Smit, Christian, "International Crises of Legitimacy," *International Politics* 44, 2&3 (2007), pp. 157–74.

Rich, Roland and Edward Newman, *The UN Role in Promoting Democracy: Between Ideals and Reality* (Tokyo: United Nations University Press, 2004).

Richards, Paul, *Fighting for the Rain Forest: War, Youth and Resources in Sierra Leone* (Oxford: James Currey, 1996).

Richmond, Oliver, *The Transformation of Peace* (Basingstoke: Palgrave, 2005).

Richmond, Oliver and Jason Franks, "Liberal Peacebuilding in Timor Leste: The Emperor's new Clothes?," *International Peacekeeping* 15, 2 (2008), pp. 185–200.

Ricks, Thomas E., *Fiasco* (London: Allan Lane, 2006).

Rieff, David, *A Bed for the Night: Humanitarianism in Crisis* (London: Vintage, 2002).

Robinson, Kenneth, *The Dilemmas of Trusteeship: Aspects of British Colonial Policy between the Wars* (London: Oxford University Press, 1965).

Robinson, Ronald, *The Dilemmas of Trusteeship: Aspects of British Colonial Policy Between the Wars* (London: Oxford University Press, 1965).

Robinson, Thomas W. and David Shambaugh, *Chinese Foreign Policy: Theory and Practice* (Oxford: Clarendon Press, 1994).

Rohland, Klaus and Sarah Cliffe, *The East Timor Reconstruction Program: Successes, Problems, and Tradeoffs* (Washington, DC: The World Bank, 2002).

Ross, Stephen A., "The Economic Theory of Agency: The Principal's Problem," *American Economic Review* 63, 2 (1973), pp. 134–9.

Rotberg, Robert I., "The New Nature of Nation-State Failure," *Washington Quarterly* 25, 3 (2002), pp. 85–96.

Rotberg, Robert I. (ed.), *When States Fail: Causes and Consequences* (Princeton: Princeton University Press, 2004).

Roy, Denny, "China and the War on Terrorism," *Orbis* 46, 3 (Summer 2002), pp. 511–21.

——— "The China Threat" Issue: Major Arguments," *Asian Survey* 36, 8 (1996), pp. 758–71.

Rubin, Barnett, "The Political Economy of War and Peace in Afghanistan," *World Development* 28, 10 (2000), pp. 1789–1803.

Rubin, Barnett, Humayun Hamidzada, and Abby Stoddard, *Through the Fog of Peacebuilding: Evaluating the Reconstruction of Afghanistan*. Center on International Cooperation, Program in Conflict Prevention, Recovery and Peacebuilding, http://www.cmi.no/pdf/?file=/afghanistan/doc/CIC-EvaluatingTheReconstructionOfAfghanistan.pdf (2003).

Ruggie, John, *Constructing the World Polity: Essays on International Institutionalization* (London: Routledge, 1998).

Ryan, Paul B., *The Panama Canal Controversy: U.S. Diplomacy and Defense Interests* (Stanford, CA: Hoover Institution Press, 1977).

Scharpf, Fritz, *Governing Europe: Effective and Democratic?* (Oxford: Oxford University Press, 1990).

Schimmelfennig, Frank and Ulrich Sedelmeier (eds), *The Europeanization of Central and Eastern Europe* (Ithaca, NY: Cornell University Press, 2005).

Schmidt, Bettina E. and Ingo W. Schroeder (eds), *Anthropology of Violence and Conflict* (London: Routledge, 2001).

Schnabel, Albrecht and Ramesh Thakur (eds), *Kosovo and the Challenge of Humanitarian Intervention: Selective Indignation, Collective Action and International Citizenship* (Tokyo: United Nations University Press, 2000).

Scholte, Jan Aart, *Globalization: A Critical Introduction* (London: Palgrave Macmillan, 2005).

Scott, Amy, "The United Nations Peacebuilding Commission: An Early Assessment," *Journal of Peacebuilding & Development* 4, 2 (2008).

Scott, James, *Seeing Like a State* (New Haven: Yale University Press, 1998).

Secretary-General's High-Level Panel on Threats, *Report: A More Secure World. Our Shared Responsibility Challenges and Change* (New York: United Nations, 2004).

Seibel, Wolfgang, "Successful Failure: An Alternative View on Organizational Coping," *American Behavorial Scientist* 39, 8 (1996), pp. 1011–1024.

Simmons, Alan J., "Justification and Legitimacy," *Ethics* 109, 4 (1999), pp. 739–71.

Simpson, Gerry, *Great Powers and Outlaw States: Unequal Sovereigns in the International Legal Order* (Cambridge: Cambridge University Press, 2004).

Sismandis, Roxanne V., *Police Functions in Peace Operations: Reports from a Workship Organized by the United States Institute for Peace* (Washington, DC: US Institute for Peace, 1997).

Slaughter, Anne-Marie, "America's Edge: Power in the Networked Century," *Foreign Affairs*, January–February 2009.

Smith, General Sir Rupert, *The Utility of Force* (London: Allen Lane, 2005).

Smith, Karen E., *The Making of EU Foreign Policy: The Case of Eastern Europe* (Basingstoke: Palgrave, 2004).

Smith, Mike (Major General) [deputy commander of UN forces in East Timor], with Moren Dee, *Peacekeeping in East Timor: The Path to Independence* (Boulder, CO: Lynne Rienner, 2003).

Smith Jnr, Warren W., *China's Tibet? Autonomy or Assimilation* (Lanham, MD: Rowman and Littlefield, 2008).

Soares de Oliveira, Ricardo, "Illiberal Peacebuilding in Angola," *Journal of Modern African Studies*, 49, 2 (2011), pp. 287–314.

Stafford, F.E., "The Ex-Italian Colonies," *International Affairs* 25, 1 (January 1949), pp. 47–55.

Stebbins, Richard P., *The United States in World Affairs* (New York, 1952).

Stedman, Stephen J., "Spoiler Problems in Peace Processes," *International Security* 22, 2 (Fall 1997), pp. 5–53.

Stephen, James Fitzjames, "Foundations of the Government in India," *Nineteenth Century* 80 (1883), pp. 541–68.

Stewart, Rory, *The Prince of the Marshes, and Other Occupational Hazards of a Year in Iraq* (New York: Harcourt, 2006).

Stokes, Eric, *The English Utilitarians and India* (Oxford: Oxford University Press, 1959).

Strazzari, Francesco, "*L'Oevre au Noir*: The Shadow Economy of Kosovo's Independence," *International Peacekeeping* 15, 2 (2008), pp. 155–70.

Suchman, Mark, "Managing Legitimacy: Strategic and Institutional Approaches," *Academy of Management Review* 20, 3 (1995), pp. 571–610.

Suhrke, Astri, "Peacekeepers as Nation-builders: The Dilemmas of the UN in East Timor," *International Peacekeeping* 8, 4 (2001), pp. 1–20.

Suzuki, Shogo, "Chinese Soft Power, Insecurity Studies, Myopia and Fantasy," *Third World Quarterly* 30, 4 (2009), pp. 779–93.

———— *Civilization and Empire: China and Japan's Encounter with European International Society* (London: Routledge, 2009).

———— "Seeking 'Legitimate' Great Power Status in Post-Cold War International Society: China and Japan's Participation in UNPKO," *International Relations* 22, 1 (2008), pp. 45–63.

Tabeau, Ewa and Jakub Bijak, "War-related Deaths in the 1992–1995 Armed Conflicts in Bosnia and Herzegovina: A Critique of Previous Estimates and Recent Results," *European Journal of Population* 21, 2/3 (2005), pp. 187–215.

Tao, Jiang, "Meiguo waijiao zhengce zhong de 'guojia chongjian' wenti," *Waijiao pinglun* 87 (February 2006), pp. 83–7.

Theidon, Kimberly, "Reconstructing Masculinities: The Disarmament, Demobilization, and Reintegration of Former Combatants in Colombia," *Human Rights Quarterly* 31 (2009), pp. 1–34.

Thomas, Lanny, "The Imperial Republic: A Comparison of the Insular Territories under US. Dominion after 1898," *Pacific Historical Review* 71, 4 (November 2002), pp. 535–74.

Thornton, Archibald P., *Doctrines of Imperialism* (New York: John Wiley, 1965).

Tierney, Brian, "The Prince is Not Bound by the Laws—Accursius and the Origins of the Modern State," *Comparative Studies in Society and History* 5, 4 (1963), pp. 378–400.

Tilly, Charles, "War Making and State Making as Organized Crime" in Peter B. Evans, Dietrich Rueschmeyer, and Theda Skocpol (eds), *Bringing the State Back In* (Cambridge: Cambridge University Press, 1985).

Todorova, Maria, *Imagining the Balkans* (Oxford: Oxford University Press, 1997).

Trivkovic, Srdja, *The Krajina Chronicle, A History of Serbs in Croatia, Slavonia and Dalmatia* (Chicago, Ottawa and London: the Lord Byron Foundation of Balkan Studies, 2010).

Tsebelis, George, *Veto Players* (Princeton: Princeton University Press, 2002).

Tripp, Charles, "After Saddam," *Survival* 44, 4 (October 2002), pp. 23–37.

Tucker, Robert and David Hendrickson, *The Imperial Temptation: the World Order and America's Purpose* (New York: Council on Foreign Relations Press, 1992).

UN Document A/47/285, 25 June 1992.

UN Document A/59/565, Report of the High Level Panel on Threats, Challenges and Change, "A More Secure World: Our Shared Responsibility," 2 December 2004.

UN Document S/24183, 25 June 1992.

UN Document A/RES/47/209, 24 March 1993.

UN Document A/55/305-S/2000/809, 21 August 2000.

UN Document A/63/677.

UN Docment A/55/305-S/2000/809 Report of the Panel on United Nations Peace Operations, 21 August 2000.

UN Document (Internal), "Monthly Military and Civilian Police Contributions," 31 December 1999.

UN Document S/2006/976, Report of the Panel of Experts concerning Liberia, 15 December 2006.

UN Document A/47/277-S/24111, UN Secretary-General, "An Agenda for Peace," June 17 1992.

UN Document A/59/2005, UN Secretary-General, "In Larger Freedom: Towards Development, Security and Human Rights for All," 21 March 2005.

UN Document A/RES/60/1, "Resolution adopted by the General Assembly: 60/1. 2005 World Summit Outcome," 24 October 2005.

UN Document S/20168, Report of the Trusteeship Council to the Security Council on the Trust Territory of the Pacific Islands, 17 December 1987–19 July 1988.

UN Document S/1994/346, Report of the Trusteeship Council to the Security Council on the Trust Territory of the Pacific Islands, 22 December 1992–18 January 1993.

UN Document S/1999/987, Report of the Secretary General on the United Nations Interim Administration Mission in Kosovo, 16 September 1999.

UN Document S/1999/1024, Report of the UN Secretary-General on the Situation in East Timor.

UN Document A/59/2005, *In Larger Freedom: Towards Development, Security and Human Rights for All: Report of the Secretary-General*, 21 March 2005.

UN Document S/2001/42, Report of the Panel on United Nations Peace Operations (The Brahimi Report), 21 August 2000.

UN Document S/PV.4011, Ambassador Shen Guofang's statement at the 4011th UNSC meeting, 10 June 1999.

UN Document S/PV.4844, Minutes of the 4844th meeting of UNSC, 16 October 2003.

UN Document. S/PV.5839 of 18 Febuary 2008.

UN Document S/RES/1511, United Nations Security Council Resolution (UNSC) 1511 (2003), 16 October 2003 (2003).

UN Document S/23500, "Note by President of the Security Council concerning the Responsibility of the Security Council in the Maintenance of International Peace and Security," 31 January 1992.

UN Document A/47/277, Boutros Boutros-Ghali, "An Agenda for Peace," 17 June 1992.

UN General Assembly Official Records, 929th Plenary Meeting, A/PV 929, 1047.

UN General Assembly, "Responsibility to Protect Populations from Genocide, War Crimes, Ethnic Cleansing and Crimes against Humanity."

UN Document S/2006/1696, UN Security Council, "Non-Proliferation," July 31 2006.

UNMIK Regulation 2000/38, On the Establishment of an Ombudsperson Institution in Kosovo, 30 June 2000.

UNMIK, Regulation 1999/1, On the Authority of the Interim Administration in Kosovo, 25 July 1999.

UNTAET, Regulation 1999/1, On the Authority of the Transitional Administration in East Timor, 27 November 1999.

UN General Assembly Resolution 60/180 of 30 December 2005.

UN Security Council Resolution 1244 of 10 June 1999.

UN Security Council Resolution 1272 of 25 October 1999.

UN Security Council Resolution 1483 of 22 May 2003.

UN Security Council Resolution 1645 of 20 December 2005.

UN Development Programme *Human Development Report, 1994* (Oxford: Oxford University Press, 1994).

US Government, *The National Security Strategy of the United States of America* (September 2002).

Urquhart, Brian, *A Life of Peace and War* (New York: Harper and Row, 1987).

US National Institute of Justice and the Bureau of Narcotics and Law Enforcement Affairs, U.S. Department of State, *Policing in Emerging Democracies* (Washington, DC: US Department of State, 1997).

Van den Boogert, Maurits H., *The Capitulations and the Ottoman Legal System, Qadis, Consuls, and Baraths in the Eighteenth Century* (Leiden: Brill, 2005).

Van Meurs, Wim (ed.), *Prospects and Risks Beyond EU Enlargement: Southeastern Europe: Weak States and Strong International Support* (Opladen: Leske-Budrich, 2003).

Vlassenroot, Koen and Timothy Raeymaekers, "Briefing: Kivu's Intractable Security Conundrum," *African Affairs* 108, 432 (July 2009), pp. 1–10.

Warner, Stuart (ed.), *Liberty, Equality, Fraternity* (Indianapolis: Liberty Fund, 1993).

Weeks Jr, Charles J., "The New Frontier, the Great Society, and American Imperialism in Oceania," *The Pacific Historical Review* 71, 1 (Febuary 2002), pp. 91–125.

Wei, Da and Li Shaoxian, "Cuiruo de guojia chongjian: dui zhuquan yijiao zhi ji meiguo de yilake zhengce pinggu," *Xiya feizhou* 4 (2004), pp. 10–16.

Weinstein, Jeremy M., "Autonomous Recovery and International Intervention in Comparative Perspective," Working Paper 57, Center for Global Development, April 2005.

Weiss, Thomas G., "Civilian-Military Interactions and Ongoing UN Reforms: DHA's Past and OCHA's Remaining Challenges," *International Peacekeeping* 5, 4 (1998), pp. 49–70.

Weissman, Fabrice, *In the Shadow of "Just Wars": Violence, Politics and Humanitarian Action* (London: Hurst, 2004).

Weller, Marc, "Kosovo's final status," *International Affairs* 84, 6 (2008), pp. 1223–43.

Weller, Marc, "The Vienna Negotiations on the Final Status for Kosovo," *International Affairs* 84, 4 (2008), pp. 659–81.

Welsh, Jennifer M. (ed.), *Humanitarian Intervention and International Relations*, (Oxford: Oxford University Press, 2004).

Wen, Wang, "Lun lianheguo zai tuidong shijie feizhiminhua jinchengzhong de lishi zuoyong."

Wenzong, Liu, "Lun guojifa zhong de zhuquan yu renquan: mo 'renquan gaoyu zhuquan' miulun," *Waijiao xueyuan xuebao* 3 (1999), pp. 38–43.

Wesley, Michael, *Casualties of the New World Order: The Causes of Failure of UN Missions to Civil Wars* (Basingstoke: Macmillan, 1997).

Wheeler, Nicholas J., *Saving Strangers: Humanitarian Intervention in International Society* (Oxford: Oxford University Press, 2000).

White, Brian, *Understanding European Foreign Policy* (Basingstoke: Palgrave, 2001).

White, Joshua T., "The Shape of Frontier Rule: From the Raj to the Modern Pakistan Frontier," *Asian Security* 4, 3 (September 2008), pp. 219–43.

Whitehead, J., "The Rev. J. Whitehead to Governor-General of the Congo State, July 28, 1903" and "The Rev. J. Whitehead to Governor-General of the Congo State, September, 7, 1903," Cmd. 1933 lxii (1904), pp. 65–9.

Wilde, Ralph, *International Territorial Administration: How Trusteeship and the Civilizing Mission Never Went Away* (Oxford: Oxford University Press, 2008).

Williams, Andrew, *Liberalism and War* (London: Routledge, 2006).

Williams, Paul D. and Alex J. Bellamy, "The Responsibility to Protect and the Crisis in Darfur," *Security Dialogue* 36, 1 (2005), pp. 27–47.

Williams, Phil, "Organised Crime and Corruption in Iraq," *International Peacekeeping* 16, 1 (2009), pp. 115–35.

Winter, Jay, *Dreams of Peace and Freedom: Utopian Moments in the Twentieth Century* (New Haven: Yale University Press, 2002).

Xinbo, Wu, "Four Contradictions Constraining China's Foreign Policy Behavior," *Journal of Contemporary China* 10, 27 (2001), pp. 293–301.

Yonglei, Tan, "Cong weichi heping dao qiangzhi heping—lun lengzhan hou lianheguo weihe xingdong de bianhua," *Lanzhou xuekan* 80 (1994), pp. 50–53.

Yongsheng, Tang, "Zhongguo yu lianheguo weihe xingdong," *Shijie jingji yu zhengzhi* 9 (2002), pp. 39–44.

Yuchun, Xing, "Guojia zhuquan yuanze de jichu diwei yu mianlin de tiaozhan," *Guoji wenti yanjiu* 6, (2003), pp. 45–9.

Yugang, Chen and Yuan Jianhua (eds), *Chaoyue weisitefaliya?: ershiyi shiji guoji guanxi de jiedu* (Beijing: Shishi chubanshe, 2004).

Zartman, I. William (ed.), *Collapsed States: The Disintegration and Restoration of Legitimate Authority* (Boulder, CO: Lynne Rienner, 1995).

Zaum, Dominik, *States of Conflict: A Case Study of Statebuilding in Kosovo* (London: IPPR, 2009).

————— "The Authority of International Administrations in International Society," *Review of International Studies* 32, 3 (2006), pp. 463–5.

————— "The Norms and Politics of Exit: Ending Post-Conflict Transitional Administrations," *Ethics and International Affairs* 23, 2 (2009), pp. 189–208.

————— "The Paradox of Sovereignty: International Involvement in Civil Service Reform in Bosnia and Herzegovina," *International Peacekeeping* 10, 3 (2003), pp. 102–20.

————— *The Sovereignty Paradox: The Norms and Politics of International Statebuilding* (Oxford: Oxford University Press, 2007).

# BIBLIOGRAPHY

Zhang, Yongjin, "China's Entry into International Society: Beyond the Standard of "Civilisation'," *Review of International Studies* 17, 1 (1991), pp. 3–16.

——— "Problematizing China's Security: Sociological Insights," *Pacifica Review* 13, 3 (2001), pp. 241–53.

Zhang, Yongjin and Rouben Azizian (eds), *Ethnic Challenges Beyond Borders: Chinese and Russian Perspectives of the Central Asian Conundrum* (Basingstoke: Macmillan, 1998).

Zhigang, Lai, "Weihe xingdong yu guojia zhuquan," *Xi'an zhengzhi xueyuan xuebao* 12, 3 (June 2000), pp. 64–8.

Zhongying, Pang, "China's Changing Attitude to UN Peacekeeping," *International Peacekeeping* 12, 1 (Spring 2005), pp. 87–104.

Zielonka, Jan, *Europe as Empire: the Nature of the Enlarged European Union* (Oxford: Oxford University Press, 2006).

Zielonka, Jan (ed.), *Paradoxes of European Foreign Policy* (Boston: Kluwer Law International, 1998).

Zuercher, Christoph, "Is More Better? Evaluating External-Led State Building After 1989," *Center on Democracy, Development, and The Rule of Law*, 54 (April 2006).

# INDEX